Tamil Computing

Tamil Computing

Dr R. Ponnusamy

ALLIED PUBLISHERS PVT. LTD.

Noida • Mumbai • Kolkata • Chennai • Bangalore

ALLIED PUBLISHERS PRIVATE LIMITED

D-5, Sector-2, **Noida**–201 301
Ph. Nos.: 0120-4320295/2542557/4352866 • E-mail: delhi.books@alliedpublishers.com

17 Chittaranjan Avenue, **Kolkata**–700072
Ph.: 033-22129618 • E-mail: cal.books@alliedpublishers.com

15 J.N. Heredia Marg, Ballard Estate, **Mumbai**–400001
Ph.: 022-42126969 • E-mail: mumbai.books@alliedpublishers.com

No. 25/10, Commander-in-Chief Road, Ethiraj Lane (Next to Post Office)
Egmore, **Chennai**–600008
Ph.: 044-28223938 • E-mail: chennai.books@alliedpublishers.com

P.B. No. 9932, No. 15, 3rd Floor (Next to Vijaya Bank), 5th Cross, Gandhinagar,
Karnataka, **Bangalore**–560009, Ph.: 080-41530285 / 22386239
E-mail: bngl.books@alliedpublishers.com

Website: www.alliedpublishers.com

ISBN: 978-93-90951-05-5

Published by Sunil Sachdev and printed by Ravi Sachdev
at Allied Publishers Pvt. Ltd., D-5, Sector-2, Noida–201 301

Preface

Tamil Computing is a longstanding dream of Tamil Professionals, enthusiasts, government entities and every Tamil person using the Computer. Different professionals and researchers made several efforts to realize this dream. Teaching this subject as an academic discipline is a meaningful way to consolidate these efforts holistically. However, the non-availability of the specific textbook seems to hinder this task significantly. Therefore, a full-fledged action is taken too successfully to complete this book by the author in spending a few years studying and consolidating the works of various researchers. This book will be a textbook for the undergraduate, postgraduate and research scholars to understand the subject.

This book first introduces Tamil and its importance, basics like characters, words and grammar in a straightforward way. It presents Tamil Computing, Tamil Computing History, encoding standards, fonts, keyboards and standards in a detailed manner. It elaborates on the issues arising while straightforwardly performing Tamil Computing.

Further, this book gives Tamil Phonology, Morphology, Syntax, Semantics and Pragmatics in a detailed manner. It also presents the tools that enable the basic Tamil language processing from a larger perspective. Then the different applications of Tamil Computing are discussed in detail. It also gives the method of accessing MS Office and Google Applications in Tamil. The database is an essential element for storing and retrieving data effectively. Therefore, it provides an idea about how to access the databases in Tamil.

Open Tamil is one of the packages developed by a group of Tamil Computing professionals to make the Tamil Open world. This book presents a method to access the Open Tamil packages and supported operations in a detailed manner.

Speech processing is one of the critical activities in processing the language. This book gives a method for dealing with automatic Tamil speech processing. This book also deals with another application is handwritten character recognition. It is also difficult for any language processing and more handwritten-oriented applications are in place in the modern world. This book gives an outline of how to do Tamil character recognition elaborately. Input and Output handling of Characters is one of the essential activities in any computing system. This book gives an example of how to give and get the output of Tamil characters. Finally, it presents the MS-Windows Tamil customization method to make the Windows System work as a Tamil machine. In addition to this, details about Indic Libraries and Large Language Models have also been included.

The author wishes to state that this book is mostly a collection of information from various sources, arranged in a coherent manner presented to help all the courses, including my views at possible places to consolidate and support the Tamil Computing professionals to pursue their study and research.

முனைவர் மு.பொன்னவைக்கோ

முன்னைத் துணைவேந்தர்
பாரதிதாசன், SRM, பாரத், மற்றும் தமிழ் இணையப் பல்கலைக்கழகங்கள்

பேராசிரியர் பொன்னுசாமி அவரகளின்

Tamil Computing
என்னும் நூலுக்கு முகவுரை

Tamil Computing என்னும் இன்னூல் கணிப்பொறியில் தமிழ் மொழியில் பல்வேறு வகையான கணிப்பீடுகளை செய்யும் முறைகள் பற்றி மிகவும் விரிவாக வழங்கும் ஒரு முழு நூல். இந்நூல் 15 அத்தியாயங்களைக் கொண்டுள்ளது.

முதல் அத்தியாயம், தமிழ் மொழியைப்பற்றியும் தமிழ் இலக்கண, குறிப்புகள் பற்றியும், இரண்டாவது அத்தியாயம் தமிழ் கணிப்பீடு தொடர்பான அடிப்படை-களையும், மூன்றாவது அத்தியாயம் தமிழ் கணிப்பீடு பற்றிய சிக்கல்கள் மற்றும் தீர்வுகள் பற்றியும், நான்காவது அத்தியாயம் பேச்சுத்தமிழ் தொடர்பான இலக்கண முறைகள் பற்றியும், ஐந்தாவது அத்தியாயம் தமிழ் கணிப்பீட்டிற்கான கருவிகள் மற்றும் ஆதாரங்கள் பற்றியும், ஆறாவது அத்தியாயம் தமிழ்த் தகவல் அமைப்பு முறைகளை கணிப்பொறியில் செயல்படுத்துவது தொடர்பாகவும், ஏழாவது அத்தியாயம் MS-Office, Google ஆகியவற்றில் தமிழைப் பயன்படுத்துவது பற்றியும், எட்டாவது அத்தியாயம் தமிழில் தகவல் தொழில்நுட்ப அமைப்புகள் மற்றும் கருவிகள் பற்றியும், ஒன்பதாவது அத்தியாயம் தமிழ் open-source பற்றியும், பத்தாவது அத்தியாயம் கணிப்பொறியில் பேச்சுத்தமிழ் செய்முறை பற்றியும், பதினோராவது அத்தியாயம் கணிப்பொறியில் கையெழுத்துத் தமிழை படித்தறிதல் பற்றியும், பன்னிரெண்டாவது அத்தியாயம் கணிப்பொறியில் தமிழ் உள்ளீடு வெளீடு முறைகள் பற்றியும், பதின்மூன்றாவது அத்தியாயம் கணிப்பொறி இயக்க முறைமையை தனிப்பயனாக்கல் பற்றியும், இறுதியாக, அத்தியாயம் பதினான்கு மற்றும் பதினைந்தில், இது இந்திய மொழி நூலகங்கள்

மற்றும் பெரிய மொழி மாதிரிகள் பற்றியும் விவாதிக்கிறது. ஒரு கல்வி பாடத்திட்டத்திற்கு ஏற்றவாறு மிக அருமையாக விவரிக்கப்பட்டுள்ளன.

இந்நூல், பல்கலைக்கழங்களின் பட்டப்படிப்பிற்கு ஏற்ற ஒரு சிறந்த நூல். இந்நூலைப் படைத்துள்ள பேராசிரியர் முனைவர் பொன்னுசாமி அவர்களுக்கு எனது உளம் நிறைந்த பாராட்டுகள். அவரது கல்விப்பணி மேன்மேலும் சிறக்க எனது அன்பு வாழ்த்துக்கள்.

அன்புடன்,

மு.பொன்னவைக்கோ.

About this Book

This book aims to outline current **Tamil Computing** technologies available around us in the present context to all participants like students, academicians, researchers and others who are interested in this field. Most of the books available in the market deal with Natural Language Processing, specifically English Language Processing. Therefore, the author hopes this book will be of utmost use to the undergraduate, postgraduate and researchers.

This book provides an overall picture of Tamil Computing, covering different aspects. Specifically, starting with the basics of Tamil, Tamil Computing, Coding standards, fonts, keyboards, issues related to it, morphology, phonology, syntax, semantics and pragmatics of Tamil, Tools and resources and applications of Tamil Computing in detail.

The purpose of this book is also to give an insight into Tamil Handwritten character recognition and Speech processing in detail. Automatic Speech Recognition in one of the critical issues in any language. Recognizing handwritten characters using a machine is necessary in today's modern world. A computer system should be intelligent enough to receive and interpret the handwritten input. These two aspects are explained in detail.

This book elaborates on the existing corporate packages like Ms-Office and its usage in Tamil, Database Processing and open Tamil. The book also explains input-outputting methods in detail with simple python programs. The use of the MS Windows Operating System is widespread worldwide in different languages. This book describes the practices of customization of MS Windows software for Tamil. Usage of the MS Windows Operating System is famous worldwide in other languages. This book has also added details concerning Indic Libraries and Large Language Models.

Acknowledgements

Writing a technical book is more complicated than I thought and more rewarding than I could have imagined. None of this would have been possible without my best friends and philosophers. He is the best friend and philosopher I made when I moved to Dr R. Raghavan, Former Principal of Anjalai Ammal Mahalingam Engineering College, Tamilnadu. He stood by me during every struggle and all my successes. I'm eternally grateful to my Professor and philosopher, Dr S. Kuppuswami, Former Dean of Ramanujam School of Mathematics & Computer Science Pondicherry University, who made an extra effort to feed when he didn't have to. He taught me discipline, tough love, manners, respect and much more, which has helped me succeed in life.

I sincerely thank my postgraduate guides Dr. T. Chitralekha, Professor, Department of Computer Science, Dr. V. Prasanna Venkatesan, Professor, Department of Banking Technology, Pondicherry University for introducing this subject to me. Although this period of my life was filled with many ups and downs, my time in the different institutes was worth it because of my Doctoral guide Dr T.V. Gopal, Professor, Department of Computer Science & Engineering, Anna University. Therefore, my heartfelt thanks to him.

My thanks are due to Prof. V. Rajaraman, Honorary Professor, Super Computer Education & Research Centre, Indian Institute of Science for having inspired me to author books.

I thank the Chairman of Chennai Institute of Technology Mr. P. Shriram and the Principal Dr A. Ramesh of Chennai Institute of Technology for motivating me to write this book.

My special thanks to Dr M. Ponnavaikko, Former Vice-Chancellor Bharathidasan University and SRM Institute of Science and Technology, who extended all support and morale whenever I reached him on different occasions and provided an introductory note for this book.

I sincerely thank Ms. Dikashma Shree Selvakumaran and Mr. Anish K, both first-year students at Chennai Institute of Technology, enrolled in B.E. in Computer Science and Engineering with a specialization in Artificial Intelligence and Machine Learning. Their dedicated efforts in creating the program for Tamil Translation using a large language model are genuinely valued.

Writing a book about Tamil Computing is a strange process. I'm forever indebted to Ms. Ezhilvithya R, CEO, Claspintech, Prof. N. Lakshmana Perumal, Former Professor of English, SRM Valliammai Engineering College, Mr S. Senthilkumar, Asst. Professor, Department of Computer Science and Engineering, Chennai Institute of Technology for their editorial help, keen insight and ongoing support in bringing out this book.

My sincere thanks to Allied Publishers, Noida and its Editor, Mr Jagdish Singh for his support in publishing this book.

Finally, to all those who have been a part of the open Tamil team members for sharing the open source code Mr Arulanan T., Mr Arunmozhi, Mr S. Buvaneshkumar, Mr A.T.V. Kumar, Mr M. Kumaran, Dr Muthiah Annamalai, Mr Mahadevan Sathia, Mr K. Sengottuvel, Mr T. Shrinivasan, Mr Subramani Ramanathan, Mr R. Surendhar, Mr Syed Abuthahir, Mr Varun Soundarajan, Mr R. Ashok, Mr Parathan Thiyagalingam, Mr Damodharan Rajalingam, Mr Yoshiki Shibukawa, Mr Ashok Ramachandran.

About the Author

Dr. R. Ponnusamy graduated in Computer Science from A.V.C. College (Autonomous) in 1994 and obtained his M.Sc. in Computer Science from the same institution in 1996. He also received an M.Tech. in Computer Science & Engineering from Pondicherry University, Pondicherry, India, in 2000. He has a Ph.D. in Computer Science & Engineering from the Department of Computer Science & Engineering, College of Engineering, Anna University, Chennai, in 2008. He has also received a D.C.Sc. (Engg.) (Post-Doctoral Degree), from the Universita Popolare Degli Studi De Milano, Italy in 2015. He is a Computer Science and Engineering professor and has more than 26 years of collegiate service in Tamilnadu and Telangana, India. He is currently the Professor and Dean in the Computer Science and Engineering Department at Chennai Institute of Technology, Chennai. His areas of interest are Artificial Intelligence, Human-Computer Interaction, Information Systems, Tamil Computing and Higher Education. He has authored and co-authored more than 120 papers in various international conferences and journals. He has guided 14 scholars and guiding eight research scholars for Ph.D. The Tamilnadu State Council for Science & Technology awarded him the Young Scientist Fellowship Award and he visited the Super Computer Education Research Centre of Indian Institute of Science, Bangalore, India during 2005–2006. He is a Management Council Member of Computer Society of India Chennai Chapter 2023–2025. He is also a Former Executive Director of INFITT (International Forum for Information Technology in Tamil). He is also a Fellow and Member of Professional Societies IETE, IE(I), CSI, ACM, IEEE, ISTE and ISCA. He also received GISR Foundation IARE Best Faculty Award 2020, Fox Story India 50 Aspiring Authors and Researchers 2022, Glantor X 100 Powerful Personalities Award 2022 for being a great leader and an Inspiration to masses in the society.

Contents

CHAPTER 1

Tamil Basics and Grammar

TAMIL BASICS AND GRAMMAR

It is said that,

> "கல்தோன்றி மண்தோன்றாக் காலத்தே
> வாளோடு முன்தோன்றிய மூத்தகுடி."
>
> *"Before the birth of stones and sand,*
> *Brave Tamil man was born"*

The above verse explains the legacy of the Tamil language. The Sangam literature has valued literature with the devotional inspiration and the outline of grammar treatise of Tholkaapiyar and the structure of the language. Furthermore, the Tamil-speaking people have significant prominence across the countries. The birth and the developmental growth of the language, the letters, the rules of language, the sound variations and the source of unique characters, symbols for the Tamil have also been dealt within this book.

1.1 INTRODUCTION

Tamil is the oldest of the Dravidian languages. It is one of the world's classical languages, along with Chinese, Greek, and Sanskrit. Tamil literature spans 4000 years. This language was the first to develop a distinct prose form of writing among the world's classical languages. Tamil is the only language among the old languages that has a history of 2000 or more years of existence. With slight variations in scripts and usage, the language still thrives. The literature written in 200 BC is still learned and used in normal speeches. The Tamil *Thirukkural* is second only to the Bible in several published translations. Many words from other languages have been absorbed throughout the language's development. For instance, Tamil, spoken in Tamil Nadu, has many words from Sanskrit, English, Dutch, French, and Urdu.

It flourished in India as a language with rich literature during the Sangam period (300 BCE to 300 CE). Tamil scholars categorize the history of the language into three periods: Old Tamil (300 BC – 700 CE), Middle Tamil

(700 CE – 1600 CE), and Modern Tamil (1600–present). In ancient times, the epigraphic attestation of the Tamils began with rock imprinting from the 3rd century BC. “The Tamil scripts were originally inscribed in Tamil-Brahmi and later recognized as the Brahmi Script in Tamil”. The older or earliest extant literary text is the தொல்காப்பியம் (tholkAppiyam). The period that describes the classical period, this time works on the grammar and poetic portion. The Sangam literature has 2381 poems containing 50,000 lines of poetry with the attributes of the 473 poets. In the early 20th century, the modern Tamil movement was called the ‘Tani Tamil Iyakkam’ (Tamil Purist Movement), which was to erase the Sanskrit and the other foreign components from Tamil. The critical number of the Sanskrit words and the substitution of words equivalent to Tamil. The essential feature is to specify the presence of the two main varieties of the languages, informal and formal Tamil செந்தமிழ் (sewthamiz); this divergent are sufficient for the language to become to the diglossia class.

The informal Tamil language is used for regular spoken communication, while formal Tamil is used in high-class contexts, such as lectures, news bulletins, and legal writings. They are distinguished among the lexis, morphology, and segmental phonology.

The official language of the Indian state of Tamilnadu is Tamil, one of the 22 languages under the list of the eighth schedule of the constitution of India. Tamil is the primary language spoken in Tamilnadu, and more than eight crore Tamils live in Tamilnadu and Pondicherry. The other official language of this place is the Union Territories of Puducherry, Andaman & Nicobar Islands. Tamil became India’s first legally recognized classical language in 2004. Tamils are also found residing in other countries, including Sri Lanka, Malaysia, Burma, Indonesia, South Africa, Fiji, Mauritius, and Singapore.

1.2 TAMIL CHARACTERS AND CLASSIFICATIONS

The writing script of the Tamil is called vattEzuththu. The Tamil characters are classified into three classes. The Tamil scripts have twelve vowels uyirezuththu (உயிரெழுத்து) “soul-letters,” eighteen consonants meyyezuththu (மெய்யெழுத்து) “body-letters” and one character, the Aythaezuththu (ஆய்த எழுத்து) “the hermaphrodite letter,” in Tamil grammar it is being neither a consonant nor a vowel through considered as the part of the vowel sets. The script, however, is syllabic. Therefore, the whole script consists of thirty-one letters in their independent forms. The additional 216 compound letters represent the total number of the 247 combinations displayed in the Table 1.3. These compound letters are produced by adding and mixing vowel markers and consonants. The Tamil vowels are given in the 1.1 table; Table 1.2 lists the consonant letters, and the side combination that gives all the Tamil compounds (uyirmei) notes.

1.2.1 Vowels

There are twelve vowels in Tamil. They are:

அ, ஆ, இ, ஈ, உ, ஊ, எ, ஏ, ஐ, ஒ, ஓ, ஔ

The Tamil script is written from left to write. Vowels are called the 'life' (uyiṛ) or 'soul' letters. Tamil vowels are divided into the short and the long Kuril (குறில்) and nedil (நெடில்)—five of each type) and two diphthongs, depending on the duration of the utterance.

Table 1.1: Tamil Vowels

Short Vowel (Kuril)	*Long Vowel (Nedil)*	*Diphthong*
அ	ஆ	ஐ
இ	ஈ	
உ	ஊ	ஔ
எ	ஏ	
ஒ	ஓ	

There are eighteen consonants in Tamil. They are: க், ங், ச், ஞ், ட், ண், த், ந், ப், ம், ய், ர், ல், வ், ழ், ள், ற், ன்.

Table 1.2: List of Consonants

க்	[k] like kiss	ங்	[ṅ] like nice	ச்	[c] like cat	ஞ்	[ñ] like new	ட்	[ṭ] like top
ண்	[ṇ] like news	த்	[t] like time	ந்	[n] like noon	ப்	[p] like play	ம்	[m] like me
ய்	[y] like yes	ர்	[r] like ring	ல்	[l] like love	வ்	[v] like vast	ழ்	[ḻ] like rag
ள்	[ḷ] like look	ற்	[ṟ] like rice	ன்	[ṉ] like nine				

Vallinam வல்லினம்) க், ச், ட், த், ப், ற்

Mellinam (மெல்லினம்) ங், ஞ், ண், ந், ம், ன்

Idayinam (இடயினம்) ய், ர், ல், வ், ழ், ள்

Aaydham, there is one aaydham type of character in Tamil, namely ஃ.

1.2.2 Unique Characteristics of some Tamil Characters

A few Tamil characters shown below having the semantic functions with their normal functioning.

Demonstrative Letters (suttu)

The three short vowels அ, இ & உ are used to sing the proximity; in other words, to point objects called the pointing characters of suttezhuthukkaL. AmmaaNavan (அம்மாணவன்)—the student, immaram (இம்மரம்)—this tree, upputhakam (உப்புத்தகம்).

Interrogative Characters (vinaa)

The interrogative character called and conveyed the questions semantically, ஆஎஏஓயா.

Prolongation (aLabedai)

In the poetry, the poem has a different format and adjusts to the "maathras" to make the poem's structure. In this structure, the long vowels and consonants are used to raise the vowels and extra "maathras" (ala). This property of the Tamil is called aLabedai.

1.2.3 Position of Characters in a Word

The vowels and consonants that allow arranging the end of the words, in these characters are the twelve vowels and ten consonant words such as கசதநபமவயஞங.

The twelve vowels, eleven consonants ஞ்ண்ந்ம்ன்ய்ர்ல்வ்ழ்ள் and the shortened குசுடுதுபுறு are all allowed to occur at the end of words.

Table 1.3: Tamil Compound Characters

Vow→ ↓Cons	அ a	ஆ (A)	இ (i)	ஈ (I)	உ (u)	ஊ (U)	எ (e)	ஏ (E)	ஐ (ai)	ஒ (o)	ஓ (O)	ஔ (au)
க் (k)	க	கா	கி	கீ	கு	கூ	கெ	கே	கை	கொ	கோ	கௌ
ங் (ng)	ங	ஙா	ஙி	ஙீ	ஙு	ஙூ	ஙெ	ஙே	ஙை	ஙொ	ஙோ	ஙௌ
ச் (s)	ச	சா	சி	சீ	சு	சூ	செ	சே	சை	சொ	சோ	சௌ
ஞ் (nj)	ஞ	ஞா	ஞி	ஞீ	ஞு	ஞூ	ஞெ	ஞே	ஞை	ஞொ	ஞோ	ஞௌ
ட் (d)	ட	டா	டி	டீ	டு	டூ	டெ	டே	டை	டொ	டோ	டௌ
ண் (N)	ண	ணா	ணி	ணீ	ணு	ணூ	ணெ	ணே	ணை	ணொ	ணோ	ணௌ
த் (th)	த	தா	தி	தீ	து	தூ	தெ	தே	தை	தொ	தோ	தௌ
ந் (w)	ந	நா	நி	நீ	நு	நூ	நெ	நே	நை	நொ	நோ	நௌ
ப் (p)	ப	பா	பி	பீ	பு	பூ	பெ	பே	பை	பொ	போ	பௌ
ம் (m)	ம	மா	மி	மீ	மு	மூ	மெ	மே	மை	மொ	மோ	மௌ
ய் (y)	ய	யா	யி	யீ	யு	யூ	யெ	யே	யை	யொ	யோ	யௌ
ர் (r)	ர	ரா	ரி	ரீ	ரு	ரூ	ரெ	ரே	ரை	ரொ	ரோ	ரௌ
ல் (l)	ல	லா	லி	லீ	லு	லூ	லெ	லே	லை	லொ	லோ	லௌ
வ் (v)	வ	வா	வி	வீ	வு	வூ	வெ	வே	வை	வொ	வோ	வௌ
ழ் (z)	ழ	ழா	ழி	ழீ	ழு	ழூ	ழெ	ழே	ழை	ழொ	ழோ	ழௌ
ள் (L)	ள	ளா	ளி	ளீ	ளு	ளூ	ளெ	ளே	ளை	ளொ	ளோ	ளௌ
ற் (R)	ற	றா	றி	றீ	று	றூ	றெ	றே	றை	றொ	றோ	றௌ
ன் (n)	ன	னா	னி	னீ	னு	னூ	னெ	னே	னை	னொ	னோ	னௌ

1.3 TAMIL GRAMMAR

The oldest grammar book Tolkāppiyam considerably explains the Tamil grammar. The modern writing of Tamil is created based on the 13th-century grammar Naṉṉūl, which restated and clarified the rules of Tolkāppiyam with a few modifications. Tamil grammar is divided into five portions, namely ezuthu (Letter), sol (Word), porul (Meaning), Yaappu (poetic structure), and aNi (Poetic decoration). The first book was Agathiyam which was based on Tamil grammar. But the scripts of Agathiyam were never available. The Tholkaappiyam was considered the first book of Tamil grammar. The Tholkaappiyam is categorized into three adhigaarams as ezuthadhigaaram, solladhigaaram, and poruladhigaaram. Each adhigaaram has nine chapters.

The growth and classification described by the Tamil characters, with their listing of the Tamil characters and the maathraas of the Tamil, are some of the features defined in ezuththadhigaaram. Single-letter, multi-letter, sandhi rules, classification of words according to the origin, and syntactic classification of words are the features detailed in solladhigaaram. Some of the topics discussed in the poruladhigaaram, the terms explained with the meanings, conventional use of words, metaphors, classification of nouns based on the human and nonhuman characters, expressed the emotions, with the 'living thing' in many senses.

Table 1.4: Tamil Grammars

Divisions	*Meaning*	*Main Grammar Books*
எழுத்து (Ezuththu)	Letter	தொல்காப்பியம் (tholkAppiyam), நன்னூல் (Nanoul)
சொல் (sol)	Word	தொல்காப்பியம் (tholkAppiyam), நன்னூல் (Nanoul)
பொருள் (poruL)	Meaning	தொல்காப்பியம் (tholkAppiyam)
யாப்பு (yAppu)	Form	யாப்பெருங்கலாக்காரிகை (yApperungkalAkkArikai)
அணி (aNi)	Method	தனியலங்காரம் (thaniyalangkAram)

1.4 TAMIL WORDS CLASSIFICATION (MORPHOLOGY)

Tamil is also an agglutinative language. Tamil words contain verbal roots to which one or more affixes are enclosed. Mostly, the affixes or suffixes are attached, which either change the words or their meaning, or an inflectional suffix that is marking characterized such as the person, moods, tense and numbers of emotions, etc., in agglutination has no total length and extent, the long word needs more suffixes in Tamil. For example, to give an example, the word pōkamuṭiyātavarkaḷukkāka (போகமுடியாதவர்களுக்காக) means "for the sake of those who cannot go," and consists of the following morphemes shown in Table 1.5. The word formed through the agglutinative process is often harder to translate into English.

Table 1.5: Tamil Morphemes Example

Pōka	*muṭi*	*y*	*āta*	*var*	*kaḷ*	*ukku*	*āka*
go	accomplish	word-joining letter	negation (impersonal)	nominalizer he/she who does	plural marker	to	for

1.5 PARTS OF SPEECH

1.5.1 Nouns

Tamil nouns (and pronouns) are classified into two super-classes (tiṇai)—the "rational" (uyartiṇai) and the "irrational" (ak̲r̲iṇai)—which include a total of five classes (paal, which means 'gender'). The levelheaded named the human and divinities and the wide range of things (creatures, objects, conceptual things) are delegated nonsensical. The rational nouns and pronouns partner with one of the three classes (paal)—masculine singular feminine singular and rational plural. The plural type of the good things might be utilized as an honorific, gender-natural, solitary structure. The irritational things and pronouns identify with one and two classes (paal)—irrational singular and irrational plural. As the model in the table shows, the paal is frequently shown through suffixes.

Table 1.6: Noun Classification Table

Peyarccol (Name-words)				
Uyartiṇai (rational)			ak̲r̲ iṇai (irrational)	
āṇpāl Male	peṇpāl Female	palarpāl Collective	on̲r̲ an̲pāl One	palavin̲pāl Many
For example, the Tamil words for "doer"				
ceytavan̲ He who did	ceytavaḷ She who did	ceytavar They who did	ceytatu That which did	ceytavai Those who did

Certain special suffixes in Tamil are known as case suffixes. There are about 8 case suffixes, and they are only added to nouns. The conventional grammarians endeavoured to bunch the various suffixes into 8 cases with the correspondence used in Sanskrit. These were the nominative, accusative, dative, sociative, genitive, instrumental, locative, and ablative. Current grammarians contend that the order is counterfeit and Tamil utilization is the best understanding with each postfix, or the blend of the additions is viewed as the stamping as the different cases.

Tamil nouns can also take one of four prefixes, i, a, u, and e which are functionally equivalent to demonstratives in English. For example, the word vazhi (வழி) meaning "way" can take these to produce ivvazhi (இவ்வழி) "this way," avvazhi (அவ்வழி) "that way," uvvazhi (உவ்வழி) "the medial way" and evvazhi (எவ்வழி) "which way."

The methods of agglutination measure create a few things. For instance, "he-who-does" or "that-which-will-turn into" are the alleged participial things. The mix delivers composite things of descriptors and pronouns. For example, by joining "great" and "he" into "great he," we achieve what could be compared to the English "a decent man." Consistently, the thing "great they" is interpreted as "acceptable individuals." Verbal things in Tamil are shaped from the foundations of action words and are generally identical to the English "-ing" things. For example:

Table 1.6: Lists of Nouns

English Nouns	*Tamil Nouns*
arm	kai – கை
back	muthuku – முதுகு
cheeks	kannangal – கன்னங்கள்
chest	maarpu – மார்பு
chin	mukavaaik kattai – முகவாய்க்கட்டை
ear	kaathu – காது
elbow	muzhankai – முழங்கை
eye	kan – கண்
face	mukam – முகம்
finger	viral – விரல்
fingers	viralkal – விரல்கள்
foot	paatham – பாதம்
hair	mudi – முடி
hand	kai – கை
head	thalai – தலை
heart	ithayam – இதயம்

English Nouns	*Tamil Nouns*
knee	muzhankaal – முழங்கால்
leg	kaal – கால்
lip	uthatu – உதடு
mouth	vaai – வாய்
neck	kazhuththu – கழுத்து
nose	mookku – மூக்கு
shoulder	thol – தோள்
stomach	vayiru – வயிறு
teeth	parkal – பற்கள்
thigh	thotai – தொடை
throat	thondai – தொண்டை
thumb	kattaiviral – கட்டைவிரல்
toe	kaal viral – கால்விரல்
tongue	naakku – நாக்கு
tooth	pal – பல்
nouns	peyarchsorkal – பெயர்ச்சொற்கள்
my car	yenathu kaar – எனதுகார்
green car	pachchai kaar – பச்சைகார்
three cars	moondru kaarkal – மூன்றுகார்கள்
car garage	kaar kottil – கார்கொட்டில்
outside the car	kaarin veliye – காரின்வெளியே

1.5.2 Pronouns

A pronoun is a word used instead of a noun or noun phrase. It is a specific instance of a good shape. Pronouns have customarily been viewed as grammatical features. However, some advanced scholars would not consider them to frame a solitary class considering their various capacities. Subtypes incorporate personal pronouns, reflexive and complementary, possessive, demonstrative, relative, inquisitive, and endless pronouns.

Table 1.7: Pronouns and Corresponding Possessive ('Oblique') Forms

Class	*Pronouns*	*Possessive ('oblique') Form*
I person singular	நான் 'I'	என் 'my'
I person plural (inclusive)	நாம் (நாம) 'we'	நம் (நம்ம) 'our'
I person plural (exclusive)	நாங்கள் (நாங்க) 'we'	எங்கள் (எங்க) 'our'
II person singular (impolite/intimate)	நீ 'you'	உன் 'your'
II person plural (polite)	நீங்கள் (நீங்க) 'you'	உங்கள் (உங்க) 'your'
II person plural (equals)	நீர் 'you'	உம் 'your'
III-person singular mascu-line (impolite/intimate)	அவன் 'he'	அவன் 'his'
III person singular masculine (polite)	அவர் 'he'	அவர் 'his'
III person singular feminine (impolite/intimate)	அவள் (அவ) 'she'	அவள் (அவ) 'her'
III person singular feminine/ masculine plural/polite	அவர்கள் (அவுங்க) 'they-human'	அவர்கள் (அவுங்க) 'their-human'
Neuter singular	அது 'it'	அதன் (அதோடெ) 'it's'
Neuter plural	அவை 'they-neut.'	அவைகள்/அவற் – 'their-neut'
Question word – human	யார் 'who'	யார்/யாருடைய yaaroote 'whose'
Question word – neuter	எது 'which'	எதன்/எதனுடைய எதோடெ 'whose' (its)

1.5.3 Verbs

The verb is a word that characterizes an activity, state or event and frames the fundamental piece of the predicate of a sentence, for example, hear, become, occur. Like Tamil nouns, Tamil action words are likewise arched using additions. A commonplace Tamil action word structure will have many additions, which show individual, number, temperament, tense, and voice, as is shown by the following example azhintukkoṇṭiruntēn (அழிந்து க்கொண்டிருந்தேன்) "(I) was destroying":

Table 1.8: Tamil Verb with many Suffixes

azhi	*intu*	***koṇṭu***	*irunta*	*ēn*
root destroy	voice marker past tense object voice	tense marker during	aspect marker past progressive	person marker first person, singular

Individual and number are indicated by suffixing the sideways instance of the applicable pronoun (ēn in the above model). The suffixes to demonstrate tenses and voice are framed from grammatical particles added to the stem.

Tamil has two voices. The first—used in the model above—exhibits that the sentence's subject goes through or is the object of the movement named by the activity word stem. The second shows that the sentence's subject facilitates the action suggested by the activity word stem. These voices are not indistinguishable from transitivity or causation considerations or the unique dormant or reflexive-nonreflexive division of voices found in the Indo-European lingos.

Tamil has three simple tenses—past, present and future—sign by the simple suffixes and the sequences of the perfects, the sign by the compound suffixes. Tamil is gradually reflected by the similar morphemes which mark tense classes. These signals, whether spoken in the verb, are imitation, possible, potential, or actual. The verb of Tamil is the indicator through the accumulation of the rumor clitic ām.

Table 1.9: Lists of Sample Verbs

English Verbs	*Tamil Verbs*
Verbs	vinaichsorkal – வினைச்சொற்கள்
Past	irandha kaalam – இறந்த காலம்
I spoke	naan pesinen – நான் பேசினேன்

English Verbs	*Tamil Verbs*
I wrote	naan yezhuthinen – நான் எழுதினேன்
I drove	naan ottinen – நான்ஓட்டினேன்
I loved	naan kaathaliththen – நான் காதலித்தேன்
I gave	naan koduththen – நான் கொடுத்தேன்
I smiled	naan punsiriththen – நான் புன்சிரித்தேன்
I took	naan yeduththen – நான் எடுத்தேன்
He spoke	avan pesinaan – அவன் பேசினான்
He wrote	avan yezhuthinaan – அவன் எழுதினான்
He drove	avan ottinaan – அவன் ஓட்டினான்
He loved	avan kaathaliththaan – அவன் காதலித்தான்
He gave	avan koduththaan – அவன் கொடுத்தான்
He smiled	avan punsiriththaan – அவன் புன்சிரித்தான்
He took	avan yeduththaan – அவன் எடுத்தான்
We spoke	naangal pesinom – நாங்கள் பேசினோம்
We wrote	naangal yezhuthinom – நாங்கள் எழுதினோம்
We drove	naangal ottinom – நாங்கள் ஓட்டினோம்
We loved	naangal kaathaliththom – நாங்கள் காதலித்தோம்
We gave	naangal koduththom – நாங்கள் கொடுத்தோம்
We smiled	naangal punsiriththom – நாங்கள் புன்சிரித்தோம்
We took	naangal yeduththom – நாங்கள் எடுத்தோம்
Future	yethir kaalam – எதிர்காலம்
I will speak	naan pesuven – நான் பேசுவேன்
I will write	naan yezhuthuven – நான் எழுதுவேன்
I will drive	naan ottuven – நான் ஓட்டுவேன்
I will love	naan kaathalippen – நான் காதலிப்பேன்
I will give	naan koduppen – நான் கொடுப்பேன்
I will smile	naan punsirippen – நான் புன்சிரிப்பேன்
I will take	naan yeduppen – நான் எடுப்பேன்
He will speak	avan pesuvaan – அவன் பேசுவான்
He will write	avan yezhuthuvaan – அவன் எழுதுவான்
He will drive	avan ottuvaan – அவன் ஓட்டுவான்
He will love	avan kaathalippaan – அவன் காதலிப்பான்
He will give	avan koduppaan – அவன் கொடுப்பான்

English Verbs	*Tamil Verbs*
He will smile	avan punsirippaan – அவன் புன்சிரிப்பான்
He will take	avan yeduppaan – அவன் எடுப்பான்
We will speak	naangal pesuvom – நாங்கள் பேசுவோம்
We will write	naangal yezhuthuvom – நாங்கள் எழுதுவோம்
We will drive	naangal ottuvom – நாங்கள் ஓட்டுவோம்
We will love	naangal kaathalippom – நாங்கள் காதலிப்போம்
We will give	naangal koduppom – நாங்கள் கொடுப்போம்
We will smile	naangal punsirippom – நாங்கள் புன்சிரிப்போம்
We will take	naangal yeduppom – நாங்கள் எடுப்போம்
Present	nikazh kaalam – நிகழ்காலம்
I speak	naan pesukiren – நான் பேசுகிறேன்
I write	naan yezhuthukiren – நான் எழுதுகிறேன்
I drive	naan ottukiren – நான் ஓட்டுகிறேன்
I love	naan kaathalikkiren – நான் காதலிக்கிறேன்
I give	naan kodukkiren – நான் கொடுக்கிறேன்
I smile	naan punsirikkiren – நான் புன்சிரிக்கிறேன்
I take	naan yedukkiren – நான் எடுக்கிறேன்
He speaks	avan pesukiraan – அவன் பேசுகிறான்
He writes	avan yezhuthukiraan – அவன் எழுதுகிறான்
He drives	avan ottukiraan – அவன் ஓட்டுகிறான்
He loves	avan kaathalikkiraan – அவன் காதலிக்கிறான்
He gives	avan kodukkiraan – அவன் கொடுக்கிறான்
He smiles	avan punsirikkiraan – அவன் புன்சிரிக்கிறான்
He takes	avan yedukkiraan – அவன் எடுக்கிறான்
We speak	naangal pesukirom – நாங்கள் பேசுகிறோம்
We write	naangal yezhuthukirom – நாங்கள் எழுதுகிறோம்
We drive	naangal ottukirom – நாங்கள் ஓட்டுகிறோம்
We love	naangal kaathalikkirom – நாங்கள் காதலிக்கிறோம்
We give	naangal kodukkirom – நாங்கள் கொடுக்கிறோம்
We smile	naangal punsirikkirom – நாங்கள் புன்சிரிக்கிறோம்
We take	naangal yedukkirom – நாங்கள் எடுக்கிறோம்

1.5.4 Adverb

A word belonging to one of the major form classes in any of numerous languages, typically serving as a modifier of a verb, an adjective, another adverb, a preposition, a phrase, a clause, or a sentence, expressing some relation of manner or quality, place, time, degree, number, cause, opposition, affirmation, or denial, and in Tamil also serving to connect and to express comment on clause content. Adverbs typically express manner, place, time, frequency, degree, level of certainty, etc., answering questions such as how? and in what way? When? Where? and to what extent?

Table 1.10: Lists of Adverbs

English Adverbs	*Tamil Adverbs*
adverbs of time	kaala vinai urichsorkal – காலவினைஉரிச்சொற்கள்
yesterday	netru – நேற்று
today	in – இன்று
tomorrow	naalai – நாளை
now	ippozhuthu – இப்பொழுது
then	appozhuthu – அப்பொழுது
later	piraku – பிறகு
tonight	inriravu – இன்றிரவு
right now	ippozhudhe – இப்பொழுதே
last night	netriravu – நேற்றிரவு
this morning	inru kaalai – இன்று காலை
next week	aduththa vaaram – அடுத்த வாரம்
already	yerkenave – ஏற்கெனவே
recently	anmaiyil – அண்மையில்
lately	sirithu kaalaththirku mun – சிறிது காலத்திற்கு முன்
soon	viraivil – விரைவில்
immediately	udanadiyaai – உடனடியாய்
still	innum – இன்னும்
yet	aayinum – ஆயினும்
ago	munnar – முன்னர்
adverbs of place	ita vinai urichsorkal – இடவினை உரிச்சொற்கள்
here	ivvidam – இவ்விடம்
there	avvidam – அவ்விடம்
over there	atho tholaivilulla – அதோ தொலைவிலுள்ள

English Adverbs	*Tamil Adverbs*
everywhere	yella idankalilum – எல்லா இடங்களிலும்
anywhere	yendha idaththilaavathu – எந்த இடத்திலாவது
nowhere	yenkumindri – எங்குமின்றி
home	veedu – வீடு
away	tholaivil – தொலைவில்
out	veliye – வெளியே
adverbs of manner	vakai vinai urichsorkal – வகைவினை உரிச்சொற்கள்
very	mikavum – மிகவும்
quite	murrilum – முற்றிலும்
pretty	azhaku vaaindha – அழகுவாய்ந்த
really	unmaiyaaga – உண்மையாக
fast	vekamaaga – வேகமாக
well	nanku – நன்கு
hard	kadinamaaga – கடினமாக
quickly	vekamaaga – வேகமாக
slowly	medhuvaaga – மெதுவாக
carefully	kavanamaaga – கவனமாக
hardly	apoorvamaaga – அபூர்வமாக
barely	pothum pothaamal – போதும் போதாமல்
mostly	perumpaalum – பெரும்பாலும்
almost	anekamaaka – அநேகமாக
absolutely	murrilumaaga – முற்றிலுமாக
together	onraai – ஒன்றாய்
alone	thannanthaniyaaga – தன்னந்தனியாக
adverbs of frequency	adikkadi nikazhkira vinai urichsol kal அடிக்கடி நிகழ்கிற வினைஉரிச்சொற்கள்
always	yeppozhuthum – எப்பொழுதும்
frequently	adikkadi – அடிக்கடி
usually	vazhakkamaaga – வழக்கமாக
sometimes	sila samayam – சிலசமயம்
occasionally	yeppozhuthaavathu – எப்பொழுதாவது
seldom	apoorvamaai – அபூர்வமாய்
rarely	arithaai – அரிதாய்
never	yenrum illaadha nilaiyil – என்றும் இல்லாத நிலையில்

1.5.5 Prepositions

A function word that typically combines with a noun phrase to form a phrase which usually expresses a modification or predication. The contrast between the preposition and the noun phrase is called the prepositional phrases. The groups of words, function like the simple, one-word preposition, is called the complex preposition. Prepositions commonly convey the following relationships: agency (by); comparison (like, as . . . as); direction (to, towards, through); place (at, by, on); possession (of); purpose (for); source (from, out of); and time (at, before, on).

Table 1.11: List of Prepositions

English Prepositions	*Tamil Prepositions*
about	kuriththu – குறித்து
above	mele – மேலே
across	kurukkaaga – குறுக்காக
after	piraku – பிறகு
against	yethiraaga – எதிராக
among	idaiyil – இடையில்
around	sutri/yeraththaazha – சுற்றி/ஏறத்தாழ
as	oppaaga/avvannam/athupolave – ஒப்பாக/அவ்வண்ணம்/அதுபோலவே
at	il/idaththil/arukil – இல்/இடத்தில்/அருகில்
before	yethire/munpaaga – எதிரே/ முன்பாக
behind	pinnaal – பின்னால்
below	keezhe – கீழே
beneath	keezhe/adiyil – கீழே/அடியில்
beside	melum/pakkaththil/arukil – மேலும்/பக்கத்தில்/அருகில்
between	idaiye – இடையே
beyond	appaal – அப்பால்
but	aanaal – ஆனால்
by	aal/arukil – ஆல்/அருகில்
despite	aayinum – ஆயினும்
down	keezhe – கீழே
during	kaalaththil/velaiyil/pozhuthil – காலத்தில்/வேளையில்/பொழுதில்

English Prepositions	*Tamil Prepositions*
except	thavira – தவிர
for	kaaranamaai/kuriththu/yenenraal – காரணமாய்/குறித்து/ஏனென்றால்
from	thodanki/muthalaai/irundhu – தொடங்கி/முதலாய்/இருந்து
in	il/ulle/aruke – இல்/உள்ளே/அருகே
inside	ulle/utpakkam – உள்ளே/உட்பக்கம்
into	ulle/ulnokki – உள்ளே/உள்நோக்கி
near	arukil – அருகில்
next	aduththu – அடுத்து
of	il/in/udaiya – இல்/இன்/உடைய
on	mele – மேலே
opposite	yethiraana/murrilum maaraana – எதிரான/முற்றிலும் மாறான
out	veliye – வெளியே
outside	veliye/velippuraththil – வெளியே/வெளிப்புறத்தில்
over	mele/athikamaai/mudivutra nilaiyil – மேலே/அதிகமாய்/முடிவுற்ற நிலையில்
per	vazhiyaai/moolamaai – வழியாய்/மூலமாய்
plus	kooda – கூட
round	vattamaana/urundaiyaana/sutru – வட்டமான/உருண்டையான/சுற்று
since	appozhuthilirundhu/aakaiyaal – அப்பொழுதிலிருந்து/ஆகையால்
than	kaattilum/vida – காட்டிலும்/விட
through	kurukke/moolamaai – குறுக்கே/மூலமாய்
till	varaiyil – வரையில்
to	varaiyil – வரையில்
toward	poruttu/nokki/naadi – பொருட்டு/நோக்கி/நாடி
under	keezhe/adiyil – கீழே/அடியில்
unlike	polillaadha/veru maathiriyaana – போலில்லாத/வேறுமாதிரியான
until	varaiyilum – வரையிலும்
up	mele – மேலே

English Prepositions	*Tamil Prepositions*
via	vazhiyaaga – வழியாக
with	aal/odu/udan – ஆல்/ஓடு/உடன்
within	ulle – உள்ளே
without	inri/illaamal – இன்றி/இல்லாமல்
two words	irandu vaarththaikal – இரண்டுவார்த்தைகள்
according to	inanga – இணங்க
because of	kaaranamaaga – காரணமாக
close to	pakkaththil/arukil – பக்கத்தில்/அருகில்
due to	kaaranamaai – காரணமாய்
except for	thavira – தவிர
far from	illave illai – இல்லவே இல்லை
inside of	ulle – உள்ளே
instead of	pathilaaga – பதிலாக
near to	arukil – அருகில்
next to	pakkaththil – பக்கத்தில்
outside of	veliye – வெளியே
prior to	munpaaga – முன்பாக
three words	moondru vaarththaikal – மூன்றுவார்த்தைகள்
as far as	kuriththu/varaiyil – குறித்து/வரையில்
as well as	melum/athe pondru – மேலும்/அதேபோன்று
in addition to	melum – மேலும்
in front of	munnaal – முன்னால்
in spite of	irunthapothilum – இருந்தபோதிலும்
on behalf of	saarpaai – சார்பாய்
on top of	mel/atharku mel – மேல்/அதற்குமேல்
demonstrative prepositions	suttu munn mozhivu – சுட்டு முன் மொழிவு
this	ithu – இது
that	athu – அது
these	ivaikal – இவைகள்
those	avaikal – அவைகள்

1.5.6 Adjective

A class of words that modify nouns and pronouns, primarily by describing a particular quality of the word they are changing, as wise in a wise grandmother, perfect in a perfect score, or handsome in He is extremely handsome. Other terms, such as numbers (one cup; twelve months), specific demonstrative pronouns (this magazine; those questions) and terms that impose limits (each person; no mercy) can also function adjectivally, as can some nouns that are found chiefly in fixed phrases where they immediately precede the noun they modify, like a bottle in bottle cap and bus in the bus station. Synonyms for adjectives are modifier, qualifier, identifier, describer, and describing word.

Table 1.12: List of Adjectives

English Adjectives	*Tamil Adjectives*
colors	nirangal – நிறங்கள்
black	karuppu – கருப்பு
blue	neelam – நீலம்
brown	pazhuppu – பழுப்பு
grey	saambal – சாம்பல்
green	pachchai – பச்சை
orange	semmanjal – செம்மஞ்சள்
purple	oothaa – ஊதா
red	sikappu – சிகப்பு
white	vellai – வெள்ளை
yellow	manjal – மஞ்சள்
sizes	parimaanangal – பரிமானங்கள்
big	periya – பெரிய
deep	aazhamaana – ஆழமான
long	neelamaana – நீளமான
narrow	kurukalaana – குறுகலான
short	kuttaiyaana – குட்டையான
small	siriya – சிறிய
tall	uyaramaana – உயரமான
thick	thadiyaana – தடியான
thin	olliyaana – ஒல்லியான
wide	akalamaana – அகலமான

English Adjectives	*Tamil Adjectives*
shapes	vadivangal – வடிவங்கள்
circular	vattamaana – வட்டமான
straight	neraana – நேரான
square	sathuramaana – சதுரமான
triangular	mukkonamaana – முக்கோணமான
tastes	suvaikal – சுவைகள்
bitter	kasappaana – கசப்பான
fresh	uvarppatra – உவர்ப்பற்ற
salty	uppu karikkira – உப்புகரிக்கிற
sour	pulippaana – புளிப்பான
spicy	kaarasaaramaana – காரசாரமான
sweet	inippaana – இனிப்பான
qualities	tharangal – தரங்கள்
bad	mosamaana – மோசமான
clean	suththamaana – சுத்தமான
dark	karu niramaana – கருநிறமான
difficult	kadinamaana – கடினமான
dirty	azhukkaana – அழுக்கான
dry	kaaindha – காய்ந்த
easy	yelithaana – எளிதான
empty	kaaliyaana – காலியான
expensive	kiraakkiyaana – கிராக்கியான
fast	vekamaana – வேகமான
foreign	ayalaana – அயலான
full	niraindha – நிறைந்த
good	nalla – நல்ல
hard	kettiyaana – கெட்டியான
heavy	kanamaana – கனமான
inexpensive	malivaana – மலிவான
light	ilesaana – இலேசான
local	oritaththirkuriya – ஓரிடத்திற்குரிய
new	puthiya – புதிய
noisy	saththamaana – சத்தமான
old	pazhaiya – பழைய

English Adjectives	*Tamil Adjectives*
powerful	sakthiyulla – சக்தியுள்ள
quiet	asaiyaatha – அசையாத
correct	sariyaana – சரியான
slow	methuvaana – மெதுவான
soft	miruthuvaana – மிருதுவான
very	mikavum – மிகவும்
weak	valukkuraindha – வலுக்குறைந்த
wet	eeramaana – ஈரமான
wrong	thavaraana – தவறான
young	ilamaiyaana – இளமையான
quantities	alavukal – அளவுகள்
few	kuraivaana – குறைவான
little	sirithalavaana – சிறிதளவான
many	yeraalamaana – ஏராளமான
much	mikundha – மிகுந்த
part	pakuthi – பகுதி
some	konjam – கொஞ்சம்
a few	oru sila – ஒரு சில
whole	muzhumaiyaana – முழுமையான

1.5.7 Article

Articles are words that identify a noun/an individual/spot/item or thought as being specific or unspecific. An article is a modifier, which is any word that adjusts a thing. Typically, modifiers change things through the depiction, yet articles are utilized rather than refer to nouns. We use two distinct kinds of articles recorded as hard copies and discussions to call attention to or allude to a thing or gathering of things: unequivocal and endless articles.

If you're attempting to learn Tamil Articles, you will track down some valuable assets, including a course about Definite and Indefinite Articles. Tamil articles are words that consolidate with a thing to demonstrate the reference being made by the thing. For the most part, articles determine the syntactic definiteness of the item. Models are "the, a, and an." Here are a few models.

Table 1.13: Lists of Articles

English Articles	*Tamil Articles*
articles	peyarchsorkurikal – பெயர்ச்சொற்குறிகள்
the	andha, intha – அந்த, இந்த
a	oru/or – ஒரு/ஓர்
one	onru – ஒன்று
some	konjam – கொஞ்சம்
few	kuraivaana – குறைவான
the book	andha puththakam – அந்த புத்தகம்
the books	andha puththakangal – அந்த புத்தகங்கள்
a book	oru puththakam – ஒரு புத்தகம்
one book	otraip puththakam – ஒற்றைப் புத்தகம்
some books	sila puththakangal – சில புத்தகங்கள்
few books	kuraivaana puththakangal – குறைவான புத்தகங்கள்

1.5.8 Conjunction

A Conjunction is a word used to connect clauses or sentences or coordinate terms in the same clause (e.g., and, but, if).

Table 1.14: Lists of Conjunction

English Word	*Speech*	*Definition*	*Tamil Meaning*
albeit	conj	although	இருப்பினும்.
although	conj	even though	இருப்பினும், இருந்தபோதிலும்
and	conj	besides	மேலும், மற்றும்
because	conj	due to the fact that	ஏனெனில், ஏனென்றால்
ergo	conj	therefore	ஆகவே.
if	conj	supposing that	ஒருவேளை எனக் குறிக்கும் சொல்.
lest	conj	so that	ஆகாதவாது.
nisi	conj	unless	ஒழிய.
nor	conj	not	இன்றி.
or	conj	particle to connect words suggesting alternatives	அல்லது (அ) அதாவது.

1.5.9 Interjection

An Interjection is a short utterance that usually expresses emotion and is capable of standing alone. Interjections are generally considered one of the traditional Parts of Speech. In writing, an interjection is typically followed by an exclamation point.

Table 1.15: Lists of Interjunction

English Word	*Speech*	*Definition*	*Tamil Meaning*
alack	int	cry of sorrow	அந்தோ.
alas	int	cry of sorrow	அந்தோ.
alleluia	int	praise of god	கடஉட்ப்புகழ்மாலை.
amen	int	so be it	அவ்வாறேஆகுக.
ave	int	welcome	வருக.
banzai	int	a shout of patriotic enthusiasm in Japan and wishing the emperor a long life.	அரசர் நீடூடிவாழ உவகையோடு ஜப்பானியர்கள் நாட்டுப்பற்றோடு எழுப்பும்ஒலி.
bismillah	int	(Arabic) in the name of Allah.	'பிஸ்மில்லா"; அல்லாவின் பெயரால்.
eh	int	as an expression of surprise or doubt	வியப்படையச்சொல்.
eureka	int	I have found in greek	கிரேக்கமொழியில் 'நான்கண்டுபிடித்துவிட்டேன்'
farewell	int	goodbye	சென்றுவா.
fie	int	for shame	கேவலம்.
ha	int	an expression of surprise	மகிழ்ச்சி, ஐயம் ஆகிய உணர்ச்சிகளை காண்பிக்கும் வியப்படைச்சொல், ஆ!
hallelujah	int	Praise to Lord.	கடவுட்புகழ்.
hallo	int	sound uttered to attract attention; a way of greeting	கவனத்தைத்தன்பால் ஈர்க்கும் வியப்பிடைச்சொல்.
heck	int	an expression of disgust or annoyance	சற்றேவெறுப்புள்ள மனநிலையைத்தெரிவிக்கும் ஒலிச்சொல்.
hello	int	hallo	கவனத்தைத்தன்பால்ஈர்க்கும் வியப்பிடைச்சொல்.
hey	int	the word expressed to attract attention	கவனத்தைஈர்க்கப்பயன்ப டுத்தும்கு றிப்புச்சொல்.

English Word	*Speech*	*Definition*	*Tamil Meaning*
hist	int	expressed to invite attention	கவனி என்றகவனத்தை ஈர்க்கும்சொல்.
hollo	int	an expression to attract attention	கவனத்தைஈர்க்க ஒலிக்கப்படும்சொல்.
hooray	int	hurry	கூவிமகிழ்ச்சிதெரிவிக்கும் குறிப்புச்சொல்.
hullo	int	an expression of surprise or to attract attention	கவனத்தைஈர்க்கப்பயன்படும் குறிப்புச்சொல்.
hump	int	an expression showing dissatisfaction	மனக்குறையைத்தெரிவிக்கும் ஒலி.
hurrah	int	expressing approval	பெரும்மகிழ்ச்சிக்குறிப்பு.
ichabod	int	an expression of regret for the glory that has departed	மறைந்தபுகழ்கண்டுஏங்குதல்.
lo	int	look	அதோபார்.
lor	int	lord	கடவுளே.
o	int	an exclamation of surprise	வியப்பு.
oh	int	exclamation of fear	பயம்.
oops	int	used as an expression of one's mistake, etc	வியப்பையோ, எமாற்றத்தியோ தெரிவிக்கும் ஒலி.
ouch	int	an expression of sudden pain	திடீர் என உண்டாகும் வழியை உணர்த்தும்சொல்.
pah	int	an expression of disgust	வெறுப்பைப்குறிக்கும் ஒலி.
phew	int	an expression of impatience	பொருமையின்மையை க்காட்டும் குறிப்பொலி.
quotha	int	indeed.	உண்மையாகவே

1.6 Sentence Structures and Word Ordering

The primary subjects of the object and the verb must accomplish the sentences, excluding poetry. Therefore, this subject order is frequently not standard in typical sentences, Subject-Object-Verb (SOV) though Object-Subject-Verb.

Tamil is a null-subject language. All Tamil sentences do not have subjects, verbs and objects. It is the validity of the sentences to create the possible making sentences. The verb—that is the muṭintuviṭṭatu (முடிந்துவிட்டது) "It is completed", or the just the subjects and objects, for suppose, such as atu eṉ vīṭu (அதுஎன்வீடு) "That is my house". The components must comprehend the SOV orders. The Tamil words there equal to the word '*is*', and the word is comprised just in the translation for passing on the meaning. The verb to *have* is not directly translated in the means of "to possess". In command to the say "I have a house" in Tamil" to construct the equal to and used the "There is a house to me" or "There exists a house to me".

Tamil has paucities of *relative pronouns,* but their denotation is carried by comparative participle constructions built using agglutination. For example, the English sentence "Call the boy who learned the lesson" will be said in Tamil roughly as "That-lesson-learned-boy call."

Explain the sentence formulation in Tamil.

Example

A sample passage in Tamil script with an *ITRANS*-like transliteration.

> ஆசிரியர் வகுப்புக்குள் நுழைந்தார்.
> அவர் உள்ளே நுழைந்தவுடன் மாணவர்கள் எழுந்தனர்.
> வளவன் மட்டும் தன் அருகில் நின்று கொண்டிருந்த
> மாணவி கனிமொழியுடன் பேசிக்
> கொண்டிருந்தான்.
> நான் அவனை எச்சரித்தேன்.

English tranlation of the above passage given below.

The teacher entered the classroom. When he entered, the students got up. Just Valavan was conversing with Kanimozhi, who was remaining close to him. I warned him.

Notes

1. Tamil doesn't have a definite article. The definite article utilized above is just an artifact of interpretation.
2. To comprehend why Valavan must be cautioned, it is essential to understand Indian social decorum. It is considered discourteous to be diverted when an individual of distinction (the educator for this situation) makes a section and the instructor might feel offended or insulted.

Table 1.16: Sentence Translation Table

Word (Romanized)	*Translation*	*Morphemes*	*Part of Speech*	*Person, Gender, Tense*	*Case*	*Number*	*Remarks*
aasiriyar	teacher	*aasiriyar*	***noun***	n/a, ***gender-neutral***, n/a	nominative	***honorific*** plural indicated by the ***suffix*** **ar**	The feminine gender *aasiriyai* can be used here too; the masculine gender *aasiriyan* is rarely used, considering the honored position of the teacher.
vakuppaRaiyuL	inside the class room	Vakuppu + aRai + uL	***adverb***	n/a	locative	n/a	***Sandhi*** (called *puṇarci* in Tamil) rules in Tamil require euphonic changes during ***agglutination*** (such as the introduction of *y* in this case).
nuzhainthaar	entered	*nuzhainthaar*	***verb***	third, gender-neutral, ***past***		honorific plural	In an honorific context, the masculine and feminine equivalents nuzhainth**aan** and nuzhainth**aaL** are replaced by the collective nuzhainth**aar.**
avar	He	*avar*	***pronoun***	third, gender-neutral, n/a	nominative	honorific plural indicated by the suffix **ar**	In honorific contexts, the masculine and feminine forms *avan* and *avaL* are not used.
uLLE	inside	*uLLE*	adverb	n/a		n/a	

Word (Romanized)	*Translation*	*Morphemes*	*Part of Speech*	*Person, Gender, Tense*	*Case*	*Number*	*Remarks*
nuzhainthavudan	upon entering	*nuzhaintha + udan*	adverb	n/a		n/a	***Sandhi*** rules require a *v* to be inserted between an end-vowel and a beginning-*u* during ***agglutination.***
maaNavarkaL	students	*maaNavarkaL*	***collective noun***	n/a, ***masculine,*** often used with gender-neutral connotation, n/a	nominative	***plural*** indicated by suffix**kaL**	
ezhunthanar	got up	*ezhunthanar*	verb	third, gender-neutral, past		plural	
VaLavan	VaLavan (name)	*VaLavan*	***proper noun***	n/a, masculine, usually indicated by suffix **an**, n/a	nominative	***singular***	
Mattum	Only	*mattum*	adverb	n/a		n/a	
than	his (self) own	*than*	pronoun	n/a, gender-neutral, n/a		singular	
arukil	near (lit. "in nearness")	*aruku + il*	adverb	n/a	locative	n/a	The ***postposition*** *il* indicates the ***locative case.***
ninRu kondiruntha	standing	*ninRu +kondu +iruntha*	adverb	n/a		n/a	The verb has been morphed into an adverb by the incompleteness due to the terminal **a.**

Word (Romanized)	*Translation*	*Morphemes*	*Part of Speech*	*Person, Gender, Tense*	*Case*	*Number*	*Remarks*
maaNavi	student	*maaNavi*	noun	n/a, feminine, n/a		singular	
kanimozhiyudan	with Kanimozhi (name of a person)	*kanimozhi +udan*	adjectives	n/a	comitative	n/a	The name *Kanimozhi* literally means *sweet language.*
pEsik kondirunthaan	was talking	*pEsi + kondu+irunth aan*	verb	third, masculine, past continuous		singular	Continuousness indicated by the incompleteness brought by *kondu.*
naan	I	*naan*	pronoun	first person, gender-neutral, n/a	nominative	singular	
avanai	him	*avanai*	pronoun	third, masculine, n/a	accusative	singular	The ***postposition ai*** indicates the ***accusative case.***
echarithEn	cautioned	*echarithEn*	verb	first, indicated by suffix **En**, gender-neutral, past.		singular, the plural would be indicated by substituting*En* with *Om.*	

1.7 CONCLUSION

Tamil is a classical language and ancient language. This chapter discusses the history of the language. Secondly, it gives the fundamentals of Tamil grammar, character set and classification. In particular, it describes the Parts of Speech in the Tamil Language. The chapter concludes with Sentence Structures and Word Ordering. One can get complete exposure to the basics of the Tamil language by reading this chapter. It is tough to perform Tamil Computing because of various reasons. One needs this fundamental understanding to perform the computing with the language. Hence, this chapter focuses on some of the basics of the language.

CHAPTER 2

Basics for Tamil Computing

2.1 INTRODUCTION TO TAMIL COMPUTING (WHAT IS TAMIL COMPUTING?)

The 'Tamil Computing' refers to information processing in Tamil. The word Tamil refers to the 'Tamil Language'. At the same time, computing is a general term that relates to information processing, where information is associated with data, typically a text string, a number, or an image. Computing in the Tamil language may broadly relate to computer programs that process Tamil language text strings, which may be input through a keyboard and displayed on a conventional screen display.

A primitive approach to computing in the Tamil language may be through computer programs that do string processing on texts of the Tamil language much the same way it is done for the Roman (ASCII) strings. Many existing applications may be adapted to work with text strings in the Tamil language, and this turns out not to be a simple task because of the large set of tools that will be handled. Hence, new approaches to addressing Tamil language text are required. Two universally accepted implementations are used: one uses Unicode, and one uses TSCII codes.

It is best to deal with the problem of computing in the Tamil language by first understanding how characters have been used in our ancient and modern texts. It will give us an insight into the linguistic base of our languages, allowing us to develop a universal approach to dealing with the Tamil language of the world.

2.2 HISTORY OF TAMIL COMPUTING

The journey of Tamil computing history began with the development of the first Tamil script encoding standards in the late 1970s. Dravidian Languages such as Tamil use non-roman letters as alphabets. In this section, features of some of the most commonly used Tamil font faces and software are reviewed and a possible scheme towards standardizations of Tamil Computing is also indicated.

In the last five decades, many different font faces and desktop publishing (DTP) Software have appeared for word-processing of Tamil and along with them different typing (input) methods. Font Encoding, i.e., the exact location of different Tamil characters in the standard extended ASCII table (128 or 256 slots) in the Tamil font being used determines the 'output' content of the Tamil text irrespective of the mode of 'input'.

There are growing numbers of Tamil pages being put on the Internet/WWW using fonts, packages with different font encoding schemes. So, procedures have to be designed so that ordinary/common people can put up web pages and share information electronically in Tamil worldwide without getting involved too much into the technical nitty-gritty.

Starting from the late-1970s and on into the early-1980s, when personal computers became available on a significant scale, a number of Tamil professionals around the world were enthused to undertake individual efforts to incorporate Tamil language in computers and in the then-fledgling Internet. By the late-1980s, the degree of incompatibility among these efforts had limited the value of their contributions to local contexts. Initiatives for the usage of Tamil in computers and in Information technology started as early as 1985. The Tamils living in different parts of the world started developing their own 8-bit bi-lingual encodings for Tamil using the extended ASCII area. Thus, there were a number of encodings for Tamil in use around the world. Mean time the Government of India introduced a 7-bit encoding called ISCII for all the Indian languages for transliteration purposes. In October 1991 Unicode Tamil was announced by the Unicode Consortium incorporating the 7-bit encoding of ISCII standard in the 16-bit environment of Unicode. But this standard of Unicode Tamil was not put to use until recently. The usage of many encoding schemes for Tamil posed a number of problems for the users as well as developers, causing a big concern for the Tamil computing world.

The first initiative to identify the dimensions of disorder in Tamil computing was undertaken in 1997 at a conference in Singapore (since then called the First Tamil Internet Conference). It was resolved in the conference that the Keyboard and Encoding diversities should be solved and the Tamil Nadu Government should take initiatives to evolve 8-bit Encoding and Keyboard standards for Tamil. The issues raised there were further articulated at the Second Tamil Internet Conference held in Chennai in February 1999. At this conference it was proposed that the placement of glyphs within a Tamil font would follow a recommended scheme. Both bilingual and monolingual schemes were standardized. The conference also arrived at a standard for data entry in Tamil. Despite agreements with respect to the Tamilnet-99 keyboard and encoding for TAB and TAM Tamil characters, there was a sense of non-fulfilment with respect to many other crucial tasks. As a fallout of the 1999 Chennai conference, Tamil Nadu got a Tamil Virtual University and the Tamil Software Development Fund. And, more substantially, attention came to be paid to the value of promoting Tamil computing on multiple fronts.

Later, the Sub-Committee on Tamil in Information Technology entrusted this responsibility to the Tamil Virtual University (TVU) to evolve a suitable Character encoding scheme for Tamil for adoption into the Unicode standard through appropriate testing and evaluation of the possible schemes, using the Tamil Software Development Fund. TVU formed a committee with experts pooled from KaNithamizh Sangam for evolving a suitable Character encoding scheme for Tamil for adoption into the Unicode standard. The committee developed a 16-bit All Character encoding for Tamil and the same was presented at the pre-conference session of TamilNet 2000 conference in Colombo, Sri Lanka as well as at the main TamilNet2000 conference in Singapore. This was also discussed at the TamilNet 2001 conference in Malaysia where an expert from Microsoft was present.

Recognizing the need for an institutional foundation at the international level to pay continued attention to emerging developments in Tamil Computing and Internet applications, the International Forum for Information Technology in Tamil (INFITT) was formed and located in Singapore with generous support from the Singapore government. The problem of Unicode Tamil was also discussed widely in a work group of INFITT. Subsequently the new scheme an all Character 16-bit encoding scheme for Tamil, and a vowel and consonant scheme along with the present Unicode Tamil were tested and evaluated on different applications. The results of the investigation were favorable to the 16-bit All Character Encoding for Tamil (TACE 16) in 2008 after several rounds of deliberations by various forums.

Global cooperation facilitated by momentous developments in Internet and computing technologies has since then led to many remarkable achievements. Sending and receiving e-mail with text in Tamil, or handling chat, have been greatly simplified. Text-to-speech editors have been developed for the benefit of the visually handicapped. The number of Tamil websites has become large, and it is growing. These include those of Tamil newspapers and magazines and e-journals. Then there are greeting cards, matrimonial sites, on-line learning resources, those sites devoted to cookery, beauty tips, health issues, songs, movies, tourism information, games, puzzles and so on, in Tamil. Unicode has become a world standard and many computer applications have provided Unicode support so that multilingual text can be handled.

At the same time, there are many lingering problems. Information Technology, in respect of the use of Tamil on computers, should necessarily aim to reach all the people so as to give them the benefits of this new technological power. People should be able to use computers to deal with information given in Tamil without knowledge of English on the part of the user. Some of the current research and development efforts address such issues.

The Tamil community is suddenly waking up to all the missed opportunities after realizing how far Tamil language is falling behind many other languages. This is evident from the degree of enthusiasm and cooperation seen in putting together the Tamil Internet Conference (TIC-2010) in Coimbatore to be held in conjunction with the World Classical Tamil Conference, thanks to unstinted support from the Government of Tamil Nadu. A large number of papers submitted to TIC-2010, especially from Tamil Nadu, address almost all of the advanced concepts.

The papers on Artificial Intelligence and Natural Language Processing include developments in Text to Speech, Syntactic Parsing, Character Recognition, Spell Check and so on. Several papers discuss approaches to Bilingual Data Bases, Electronic Tamil Libraries, Tamil in Mobile Devices, Tamil Search Engines, and Processing Large Data Bases in Tamil. Some explain methods of computer-assisted Tamil Teaching, Tamil Blogging and Tamil Content Development in Wikipedia. Many ideas have been advanced to carry the work forward through the next several years through special efforts in areas such as computational linguistics, and the collection of a large bank of Bi-lingual Corpora of some two million sentences.

One of the basic objectives of TIC-2010 is to stimulate the interest of the younger generation in Tamil Computing. The enthusiastic response from school and college students to the Tamil computing competition and Wikipedia has been encouraging. This needs to be sustained and expanded. The special participatory exposition of Tamil computing and Internet developments, including e-governance, Tamil periodicals, Tamil software, Tamil-related efforts of several multinational companies and so on are expected to attract the interest of lakhs of visitors. The enthusiasm and the level of expectations are evident. The spirit of cooperation needs to be sustained.

Google Translate is a free multilingual machine translation service developed by Google, to translate text, which includes Tamil. It offers a website interface, mobile apps for Android and iOS, and an application programming interface that helps developers build browser extensions and software applications. Google Translate supports over 100 languages including Tamil at various levels. Its first version released in April 2006 used a statistical machine translation service and in November 2016, Google announced that Google Translate would switch to a neural machine translation engine - Google Neural Machine Translation (GNMT) - which translates "whole sentences at a time, rather than just piece by piece. It uses this broader context to help it figure out the most relevant translation, which it then rearranges and adjusts to be more like a human speaking with proper grammar". Originally only enabled for a few languages in 2016, GNMT is used in all 103 languages in the Google Translate roster as of 2019.

There are also several supporting tools developed by the various organizations across the world, by involvement of open communities. But it should see a more change and we have to see a complete **Tamil Machine** with the support of the corporate world as well as in the open world. It is really a challenging time for the developers of Tamil Computing world.

2.3 ENCODING AND STANDARDS

Electronic processing of text in any language requires that characters (letters of the alphabet along with special symbols) be represented through unique codes. This is called encoding. Usually, this code will also correspond to the written shape of the letter. A code is basically a number associated with each letter so that computers can distinguish between different letters through their codes. The set of all the characters in a language is called a repertoire. The encoding can be further classified into glyph-based encoding and character-based encoding. A character encoding defines how sequences of numeric codes are presented as sequences of octets. The code serves the important purpose of standardizing the approach to dealing with text on different computer systems. All Indian languages have a phonetic base built on top of a fixed number of vowels and consonants; the writing systems permit many different shapes to be generated depending on the syllables in the text. Some of the character-based encodings are ASCII, ISCII, and Unicode. A glyph is the shape given to a symbol. Some of the glyph-based encodings are TAM, TAB, TSCII. In typography, a glyph is a particular graphical representation of a grapheme, or several graphemes in combination (a composed glyph), or only a part of a grapheme. In computing as well as typography, the term character refers to a grapheme. A character or grapheme is a unit of text, whereas a glyph is a graphical unit.

2.4 SBCS (Single Byte Character Set)/MBCS (Multi-byte Character Set)

In general, the character coding schemes follows a character-based approach or glyph-based approaches for encoding the letters. This is done in through SBCS/MBCS. SBCS, or Single Byte Character Set, is used to refer to character encodings that use exactly one byte for each graphic character.

The term SBCS is commonly contrasted against the terms DBCS (double-byte character set) and MBCS (multi-byte character set). The multi-byte character sets are used to accommodate languages with more characters and symbols than English and other predominantly Asian languages such as Chinese, Japanese, and Korean. These are sometimes referred to by the acronym CJK.

A variable-width encoding is a type of character encoding scheme in which codes of differing lengths are used to encode a character set (a repertoire of symbols) for representation in a computer.

Early variable width encodings using less than a byte per character were sometimes used to pack English text into fewer bytes in adventure games for early microcomputers.

Multibyte encodings are usually the result of a need to increase the number of characters which can be encoded without breaking backward compatibility with an existing constraint.

A double-byte character set (DBCS) is a character encoding in which either all characters (including control characters) are encoded in two bytes, or merely every graphic character, not representable by an accompanying single-byte character set (SBCS) is encoded in two bytes (Han characters would generally comprise most of these two-byte characters).A DBCS supports national languages that contain a large number of unique characters or symbols (the maximum number of characters that can be represented with one byte is 256 characters, while two bytes can represent up to 65,536 characters).

For example, the internationalized domain name (IDN) is an Internet domain name that contains at least one label that is displayed in software applications, in whole or in part, in a language-specific script or alphabet, such as Arabic, Chinese, Cyrillic, Tamil, Hebrew or the Latin alphabet-based characters with diacritics, such as French.

2.5 TAB/TAM ENCODING SCHEMES

Various text styles are accessible in the Tamil language. The Government of Tamil Nadu normalized the Tamil textual-style stockpiling design by introducing the TAM/TAB standard on June 13, 1999.

TAM is the Monolingual Tamil (8-bit) encoding plan of the public authority of Tamil Nadu, which has the most significant Tamil-talking population on the planet. Today, a tremendous amount of Tamil text-based data in advanced libraries, online papers, magazines, and so forth is accessible in this encoding plan. TAM, a monolingual Tamil encoding plan, is a superset of the TAB bilingual Tamil encoding plans. TAM is a glyph encoding plan,

Table 2.1: Displays the TAM Encoding Table for Tamil

TAMxxx - MONO LINGUAL CODING SCHEME FOR TAMIL																
	32	48	64	80	96	112	128	144	160	176	192	208	224	240
0		0	©	ஜி	`	ஸ்ரீ				ஒ	ஔ	ஞு	உ	ப
1	!	1	கி	ஸி	ஸீ	ஹீ		'	ன்	ஞ	ஜு	ஃ	ஊ	ம
2	"	2	ஙி	ஷி	தீ	க்ஷீ	க்	'	'	க	ஜு	'	எ	ய
3	#	3	சி	ஹி	நீ	ஏ	ங்	"	ஏ	று	கூ	'	ஏ	ர
4	$	4	ஞி	ஜீ	பீ	மீ	ச்	"	ர	ஓ	ஙூ	'	ஐ	ல
5	%	5	ணி	ஹீ	யீ	ஓம்	ஞ்	•	•	ஜு	ஒ	'	ஒ	வ
6	&	6	தி	க்ஷி	ரீ	ஸ்	ட்	ஞோ	°	து	நூ	நூ	ஓ	ழ
7	'	7	நி	கீ	லீ	ஷ்	ண்	ஷை	¬	•	ரூ	ஐ	ஃ	ள
8	(	8	பி	ஙீ	வீ	ஜ்	த்	ர்	→	நு	ஊரா	ஞூ	க	ற
9	)	9	மி	சீ	ழீ	ஹ்	ந்	ல்	©	பு	நூ	ரூ	ங	ன
10	*	:	யி	ஞீ	ளீ	க்ஷ்	ப்	வ்	ெ	மு		நூ	ச	ஸ
11	+	;	ரி	[	றீ	{	ம்	ழ்	ே	யு	நூ	ஜூ	ஞ	ஷ
12	,	<	லி	\	னீ	|	ய்	ள்	ை	ரு	டூ	அ	ட	ஜ
13	-	=	வி	]	ஸீ	}			ரு	ஜு	மூ	ஆ	ண	ஹ
14	.	>	ழி	^	ஷீ	~			டி	லு	யூ	இ	த	க்ஷ
15	/	?	ளி	_	ஜீ	DEL		ற்	டீ	வு	ரூ	ஈ	ந	ஸ்ரீ

whereas Unicode is a person encoding plan. Subsequently, a cooperative, one-to-many, many-to-one, or many-to-numerous relationship exists between the Tamil letter sets in the TAM and those in Unicode. A Tamil letter set in a TAM-encoded text can be comprised of solitary, two, or three bytes. Table 2.1 presents the TAM encoding table for Tamil.

TAB is the official Bilingual Tamil (8-bit) encoding scheme of the Tamil Nadu government. The TAB encodes Roman script along with Tamil script. The first 128 code points of the TAB encoding scheme were identical to those of the ASCII character set. The following 128 code points are a subset of the TAM monolingual Tamil encoding scheme: The TAB is also a glyph-encoding scheme. A Tamil alphabet in a TAB-encoded text consists of one, two, or three code points. Table 1 lists the TAB encoding tables for Tamil. As with any glyph encoding, TAM and TAB encoding would also suffer from problems such as learning and scripting.

Table 2.2: Presents TAB Bilingual Coding Scheme for Tamil

TABxxx - BILINGUAL CODING SCHEME FOR TAMIL														
	32	48	64	80	96	112	128	144	160	176	192	208	224	240
0		0	@	P	'	p				ஞு	ஞூ		உ	ப
1	!	1	A	Q	a	q		'		ஙு	ஜு		ஊ	ம
2	"	2	B	R	b	r		'	•	க	ஜூ	"	எ	ய
3	#	3	C	S	c	s		"	ா	ஷு	கூ	"	ஏ	ர
4	$	4	D	T	d	t		"	ி	ஒ	ஜூ	'	ஐ	ல
5	%	5	E	U	e	u		•	•	ஹு	ஞூ	'	ஒ	வ
6	&	6	F	V	f	v			ெ	ஷு	ஷூ	ஸூ	ஓ	ழ
7	'	7	G	W	g	w			¬	•	ே	ஹூ	ஃ	ள
8	(	8	H	X	h	x			ⓓ	ஜு	ஹூ	ஞெ	க	ற
9	)	9	I	Y	i	y			©	பு	ஸூ	ஞ	ங	ன
10	•	:	J	Z	j	z			ெ	மு		ஜூ	ச	ல
11	+	;	K	[	k	{			ே	யு	ஙூ	ஹூ	ஞ	ஜ
12	,	<	L	\	l	l			ை	ரு	டு	அ	ட	ஜ
13	-	=	M	]	m	}				வு	மூ	ஆ	ண	ஹ
14	.	>	N	^	n	~			ீ	நு	ஜூ	இ	த	க்ஷ
15	/	?	O	_	o	DEL			ு	ழு	ஞூ	ா	ந	ஸ்ரீ

Thus, the Tamil people, including government departments, faced double jeopardy. They bought Tamil fonts for Windows OS at an exorbitant cost and bought the Windows operating system to run it. In the above circumstances, ELCOT decided to free Tamil fonts from a single vendor so that the Government, Press, home users, Tamil Scholars, and international users could access high-quality standardized Tamil fonts for desktop use as well as database use (bilingual).

2.6 TACE16 ENCODING SCHEMES

Tamil All Character Encoding (TACE16) is a 16-bit unicode-based character encoding scheme for the Tamil language. It uses Tamil99, and Tamil Typewriter keyboard layouts approved by the Tamil Nadu Government and maps the input keystrokes to their corresponding characters in the TACE16 scheme. The Keyboard driver for this encoding scheme is available on the Tamil Virtual University website. To read the files created using the TACE16 method, the corresponding Unicode Tamil fonts for this encoding scheme are available on the same website. These fonts not only have a mapping of glyphs for characters in TACE16 format, but also have a mapping

Table 2.3: Presents a Suggested New Code for TACE-16 (18.7.2007)

A suggested new code for TACE-16 (18.7.2007)

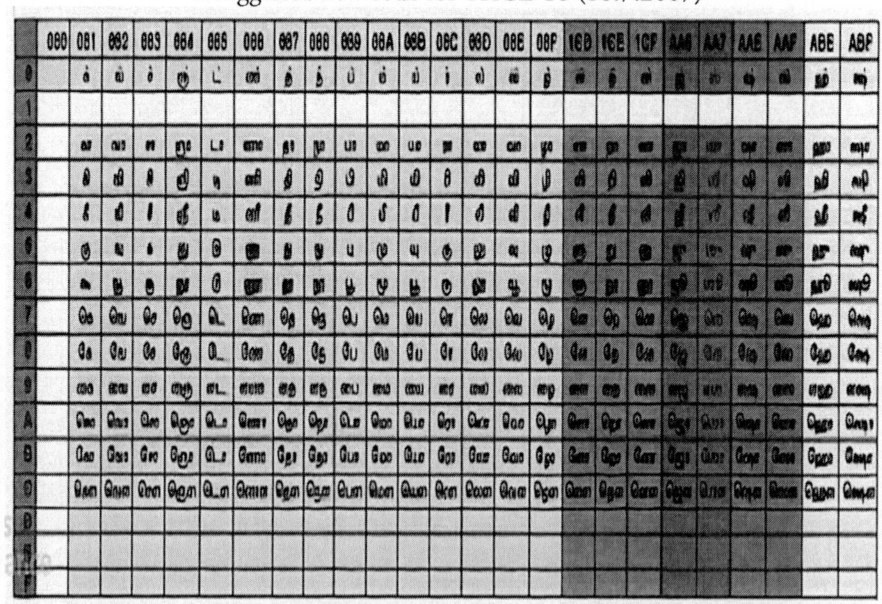

of glyphs for the present Unicode encoding for both ASCII and Tamil characters. It provides backward compatibility for reading existing files created using the current Unicode encoding scheme for Tamil.

All the fonts were designed to adapt to these coding schemes. Standard official fonts have been released on the Tamil Virtual University website.

2.7 STANDARD CODES FOR TAMIL COMPUTING

Over the years, different approaches have been taken to represent syllables for internal storage. Many of these, relied on the availability of a specific font designed to accommodate the shapes from which syllables could be composed (built). In 1991, the TSCII standard was adopted for general use and subsequently Unicode for different Indian scripts became a standard. Salient aspects of these encoding standards are discussed in these sections. Tamil Script Code for Information Interchange (TSCII) is a coding scheme for representing the Tamil script. The lower 128 code points are plain ASCII, the upper 128 code points are TSCII-specific. After long years of being used on the Internet by private agreement only, it was successfully registered with the IANA in 2007. Apart from this the system is also adopts Unicode Standards.

In computer and machine-based telecommunications terminology, a character is a unit of information that roughly corresponds to a grapheme, grapheme-like unit, or symbol, such as in an alphabet or syllabary in the written form of a natural language. Examples of characters include letters, numerical digits, common punctuation marks (such as "." or "-"), and whitespace. Computers and communication equipment represent characters using a character encoding that assigns each character to something—an integer quantity represented by a sequence of digits, typically—that can be stored or transmitted through a network. Historically, the term character has been widely used by industry professionals to refer to an encoded character, often as defined by the programming language or API. With the advent and widespread acceptance of Unicode and bit-agnostic coded character sets, a character is increasingly being seen as a unit of information, independent of any particular visual manifestation.

There are three common standard codes are used for across the world. These codes include 1. TSCII 2. ISCII and 3. UNICODE.

1. Tamil Script Code for Information Interchange (TSCII) is a coding scheme for representing the Tamil script. The lower 128 codepoints are plain ASCII, the upper 128 codepoints are TSCII-specific. After long years of being used on the Internet by private agreement only, it was

successfully registered with the IANA in 2007.TSCII encodes the characters in visual (written) order, paralleling the use of the Tamil Typewriter.

2. Indian Script Code for Information Interchange (ISCII) is a coding scheme for representing various writing systems of India. It encodes the main Indic scripts and a Roman transliteration. The supported scripts are: Assamese, Bengali (Bangla), Devanagari, Gujarati, Gurmukhi, Kannada, Malayalam, Oriya, Tamil, and Telugu. ISCII does not encode the writing systems of India based on Persian, but its writing system switching codes nonetheless provide for Kashmiri, Sindhi, Urdu, Persian, Pashto and Arabic. The Persian-based writing systems were subsequently encoded in the PASCII encoding. In 1991, the Bureau of Indian Standards adopted the Indian Standard Code for Information Interchange (ISCII), the ISCII standard that was evolved by a standardization committee, of which C-DAC was a member, under Department of Electronics during 1986–88. The ISCII document is available as IS13194:1991 from the BIS offices.

   The Indian Standard Code ISCII is an 8-bit/single byte umbrella standard, defined in such a way that all Indian languages can be treated using one single character encoding scheme. ISCII is a bilingual character encoding (not glyphs-based!) scheme. Roman characters and punctuation marks as defined in the standard lower-ASCII take up the first half the character set (first 128 slots). Characters for Indic languages are allocated to the upper slots (128–255). The Indian Standard ISCII-84 was Proposal for Tamil Standard Code TSCII 3 subsequently revised in 1991 (ISCII-91). ISCII was re-affirmed in 1997. Along with the character encoding scheme (ISCII), the Govt. of India also defined a keyboard layout for input called INSCRIPT. The research and development wing of the DOE, Govt. of India (called Center for Development of Advanced Computing, CDAC, based in Pune, India) has developed software packages based on these Indian standards. Multilingual and Multimedia products are based on Graphics and Intelligence-based Script Technology (GIST). There are only a handful of implementations of ISCII by third parties available in India.

3. Unicode is a computing industry standard for the consistent encoding, representation, and handling of text expressed in most of the world's writing systems. The standard is maintained by the Unicode Consortium, and as of May 2019 the most recent version, Unicode 12.1, contains a repertoire of 137,994 characters (consisting of 137,766 graphic characters, 163 format characters and 65 control characters) covering

150 modern and historic scripts, as well as multiple symbol sets and emoji. The character repertoire of the Unicode Standard is synchronized with ISO/IEC 10646, and both are code-for-code identical. These scripts also include Tamil Language.

These coding schemes are discussed in following sections in detail.

2.8 BASIC REQUIREMENTS FOR CODING SCHEMES

1. The codes must necessarily correspond to the syllables that form the linguistic base of the language. Furthermore, the encoding should use fixed-length codes, even if they are Multibyte. This is the best way to manage complex chain-processing problems with the phonetic nature of our language.
2. It would be helpful if the positions of the glyphs within a source for Tamil have no relationship with the codes assigned internally. This provision will help in the treatment of the chains.
3. The assigned codes must be adjusted to the classification order of the dictionary of linguistic letters.
4. The codes must also be assigned for the special symbols used in the language, the numbers included.
5. The codes must identify the consonants and vowels that form the syllable. This will help with linguistic analysis and conversion to other formats. This will also help in the synthesis of the voice.
6. Encoding must consider the syllables found in other Indian idioms so that transliteration in Tamil is easily influenced. This will help to teach other languages through Tamil.
7. The code assignment can also consider the numerical values traditionally assigned to the letters of Indian languages.
8. The codes should not have any relationship to show the letter. This recommendation is contrary to a previous observation that internal representation can influence the positioning of the glyphs. It is essential to ensure that the internal model is independent of the process of representing sources. Only then can we use software on different platforms.

2.9 UNICODE (UNICODE FOR INDIAN SCRIPTS)

The conventional Unicode idea functions admirably for Western dialects, where there is only one structure related to solitary code esteem. In this situation, a message string is essentially addressed by evenly picking the structures (glyphs) of the letters; consequently, a Unicode beginning for a Western content necessity just a glyph for each character code. The glyph file and the worth of the code can, in this manner, be, by and large, something similar. The code can be straightforwardly accounted for by a list of users. The necessary screen was reached when the glyphs were situated from one side to another. When Glyph lists are controlled, the first text is known precisely because of the planning of One Tone. Most languages have a composition framework that depends on the Latin letter set in this classification.

In Southeast Asia, composing frameworks depend on portrayal syllables, not consonants or vocals. This oversimplified view is ot helpful when the module shown is ot compared to a solitary letter. However, it is identified by a gathering of consonants and a vowel that establishes a phonetic quantum. The previously mentioned emphasized characters can likewise be found in this light, as made out of at least two structures from at least two codes.

The current issue with regard to Indian languages is one of figuring out how to show many such blends of essential letters, where every mix is perceived as a legitimate syllable. It compares to a circumstance in which a line of character codes guides a solitary shape. Regarding Indian scripts, the code for a consonant followed by a code for the vowel will, for the most part, infer a short syllable regularly delivered by adding a matra (ligature) to the consonant. However, there are sufficient exceptional cases for this standard.

Those liable to appoint Unicode esteems to Indian dialects had thought about the intricacy of delivering syllables. In any case, they felt that the allocated codes accurately mirrored the phonetic data in the syllable, thus proposing no compelling reason to allow codes for every syllable. It would be (and ought to be) feasible to distinguish something similar from a line of consonant and vowel codes (Just as syllables are recognized in English). It was explicitly suggested that a suitable delivering motor or forming motor can be utilized to produce a presentation from the multibyte portrayal of a syllable.

The Unicode developed from ISCII and a special Unicode arrangement indicates the setting in which a consonant or vowel is delivered as a syllable feature. Unicode again accommodated unequivocal portrayals accomplished by constraining the delivering utility to develop a shape for a syllable, which is not the same as what may be a default. In this manner, the Unicode for Indian content does not rigorously isolate the delivery from the inner portrayal and gives codes that determine the setting for providing. This inclination, shown by Unicode, can cause sufficient cerebral pain for designers when the Unicode text must be prepared.

Unicode acquired special significance regarding internationalization and consistency in the treatment of text-based data across the world's dialects. The primary idea driving Unicode is that message (Unicode-based message) portrayal holds an etymological substance that should be passed on. Simultaneously, this substance has been shown to have an incomprehensible structure. By obliging both of these necessities, Unicode has arisen as the ideal decision for addressing text in a COMPUTER application, explicitly one that arrangements with multilingual substance. Engineers worldwide are investing in providing unicode support for the entirety of their applications.

Table 2.4: Unicode

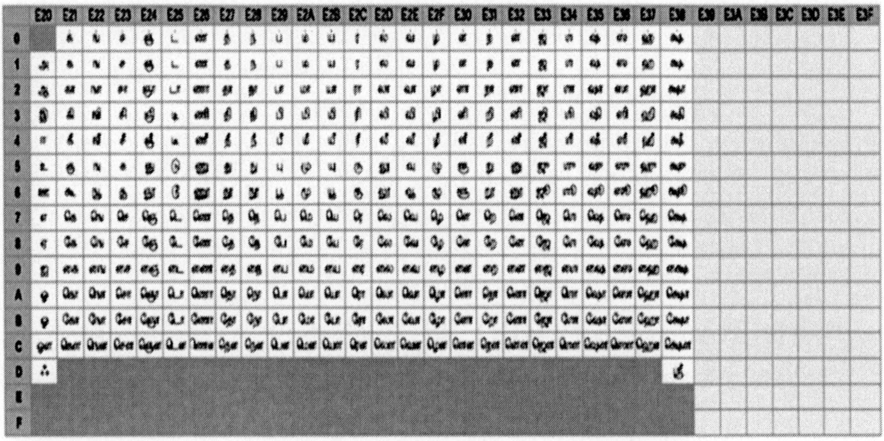

Multi-lingual information processing is one of the essential requirements when it comes to computerization in India. Here, the development of applications requires that interactive user interfaces in different regional languages must be part of each application. A specific regional language may be supported through one or more scripts even though a given script may be used for more than one language.

From a conceptual perspective, a critical issue is whether support for a script is equivalent to supporting a language. During the initial phases of the development of applications in Indian languages, one was concerned more with the rendering aspects of the text, a challenging problem in itself on account of the syllabic writing system followed by all Indian languages.

In essence, the standardization mentioned above (ISCII and Unicode) requires context-dependent text processing of each character instead of simply handling a character alone. In Western script, the writing system employs a relatively small set of shapes and symbols. It is sufficient to satisfy the requirement that the linguistic content and rendering information be specified through the same set of codes. Consequently, text processing can be comfortably achieved using a small set of codes.

Regarding our languages, the complexities of writing systems demand that many written shapes (typically thousands) be used. However, linguistic content may still be specified using a small set of codes for vowels and consonants (typically less than a hundred).

2.9.1 Limitations

Restrictions with Unicode are seen more regarding text handling than text shows. The idea of composing frameworks continued in India requires numerous presentation structures for a given syllable. It cannot be given effectively because the onus is on the developer to check whether the necessary showcase structure can be created using the given textual style. Henceforth, the application is affected by what the textual style can offer. An immediate outcome is that applications across stages cannot use a standard delivery approach, bringing about contrary qualities across applications and settings.

2.10 TSCII (TAMIL SCRIPT/STANDARD CODE FOR INFORMATION INTERCHANGE)

TSCII uses visual (written) order encoding for Tamil. Practical implementations of the ISCII and Unicode standards invoke modern font-handling techniques (such as glyph substitution) that are available only on state-of-the-art computers running under the latest versions of the OS (two of the most widely used platforms, Windows and Macintosh).

The Tamil Script Code for Information Interchange (TSCII) is a coding scheme for representing the Tamil script. After a long period of use on the Internet by private agreement, it was successfully registered with the IANA (Internet Assigned Numbers Authority) in 2007. TSCII encodes characters in a visual (written) order, paralleling the use of the Tamil Typewriter. Unicode used the logical order encoding strategy for Tamil, following ISCII, in contrast to Thai, where the visual order encoding grandfather by TIS-620 was adopted. The lower 128 code points are plain ASCII and the upper 128 are TSCII-specific. The government of Tamil Nadu endorses its own TAB/TAM standards for 8-bit encoding, and other older encoding schemes can still be found in the WWW.

Establish a consistent International Tamil character encoding standard that, in turn, leads to a self-standing Tamil font usable on all widely used computer platforms (Computers, Macintosh, and Unix), particularly on earlier models and operating systems.

The Tamil Nadu government recently embarked on an ambitious plan to provide Internet-access booths throughout the state. This will undoubtedly increase the awareness of computer utility among lay Tamils, who will be interested in getting on to Tamil computing on whatever computer they can access. In such a scenario, it is most likely that all early generation computers produced in the last decade will be used (e.g., AT/XT Computers capable of running earlier versions of Windows). All lay tamils will be a great disappointment if the standards require expensive state-of-the-art computer systems.

2.10.1 Limitations

Similarly, as with Unicode, the constraints with TSCII are seen more regarding text preparation than text show. The idea of composing frameworks continued in Tamil requires numerous showcase structures for a given

Table 2.5: Presents TSCII
(Tamil Standard Code for Information Interchange)

	0	1	2	3	4	5	6	7	8	9	A	B	C	D	E	F
0 (0-15)																
1 (16-31)																
2 (32-47)		!	"	#	$	%	&	'	(	)	*	+	,	-	.	/
3 (48-63)	0	1	2	3	4	5	6	7	8	9	:	;	<	=	>	?
4 (64-79)	@	A	B	C	D	E	F	G	H	I	J	K	L	M	N	O
5 (80-95)	P	Q	R	S	T	U	V	W	X	Y	Z	[	\	]	^	_
6 (96-111)	`	a	b	c	d	e	f	g	h	i	j	k	l	m	n	o
7 (112-127)	p	q	r	s	t	u	v	w	x	y	z	{	|	}	~	
8 (128-143)	௦	௧	ஸ்ரீ	ஜ	ஷ	ஸ	ஹ	க்ஷ	ஜ்	ஷ்	ஸ்	ஹ்	க்ஷ்	௨	௩	௪
9 (144-159)	௫	‘	’	“	”	௬	௭	௮	௯	ஙு	ஞு	ஙூ	ஞூ	௰	௱	௲
A (160-175)		ா	ி	ீ	ு	ூ	ெ	ே	ை	©	ௗ	அ	ஆ	இ	ஈ	உ
B (176-191)	ஊ	எ	ஏ	ஐ	ஒ	ஓ	ஔ	ஃ	க	ங	ச	ஞ	ட	ண	த	ந
C (192-207)	ப	ம	ய	ர	ல	வ	ழ	ள	ற	ன	டி	டீ	கு	சு	டு	ணு
D (208-223)	து	நு	பு	மு	யு	ரு	லு	வு	ழு	ளு	று	னு	கூ	சூ	டூ	ணூ
E (224-239)	தூ	நூ	பூ	மூ	யூ	ரூ	லூ	வூ	ழூ	ளூ	றூ	னூ	க்	ங்	ச்	ஞ்
F (240-255)	ட்	ண்	த்	ந்	ப்	ம்	ய்	ர்	ல்	வ்	ழ்	ள்	ற்	ன்	இ	

syllable. It cannot be given effectively because the onus is on the software engineer to check whether the necessary presentation structure can be created using the given text style. Consequently, the application is affected by the textual style. An immediate outcome is that applications across stages cannot use a standard delivery approach, bringing about contradictions across applications and settings.

2.11 ISCII (INDIAN STANDARD CODE FOR INFORMATION INTERCHANGE)

The ISCII is an eight-bit code that codes only the basic consonants and vowels of the language. Consequently, it requires more than one byte to represent a combination, although a consonant or vowel by itself requires only one byte. Thus, ISCII also amounts to a multibyte variable-length code, making the font rendering mechanism complex. Nevertheless, ISCII is a code that represents basic sounds and is helpful in practice. In the implementation, however, the ISCII encountered some problems with South Indian scripts, mainly Tamil.

The Indian Script Code for Information Interchange (ISCII) is a coding scheme that represents various writing systems in India. It encodes the main indic scripts and Roman transliteration. Assamese, Bengali (Bangla), Devanagari, Gujarati, Gurmukhi, Kannada, Malayalam, Oriya, Tamil, and Telugu supported the scripts. The ISCII does not encode the writing systems of India based on Persian, but its writing system switches codes for Kashmiri, Sindhi, Urdu, Persian, Pashto, and Arabic. Persian-based writing systems were subsequently encoded in the PASCII.

The ISCII has not been widely used outside certain government institutions and has now been rendered largely obsolete by the Unicode. Unicode uses a separate block for each indic writing system and largely preserves the ISCII layout within each block.

Brahmi-derived writing systems have a similar structure. Thus, the ISCII encodes letters with the same phonetic value at the same code point, overlaying various scripts. For example, the ISCII codes 0xB3 0xDB represent [ki]. It will be rendered as കി in Malayalam, കി in Devanagari, കി in Gurmukhi, and കി in Tamil. The writing system can be selected in rich text by markup or plain text using the ATR code described below. One motivation for using single encoding is the idea that it will allow easy transliteration from one writing system to another. However, there are insufficient incompatibilities that this is not a practical idea. See About ISCII.

The ISCII is an 8-bit encoding. The lower 128 code points are plain ASCII, and the upper 128 are ISCII-specific. In addition to the code points representing characters, ISCII uses a code point with a mnemonic ATR, indicating that the following byte contains one of the two types of information. One set of values changes the writing system until the next writing system indicator or end-of-line. Another set of values selects the display modes, such as bold and italics. The ISCII does not provide a means to indicate the default writing system.

Table 2.6: Indian Standard Code for Information Interchange

	00	01	02	03	04	05	06	07	08	09	0A	0B	0C	0D	0E	0F
20		!	"	#	$	%	&	'	(	)	*	+	,	-	.	/
30	0	1	2	3	4	5	6	7	8	9	:	;	<	=	>	?
40	@	A	B	C	D	E	F	G	H	I	J	K	L	M	N	O
50	P	Q	R	S	T	U	V	W	X	Y	Z	[	\	]		_
60		a	b	c	d	e	f	g	h	i	j	k	l	m	n	o
70	p	q	r	s	t	u	v	w	x	y	z	{	|	}		
80	. .	...	ஸ்ரீ	ஜ	ஷ	ஸ	ஹ	க்ஷ	ஜ்	ஷ்	ஸ்	ஹ்	க்ஷ்	ந	ச	ı
90		'	'	"	"	உ	ஜூ	ெ		ஙு	ஞு	ஙூ	ஞூ	ச	எ	ொ
A0		ா	்	ீ	ய	யா	ெ	ே	ை	©	ள	அ	ஆ	இ	ஈ	உ
B0	ஊ	எ	ஏ	ஐ	ஒ	ஓ	ஔ	ஃ	க	ங	ச	ஞ	ட	ண	த	ந
C0	ப	ம	ய	ர	ல	வ	ழ	ள	ற	ன	டி	டீ	கு	சு	டு	ணு
D0	து	நு	பு	மு	யு	ரு	லு	வு	ழு	ளு	று	னு	கூ	சூ	டூ	ணூ
E0	தூ	நூ	பூ	மூ	யூ	ரூ	லூ	வூ	ழூ	ளூ	றூ	னூ	க்	ங்	ச்	ஞ்
F0	ட்	ண்	த்	ந்	ப்	ம்	ய்	ர்	ல்	வ்	ழ்	ள்	ற்	ன்	ஜி	'

2.12 DIFFERENT STANDARD TAMIL FONTS

2.12.1 Introduction to Fonts

A COMPUTER textual style (or font style) is an electronic information record containing a bunch of glyphs, characters, or images, such as dingbats. Although the term text style initially alluded to a variety of metal types in a single style and size, since the 1990s, it has, for the most part, been used to indicate a versatile arrangement of advanced shapes that might be printed in a wide range of sizes.

There are three essential sorts of COMPUTER text style records in information designs:

- **Bitmap** fonts consist of a matrix of dots or pixels representing the image of each glyph for each face and size.

- **Outline** fonts (**vector** fonts) use Bezier curves, drawing instructions, and mathematical formulae to describe each glyph, thereby making the character outline scalable to any size.
- **Stroke** fonts use a series of specified lines and additional information to define the *profile*, size, and shape of the line on a specific face, which together describe the appearance of the glyph.

Bitmap font styles are quicker and simpler in computer code, yet non-adaptable, and require a different font style for each size. Diagram and stroke textual styles can be resized using a solitary textual technique and subbing various estimations for parts of every glyph, except that they are more confounded to deliver on-screen than bitmap textual styles. They require an extra COMPUTER code to provide the diagram to a bitmap for the show on screen or paper. A raster picture can be shown in an alternate size with some contortion; however, it is delivered rapidly.

Font styles are planned and made using font-style editors. Font styles explicitly intended for the COMPUTER screen and not printing are known as screen text styles. Textual styles can be monospaced (i.e., each character is plotted with a steady separation from the past character that it is close to while drawing) or relative (i.e., each character has its width).

2.12.2 Font Standards

In basic terms, text style accommodates a large number of images through precise cut shapes for every shot. The image is a non-exclusive idea, and the text style is an occurrence of the explicit portrayal of a number of images. Generally, the images referenced here are letters in order in a specific language, alongside accentuation imprints and unique characters. Textual styles used to be created by skilled workers and artisans during the times of printing machines that pre-owned portable typefaces. Today, textual styles are created by specialists and originators who work with computer-based instruments.

In a textual style, the particular shape of an image is depicted either as a computerized picture through bit maps or as a filled diagram. The previous is known as a bitmapped textual style, and the last is a blueprint textual style. Framework textual styles are being progressively utilized because of their versatility. The portrayals bring about a graphic picture or shape for every image, alluded to as a glyph. Most text styles have an arrangement for portraying up to 256 unique glyphs; however, practically speaking, somewhere around 190–240 may be available. Text mode shows on computers (DoS order shells or Unix order shells) use bitmapped textual styles, while layout text styles are utilized with Graphical UI.

Text-style guidelines have advanced over the long term and have been applied to the contents of various languages. Text styles with a limitation of eight-bit codes for choosing glyphs cannot uphold multiple scripts simultaneously. The idea of Font Encoding was utilized to permit a given 8-bit code to refer to a shape—the idea is that driving text style encoding licenses a shape related to a name. The character set is used to denote glyphs, and is mathematically portrayed.

Text styles are generally intended to facilitate detailed encoding plans. While delivering a text-produced structure to a computer application, the code for the text is first planned as a name, and the shape is situated through the interior name to glyph planning in the textual style. Internet browsers permit the decision of explicit textual styles for clear text encoding plans, which commonly vary across stages. It allows text on a site page to be shown appropriately, utilizing a suitable textual technique for which backing is provided in the program's framework.

2.12.3 Fonts for the Tamil Language

Textual styles are innately restrictive and will generally be contradictory across computer frameworks, similar to applications. In this case, the web is an archive in which its creators openly provide numerous text styles. In any case, the text style's plan, business, or uninhibitedly given manages the issues of delivering complex conjuncts and syllables when one considers Indian dialects/scripts. Today, not many non-Roman text styles are accessible for functional utilization, which is upheld under every one of the essential stages. This has forced reasonably severe limitations regarding web showcases of Indian Language text in light of the discretionary way to deal with planning the textual styles. Valid, these textual styles were not scheduled with the possibility of text handling yet more to obtain excellent printouts. In any case, when we utilize something similar to the site pages, we encounter numerous contradictions.

Standard textual styles for Western dialects. In word processors, the inward portrayal of text is the ASCII code (perhaps Unicode today) of the letter shown, and these codes are equivalent to the numeric codes appointed to the glyph areas containing the letters of the letter. Regarding textual types for Indian dialects, showcases must be developed with more than one glyph for some aksharas. Henceforth, the inward portrayal of aksharas is simply a component where the glyphs for the aksharas are situated inside the text style. In this way, one deals with the issue that the put-away text is not in a configuration that can be seen in various computer frameworks because the encoding standard may not be upheld in every framework. Additionally, glyph codes are the decision of the textual style originator and will bear no relationship to requesting aksharas in our contents. Subsequently, the phonetic preparation of the put-away message is a big assignment, as it is a text-style subordinate in any event for a similar hand.

Many text styles have been intended for Indian content, yet each plan has a particular reason that is regularly similar to a composting program. Applications managing Indian content have commonly depended on the accessibility of specific font(s). Subsequently, applications cannot move information in a straightforward manner across stages, because encoding issues become an integral factor. The matter proceeds even with Unicode, where some normalization has been influenced for message portrayal because message delivery is isolated from inward characterization (rigorously not valid for Unicode).

Unlike a site page in English that could be seen through a substitute textual style, if the predefined text style was not accessible, messages in Indian dialects would require the chosen text style to be available. This is why site pages are regularly made accessible for downloads and the textual type related to the shown data. Tragically, a solitary textual style cannot be used across stages. Indeed, even a given textual style is not ensured to show text effectively if the internal encoding varies, which is usually the case with numerous Indian language text styles.

2.12.4 A Brief Overview of the Method of Using Tamil with Fonts

Many arrangements for managing Tamil on Computers depend on utilizing novel textual styles. A textual style is a set of fundamental shapes that might be shown separately or in blends to show the letters of a content. The basic shapes (called Glyphs) are seen underneath, allowing Tamil messages to be displayed on a computer screen, as present in the textual style of Indo-Web-Kambar. Eight-bit text styles are the most commonly used textual styles with Indian content.

To understand how fonts are used, consider the string below, which is built from individual Glyphs.

தமிழ் மொழி　　த ம ி ழ ் ெ ம ா ழ ி

There are ten shapes here (each known as a glyph). However, only seven were unique. The glyphs inside the text style are designed per requirement, and the shapes shown are given positions on the computer. Ordinarily, a textual style upholds up to approximately 200 glyphs. In the Kambar textual style used to show the Tamil string over, the glyphs used in the string are (234, 235, 168, 200, 208, 226, 235, 232, 200, and 168) in the request where they will be shown. It should be noted that the string has only five Tamil letters through 10 glyphs, seven of which are particular. Consequently, passing by the number of Glyphs alone, one will ll not sort the number of letters in the string. Semantic examination of the message will be lumbering if a text-style-based portrayal is selected.

Table 2.7: Tamil with Fonts

	0	1	2	3	4	5	6	7	8	9	A	B	C	D	E	F
20																
30																
30																
50																
60																
70																
80																
90																
A0		ஸ	ஞ	ஜ	ஸ்ரீ	ஞ	-	ங	ˀ	•	˙	ூ		தா	றா	
B0		யு	வு	ஙு	ஜு	பு		பூ		யூ	ஙூ	ஜூ	ஈ	ஜா	ழூ	நா
C0	ஹு	ஹூ	க்ஷ	ஊ	ஜு	நு	கு	ழு	மூ	ஜூ	து	மு	டு	ஆ	கூ	டி
D0	˙	ஜு		ஞு	கூ	ரு	ஏ	று	ஓ	ஜு	பப	ஜூ	ஷ		டூ	மூ
E0	க்	ய	ெ	உ	ன	ந	க	ப	ா	ை	த	ம	ட	அ	ே	டி
F0	'	ளு	ச	ள	வ	ர	எ	ற	ஒ	ல	ண	ஹா	ஜு	ஓ	ஃ	

The technique frequently used to address Tamil data depends on the glyph codes of the letters. It turns out okay for a given text style; somewhat, string preparation may have likewise endeavored. Be that as it may, the reliance of the codes on the textual style impedes utilizing this methodology. The glyphs required to show a string are produced when the keystrokes are influenced. The keys on the ASCII console are planned in the Tamil letter, whose glyph is indicated through the ASCII code for the letter. A few blends require two keystrokes; however, this is acceptable because the subsequent keystroke is related to vowel augmentation.

Notwithstanding its effortlessness, this technique is unbearable because it is consistently challenging to recollect the plan between the Tamil letter and the key. However, a few blends require three keystrokes to be executed, whereas different mixes might be taken care of through only one keystroke. Depending on the text-style plan, the number of glyphs and keystrokes will shift. It illustrates the contrast between console passages for "ti" and "tu." This is not a down-to-earth approach to general acknowledgments.

It is along these lines clear that Tamil cannot be composed in a manner similar to that in English. In some ways, the blends must be considered in a textual, autonomous mode with the same number of keystrokes for mixes. Some word processors offer exceptional help by following keystrokes and joining them properly. Bundles from CDAC or word processors such as SRILIPI utilize this strategy. Here, the succession is chosen by the glyph mappings; however, in CDAC programming, extraordinary planning known as INSCRIPT is utilized, yet this is not natural for those acquainted with English. With most programming, one has almost no decision regarding the text style because the information passage technique is somehow attached to using textual styles. Neither textual-style planners concur with the glyphs or their situation inside the textual style. Regrettably, text styles are not generally viable across COMPUTER frameworks.

This key might have no phonetic comparability with Tamil letters. Indeed, for some textual styles where the originator had planned bilingual use (Roman and Tamil), the glyphs for Tamil are situated in the 128–255 territory, making the information section considerably more troublesome except if the MACRO components are conjured. Looking at the keyboard mapping issue, the glyph code fixed the way to be squeezed for a particular letter.

A few originators have prescribed one answer for placing the Tamil letters' glyphs at positions, compared to the ASCII code of the phonetically identical letter in Roman. This makes the information section more intuitive, yet varieties likewise occur when managing consonant-vowel mixes that change the consonant's basic shape.

In the plan followed at the CDAC, interior stockpiling is not as far as glyph codes yet relate to the ISCII conspire. The specific word processor changes the keystrokes into fitting letters, and a yield module changes over the ISCII or TISCII-based interior portrayal into glyph code. This strategy enjoys the benefit of being applied to all Indian dialects. However, an actual plan experiences language-explicit descriptions.

2.12.5 Installation of the Tamil Fonts

To write the content in Tamil Fonts, installing them in the system is essential. If the Windows Operating system is used, the following steps must be followed to install the fonts.

How to install Tamil Font Method-I (Windows)

Step I: Download Tamil font from the given link.

Step II: After downloading the Tamil fonts zip file -> Extract it -> Now, you will find. ttf file.

Step III: Double-click on ttf font file ->: when the file is open, it shows a button to install.

Step IV: Click on the install button; the Tamil font will be installed on your system, and you can now select the Tamil font in MS Word or type in Tamil font.

How to install Tamil Font Method - II (Windows).

Step I: Download Tamil Font from the given link.

Step II: After downloading the zip file -> Extract it -> Now, find. ttf file.

Step III: Go to Start -> Control Panel -> Fonts -> Paste the font file.

Step IV: When doing all this, go to MS Word, select Tamil font from the drop-down, and then type in Tamil font.

After installing the respective fonts, one can use the Tamil language system.

2.12.6 Recommendations for the Design of Fonts

1. It will be helpful to fix the glyphs in the displayable reach for ASCII because word processors can influence information passage. In the 128–255 range, the glyphs might be situated at positions related to the identical ASCII in the lower range. Thus, alteration should be possible on a text string that utilizes regular word processors. This is plausible for Tamil.
2. It is wise to offer a basic arrangement of glyphs for each content and to fix their areas. It will make it simpler to see similar text in various textual styles, insofar as the text does not join extraordinary images.
3. Textual-style delivery techniques have shifted across frameworks. It is intelligent to construct textual styles with standard encodings to be provided at various stages utilizing a similar glyph code. This determination is fundamental for electronic applications. The default encoding liked for Tamil is Latin-8859-1 encoding, which is upheld in every three stages. Additionally, the insignificant arrangement of glyphs might be utilized in every text style with some benefit.
4. It is a smart thought to remember accentuation and uncommon images of glyphs in the language. Accentuation should incorporate period, comma,

interjection, and question marks. Along these lines, it is feasible to regard unique images as features of the actual language.

5. It will be helpful to give some exceptional images utilized in old compositions of Tamil (e.g., shapes for some twofold consonants).
6. It is unavoidable that variable-width characteristics are planned. In the glyphs, it is suggested that the width is made of a variety of fundamental units (say 2 pixels). This will assist in holding a vertical arrangement in the text without turning to a unique organization. One glyph might be preserved as an uncommon space with an odd number of units. This glyph is valuable in terms of having an arrangement.

2.13 TAMIL KEYBOARD AND STANDARDS—INTRODUCTION

In computing, a keyboard is a typewriter-style device that uses an arrangement of buttons or keys to act as a mechanical lever or electronic switch. A keyboard typically has characters engraved or printed on the keys, and each keyboard press typically corresponds to a single written symbol. In everyday usage, the keyboard is used to type text and numbers into a word processor, text editor, or other program. Keyboards are also used in computer games, either with regular keyboards or keyboards with unique game features, which can expedite frequently used keystroke combinations.

2.13.1 The COMPUTER Keyboard Operation

Globally, two types of keyboard have been used. IBM COMPUTER was equipped with a keyboard with 84 keys, with function keys on the left side of the keyboard. The other is that IBM AT introduced a 101-key keyboard, which soon became the standard for most COMPUTER clones. This keyboard has function keys along the top and a Numeric Keypad at the right-hand end.

2.13.2 Keyboard Basics and issues for Tamil Keyboards

A typical modern computer keyboard consists of a processor chip connected to a matrix of keys arranged in an array of X- and Y-scan lines. The keyboard processor puts an active low, "one-off" count on each output line, and then scans the input lines for a low one at a time. The first COMPUTER keyboard used an 8048-processor chip and eight × 11 or 12 matrices. The matrix typically consists of eight output lines and 11 or 12 input lines. The keyboard processor uses a lookup table to find code that represents the key that has been pressed. When the keyboard processor finds a "Key Press" during its matrix scanning, it sends a code to indicate that key to the keyboard interface circuit in the computer.

There are only 26 letters in the English language, but in the Tamil Language, 248 letters exist and directly accommodate the complexity of the English language. Hence, different glyph- or phonetic-based approaches are used to design keyboards. Moreover, other keyboards are designed, used, and standardized by community groups, Governments, and Organizations. These standardized layouts are explained in detail in the following sections.

2.13.3 Tamil Keyboard Standards and Features

Various types of keyboard exist worldwide. There are standards for the keyboard types. The keyboard standards were as follows:

2.13.3.1 *Tamil 99 Keyboard*

Tamil 99 is a keyboard format endorsed by the Tamil Nadu Government. The design, alongside a few monolingual and bilingual textual styles for use with Tamil, was supported by the public authority request on June 13, 1999. Tamil consoles are regular bilingual keyboards fundamentally joined with the English Language for simple access. This console permits you to type using the Tamil Phonetic Keyboard, creating a content message in this language.

Figure 2.1: Presents Script Text in Tamil 99 Keyboard

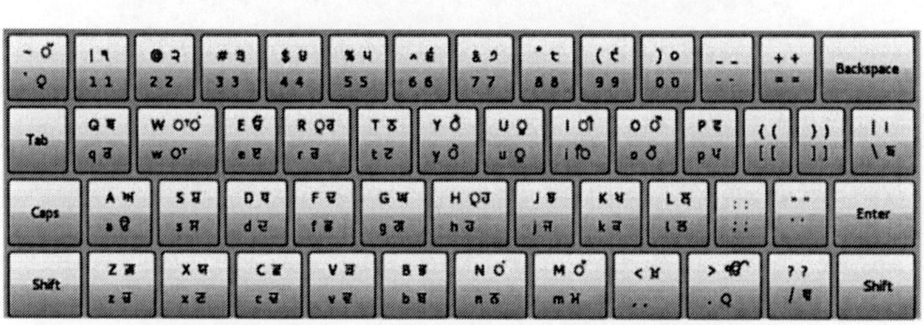

Figure 2.2: Tamil Typing Phonetic Keyboard

Figure 2.3: Tamil 99 Keyboard Typing Phonetic Keyboard

The government of Tamil Nadu constituted a technical committee to standardize the keyboard. A functioning Group and an International Technical Committee were included to assess the specialized issues and finish coding principles for Tamil because the agreement was reached during the International Conference and Seminar on Tamil in Information Technology (Tamil net 99) held in Chennai on February seventh and eighth February 1999.

Because of the last ideas of the International Technical Committee, the Subcommittee on Tamil in Information Technology of the State Information Technology Task Force proposed monolingual and bilingual encoding plans for Tamil glyphs and a standard Tamil Keyboard format. The Government of India normalizes this keyboard design for contributing text in the Indian dialects written in Brahmic scripts and the Santali language, registered in the non-Brahmic OlChiki hand. It was created by the Indian government and upheld by several public and private associations.

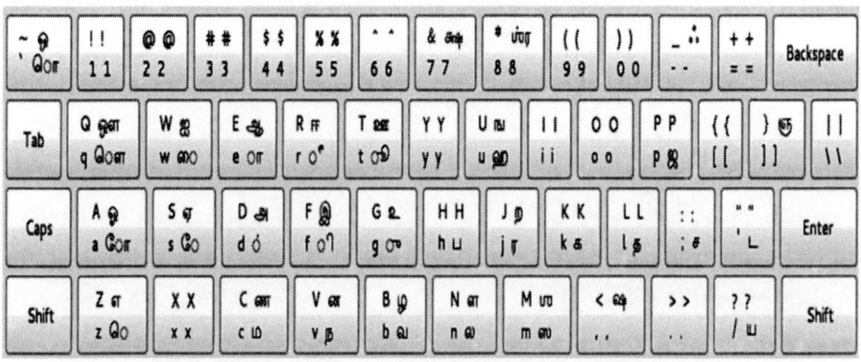

Figure 2.3: C-DAC Designed the Inscript Keyboard

C-DAC designed an inscription keyboard. The Central Government standardized the keyboard. India for typing the Indic text.

Keyboard Features

Separate keys are used for typing *Swara* (independent vowel) and the corresponding *matra* (dependent vowel sign). However, if *matra* keys are typed alone, *Swara* is produced instead.

Matra cannot be added to existing consonants. The complete Consonant + Vowel (CV) combination must be typed simultaneously.

The 'a' matra is implicit in the consonants. The d key should be explicitly used to add a *halant* symbol.

The asciicircum key ^ is used for the ZWNJ (Zero Width Non-Joiner). The ampersand key & is used for the ZWJ (Zero Width Joiner). These are required in some scripts to produce an alternate rendering of a character.

2.13.3.2 *English Keyboard*

விசைப்பலகை வடிவமைப்பு

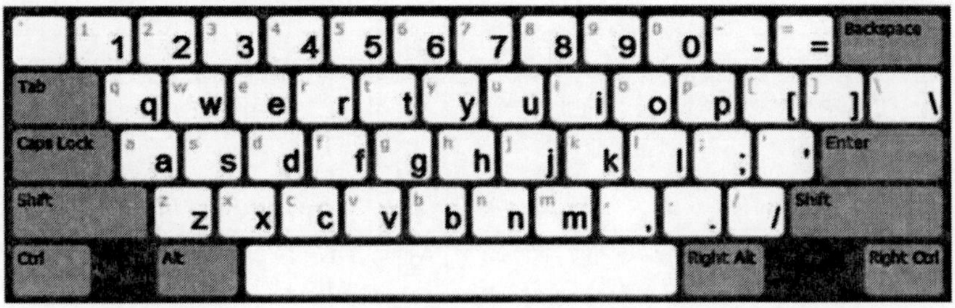

Figure 2.4: English Keyboard

This is an English keyboard used to enter English letters. However, this keyboard is sometimes used in Tamil transliteration.

2.13.3.3 *Roman Keyboard*

This keyboard is helpful for people who are e unaware of Tamil typewriting. When they type Roman letters, they will automatically transfer them to Tamil letters. To type extended Tamil characters ('nadil'), one must press the short letters ('kuril') twice. To type 'ஆ,' press the 'aa' in English.

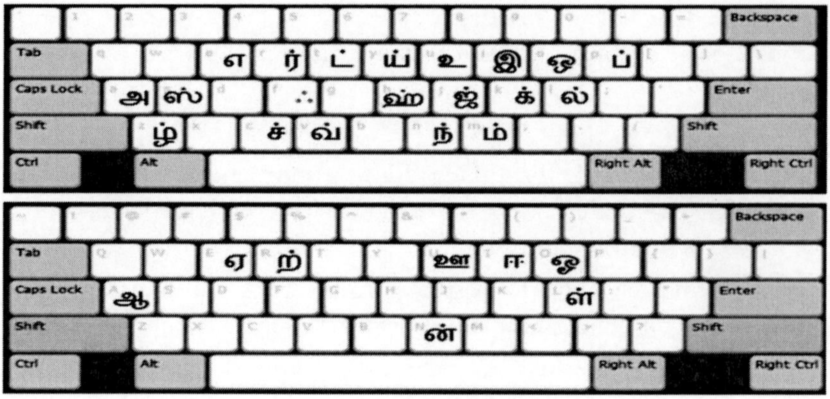

Figure 2.5: Roman Keyboard

Table 2.8: Shows Roman Keyboard

விசைஅழுத்தி	A	aa	i	ii\I	U	uu\U	E	ee\E	Ai
உயிரெழுத்துகள்	அ	ஆ	இ	ஈ	உ	ஊ	எ	ஏ	ஐ
விசைஅழுத்தி	O	oo\O	Au	F					
உயிரெழுத்துகள்	ஒ	ஓ	ஔ	ஃ					
விசைஅழுத்தி	K	Nk	C	Nc	T	Nn	Th	N	P
மெய்யெழுத்துகள்	க்	ங்	ச்	ஞ்	ட்	ண்	த்	ந்	ப்
விசைஅழுத்தி	M	Y	R	L	V	Z	R	L	N
மெய்யெழுத்துகள்	ம்	ய்	ர்	ல்	வ்	ழ்	ற்	ள்	ன்
விசைஅழுத்தி M - மெய்யெழுத்து	M + aa/A	M + i	M+ ii/l	M+ u	M+ uu/U	M+ e	M+ ee/E	M+ ai	M+ o
துணைவரிவடிவம்	◌ா	◌ி	◌ீ	◌ு	◌ூ	ெ◌	ே◌	ை◌	ெ◌ா
விசைஅழுத்தி M - மெய்யெழுத்து	M+ oo/O	M+ au							
துணைவரிவடிவம்	ே◌ா	ெ◌ள							

2.13.3.4 *Tamilanjal Keyboard*

The Tamilanjal keyboard is very valuable for those who are familiar with Tamil typewriting. Popularly used in eKalappai, this keyboard follows the Anjal phonetic standards. It is the easiest to use when learning about Tamil. This keyboard follows the Tamil99 standard recommended by the Tamil Nadu government. It is also used to type the standardized transliteration of Tamil fonts while typing Roman letters in English.

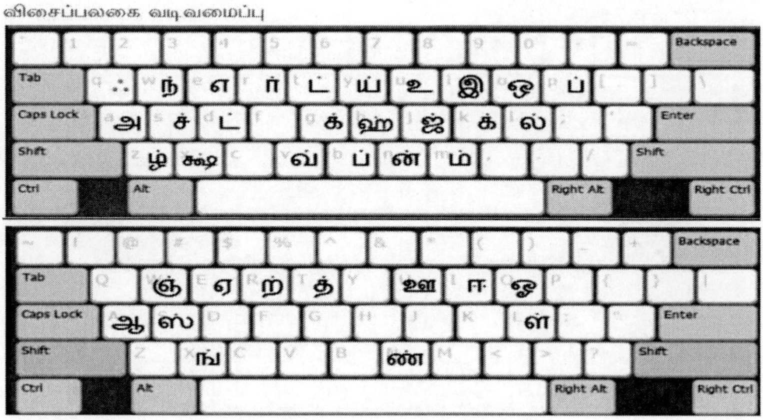

Figure 2.6: Tamilanjal Keyboard

Table 9: Shows Tamilanjal Keyboard

விசைஅழுத்தி	a	aa\A	i	ii\I	u	uu\U	e	ee\E	ai
உயிரெழுத்துகள்	அ	ஆ	இ	ஈ	உ	ஊ	எ	ஏ	ஐ
விசைஅழுத்தி	o	oo\O	au	q					
உயிரெழுத்துகள்	ஒ	ஓ	ஔ	ஃ					
விசைஅழுத்தி	k	X	s	W	t	N	T	w	p
மெய்யெழுத்துகள்	க்	ங்	ச்	ஞ்	ட்	ண்	த்	ந்	ப்
விசைஅழுத்தி	m	y	r	l	v	z	R	L	n
மெய்யெழுத்துகள்	ம்	ய்	ர்	ல்	வ்	ழ்	ற்	ள்	ன்
விசைஅழுத்தி	S	sh	j	h	x	shri			
மெய்யெழுத்துகள்	ஸ்	ஷ்	ஜ்	ஹ்	க்ஷ்	ஸ்ரீ			
விசைஅழுத்தி M - மெய்யெழுத்து	M + aa/A	M + i	M+ ii/I	M+ u	M+ uu/U	M+ e	M+ ee/E	M+ ai	M+ o
துணைவரிவடிவம்	◌ா	◌ி	◌ீ	◌ு	◌ூ	ெ◌	ே◌	ை◌	ெ◌ா
விசைஅழுத்தி M - மெய்யெழுத்து	M+ oo/O	M+ au							
துணைவரிவடிவம்	ே◌ா	ெ◌ள							

2.13.3.5 *Tamil Bamini Keyboard*

The Tamil Bamini keyboard is also known as the Tamil Inayam 99 keyboard. This keyboard is popularly used in eKalappai, which follows the

Figure 2.7: Tamil Bamini Keyboard

Bamini standard common in Sri Lanka based on old Tamil typewriters. Bamini font is a well-known font for Tamil Typing; it is the typewriter font for Tamil Typing. Here, we show the layout of the Bamini font Keyboard style. Candidates seeking to learn Tamil Typing can start typing by mapping the following image of the Bamini font and English key mapping. This keyboard uses a standardized transliteration method for typing Tamil letters. To type the vowel- consonants '**ஊயிர் – மெய்எழுத்துக்கு**', first type the consonants followed by type:

Table 2.10: Shows Tamil Bamini Keyboard

விசைஅழுத்தி	M	M	,	<	C	C	V	V	I
உயிரெழுத்துகள்	**அ**	**ஆ**	**இ**	**ஈ**	**உ**	**ஊ**	**எ**	**ஏ**	**ஐ**
விசைஅழுத்தி	X	X	Xs	/					
உயிரெழுத்துகள்	ஒ	ஓ	ஔ	ஃ					
விசைஅழுத்தி	F	Q	R	Q	L	Z	J	E	G
உயிர்மெய்யெழுத்துகள்	க	ங	ச	ஞ	ட	ண	த	ந	ப
விசைஅழுத்தி	K	A	U	Y	T	O	S	W	D
உயிர்மெய்யெழுத்துகள்	ம	ய	ர	ல	வ	ழ	ற	ள	ன
விசைஅழுத்தி	F	Nil	R	Nil	L	Z	J	E	G

உயிர்மெய்யெழுத்துகள்	கு	ஙு	சு	ஞு	டு	ணு	து	நு	பு
விசைஅழுத்தி	K	A	U	Y	T	O	S	W	D
உயிர்மெய்யெழுத்துகள்	மு	யு	ரு	லு	வு	ழு	ளு	று	னு
விசைஅழுத்தி	Nil	^	%	Nil	*	F	Nil		
உயிர்மெய்யெழுத்துகள்	ஹூ	டூ	மூ	ரூ	ழூ	கூ	சூ		
விசைஅழுத்தி M - மெய்யெழுத்து	;	H	P	P	Nil	Nil	N	N	l
துணைவரிவடிவம்	◌்	◌ா	◌ி	◌ீ	◌ு	◌ூ	ெ◌	ே◌	ை◌
விசைஅழுத்தி M - மெய்யெழுத்து	n+M+h	N+M+h	n+M+s						
துணைவரிவடிவம்	ொ	ோ	ௌ						

2.13.3.6 *Tamil Inscript Keyboard*

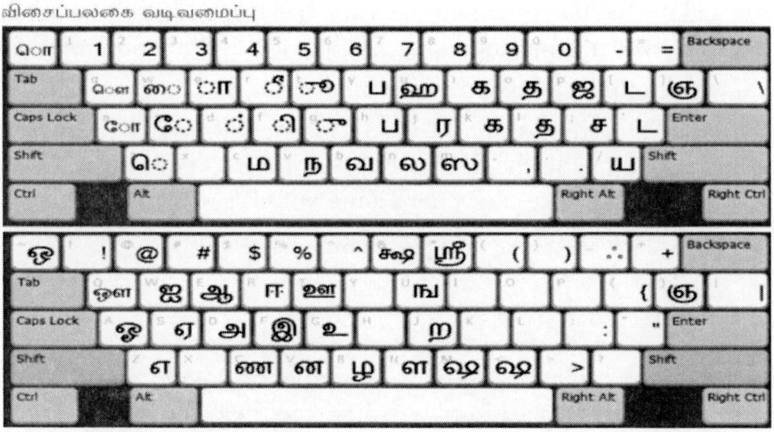

Figure 2.8: Tamil Inscript Keyboard

Table 2.11: Shows Tamil Inscript Keyboard

விசைஅழுத்தி	D	E	F	R	G	T	Z	S	W
உயிரெழுத்துகள்	அ	ஆ	இ	ஈ	உ	ஊ	எ	ஏ	ஐ
விசைஅழுத்தி	~	A	Q	-					
உயிரெழுத்துகள்	ஒ	ஓ	ஔ	ஃ					
விசைஅழுத்தி	k or i	U	;	} or]	, or [	C	I or o	V	h or y

உயிர்மெய்யெழுத்துகள்	க	ங	ச	ஞ	ட	ண	த	ந	ப
விசைஅழுத்தி	C	/	J	N	B	B	N	J	V
உயிர்மெய்யெழுத்துகள்	ம	ய	ர	ல	வ	ழ	ற	ள	ன
விசைஅழுத்தி	M	< or M	P	U	&	* or *r			
கிரந்தயெழுத்துகள்	ஸ	ஷ	ஜ	ஹ	க்ஷ	ஸ்ரீ			
விசைஅழுத்தி M - மெய்யெழுத்து	M+ d	M+ e	M+ f	M+ r	M+ g	M+ t	M+ z	M+ s	M+ w
துணைவரிவடிவம்	◌்	◌ா	◌ி	◌ீ	◌ு	◌ூ	ெ◌	ே◌	ை◌
விசைஅழுத்தி M - மெய்யெழுத்து	M+ ,	M+ a	M+ q						
துணைவரிவடிவம்	ெ◌ா	ே◌ா	ெ◌ள						

2.13.3.7 *Murasu Anjal Keyboard*

Murasu Anjal is a popular Tamil input method technology developed by Murasu Systems, a software company based in Singapore. It is a virtual keyboard layout specifically designed for typing in the Tamil language. It's also designed to facilitate typing in the Tamil language using standard English (QWERTY) keyboards by employing a phonetic transliteration method.

Here's how Murasu Anjal typically works:

1. **Phonetic Transliteration:** Murasu Anjal allows users to type Tamil characters phonetically using English letters. For example, typing "vanakkam" would result in the Tamil word "*வணக்கம்*".
2. **Intuitive Layout:** The keyboard layout is designed to be intuitive for users familiar with English keyboards. It maps English characters to Tamil letters in a logical and consistent manner.
3. **Wide Adoption:** Murasu Anjal is widely adopted across various digital platforms, including computers, smartphones, and tablets. It's often used in software applications, websites, and digital communication tools to enable Tamil speakers to input text in their language.
4. **Versatility:** Murasu Anjal supports various Tamil language features, including consonant-vowel combinations (*க* + *◌ா* = *கா*), Grantha characters, and special symbols used in Tamil script.
5. **Customization:** Users can customize and adapt Murasu Anjal to suit their preferences and typing style, making it a versatile and user-friendly Tamil input method.

Overall, Murasu Anjal has played a significant role in enabling Tamil speakers to communicate and type in their language across different devices and applications, contributing to the preservation and promotion of the Tamil language in digital spaces.

Murasu Anjal keyboard lets you type Tamil with English letters. The keys will generate Tamil letters based on the keymap provided in the table below. The keys approximate the sound of the Tamil letters.

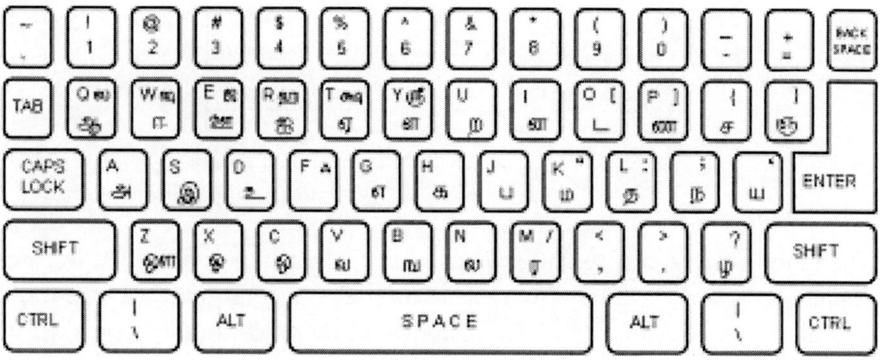

Murasu Anjal Keymap

அ	a	க்	k	வ்	v
ஆ	aa	ங்	ng	ழ்	z
இ	i	ச்	c	ள்	L
ஈ	ii	ஞ்	nj	ற்	R
உ	u	ட்	d	ன்	n
ஊ	uu	ண்	N	ஜ்	j
எ	e	த்	t	ஷ்	sh
ஏ	ee	ந்	w	ஸ்	S
ஐ	ai	ப்	p	ஹ்	h
ஒ	o	ம்	m	க்ஷ்	x
ஓ	oo	ய்	y	ஸ்ரீ	sr
ஔ	au	ர்	r	ௐ	OM
ஃ	q	ல்	l		

Pulli (புள்ளி)

Consonant keys by default generate letters with pulli (மெய் எழுத்துகள்). The pulli is removed when the 'a' key is typed.

Examples:

Typing 'a' to remove pulli

keystrokes	*output*
k	க்
ka	க
p	ப்
pa	ப

Vowel signs

When a vowel key is typed after a consonant, the key generates a vowel sign instead of a vowel. To explicitly type a vowel after a consonant, change mode to English and back to Tamil. You can do this by touching the toggle button twice.

Example:

Vowel Signs

keystrokes	*output*
ki	கி
k[toggle toggle]i	கஇ

Paired consonants

The following consonant pairs can be typed with alternate key sequences:

1. ன்ற்

Type ndr to get ன்ற்

keystrokes	*output*
mandram	மன்றம்
kandru	கன்று
toondri	தோன்றி

2. ற்ற்

Type tr to get ற்ற்.

keystrokes	*output*
patru	பற்று
pootri	போற்றி
petraal	பெற்றால்

3. ண்ட்

Type nd to get ண்ட்.

keystrokes	*output*
mandapam	மண்டபம்
kandu	கண்டு
veendaam	வேண்டாம்

4. ந்த்

Type nt to get ந்த்.

keystrokes	*output*
sontam	சொந்தம்
anti	அந்தி
vantu	வந்து

5. ஞ்ச்

Type njj to get ஞ்ச்.

keystrokes	*output*
manjjaL	மஞ்சள்
tanjjam	தஞ்சம்
konjji	கொஞ்சி

6. *Words beginning with ந*

When ‘n’ is typed after a space, tab or return key, it will automatically produce ந். To explicitly get ன், type upper case ‘W’

keystrokes	*output*
<space>n	ந்
W	ன்

2.13.3.8 *Tamil Modular Keyboard*

The Tamil Modular keyboard is designed based on Tamil writers or Tamilinayam 99 keyboards. This is also helpful for those who know Tamil typewriting. It is also based on a standardized transliteration-based approach. While typing in Roman letters, it automatically transforms into Tamil letters.

Figure 2.10: Tamil Modular Keyboard

Table 2.13: Shows Tamil Modular Keyboard

விசைஅழுத்தி	F	T	H	J	>	‘	V	B	U
உயிரெழுத்துகள்	அ	ஆ	இ	ஈ	உ	ஊ	எ	ஏ	ஐ
விசைஅழுத்தி	Z	Z	Not Used	]					
உயிரெழுத்துகள்	ஒ	ஓ	ஔ	ஃ					

விசைஅழுத்தி	G	N	R	N	I	D	Y	L	K
உயிர்மெய்யெழுத்துகள்	க	ங	ச	ஞ	ட	ண	த	ந	ப
விசைஅழுத்தி	E	C	A	M	O	X	W	S	P
உயிர்மெய்யெழுத்துகள்	ம	ய	ர	ல	வ	ழ	ற	ள	ன
விசைஅழுத்தி	Q	{	[	}	\	|			
மெய்யெழுத்துகள்	ஸ	ஷ	ஜ	ஹ	க்ஷ	ஸ்ரீ			
விசைஅழுத்தி M - மெய்யெழுத்து	M+ t	M+ t	M+ h	M+ j	M+ (/)				
துணைவரிவடிவம்	◌்	◌ா	◌ி	◌ீ	◌ௌ				
விசைஅழுத்தி	W	E	R	Y	O	P	S	D	K
துணைவரிவடிவம்	ளு	மு	சு	து	வு	னு	று	ணு	பு
விசைஅழுத்தி	L	X	C	M	I	A	G	Vg	Vn
துணைவரிவடிவம்	நு	ழு	யு	லு	டு	ரு	கு	கெ	ஙெ
விசைஅழுத்தி	Vr	v[	vN	Vi	Vd	Vy	VI	Vp	Vk
துணைவரிவடிவம்	செ	ஜெ	ஞெ	டெ	ணெ	தெ	நெ	னெ	நெ
விசைஅழுத்தி	Vp	Vk	Ve	Vc	Va	Vs	Vm	Vw	Vo
துணைவரிவடிவம்	னெ	பெ	மெ	யெ	ரெ	றெ	லெ	ளெ	வெ
விசைஅழுத்தி	V{	vQ	V}	Vx	Bg	Bn	Br	B[	bN
துணைவரிவடிவம்	ஷெ	ஸெ	ஹெ	ழெ	கே	ஙே	சே	ஜே	ஞே
விசைஅழுத்தி	Bi	Bd	By	BI	Bp	Bk	Be	Bo	Ba
துணைவரிவடிவம்	டே	ணே	தே	நே	னே	பே	மே	யே	ரே
விசைஅழுத்தி	Bs	Bm	Bw	Bo	b{	bQ	b)	Bx	Ug
துணைவரிவடிவம்	றே	லே	ளே	வே	ஷே	ஸே	ஹே	ழே	கை
விசைஅழுத்தி	Un	Ur	u[	uN	Ui	Ud	Uy	UI	Up

துணைவரிவடிவம்	ஙை	சை	ஜை	ஞை	டை	ணை	தை	நை	னை
விசைஅழுத்தி	Uk	Ue	Uc	Ua	Us	Um	Uw	Uo	u}
துணைவரிவடிவம்	பை	மை	யை	ரை	றை	லை	ளை	வை	ஷை
விசைஅழுத்தி	Ux	n$	[$	N$	{$	Q$	}$	[$	
துணைவரிவடிவம்	ழை	ஙூ	ஜூ	ஜு	ஷூ	ஸூ	ஹூ	ஜூ	
விசைஅழுத்தி	!	1	2	3	4	5	6	7	8
துணைவரிவடிவம்	!	1	2	3	4	5	6	7	8
விசைஅழுத்தி	9	0	(	)	1\	,	.	?	#
துணைவரிவடிவம்	9	0	(	)	Rs	,	.	?	‘
விசைஅழுத்தி	@	%	=	_	;	:			
துணைவரிவடிவம்	‘	%	=	_	;	:			

2.13.3.9 *Tamil Singapore Keyboard*

The Tamil Singapore keyboard was a glib-based keyboard. To type the vowel-consonant letter, first, the consonant letter is followed by vowel letters in Tamil. To input the independent consonant letter alone, we type the letter followed by g (ஃ) instead.

Figure 2.11: Tamil Singapore Keyboard

Table 2.14: Tamil Singapore Keyboard

விசைஅழுத்தி	b/B	s	d/D	e/E	f/F	w/W	r/R	t/T	a/A
உயிரெழுத்துகள்	அ	ஆ	இ	ஈ	உ	ஊ	எ	ஏ	ஐ
விசைஅழுத்தி	v/V	c/C	x/X	g/G, z/Z /q					
உயிரெழுத்துகள்	ஒ	ஓ	ஔ	ஃ					
விசைஅழுத்தி	j	J	/	k	;/:	[	h/H	'/'	I/L
உயிர்மெய்யெழுத்துகள்	க	ங	ச	ஞ	ட	ண	த	ந	ப
விசைஅழுத்தி	k	p	n/N	i	u	]	m/M	y	o
உயிர்மெய்யெழுத்துகள்	ம	ய	ர	ல	வ	ழ	ற	ள	ன
விசைஅழுத்தி	Y	I	O	P	U				
கிரந்தயெழுத்துகள்	ஸ	ஷ	ஜ	க்ஷ	ஸ்ரீ				
விசைஅழுத்தி M - மெய்யெழுத்து	g	s	d	e	f	w	r	t	a
துணைவரிவடிவம்	◌்	◌ா	◌ி	◌ீ	◌ு	◌ூ	ெ◌	ே◌	ை◌
விசைஅழுத்தி M - மெய்யெழுத்து	v	c	x						
துணைவரிவடிவம்	ொ	ோ	ௌ						
விசைஅழுத்தி	1	2	3	4	5	6	7	8	9
தமிழ்எண்கள்	1	2	3	4	5	6	7	8	9
விசைஅழுத்தி	0	(	)	1\	\	,	.	?	!
தமிழ்எண்கள்	0	(	)	Rs	\	,	.	?	!

2.13.3.10 *Tamil Inayam 99 Keyboard*

The Tamil Nadu Government also released a Gazette to accept the same on 18.06.1999. The Tamil Nadu Government agrees with this, based on the recommendation of the Tamil Inayam 99 International Conference Technical Committee.

Table 2.15: Tamil Inayam 99 Keyboard

விசைஅழுத்தி	A	Q	S	W	D	E	G	T	R
உயிரெழுத்துகள்	அ	ஆ	இ	ஈ	உ	ஊ	எ	ஏ	ஐ
விசைஅழுத்தி	C	X	Z	F					
உயிரெழுத்துகள்	ஒ	ஓ	ஔ	ஃ					
விசைஅழுத்தி	H	B	[	]	O	P	L	:	J
உயிர்மெய்யெழுத்துகள்	க	ங	ச	ஞ	ட	ண	த	ந	ப

விசைஅழுத்தி	K	‘	M	N	V	/	U	Y	I
உயிர்மெய்யெழுத்துகள்	ம	ய	ர	ல	வ	ழ	ற	ள	ன
விசைஅழுத்தி	Q	W	E	R	T	Y			
கிரந்தயெழுத்துகள்	ஸ	ஷ	ஜ	ஹ	க்ஷ	ஸ்ரீ			
விசைஅழுத்தி M - மெய்யெழுத்து	Q	S	W	D	E	G	T	R	C
துணைவரிவடிவம்	◌ா	◌ி	◌ீ	◌ு	◌ூ	ெ◌	ே◌	ை◌	ெ◌ா
விசைஅழுத்தி M - மெய்யெழுத்து	X	Z							
துணைவரிவடிவம்	ே◌ா	ெ◌ள							
விசைஅழுத்தி	U	I	A	D	G	H	J	B	V
தமிழ்எண்கள்	௲	௱	௰	௧	௨	௩	௪	௯	௮
விசைஅழுத்தி	C	X	Z						
தமிழ்எண்கள்	௭	௬	௫						

விசைப்பலகை வடிவமைப்பு

Figure 2.12: Tamil Inayam 99 Keyboard

2.13.3.11 *Tamil Inayam MOE Keyboard*

The Tamil Inayam MOE Keyboard is shown in the following figure. Vowel letters and left-side consonant letters were fixed on the right side of the keyboard.

Table 2.16: Tamil Inayam MOE Keyboard

விசைஅழுத்தி	A	Q	S	W	D	E	G	T	R
உயிரெழுத்துகள்	அ	ஆ	இ	ஈ	உ	ஊ	எ	ஏ	ஐ
விசைஅழுத்தி	C	X	Z	F					
உயிரெழுத்துகள்	ஒ	ஓ	ஔ	ஃ					
விசைஅழுத்தி	H	B	[	]	O	P	L	:	J
உயிர்மெய்யெழுத்துகள்	க	ங	ச	ஞ	ட	ண	த	ந	ப
விசைஅழுத்தி	K	‘	M	N	V	/	U	Y	I
உயிர்மெய்யெழுத்துகள்	ம	ய	ர	ல	வ	ழ	ற	ள	ன
விசைஅழுத்தி	Q	W	E	R	T	Y			
கிரந்தயெழுத்துகள்	ஸ	ஷ	ஜ	ஹ	க்ஷ	ஸ்ரீ			
விசைஅழுத்தி M - மெய்யெழுத்து	Q	S	W	D	E	G	T	R	C
துணைவரிவடிவம்	◌ா	◌ி	◌ீ	◌ு	◌ூ	ெ◌	ே◌	ை◌	ொ
விசைஅழுத்தி M - மெய்யெழுத்து	X	Z							
துணைவரிவடிவம்	ோ	ௌ							
விசைஅழுத்தி	U	I	A	D	G	H	J	B	V
தமிழ்எண்கள்	௲	௱	௰	௧	௨	௩	௪	௯	௮
விசைஅழுத்தி	C	X	Z						
தமிழ்எண்கள்	௭	௬	௫						

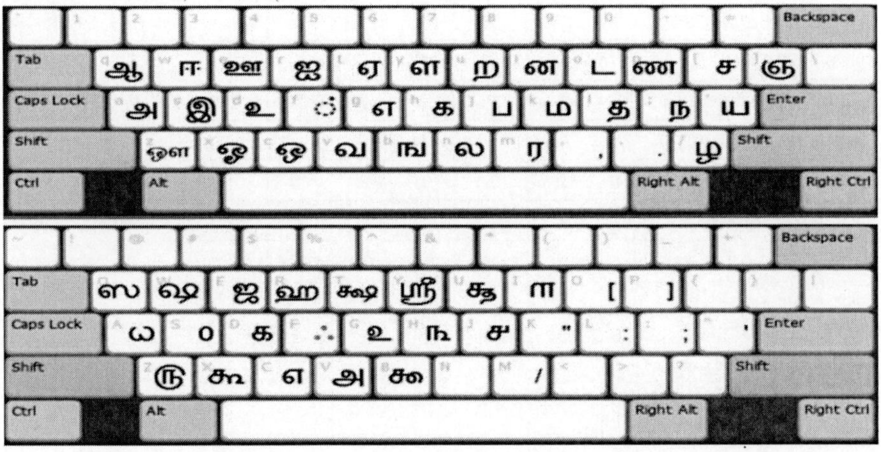

Figure 2.13: Tamil Inayam MOE Keyboard

2.13.3.12 *Tamil Typewriting Keyboard*

The Tamil Typewriting Keyboard is the same as the Tamil typewriter keyboard, and those who know Tamil typing can use it.

Figure 2.14: Tamil Typewriting Keyboard

Table 2.17: Tamil Typewriting Keyboard

விசைஅழுத்தி	M	M	,	<	C	C	V	V	I
உயிரெழுத்துகள்	அ	ஆ	இ	ஈ	உ	ஊ	எ	ஏ	ஐ
விசைஅழுத்தி	X	X	x +s						
உயிரெழுத்துகள்	ஒ	ஓ	ஔ						
விசைஅழுத்தி	F	‘	R	‘	L	Z	J	E	G
உயிர்மெய்யெழுத்துகள்	க	ங	ச	ஞ	ட	ண	த	ந	ப
விசைஅழுத்தி	K	A	U	Y	T	H	W	S	D
உயிர்மெய்யெழுத்துகள்	ம	ய	ர	ல	வ	ழ	ற	ள	ன
விசைஅழுத்தி	!	Z	$	]	c	-			
கிரந்தயெழுத்துகள்	ஸ	ஷ	ஜ	ஹ	க்ஷ	ஸ்ரீ			
விசைஅழுத்தி M - மெய்யெழுத்து	; + M	M+ h	p+M	p+M	‘[‘ / %	‘{‘ / ‘:’ / ‘^’ / ‘}’	b+M	n+M	i+M
துணைவரிவடிவம்	◌்	◌ா	◌ி	◌ீ	◌ு	◌ூ	ெ◌	ே◌	ை◌
விசைஅழுத்தி M - மெய்யெழுத்து	b+M+h	n+M+h	b+M+s						
துணைவரிவடிவம்	ெ◌ா	ே◌ா	ெ◌ள						

2.13.3.13 *Tamil Audio Keyboard*

This keyboard is also based on the Tamil letters sound system.

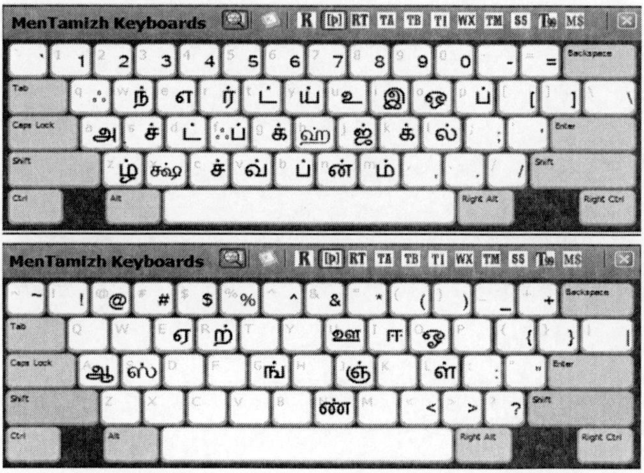

Figure 2.15: Tamil Audio Keyboard

Table 2.18: Tamil Audio Keyboard

விசைஅழுத்தி	a	aa\A	i	ii\I	u	uu\U	e	ee\E	ai
உயிரெழுத்துகள்	அ	ஆ	இ	ஈ	உ	ஊ	எ	ஏ	ஐ
விசைஅழுத்தி	o	oo\O	au	q					
உயிரெழுத்துகள்	ஒ	ஓ	ஔ	ஃ					
விசைஅழுத்தி	K \ g	G / ng	c/s	j/ gn	t /d	N	th/dh	w / n-	p
மெய்யெழுத்துகள்	க்	ங்	ச்	ஞ்	ட்	ண்	த்	ந்	ப்
விசைஅழுத்தி	m	y	r	l	v	z	L	R	n
மெய்யெழுத்துகள்	ம்	ய்	ர்	ல்	வ்	ழ்	ள்	ற்	ன்
விசைஅழுத்தி	S	sh	J	h	X	sr			
மெய்யெழுத்துகள்	ஸ்	ஷ்	ஜ்	ஹ்	க்ஷ்	ஸ்ரீ			
விசைஅழுத்தி M - மெய்யெழுத்து	M+ Aa/A	M+ i	M+ r	M+ g	M+ t	M+ z	M+ s	M+ w	M+ ,
துணைவரிவடிவம்	◌ா	◌ி	◌ீ	◌ு	◌ூ	ெ◌	ே◌	ை◌	ெ◌ா
விசைஅழுத்தி M - மெய்யெழுத்து	M+ a	M+ au							
துணைவரிவடிவம்	ே◌ா	ெ◌ள							

Figure 2.16: Tamil Unicode Keyboard

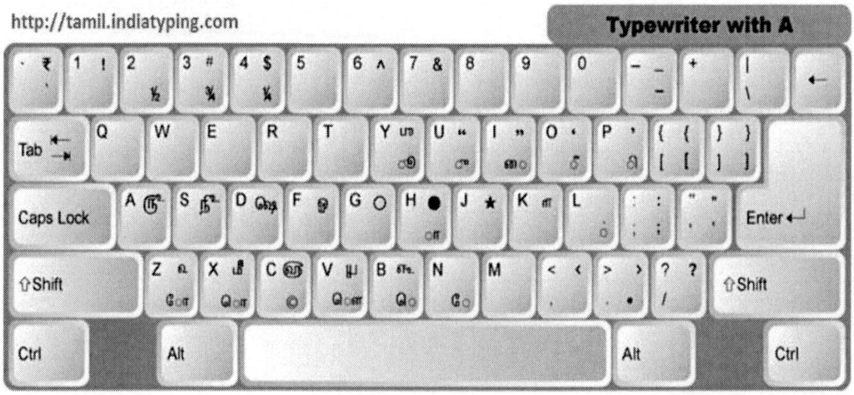

Figure 2.17: Tamil Unicode Keyboard

2.13.4 Input Software and Keyboard Layouts Mapping

Software plays a vital role in this study. It is essential to enable the software to use specific keyboard layouts. This section explains how to allow particular keyboard layouts on Windows platforms.

For composing in Tamil on Windows stages, the SALRC suggests the accompanying alternatives:

- **Windows Keyboard Layouts:** Microsoft Windows offers full help in composing Tamil console formats in its multilingual support. These might be gotten to through **Control Panel >System>Languages** and are a discretionary establishment (Click "On the best way to Install Fonts and

Layouts" in the left route bar for more data). The console might be seen with the On-screen Keyboard Viewer (**Start>Program Files>Utilities> Accessibility >On Screen Keyboard**). See Microsoft's Keyboard Layouts page for different designs accessible for Windows.

- **Tamil Indic IME:** Microsoft's **Bhasha India** (https://www.microsoft.com/en-in/bhashaindia/downloads.aspx) webpage provides a number of phonetic information technique editors (IMEs), viable with Windows, for Hindi, Bengali, Gujarati, Kannada, Malayalam, and Tamil. IME is a different application that should run close to Microsoft Office programming.

2.13.5 *Installing Fonts and Keyboard Layouts*

To type in South Asian languages, you must set up a keyboard. The following instructions were used to activate the keyboard. Most modern operating systems have fonts that can display the South Asian languages. If you want to add other fonts, use the "Installing Fonts' instructions below. If you are just learning to type in a South Asian language, you may want to activate an onscreen keyboard.

1. *Enabling South Asian Language Support*

Windows:

(a) Navigate to Start > Control Panel > Regional and Language Options
(b) Select the "Languages" tab
(c) Check "Install files for complex script and right-to-left languages and click "Okay." Windows may require insertion of the original installation CD to complete the installation.
(e) Reboot the computer.

2. *Activating Keyboard Layouts:*

Windows:

(a) Complete "Enabling South Asian Language Support
(b) Navigate to Start > Control Panel > Language and Regional Options
(c) In the dialogue window, select the "Languages" tab.
(d) Click on "Details" under the "Text Services and Input Languages" header.
(e) Under the "Installed Services" menu, select "Add." It will take you to a dialogue window that will allow you to add language input services,

including various keyboard layouts for the South Asian languages. Select the language under the language under "Input language." Press "Okay."

(f) Repeat Steps 4 and 5 to add an additional language. Click "OK" and then "OK" OK.

(g) At the bottom of your screen, you will see a language bar that probably says "EN" for English. Click on it to change the input language. You can also move between languages by pressing "Alt-Left Shift."

3. *Installing Fonts*

Windows:

(a) Download the font (or. zip file containing the font) to a temporary location (e.g., desktop).

(b) Open the 'Fonts' folder (Windows: Start > Control Panel > Fonts; Windows: Start > Control Panel > Appearances and Themes > Fonts).

(c) Drag a font file (not the). zip file) into the Fonts folder. Applications must be restarted to recognize fonts.

4. *Displaying On-Screen Keyboard*

Windows:

1. Select Start > All Programs > Accessories > Accessibility Options > On-Screen Keyboard

2.13.6 *Recommendations on the Use of the Keyboard*

Key mappings might be appointed discretionarily, and programming can perform the necessary planning of the inside codes. However, in primary areas, we alluded to mappings that drag some relationship to the text-style glyphs; taking a gander at console mappings according to the client perspective as opposed to programming accommodation is helpful. The next section is a portion of the suggestions.

1. The information section should be regular and identified using Tamil letters. It ought to be sufficiently simple to prepare people to utilize the standard QWERTY console, which is what one will see in all COMPUTERs.
2. Quite far, utilize the standard keys to plan the letters. Not every console will have all the keys found in the COMPUTER consoles.
3. Normalize the information strategy for entering a consonant-vowel blend.

4. A manual typewriter console (for Tamil) is a decision that should not be disregarded. This is the current norm and many have been prepared for it. This console is satisfactory for present-day Tamil compositions. Programming can generally utilize a console channel to change the arrangement of keystrokes into suitable letters. It can be refined using Macros in most word processors.
5. Try not to fix or relate essential planning to any text style; however, this methodology might permit practically any word processor to deal with the information passage in Tamil. It is attractive that the inner portrayal is exportable to some word processors, so incredible organizing offices might be used.
6. Likewise, keyboard mappings ought not to be identified using the codes appointed to the characters. This guarantees that the inward portrayal is autonomous of the framework we are handling the text. It is consistently simpler to work with standard codes that do not straightforwardly identify with any equipment-explicit part of a COMPUTER. Tables can relate the inner portrayal to the glyphs or console mappings, consequently permitting extraordinary adaptability in managing information and presentation.
7. Keyboard mappings depended on specific investigations of the observed letter frequencies in a typical Tamil composition, which is doubtlessly supportive. It just happens that composing styles shift so much that the frequencies found in old texts are not the same as in present-day messages. Subsequently, it is desirable to consider the speculation interaction as one kind and dole out the key mapping dependent on client suggestions.

2.14 CONCLUSION

In this chapter's opening, "Tamil Computing" is introduced, followed by an explanation about History of Tamil Computing. The chapter also gives various coding standards and approaches. The narrative extends to encompass diverse font styles and their standards within Tamil typography. Furthermore, detailed explanations are provided regarding font installation procedures. Delving deeper, the discourse extends to the array of keyboards and their respective standards. Comprehensive insights are offered into the meticulous process of installing keyboard drivers. Through systematic elucidation, readers gain a holistic understanding of Tamil Computing's technical nuances.

CHAPTER 3

Tamil Computing Issues and Challenges

In general, there are different issues exists in Tamil Computing. There issues are software design issues, rendering text, encoding standards, font standards, Language enabling, localization, Data entry methods, Transliteration, Linguistic considerations, Writing Systems, Text analysis, Translation, Text to Speech (Software for the Disabled), Specific technical problems with TSCII/ISCII and Unicode. There are several technical issues to be considered as also the viability of solutions for implementations that will gain acceptance by the users. The discussions in the chapter of this site highlight the issues involved in computing with Tamil language. In this chapter it highlights these problems in detail.

3.1 SOFTWARE DESIGN ISSUES

The writing systems in use in the South Asian Region Languages are based on syllable representation and for this reason; it has generally been difficult to develop user interfaces supporting them. Tamil text representation has however been made possible through Unicode or TSCII/ISCII, the scheme that supports representation for the scripts of the world so that computer applications could really be Tamil in terms of user interaction.

It turns out that it has not been easy to adapt the methodologies suggested by Unicode to text in Indian languages on account of the complexities of the writing systems. While in principle, methods have been suggested for handling syllable level information through multi-byte Unicode strings, practical difficulties arise in developing applications based on Unicode (or for that matter ISCII or TSCII) where text or linguistic processing is involved. Basically, the problem has to do with the issue of internal text representation which has to be necessarily different from the representation for rendering the text. Technical solutions have been recommended to handle this but one cannot assert that the results have been satisfactory.

3.2 RENDERING TEXT

An interactive computer application should permit data entry and display in the script of interest to the user. With writing systems that are syllabic in nature, data entry has to ultimately lead to the formation of syllables, if needed, through multiple key strokes. The problem of text rendering deals with approaches that can be taken to represent syllables in such a way they can be displayed correctly.

In most computer applications today, the internal representation involves codes for each key stroke and hence the syllable is specified through a variable number of codes. From a variable length code (internal representation) one has to generate the display using appropriate fonts. Dealing with variable length codes is a difficult problem. It is for this reason generally in application system development has recommended the use of fixed length syllable level codes for text.

3.3 ENCODING STANDARDS

Over the years, different approaches have been taken to represent syllables for internal storage. Many of these, relied on the availability of a specific font designed to accommodate the shapes from which syllables could be composed (built). In 1991, the TSCII standard was adopted for general use and subsequently Unicode for different Indian scripts became a standard. Salient aspects of these encoding standards are discussed in these sections. Tamil Script Code for Information Interchange (TSCII) is a coding scheme for representing the Tamil script. The lower 128 code points are plain ASCII, the upper 128 code points are TSCII-specific. After long years of being used on the Internet by private agreement only, it was successfully registered with the IANA in 2007. Apart from this the system is also adopts Unicode Standards.

3.3.1 Unicode

Unicode for Indian Scripts

The generic concept of Unicode works well for the western languages where there is only one shape associated with one and only one code value. That is, each code value can directly refer to a glyph index and when the glyphs are placed side by side, the required display is achieved. In this case, a text string is rendered simply by horizontally concatenating the shapes (Glyphs) of the letters. Thus, a Unicode font for a western script need have only one glyph for each character code. The Glyph index and the code value can therefore be exactly the same. When the glyph indices are given, the original text is also known exactly due to the one-to-one mapping. Most languages whose writing system is based on the Latin alphabet come under this category.

This simplistic view does not help when the displayed shape does not correspond to a single letter but relates to a group of consonants and a vowel which constitute a linguistic quantum. In the South East Asian region, writing systems are based on rendering syllables and not the consonants and vowels. The accented characters mentioned earlier may also be viewed in this light as being made up of two or more shapes derived from two or more codes.

The problem at hand in respect of Indian languages is one of finding a way to display thousands of such combinations of basic letters where each combination is recognized as a proper syllable. This corresponds to a situation where a string of character codes map to a single shape. In the context of Indian scripts, the code for a consonant followed by a code for the vowel will usually imply a simple syllable often rendered by adding a matra (ligature) to the consonant, though there are enough exceptions to this rule.

Those responsible for assigning Unicode values to Indian languages had known about the complexity of rendering syllables. But they felt that the assigned codes correctly reflected the linguistic information in the syllable and so suggested that there was no need to assign codes to each syllable. It would be (and should be) possible to identify the same from a string of consonant and vowel codes (Just as syllables are identified in English). What was specifically recommended was that an appropriate rendering engine or shaping engine should be used to actually generate the display from the multi-byte representation of a syllable.

Since Unicode evolved from ISCII, there was also the special provision of Unicode values to specify the context in which a consonant or vowel was being rendered as part of a syllable. In other words, Unicode also provided for explicit representations achieved by forcing the rendering utility to build up a shape for a syllable, different from what might be a default. Thus Unicode for Indian scripts does not strictly separate the rendering from the internal representation and provides codes which specify the context for rendering. This bias, exhibited by Unicode can cause enough headaches for developers when Unicode text has to be processed.

Limitations

Limitations with Unicode are seen more in respect of text processing than text display. The nature of the writing systems followed in India require multiple display forms for a given syllable and this cannot be provided easily, for the onus is on the programmer to check if the required display form can be generated using the given font. Hence the application is influenced by what the font can offer. A direct consequence of this is that applications across platforms will not be in a position to utilize a standard rendering approach resulting in incompatibilities across applications and platforms.

3.3.2 TISCII

Tamil Script Code for Information Interchange (TSCII) is a coding scheme for representing the Tamil script. The lower 128 code points are plain ASCII, the upper 128 code points are TSCII-specific. After long years of being used on the Internet by private agreement only, it was successfully registered with the IANA (Internet Assigned Numbers Authority) in 2007. TSCII encodes the characters in visual (written) order, paralleling the use of the Tamil Typewriter. Unicode has used the logical order encoding strategy for Tamil, following ISCII, in contrast to the case of Thai, where the visual order encoding grandfathered by TIS-620 was adopted. The government of Tamil Nadu endorses its own TAB/TAM standards for 8-bit encoding and other, older encoding schemes can still be found on the WWW.

Limitations

As like the Unicode here also, the limitations with TISCII are seen more in respect of text processing than text display. The nature of the writing systems followed in Tamil require multiple display forms for a given syllable and this cannot be provided easily, for the onus is on the programmer to check if the required display form can be generated using the given font. Hence the application is influenced by what the font can offer. A direct consequence of this is that applications across platforms will not be in a position to utilize a standard rendering approach resulting in incompatibilities across applications and platforms.

3.4 FONT STANDARDS

In simple terms, a font provides for displaying a set of symbols through well defined shapes for each symbol. The symbol is a generic concept and the font is an instance of specific representation of a set of symbols. Traditionally, the symbols mentioned here have been the letters of the alphabet in a particular language along with punctuation marks and special characters. Fonts used to be created by craftsmen and artists during the days of printing machines that used movable type faces. Today, fonts are created by artists and designers who work with computer based tools.

Inside a font, the specific shape for a symbol is described either in terms of a digital image through bit maps or in terms of a filled outline. The former is called a bit mapped font and the latter, an outline font. Outline fonts are increasingly being used on account of their scalability. The descriptions result in a pictorial representation or shape for each symbol, which is referred to as a glyph. Most fonts have a provision for describing up to 256 different glyphs, though in practice only about 190 - 240 may be present. Text mode displays on computers (Dos command shells or Unix command shells) use bit mapped fonts while outline fonts are used with Graphical user interfaces.

Font standards have evolved over the years and apply to the scripts of different languages. Fonts with a restriction of eight bit codes for selecting the glyphs cannot support multiple scripts at the same time. Traditionally, to allow a given 8 bit code to refer to a shape, the concept of Font Encoding was employed. The concept behind font encoding permits a shape to be identified with a name (may be even different names). Thus the name for a shape is mapped to a geometrical description of the shape. Such mapping implies that the code for a given name is located through a table mapping names to codes and the resulting code used as an index into the set of glyphs to select the shape appropriate to the name.

Fonts are typically designed to support specific encoding schemes. While rendering text generated form a computer application, the code for the text is first mapped to a name and the shape corresponding to the named character is located through the internal name to glyph mapping in the font. Web browsers allow the choice of specific fonts for specific text encoding schemes which typically differed across platforms. This will permit text in a web page to be displayed properly using an appropriate font for which support is provided in the system on which the browser is running.

3.4.1 Fonts for Tamil Language

Fonts are inherently proprietary in nature and tend to be incompatible across computer systems as well as applications. It is true that the internet is a repository where many fonts are freely given by their designers. However, the design of a font, commercial or freely given, deals with issues of rendering of complex conjuncts and syllables when one thinks of Indian languages/scripts. Today, it appears that very few non-Roman fonts are available for practical uses which are supported under all the important platforms. This has imposed fairly severe restrictions in respect of web displays of Indian Language text on account of the totally arbitrary approach to designing the fonts. True, these fonts were not designed with the idea of text processing but more for getting good printouts. However when we use the same for web pages, we run into many incompatibilities.

In text editors and word processors, the internal representation of text is usually the ASCII codes (possibly Unicode today) of the letter displayed and these codes happen to be the same as the numeric codes assigned to the glyph locations containing the letters of the alphabet in standard fonts for the western languages. When it comes to fonts for Indian languages, the display has to be built up with more than one glyph for many aksharas and hence the internal representation of the aksharas is purely a function of where the glyphs for the aksharas are located within the font. Thus, one faces the problem that, the stored text is not in a format that can be viewed on different computer systems because; the encoding standard may not be supported in each system. Also, glyph codes are the choice of the font designer and will bear no relationship to the ordering of the aksharas in our scripts. Thus, linguistic processing of the stored text is a formidable task, being font dependent even for the same script.

Thousands of fonts have been designed for Indian scripts but each design has its own specific purpose, often compatibility with a typing scheme. Applications dealing with Indian scripts have generally relied on the availability of a specific font(s) for a script. Consequently, applications could not move data transparently across platforms since encoding issues come into play. The problem continues even with Unicode where some standardization has been effected for text representation because text rendering is separated from internal representation (strictly not true for Unicode).

Unlike a web page in English which could be seen through a substitute font, if the specified font were not available, text in Indian languages will require the specified font to be present. This is the reason why web pages often make available for download, the font associated with the displayed information. Unfortunately, a single font cannot be used across platforms and even a given font is not guaranteed to display text properly if the internal encoding differs, which is usually the case with many Indian language fonts.

A Brief Overview of the Method of Using Tamil with Fonts

Many of the solutions provided in the past for dealing with Tamil on computers have relied on the use of special fonts. A font is essentially a set of basic shapes which may be shown individually or in combinations to display the letters of a script. Eight-bit fonts are the most commonly used fonts with Indian scripts. Seen below are the basic shapes (called Glyphs) which permit

Tamil text to be displayed on a computer screen, as present in the font known as Indo-Web-Kambar.

	0	1	2	3	4	5	6	7	8	9	A	B	C	D	E	F
20																
30																
30																
50																
60																
70																
80																
90																
A0		ஸ	ஞ	ஜ	ஸ்ரீ	ஹ	ு	ஙு	ி	ீ	்	ூ		தூ	றூ	
B0		யு	வு	நு	ஜு	பு		டு		யூ	நூ	ஞா	ஈ	ஞூ	லூ	நா
C0	ஷு	ஹூ	க்ஷ	உள	ஜு	நு	கு	ழு	ழ	ஜு	து	மு	டு	ஆ	கு	டீ
D0	்	ஞு		ஞு	க	ரு	ஏ	று	ஓ	ஜு	பப	ஞூ	ஷ		டீ	மூ
E0	க	ய	ெ	உ	ன	ந	க	ப	ா	ை	த	ம	ட	அ	ே	டி
F0	'	ஹ	ச	ள	வ	ர	எ	ற	ஒ	ல	ண	ஜு	ஜு	ஷ	ஃ	

To understand how fonts are used, consider the string shown below which string is built up from individual Glyphs.

தமிழ் மொழி   த ம ி ழ ் ெ ம ா ழ ி

There are 10 shapes here (each is known as a glyph) but only seven of them are distinct. The glyphs within a font are arranged in some order and inside the computer the shapes to be displayed are given in terms of the positions occupied by the glyphs in the fonts. Typically a font will support up to about 200 glyphs. In the Kambar font used in displaying the Tamil string above, the glyphs used in the string are (234, 235, 168, 200, 208, 226, 235, 232, 200, 168) in the order in which they will be displayed. It may be noted that the string has only 5 Tamil letters though 10 glyphs are used, 7 being distinct. Thus going by the number of Glyphs alone, one will not be able to figure out the number of letters in the string. In other words, linguistic analysis of text will be cumbersome if font based representation is chosen.

The method most often used for representing information in Tamil is based on glyph codes for the letters. This works alright for a given font and to some extent string processing may also be attempted. However the dependence of the codes on the font is a major deterrent to using this approach. The glyphs required to display a string are generated when the keystrokes are effected. For this, the keys on the ASCII keyboard are mapped into the Tamil letter whose glyph is specified through the ASCII code for the letter. Some combinations will require two keystrokes but this is alright since the second keystroke will correspond to a vowel extension.

Inspite of its simplicity, this method is quite painful in practice, for it is always not easy to remember the mapping between the Tamil letter and the key. Worse still, some combinations require three keystrokes to be executed whereas other combinations may be handled through just one keystroke. An example of this is the difference between keyboard entries for "ti" and "tu". Depending on the font design, the number of glyphs and therefore the number of keystrokes will vary. This is not a useful approach for general acceptance.

It is thus apparent that Tamil cannot be typed in just as English is. Somehow the combinations have to be handled in a font independent manner with a uniformly same number of keystrokes for combinations. Some word processors provide special support by tracking the keystrokes and combining them appropriately. Packages from CDAC or word processors such as SRILIPI use this method. Here too, the sequence is decided by the glyph mappings though in the CDAC software, a special mapping known as the INSCRIPT is used but this is not intuitive for those familiar with English. With most software, one has very little choice for the fonts since the data entry method is in some way tied to the use of fonts. No two font designers agree on the glyphs nor their placement within the font. Worse still, fonts are not always compatible across computer systems.

Looking at the problem of keyboard mapping itself, the key to be pressed for a specific letter is fixed by the glyph code. This key may have no phonetic equivalence with the Tamil letter. In fact for many fonts where the designer had intended bilingual use (Roman and Tamil), the glyphs for Tamil are located in the 128–255 range making data entry even more difficult, unless the MACRO features are invoked.

One solution recommended by some designers has been to place the glyphs of the Tamil letters at positions corresponding to the ASCII code of the phonetically equivalent letter in Roman. This makes data entry a bit more intuitive but here too variations occur when dealing with consonant vowel combinations which change the basic shape of the consonant.

In the scheme followed at CDAC, internal storage is not in terms of glyph codes but correspond to the ISCII scheme. The special word processor transforms the keystrokes into appropriate letters and an output module converts the ISCII or TISCII based internal representation into glyph codes. This method has the advantage that it applies to all the Indian languages. But the scheme itself suffers from some language specific representations.

The ISCII code is an eight-bit code that codes only the basic consonants and vowels of the language. Consequently, it requires more than one byte to represent a combination though a consonant or a vowel by itself requires only one byte. Thus, ISCII also amounts to a multi-byte variable length code making the font rendering mechanism quite complex. Nevertheless, ISCII is a code that represents basic sounds and hence is quite useful in practice. In implementation however, ISCII has run into some problems for South Indian scripts, especially Tamil.

3.5 LANGUAGE ENABLING

Language enabling is a concept where a computer application will be able to allow data entry and display in the required language by allowing dynamic selection of the language during data entry. In an application that is enabled for a particular language, what is seen on the screen or printed will have text in that language. Data entry may not always be straightforward if the letters of the language bear no resemblance to the Roman alphabet. Yet many applications may project a keyboard on the screen and allow data entry through mouse clicks. In all these cases, the current practice is largely, one keystroke, one glyph, where each glyph shown on the screen corresponds to an individual letter of the alphabet. This approach does pose difficulties for languages where the representation of the characters involves combinations of two or more glyphs to display a single conjunct character.

Language enabling methods rely on switching keyboard input for the entry of text in different scripts. Current approach is to effect this switch through services in the Operating system (typically called Locales). It often happens that one is required to switch locales to permit text input in respect of punctuation or special symbols that are often required in a script but these symbols may not be part of the traditional writing system using the script. This happens quite frequently with Indian scripts which today, employ standard punctuation. Often the keyboard assignments are tight and one may not be able to accommodate the newer symbols unless the locale is switched or multiple keystrokes are employed even for simple punctuation. In other words, keyboard switching becomes inevitable when multilingual text is to be entered and the required locales have to be included in the OS for this to work properly.

3.6 LOCALIZATION

Language Localization is a totally different concept in which the entire interaction with the application, including all the commands, is done in the specific script for the language. This calls for major enhancements to the system software to allow interpretation of text strings in different languages. In an application that is localized for a particular language, one may never see Roman text on the screen and all computing, including naming of files, may be done in the specified language. In other words, an application supporting localization for a language can provide an effective user interface in that language. Thus a person need not know English to run the application.

Localization is difficult to achieve for languages which have large number of letters such as Indian languages. This is a consequence of the fact that localization of applications still rely the assumption that a small set of letters (128) is all that will be encountered for text processing! It turns out that while one sees improvements in rendering multilingual text, the interpretation of the text string continues to pose problems. The real problem is that of having to work with syllables for the purpose of interpretation while the rendering of text has to do with the shapes of the written characters.

3.7 DATA ENTRY METHODS

The specific problem discussed here is the use of the standard QWERTY keyboard to key in data in Indian scripts. This is a fairly well understood problem and several solutions are available. Data entry rules should be easy to follow while at the same time permit the formation of complex conjunct aksharas consistent with the rules of the writing system. In respect of Indian scripts, one sees additional requirements brought about by the use of punctuation marks from the Roman Script.

3.8 TRANSLITERATION

Transliteration serves as a bridge between languages, facilitating the conversion of text from one script to another while retaining the phonetic and sometimes semantic integrity. It involves mapping the characters of one writing system to those of another, often phonetically similar, system. This process aids in communication and comprehension across linguistic boundaries. Various methods exist, ranging from straightforward phonetic mappings to more complex algorithms based on linguistic rules. Transliteration can be both manual, involving individual character substitutions, or automated, leveraging computational algorithms. It plays a crucial role in language learning, multilingual communication, and information dissemination. Challenges arise due to differences in phonetic systems, ambiguities, and the absence of one-to-one mappings between characters. However, advancements in technology have led to the development of robust transliteration tools and systems, enriching cross-cultural interactions and accessibility to diverse linguistic content.

3.9 LINGUISTIC CONSIDERATIONS

Linguistic processing refers to the analysis of syllables or text strings in a language. This requirement comes up whenever one is trying to study the grammatical information in a text string or just interpret the string as a command. Very often, linguistic processing will require the use of a corpus. The creation of the corpus should also take into account the linguistic aspects of the language such as verb forms associated with different tenses etc.

In respect of Indian languages, linguistic processing is to be attempted at the level of a syllable since the writing systems are syllabic in nature. Almost all the Indian languages have a structure that is based on root syllables from which actual words are derived. The scriptures exhibit remarkable consistency in the number of syllables used in a verse and this consistency is also an indirect means to checking the correctness of text.

The pages on Linguistics and computation contain useful information on this subject. You will also see amazing word structures and long palindromes from some noted poetic works in Tamil.

3.10 WRITING SYSTEMS

Writing systems employed for Tamil language work on the principle of syllables where individual syllables are identified through individual shapes. In essence a syllable is composed from basic shape following the rules of the writing system which employ special shapes for the medial vowels as well as ligatures for specific combinations of consonants and vowels. Though the languages of India are phonetic in nature, each language is free to use a script which can display the syllables correctly so as to map to the correct sound. Hence, the basic sounds are fundamental to the writing system for any Indian language and not the script. When text processing is to be attempted, one faces the problem of identifying the syllables corresponding to the displayed text. Systems which emphasize the script (and hence code the syllables consistent with the requirements of the script) often run into problems if the text for the language is to be displayed in another script. This happens to be the case with Unicode.

3.11 TEXT ANALYSIS

Text analysis refers to the process of interpreting text for a specific purpose; say to find out if a specific combination of sounds is present in the text. Text analysis involves string processing of syllables and the coding scheme employed for text often decides the complexity of the algorithms required for string manipulations. Fixed length codes are much more effective for this purpose (based on the principles of regular expression matching) than variable length codes.

3.12 TRANSLATION

Machine translation (MT) is playing the most dominant role in NLP which requires aggressive development and research to apply in various applications. The MT systems act as a bridge to access cross lingual information by making the text available in one language to another language. Such systems are inexpensive, instantaneous and multiplicative when compared to human translation. Building such a system across a pair of languages is nontrivial. Each language has its own style and its special characteristics. Sentence level ambiguities are referred as syntactic while the ambiguities that arise at the word level are semantic. The most characteristic features of the Dravidian languages are that they show high agglutination and exhibit the inclusive and exclusive feature, with a completely different structure.

A hybrid approach is used to develop the MT system comprising paradigm, rule and machine learning methods at various levels. The MT system mainly deals with the analysis, transfer, and generation process. The issues being raised in the analysis part is discussed here. The challenges can be found at the syntactic and semantic levels. A word may belong to more than one Parts Of Speech (POS) category, resulting in the syntactic ambiguity. Words can have more than one meaning and sometimes group of words or whole sentence may have more than one meaning in a language resulting in the ambiguities. After the analysis process; the next step is to map it appropriately into the target language.

The divergences between the source and the target language lead to the problems in this transfer. English has 26 characters while Tamil has only 30. This marks the necessity for a good transliteration. A large coverage of words in the bilingual dictionary can solve most of the transliteration issues. The problem due to the lexical gap, an instance where there is an absence of a word to express a specific concept of the source word in the target language during the translation process. The most important challenge in developing English Tamil MT is to handle in MT system is the subject verb agreement of the target language. English is relatively a free order language without any subject verb agreement. But Tamil verbs inflect for person, number, and gender.

3.13 TEXT TO SPEECH (SOFTWARE FOR THE DISABLED)

The availability of the computer opens up several possibilities for helping the disabled gain basic educational and professional skills. Many countries of the world have provided very useful applications suited to specific disabilities and these have won appreciation from experts all over the world. Unfortunately, most of these applications require knowledge of English. It is essential for us to develop such system in Tamil.

3.14 SPECIFIC TECHNICAL PROBLEMS WITH ISCII AND UNICODE

It must be observed, in the light of the above discussion that displaying a Unicode string in Indian language requires a complex piece of processing software to identify the syllables and get the corresponding glyphs from an appropriate font for the script. The multibyte nature of Unicode (for a syllable) makes a table driven approach to this quite difficult. Even though it is possible to write such modules which can go from Unicode to the display of text using some font, one faces a formidable problem in respect of data entry, where formation of syllables from multiple key sequences Is truly overwhelming. With limited number of keys available in standard keyboards, it is often not possible to accommodate all the symbols one would require to produce meaningful printouts in each script consistent with quality typesetting systems.

Unicode based applications employ the concept of "Locales" to permit data entry of multilingual text. Each Locale is associated with its own keyboard mapping and application software can switch Locales to permit data entry of multilingual text. It will be seen that for Indian scripts, the Locales themselves have limitations since they do not permit a full complement of letters and special characters to be typed in, much less the standard punctuation that has become part of Indian scripts today.

While it is possible to write special keyboard driver programs which implement a state machine to handle key sequences to produce syllables, the approach is not universal enough to be included into the Operating Systems, certainly not when a single driver should cater to all the Indian scripts. There is no meaning in having a Hindi version of OS with its own Data entry convention which differs substantially from a Tamil or Telugu version.

Here is a summary of the issues that confront us when dealing with Unicode for Indian scripts.

- Rendering text in a manner that is uniform across applications is quite difficult. Windowing applications with cut, copy/paste features suffer due to problems in correctly identifying the width of each syllable on the screen. Also, applications have to worry about specific rendering issues when modifier codes are present. How applications run into difficulties in rendering even simple strings is illustrated with examples in a separate page.

- Interpreting the syllabic content involves context dependent processing, that too with a variable number of codes for each syllable.
- A complete set of symbols used in standard printed text has not been included in Unicode for almost all the Indian scripts.
- Displaying text in scripts other that what Unicode supports is not possible. For instance, many of the scripts used in the past such as the Grantha Script, Modi, Sharada etc., cannot be used to display Sanskrit text. This will be a fairly serious limitation in practice when thousands of manuscripts written over the centuries have to be preserved and interpreted.
- Transliteration across Indian scripts will not be easy to implement since appropriate symbols currently recommended for transliteration are not part of the Unicode set. In the Indian context, transliteration very much a requirement.
- The Unicode assignments bear little resemblance to the linguistic base on which the aksharas of Indian scripts are founded. While this is not a critical issue, it is desirable to have codes whose values are based on some linguistic properties assigned to the vowels and consonants, as has been the practice in India.
- In a separate web page, we discuss the problems associated with UNICODE for linguistic processing of text in Indian languages.

Details of Unicode for Indian scripts have been published in the standard available from the Unicode consortium. The Unicode web site (www.unicode.org) does have useful information but one will have to resort to the printed text to get the real details. These are also available in PDF format from the above web site.

Unicode for Indian Languages

Unicode was the first attempt at producing a standard for multilingual documents. Unicode owes its origin to the concept of the ASCII code extended to accommodate International Languages and scripts.

Short character codes (7 bits or 8 bits) are adequate to represent the letters of the alphabets of many languages of the world. The fundamental idea behind Unicode is that a superset of characters from all the different languages/scripts of the world be formed so that a single coding scheme could effectively handle almost all the alphabets of all the languages. What this implies is that the different scripts used in the writing systems followed by different languages be accommodated in the coding scheme. In Unicode more than 65000 different characters can be referenced. This large set includes not only the letters of the alphabet from many different languages of the world but also punctuation, special shapes such as mathematical symbols, Currency symbols etc. The term Code Space is often used to refer to the full set of codes and in Unicode, the Code space is divided into consecutive regions spanning typically 128 code values. Essentially this assignment retains the ordering of the characters within the assigned group and is therefore very similar to the ASCII assignments which were in vogue earlier.

Unicode assignments may be viewed geometrically as a stack of planes, each plane having one and possibly multiple chunks of 128 consecutive code values. Logically related characters or symbols have been grouped together in Unicode to span one or more regions of 128 code values. We may view these regions as different planes in the Code Space as illustrated in the figure below. Data processing software using Unicode will be able to identify the Language of the text for each character by identifying the plane the character is located in and use appropriate font to display the same or invoke some meaningful linguistic processing.

Technically, Unicode can handle many more languages than the supported scripts if these languages use the same script in their writing systems. By consolidating a complete set of symbols used in the writing systems across a family of languages, one can get a script that caters to all of them. The Latin script with its supplementary characters and extended symbol has about 550 different characters and this is quite adequate to handle almost anything that has appeared in print in respect of the Latin script. Hence in the geometrical view above, some planes may be larger (wider) than others and more than one script could have characters from logically similar groups specified in a plane.

The fact that several languages/scripts of the world require many more than 128 codes has necessitated assignments of more than one basic plane (i.e., multiples of 128 code values) for them. Languages such as Greek, Arabic or Chinese have larger planes assigned to them. In particular, Unicode has allowed nearly 20000 characters of Chinese, Japanese and Korean scripts to be included in a contiguous region of the Code Space. Currently fewer than a hundred different groups of symbols or specific scripts are included in Unicode.

Even though it is a sixteen bit code and can therefore handle more than 65000 code values, Unicode should not be viewed as a scheme which allows several thousand characters for each and every language. That it has provision for fewer than 128 characters for many scripts is a general observation since many languages do not require more than 128 characters to display text.

In respect of Indian languages which use syllabic writing systems, one might think that Unicode would have provided several thousands of codes for the syllables similar to the nearly 11000 Hangul syllables already included. On the contrary, Unicode has pretty much accepted the concept behind ISCII and has provided only for the most basic units of the writing systems which include the vowels, consonants and the vowel modifiers.

Unlike ISCII, which has a uniform coding scheme for all the languages, Unicode has provided individual planes for the nine major scripts of India. Within these planes of 128 code values each, assignments are language specific though the ISCII base has been more or less retained. Consequently, Unicode suffers from the same limitations that ISCII runs into. There are some questionable assignments in Unicode in respect of Matras. A Matra is not a character by itself. It is a representation of a combination of a vowel and consonant, in other words the representation of a medial vowel. A vowel and NOT its Matra is the basic linguistic unit. Consequently, linguistic processing will be difficult with Unicode with Indian languages, just as in ISCII.

Here is the Unicode assignment for Sanskrit (Devanagari). The language code for Sanskrit (Devanagari) is 09 (hex) and so the codes span the range 0901 to 097f (Hexadecimal values). In this chart, the characters of Devanagari with a dot beneath, are grouped in the range 0958 to 095f. These are the characters used in Hindi which are derived from Persian and seen in Urdu as well. Likewise in locations 0929, 0931 and 0934 the letters are dotted. The codes are similar to ISCII in ordering but Unicode includes characters not specified in ISCII. Also, the assignments for each language more or less adhere to the same relative locations for the basic vowels and consonants as in ISCII but include many languages dependent codes. The code positions in Unicode will not exactly match the corresponding ISCII assignments.

3.15 CONCLUSION

In this chapter at first section introduces the main issues of "Tamil Computing". In the subsequent Sections highlights various specific issues relating to the design of the software. By finding the suitable solution to these technical issues one can design a very good Tamil computing system. Most of the issues are fundamental in nature and it is essential to fix the solutions in the different layer level according the requirements.

CHAPTER 4

Tamil Phonology, Morphology, Syntax, Semantics, and Pragmatic

4.1 INTRODUCTION

4.1.1 Tamil Phonology

Tamil is one of the world's most important languages. It is admired for its history, vocabulary, and grammar perfection. It is also admired for its majesty, and Tolka:ppiyam, an ancient Tamil grammar, vividly demonstrates its grammatical qualities. Tolka:ppiyam examines the grammatical legacy and socioeconomic framework of Tamil society at the time. It also represents all old Tamil's linguistic structures, literature issues, phrasing, poetics, emotions, etc. From the perspective of Tamil literature, as well as the background of general linguistics and literary theory, the analysis of Tolka:ppiyam is fascinating. The themes presented in this paper are linked to a language perspective. Annamalai says, "Language is a substantial attribute utilized by humans. The purpose of grammar is to explain the meaning and offer a mechanism for the users' grasp of the meaning." Tolka: Understanding ppiyar's language is comprehensive, encompassing spoken and written language. Thus, the definition is broadened to cover not only the description but also the suggestive aspect. For him, grammar represents language and its sense in the clearest manner possible.

The grammatical framework varies over time, and there is a distinction between the development of grammatical principles in Tamil tradition and modernity. The current scenario is more advanced than that in the past. Due to the present political and other circumstances, sociological, cultural, economic, and socioeconomic situations are bound to change. The Language used in newspapers is affected by this.

This section provides a quick overview of Tamil and its basic phonological framework. The phonetic characteristics of nasalization and voice have been extensively explored. It also explains the differences in the pattern of Tamil phonology observed during the Tolkappiyam period and today. The main goal of this section is to disclose the standard Tamil phonological structure and relate it to the phonological attributes acquired from the sources, to uncover the differences in Tamil phonological components.

Tamil is a good representation of the diglossic and dialectal variety of a language. The diglossic situation in Tamil indicates the use of two languages in the Tamil speech community, each with structural and functional differences. High variety and low variety or written variety and spoken variety are the names of these types. In official contexts, a high or written variety is employed, whereas in casual settings, a low or spoken variety is utilized. Dialect is a type of language spoken by a group of people in a particular area or culture. As Tamil is a widely spoken language, it has acquired various societal and regional dialects. People are separated by geographical borders and social divisions in society, which organize them into small communities. Amidst these differences, Tamil is spoken in a conventional form for official affairs and public discussion. Despite being classified as varieties, these dialects represent the diversity of the language and are frequently used to form functional and standard varieties.

4.2 SPEECH SOUNDS

In general, speech sounds are divided into two categories: vowels and consonants.

4.2.1 *Vowels*

Jones defined a vowel as a voiced sound in which the air passes through the pharynx and mouth in a continuous stream, with no obstruction or narrowing that generates audible friction.

The vowels are divided into two groups based on two parameters:

1. Tongue position and
2. Lip position

4.2.1.1 *Tongue Position*

(A) *Height of the Tongue*

1. Close vowels
2. Half-close vowels
3. Half-open vowels
4. Open vowels

(B) *Raising of Part of the Tongue*

1. Front vowels
2. Central vowels
3. Back vowels

4.2.1.2 *Lip Position*

1. Rounded
2. Unrounded

4.2.2 Consonants

Consonants refer to all additional sounds. Jones has stated that consonants comprise:

1. All sounds that are not voiced (e.g., p, s, /)
2. All noises obstructing the air in its passage through the mouth (e.g., b, l, rolled r).
3. All sounds in which the air does not enter through the mouth during generation (e.g., m)
4. All sounds containing detectable friction (e.g., v, s, z, h).

The principle for the categorization of consonants is described below.

4.2.2.1 *The Manner of Articulation*

1. Stops
2. Nasals
3. Fricatives
4. Laterals
5. Flap
6. Trill
7. Semi-vowels

4.2.2.2 *The Place of Articulation*

1. Bilabial
2. Labio-dental
3. Dental
4. Alveolar
5. Retroflex

6. Palatal
7. Retroflex continuant lateral
8. Velar
9. Glottal

4.3 Tolkappiyar's Phonological Pattern

Here is a quick summary of the phonological patterns that occurred during Tolkappiyam. This allowed a comparative analysis of the ancient Tamil phonological structure and the advanced Tamil phonological structure.

4.3.1 *Tamil Speech Sounds*

Tolkappiyar classifies 12 vowels and 18 consonants in Tamil. They are described as:

4.3.1.1 *Vowels*

kurreluttu (short) – /a, i, u, e, o/
netteluttu (long) – /aa, ii, uu, ee, ai, oo, au

4.3.1.2 *Consonants*

Vallinam (plosives) – /k. c, t, t, *P*. r/
Mellinam (nasals) /n. h, n. n, m, n/
itaiyinam (midlings)- /y. r, v. *1*. 1/

4.3.1.3 *Dependant sounds (caarpeluttu)*

These sounds only happen if certain conditions are met.

1. kurriyalikaram (shortened '-i')
2. kurriyalukaram (shortened '-u')
3. aaytam (k)

4.3.2 Phonotactics

4.3.2.1 *Initial Position*

(A) *Vowels*

In the firstplace, all the vowels happen.
Short vowels – /a, i, u, e, o/
Long vowels–/aa, ii, uu, ee, ai, oo, au

(B) *Consonants*

The subsequent consonants happen primarily
/k, t, n, p, m, c, v, n, y, t/

4.3.2.2 *Final Position*

(A) *Vowels*

All vowels save the diphthong /au/ that appeared during the Tolkappiyam era. The diphthong /au/ appeared eventually but only if it was preceded by /k/ or /v/.

(B) *Consonants*

The resulting consonants (11) appeared in word-final position in Tolkappiyar's writings out of the 18 consonants.

/*n,* n, n, m, n, y, r, 1, v, 1, 1/

4.3.2.3 *Sequential Occurrence of Phonemes*

(A) *Vowels (alapetai)*

A short vowel was introduced following a long vowel in the Tolkappiyam period to compensate for metrical weakness.

(B) *Consonants*

(a) Medial Position

Two types of consonantal clusters that occurred medially were found in Tamil during the Tolkappiyar era. They are:

1. Cluster with non-identical consonants (meymayanku)
2. Presence of identical consonants in a sequence (utanilai) - i.e., germination.

(i) Clustering of Identical Consonants

Seven clusters were generated by combining the sounds of one group with the sounds of another. Sucha as:

1. The grouping of the first set

$$\begin{bmatrix} \text{ṭ} \\ \text{ṟ} \\ \text{l} \\ \text{ḷ} \end{bmatrix} + \begin{bmatrix} k \\ c \\ p \end{bmatrix}$$

The clusters generated are:

/-•tk-, -tc-, -tp-, -rk-, -rc-, -rp-, -lk-, -lc-, -lp-, -lk-, -lc-, -lp-/

2.

$$\begin{bmatrix} \text{l} \\ \text{ḷ} \end{bmatrix} + \begin{bmatrix} y \\ v \end{bmatrix}$$

The clusters formed by such combination are:

/-ly-, -lv-, -ly-, -lv-/

3. In this set, /n, n, n, n, m, o/ is from the first group, and /k, c, t, t, p, and r/ belong to the second group. Individually, the normal consonants were blended with the group's homorganic consonants.

$$\begin{bmatrix} \text{ṅ} \\ \text{ñ} \\ \text{ṇ} \\ n \\ m \\ \text{ṉ} \end{bmatrix} + \begin{bmatrix} k \\ c \\ \text{ṭ} \\ t \\ p \\ \text{ṟ} \end{bmatrix}$$

The clusters were,

/-nk-, -he-, -nt-, -nt-, -mp-, -nr-/

4. This set had clusters like:

/-nk-, -nc-, -nn-, -np-, -run- , -ny- , -nv- ,
-nk-, –nc–, -nn-, -np-, -nro-, -ny-, -nv-/

These clusters were designed by the nextgroups.

$$\begin{bmatrix} \text{ṇ} \\ \text{ṉ} \end{bmatrix} + \begin{bmatrix} k \\ c \\ \text{ñ} \\ p \\ m \\ y \\ v \end{bmatrix}$$

5.

$$\begin{bmatrix} \tilde{n} \\ n \\ m \\ v \end{bmatrix} + [y]$$

were combined with having the following clusters.
/-ny-, -ny-, -my-, -vy-/

6. In the sixth set, /m/ and /v/ were combined to form the cluster /-mv-/. This set grouping the following sets of sounds.

$$\begin{bmatrix} \underline{y} \\ r \\ \underline{1} \end{bmatrix} + \begin{bmatrix} k \\ t \\ n \\ p \\ m \\ c \\ \tilde{n} \\ y \\ v \\ \dot{n} \end{bmatrix}$$

The clusters that are result from these sets are:
/-yk-, -yt-, -yn-, -yp-, -ym-, -yc-, -yn-, -yy-, -yv-, -yn-, -rk-, -rt-, -rn-, -rp-, -rm-, -rc- , -rn-,' -ry- , -rv-, -rn-, -lk-, -It-, -In-, -lp-, -lm-, -lc-, -In-, -ly-, -lv-, -In-,/

(ii) Gemination

All the consonants except /r/ and /!/occurred in gemination.

/-kk-, -cc-, -tt-, -tt-, -pp-, -rr-, -nn-, -nn-,
-nn-, -nn-, -mm-, -nn-, -yy-, -11-, -vv-, -11-/

Three Consonantal Clusters

The midlings /y, r, 1/ were combined with the following ge minations /-kk-, -cc-, -tt-, -pp-, -hn-, -hn-, -nn-and -mm-/ to form the following clusters:

$$\begin{bmatrix} \underline{y} \\ r \\ \underline{l} \end{bmatrix} + \begin{bmatrix} kk \\ cc \\ tt \\ pp \\ \dot{n}\dot{n} \\ \tilde{n}\tilde{n} \\ nn \end{bmatrix}$$

/-ykk-, -ycc-, -ytt-, -ypp-, -ynn-, -ynn-, -ynn-, -ymm-,
-rkk-, -rcc-, -rtt-, -rpp-, -rnn-, -rnn-, -rnn-, -rmm-,
-Ikk-, -lee-, -ltt-, -Ipp-, -Inn-, -Inn-, -Inn-, -1mm-,/

(b) Final Position

Only one cluster was documented in the word-ending place in the Tamil of the Tolkappiyam period. The alveolar nasal,/n/, and labial nasal /m/ are present in a cluster form /nm/ in poetry. This cluster is not present in any other work by Tolkappiyam (e.g., /poonm/'poolum').

4.4 THE MODERN TAMIL PHONOLOGICAL STRUCTURE

This section provides a detailed understanding of the modern Tamil phonology. The phonological framework of Tamil, presented by Tolkappiyar, differs from Tamil in several ways. This section describes the structure of segmental phonology and the phonetic aspects studied, such as nasalization and voice.

4.4.1 Segmental Phonology

The sounds are divided into vowels, diphthongs, and consonants in segmental phonology.

4.4.1.1 *Vowels*

10 vowels are present in modern Tamil. 5 areshort vowels, and 5 are long vowels. They are:

Short vowels: /i, e, a, o, u/

Long vowels: /ii, ee, aa, oo, uu/

In these

/i, ii, e, ee/

are known as front vowels,

/a, aa/

as central vowels, and

/o, oo, u, uu/

as back vowels. The height of the tongue was also used to classify vowels, as shown below:

High vowels – /i. ii, u, uu/

Mid vowels – /e. ee, o, oo/

Low vowels – /a, aa/

Table 3.1: Tamil Vowels

Tongue Position / *Tongue Height*	*Front Vowels*		*Central Vowels*		*Back Vwels*	
	Short	*Long*	*Short*	*Long*	*Short*	*Long*
High	i	ii			u	uu
Mid	e	ee			o	oo
Low			a	aa		

4.4.1.2 *Diphthongs*

Jones defines a diphthong as an independent vowel-glide that does not contain either a 'peak' or a 'trough' of importance.

Diphthongs can be long or short depending on how they are saying, and can also be broad or narrow depending on how far they have moved from their starting place. They are called 'rising diphthongs' and 'falling diphthongs,' depending on how prominent the diphthongs are. There are two diphthongs in Tamil, /ai/ and /au/. For the same, there were a few differences. The purpose of this study was not to examine the quality of diphthongs. However, this study concentrates on the underlying characteristics.

1. Is there a difference in how diphthongs are pronounced?
2. Is the difference between the diphthongs retained?

a. *If not, how will they be altered?*

The focus of this research was not on the quality of the diphthongs. Instead, it looks to see whether the contrasts between the diphthongs are preserved. If so, the circumstances in which they are maintained and the people who maintain them will be investigated. If modifications are introduced, how they are introduced is noted. The two diphthongs were tested for their presence in all word positions and in all five situations selected in this research.

4.4.1.3 *Consonants*

Consonants are categorized according to consonantal categorization, which considers the way and location of articulation. There are 26 consonants in the modern Tamil (Table 3.2).

Table 3.2: Tamil Consonants

ARTICULATION PLACE / MANNER	Bilabial	Labio-dental	Dental	Alveolar	Retroflex	Palatal	Velar	Glottal
Stops	p,b		ṯ,ḏ		ṭ,ḍ	c,j	k,g	
Fricatives				s	ṣ			h
Nasals	m		ṉ	n	ṇ	ñ	ṅ	
Laterals				l	ḷ			
Flap				r				
Trill				ṟ				
Continuant					ḻ			
Semi-vowels		v				y		

Regarding consonants, some sounds were discovered to be unique to Tamil. The dental and retroflex nasals (n, n), retroflex lateral (1), alveolar trill (r), and voiced retroflex continuant lateral (1) are all regarded as unique to Tamil. There are several rules to remember when pronouncing these uncommon sounds, and suggestions for generating these consonants, considering the style and location of articulation, can be provided. If informants know the correct pronunciation of these sounds, they are unlikely to change their pronunciation.

(A) *Manner of Articulation*

1. ***Stops:*** Stop consonants are generated by restricting airflow with the lips or any part of the tongue. In this method of articulation, the air passing

through the mouth is prevented at a certain point and is then expelled with a rapid burst. In Tamil, there were five pairs of stop consonants.

/p, b, t, d. t, d, c, j, k, g/

2. ***Nasals:*** Nasal consonants are created by closing the mouth and lowering the soft palate, allowing air to enter through the nasal cavity. Tamil contains six nasal consonants.

   /m, n. n, n, n, n/

3. ***Fricatives:*** The vocal cords were maintained in a narrow posture when generating fricative consonants. Air flowing via the trachea pushes against the vocal cords, producing friction, and exits through the mouth cavity. Tamil has three types of fricatives.

   /s, s, h/

4. ***Laterals:*** The tongue in the center of the mouth blocks air from reaching the oral cavity, and the air moves down both sides of the tongue. In Tamil, the laterals are:

   /l, 1, 1/

5. ***Flap:*** The tongue is curved back slightly and tapped against the alveolar ridge to produce a continuous flap. Only a single flap consonant was present in Tamil.

   /r/

6. ***Trill:*** The tongue end touches the alveolar ridge and creates more than one or two taps, as it does with the flap consonant. Only a single trill consonant was present in Tamil.

   /r/

7. ***Semi-vowels:*** This sound behaves as a consonant but lacks the phonetic characteristics normally linked with consonants. It has the phonological property of a vowel, although its duration is substantially shorter than that of usual vowels. Tamil semi-vowels are as follows:

   /v. y/

(B) *Place of Articulation*

Two types of articulators are involved in the production of consonants: passive and active. The phrase 'place of articulation' refers to the point at which the active articulator meets the passive articulator. The following types of consonant-based articulation places can be found in Tamil speech sounds:

1. ***Bilabial:*** In this case, the top and lower lips are engaged in articulation. The active articulator, the lower lip, contacts the passive articulator and the upper lip. They are referred to as bilabials, because both lips are engaged in the emergence of these sounds. The Tamil bilabial consonants are as follows.

   /p, b, m/

2. ***Labio-dental:*** The lower lip and upper front teeth were engaged. The lower lip acts as an active articulator whereas the higher front teeth act as passive articulators. Only a single labio-dental consonant was present in Tamil.

   /v/

3. ***Dental:*** To make this sound, the active articulator, the tip of the tongue, contacts the passive articulator and upper front teeth. The three dental sounds in Tamil are as follows.

   /t. d, n/

4. ***Alveolar:*** The active articulator, that is, the edge of the tongue, interacts with the passive articulator, that is, the tooth ridge. The five alveolar sounds in Tamil are as follows.

   /s, n, 1, r, r/

5. ***Retroflex:*** The tongue is an active articulator in the production of retroflex consonants, whereas the alveolar ridge or hard palate is a passive articulator. The tongue contacts the passive articulator and folds back during retroflex articulation. The five retroflexes in Tamil are as follows:

   ft, d, s, n, 1/

6. ***Palatal:*** In the articulation of palatal consonants, the active articulator contacts the hard palate, which is the passive articulator, in front of the tongue. Four palatal consonants are present in Tamil.

   /c, j, n, y/

7. ***Retroflex continuant lateral:*** The creation of this consonant is comparable to that of the retroflex sound. The tip of the tongue comes close to, but does not contact, the hard palate. A single sound of this type is

   /y

8. ***Velar:*** The active articulator is the base of the tongue, whereas the passive articulator is the softer palate. The base of the tongue lifts and contacts the soft palate to produce this sound. The three velar consonants in Tamil are as follows.

   /k, g, n/

9. *Glottal:* Glottal sounds were generated at the glottis. In this case, the articulators were vocal cords. When air travels through the open glottis with little friction, a glottal sound is generated. Although there can be a glottalic hold in oral language sounds, Tamil has only one such sound in this category.

   /h/

4.4.2 Phonemic Contrasts

In Tamil, the semantic differences between words are clearly articulated by opposing morphemes under the same circumstances. Both vowels and consonants have phonemic contrast.

4.4.2.1 *Vowels*

There are two types of contrasts in vowels.

1. Qualitative contrasts
2. Quantitative contrasts

When phonemes with distinct articulatory features occur in the same context, they display qualitative contrast.

/aa, ee/	aakkam	'productivity'
	eekkam	'longing'
/a, i/	alai	'wave'
	ilai	'leaf'
/a, ii/	ṯarkkam	'argue'
	ṯiirkkam	'foresight'
/aa, i/	aaṭi	'name of a Tamil month'
	iṭi	'hit'
/aa, ii/	aaṭu	'dance'
	iiṭu	'equal'
/a, o/	aṭi	'beat'
	oṭi	'break'

/a, oo/	alai	'wave'
	oolai	'palm leaf'
/aa, o/	aaṭṭu	'shake'
	oṭṭu	'stick'
/aa, oo/	aaṭṭam	'dance'
	ooṭṭam	'run'
/a, u/	aṭuppu	'oven'
	uṭuppu	'dress'
/a, uu/	añcal	'post
	uuñcal	'swing'
/aa, u/	aaṇmai	'manliness'
	uṇmai	'truth'
/a, e/	annai	'mother'
	ennai	'me'
/aa, e/	aaṭu	'dance'
	eṭu	'take'
/a, ee/	appam	'an edible item'
	eeppam	'belch'
/aa, uu/	aakkam	'productivity'
	uukkam	'encouragement'
/e, i/	eṭu	'take'
	iṭu	'put'
/e, ii/	eṭṭu	'eight'
	iiṭṭu	'earn'
/ee, i/	eeṭu	'leaf'
	iṭu	'put'

/ee, ii/	eeṭu	'leaf'
	iiṭu	'equal'
/e, o/	eṭṭu	'eight'
	oṭṭu	'stick'
/e, oo/	eṭai	'weight'
	ooṭai	'stream'
/ee, o/	eeppam	'belch'
	oppam	'agreement'
/ee, oo/	eeṭu	'leaf'
	ooṭu	'run'
/e, u/	eṭai	'weight'
	uṭai	'dress'
/e, uu/	eṇ	'number'
	uuṇ	'flesh'
/ee, u/	eeṉṯu	'to stretch (as in hands)'
	unṭu	'propel'
/ee, uu/	eekkam	'longing'
	uukkam	'encouragement'
/i, o/	iṭi	'thunder'
	oṭi	'break'
/i, oo/	iṭu	'put'
	ooṭu	'run'
/ii, o/	iiṭṭu	'earn'
	oṭṭu	'stick'

/ii, oo/	iiṭu	'equal
	ooṭu	'run'
/i, u/	iṭai	'hip'
	uṭai	'dress'
/i, uu/	imai	'eye lash'
	uumai	'dumb'
/ii, u/	iiṭu	'equal'
	uṭu	'wear'
/ii, uu/	iiṭṭu	'earn'
	uuṭṭu	'feed'
/o, u/	oppu	'agree'
	uppu	'salt'
/o, uu/	oṭṭu	'stick'
	uuṭṭu	'feed'
/oo, u/	ooṭai	'stream'
	uṭai	'dress'
/oo, uu/	ooṭṭam	'run'
	uuṭṭam	'nutrition'

(B) *Qualitative Contrasts*

In this example, short vowels are compared with long vowels.

/a, aa/	appam	'an edible item'
	aappam	'an edible item'
/e, ee/	eṭu	'take'
	eeṭu	'leaf'
/i, ii/	iṭu	'put'
	iiṭu	'equal'
/o, oo/	oṭi	'break'
	ooṭi	'having run'

/u, uu/	uṭal	'body'
	uuṭal	'petty quarrel'

3.4.2.2 *Consonants*

The consonants are contrasted in the table beneath.

(A) *Plosives*

/p, b/	palam	'a measurement'
	balam	'strength'
/ṯ, ḏ/	ṯai	'name of a Tamil month'
	kaḏai	'story'
/ṭ, ṯ/	caṭṭam	'law'
	caṯṯam	'sound'
/ḍ, ḏ/	maḍam	'Choultry'
	maḏam	'religion'
/ṯ, ḍ/	ṯaṭṭam	'plate'
	ṯaḍam	'way'
/c, j/	caṯai	'flesh'
	jaṯai	'pair'
/k, g/	keṭu	'to spoil'
	geṭu	'dead-line'

(B) *Nasals*

/m, n/	makam	'a star'
	nakam	'finger nail'
/m, ṇ/	aamai	'tortoise'
	aaṇai	'order'
/n, ṇ/	aani	'a name of a Tamil month'
	aaṇi	'nail'

(C) *Laterals*

/l, ḷ/	muulai	'corner'
	muuḷai	'brain'
/l, ḻ/	palam	'a measurement'
	paḻam	'fruit'
/ḷ, ḻ/	vaḷi	'air'
	vaḻi	'way'

(D) *Laterals and Flap*

/l, r/	kalai	'art'
	karai	'river bank'
/ḷ, r/	vaḷi	'air'
	vari	'line/tax'
/ḻ, r/	kaḻi	'subtract'
	kari	'coal'

(E) *Laterals and Trill*

/l, ṟ/	kalai	'art'
	kaṟai	'stain'
/ḷ, ṟ/	kuḷi	'bath'
	kuṟi	'mark/target'
/ḻ, ṟ/	maḻai	'rain'
	maṟai	'hide'

(F) *Fricatives and Stops*

/s, ṯ/	saram	'string'
	ṯaram	'quality'
/h, k/	hari	'a personal name'
	kari	'coal'

(G) *Semi-vowels*

/v, y/	vaar	'strap'
	yaar	'who?'

4.4.3 Phonemic Distribution

4.4.3.1 *Vowel Distribution*

Except for the letter 'o,' all vowels appear at the beginning, middle, and end of a word. The adjacent table shows the number of times each vowel appears at each of the three locations in a word.

S.No.	Phoneme	Initial	Medial	Final
1.	i	ilai 'leaf'	paṭippu 'studies'	paḷḷi 'school'
2.	ii	iiṭu 'mortgage'	panniirṯṯuḷi 'drop of rose water'	ṯeenii 'bee'
3.	e	eli 'mouse'	kaṭṭerumpu 'a kind of ant'	enne? 'what?'
4.	ee	eeṭu 'leaf'	raaniṯṯeenii 'a kind of bee'	avanee 'that-he only'
5.	a	aṇil 'squirrel'	ṭavaḷai 'frog'	inṯa 'this-adj'
6.	aa	aaṭu 'dance'	paṭṭaasu 'cracker'	ammaa 'mother'
7.	o	onṟu 'one'	paṭinonṟu 'eleven'	-
8.	oo	ooviyam 'painting'	paṭṭooviyam 'silk painting'	avanoo? 'oh-he?'
9.	u	uṇmai 'truth'	pasumai 'green'	karuppu 'black-adj'
10.	uu	uuñcal 'swing'	vaanauurṯi 'aeroplane'	roojaappuu 'rose'

3.4.2.2 *Diphthongs*

The Tamil diphthongs, /ai/ and /au/, appear in all locations, with /ai/ occurring first and medially.

S.No.	Phoneme	Initial	Medial	Final
1.	ai	aivar 'five people'	auvaiyaar 'a personal name'	puṭavai 'saree'
2.	au	auvaiyaar 'a personal name'	vauvaal 'bat'	-

4.4.3.3 *Consonants*

None of the consonants were present in al1. The circulation is expressed as follows:

S.No.	Phoneme	Initial	Medial	Final
1.	p	pan̲t̲u 'ball'	t̲appu 'wrong'	-
2.	b	balam 'strength'	aabat̲t̲u 'danger'	-
3.	t̲	t̲avaḷai 'frog'	pat̲inonr̲u 'eleven'	-
4.	d̲	d̲armam 'dharma'	kad̲avu 'door'	-
5.	ṭ	-	paṭṭaasu 'cracker'	-
6.	ḍ	-	aḍimai 'slave'	-
7.	c	cakkaram 'wheel'	paccai 'green'	-

8.	j	jaṯai 'pair'	paṅkajam 'a personal name'	-
9.	k	kaṯavu 'door'	pakkam 'side/near'	-
10.	g	guṇṭu 'bomb'	vigrakam 'idol of a deity'	-
11.	s	sarasvaṯi 'a personal name'	kasappu 'bitter'	-
12.	ṣ	ṣanmukam 'a personal name'	viṣam 'poison'	-
13.	h	hanumaan 'a deity'	mahaan 'great person'	-
14.	m	mayil 'peacock'	ṯaamarai 'lotus'	maram 'tree'
15*.	ṉ	ṉallaṯu 'good'	paṉṯam 'relation-ship'	-
16.	n	-	manam 'mind'	makan 'son'
17.	ṇ	-	paṇam 'money'	maṇ 'soil'
18*.	ñ	ñaayiru 'sun'	pañcam 'famine'	-
19*.	n	-	ṯaṅkam 'gold'	-
20.	l	laṭṭu 'sweet'	valam 'right side'	paaṭal 'song'
21.	ḷ	-	kaḷam 'field'	taalppaaḷ 'latch;

22.	l̲	-	pal̲am 'fruit'	t̲amil̲ 'Tamil language'
23.	r	-	maram 'tree'	amar 'sit'
24.	r̲	-	manr̲am 'forum'	paar̲ai 'stone'
25.	v	vayiru 'stomach'	t̲avippu 'curiosity'	paavai 'woman'
26.	y	yaanai 'elephant'	kayir̲u 'robe'	varuvaay 'income'

* Marginal phonemes

4.4.4 Allophonic Distribution

The following table shows the allophonic distribution of Tamil speaking sounds.

4.4.4.1 *Vowels*

1. /i/

   /i/ has two allophones: [i] and [X].

   (i) [i] – A high-front ordinal short vowel appears in the central and ultimate locations.

   /put[i]ya/ 'new-adj'

   /paat[i]/ 'half'

   (ii) [I] "A lower high front unrounded short vowel that can be found anywhere."

   /[I]tu/ 'put'

   /[I]lai/ 'leaf'

2. /ii/

   /ii/ contains a single allophone [ii].

   (i) [ii] Long unrounded vowel with a high front that occurs in all places.

   /[ii]tu/ 'indemnity'

3. /e/

   /e/ has two allophones: [E] and [e].

   (i) [E]–Finally, a lower-mid frontal unrounded short vowel appears.

   /mak[E]/ 'son'

(ii) [e] – Unrounded short vowel in the upper-mid front that occurs anywhere.

/[e]li/ 'mouse'

4. /ee/

/ee/ contains a single allophone [ee].

[ee]: Unrounded long vowel in the upper-mid front. This can be observed at any position.

/[ee]ru/ 'climb/

/enk[ee]/ 'where'

5. /a/

/a/ has two allophones, [a] and [a].

(i) [A] – Unrounded short vowels on the lower mid-back. This can be observed in the middle and end regions.

/pat[A]vi/ 'post/position'

(ii) [a] Low central unrounded short vowels. It happens elsewhere.

/[a]nai/ 'hug'

6. /aa/

/aa/ contains a single allophone [aa].

[aa]: Low central unrounded long vowels. It happens throughout.

/[aa]tu/ 'dance'

/parih[aa]ram/ 'remedy'

/amm[aa]/ 'mother'

7. /o/

/o/ has two allophones, [o] and p].

(i) [o] – Unrounded short vowels in the upper-mid back. This can be observed at the first and middle locations.

/[o]ttu/ 'stick'

/patin[o]nru/ 'eleven'

[p] – Unrounded short vowel in the lower mid-back. This can also be observed in other places.

/patakkp]/ 'pendant*

8. /oo/

/oo/ contains a single allophone [oo].

[oo] – Higher-mid-back unrounded long vowels. It was present in all locations.

/[oo]tai/ 'stream'

/katal[oo]ram/ 'sea shore'

/p[oo]/ 'go'

9. /u/

/u/ has two allophones, [U] and [i].

[U]: Lower high back unrounded short vowel. It occurs elsewhere.

/[U]varppu/ 'sour'

/K[U]r[U]mpu/ 'mischief/

[ij – Short unrounded vowel with a highly centralized location. This can be observed in the middle and end regions.

/el[ijmpu/ 'bone'

/karupp[i]/ 'black'

10. /uu/

/uu/ contains a single allophone [u].

(i) [uu] Long, rounded vowel with high back. This can be observed at any location.

/[uu]r/ 'town'

/m[uu]lai/ 'brain'

/roojaapp[uu]/ 'rose'

3.4.4.2 *Consonants*

1. /P/

/p/ Bilabial voiceless plosive with three allophones.

[p] – Bilabial voiced slit fricative that occurs inter-vocally or between liquids and vowels.

/ka[p]am/ 'phlegm'

/maar[p]u/ 'chest'

[£]

[P]

2. /b/

/b/ the

[b] -

3. /%/

/%/ the

[*] -

[&]

After contact as the initial element of synergies, bilabial voiceless unaspirated lax oral plosives occur.

/pattu+t.pjpuucci/ 'butterfly/

/inta + [£]paiyan/ 'this boy'

- The bilabial voiceless unaspirated oral plosives occur elsewhere.

/[Pjaavai/ 'woman'

/[P]ottu/ 'forehead mark'

Bilabial voiced plosive has one allophone.

The bilabial voiced unaspirated oral plosive. It occurs in all the positions.

/[b]alam/ 'strength'

/[b]aavam/ 'expression'

Dental voiceless ploves. It had three allophones. The apicodental-voiced slits were fricative. It is present between liquids and vowels.

/ka[5]avu/ 'door'

/avar[$]aan/ 'that he (hon)'

It appears as the first member of synergies after the intersection.

/tanni+j^]totti/ 'water tank'

(iii) [t] – Unaspirated apico-dental voiceless oral plosives. This can also be observed in other locations.

/[t]avil/ 'a musical instrument'

/pa[tt]u/ 'ten'

4. /d/

/d/ There is only a single allophone in the dental voiced oral plosives.

[d] Unaspirated oral plosives with an apico-dental voice. This can be observed at any location.

/[d]aanam/ 'alms'

5. /t/

/t/ There are two allophones in the domal/retroflex voiceless plosives.

(i) *[T]* – The voiced apicodomal retroflex flap. It appears in liquids and vowels as well as intervocally.

/et^am/ 'place'

/ta['?]am/ 'route'

(ii) [t] – Apicodomal retroflex voiceless unaspirated oral plosive. This can also be observed in other locations.

/pa[tt]u/ 'silk'

/kee[tt]aan/ 'listened-he'

6. */a/*

/d/ The domal retroflexed voiced plosive possesses a single allophone.

[d] – Apico-dental retroflex-voiced unaspirated oral plosives. This can also be observed in other locations.

/la[dd]u/ 'an edible'

7. */c/*

/c/ The palatal voiceless oral plosives possess three allophones.

(i) [s] – Apico-alveolar voiceless groove fricative. This might happen before or after a vowel, or it can happen between liquids and vowels.

/[s]uvar/ 'wall'

/pa[s]i/ 'hungry'

/a[s]ti vaaram/ 'foundation'

(ii) [gj – Palatal voiceless lax affricate. It occurs after the juncture as the first member of a gemination.

/karuppu+t^Jcaami/ 'personal name'

/manca+tj^cattai/ 'yellow shirt'

(iii) [c] Palatal voiceless unaspirated affricates. It occurs elsewhere.

/pa[cc]ai/ 'green'

/ka[cc]eeri/ 'music concert/office'

8. */j/*

/j/ The palatal voiced oral plosive has only one allophone.

[j] " The palatal voiced unaspirated affricate. This occurs at all positions.

/raa[j]aa/ 'king'

/[j]aanaki/ 'a personal name'

9. */k/*

/k/ The velar voiceless plosive has five allophones:

(i) [c] – Fronto-palatal voiceless slit fricative. This occurs inter-vocally when followed by /i/.

/aa[c]iya/ 'such'

/raa[q]i/ 'a kind of millet'

(ii) [x] – Dorso-Velar voiceless slit fricative. It occurs inter-vocally when not followed by /i/ and between liquids and vowels (except /i/).

/ma[x]an/ 'son'

/varu[x]a/ 'let (it) come'

(iii) [k*] – Dorso-velar voiceless unaspirated palatalized oral plosives. This occurs in gemination, either preceded or followed by

/y /•

/vaa[k k^yam/ 'sentence'

/taa[kfk^yatu/ 'that-it hit'

(iv) [,k,] ~ Dorso-velar voiceless unaspirated lax oral plosives. It occurs after the juncture as the first member of a gemination.

/velli+tJsJkilamai/ 'Friday'

/talai+tjcjkat^u/ 'bandage or cloth tied around the head'

(v) [k] – Dorso-velar voiceless unaspirated oral plosives. It occurs elsewhere.

/[k]ayiru/ 'robe'

/pa[kk]am/ 'side/near'

10. /g/

/g/ Velar-voiced plosives have two allophones

(i) [g*J – Dorso-velar voiced unaspirated oral plosives.

It occurs before */if.*

/cantg^ili/ 'chain'

/ititaan[g*]i/ 'lightening conductor'

(ii) [g] – Dorso-velar voiced unaspirated oral plosives. It occurs elsewhere.

/tan[g]am/ 'gold'

/pan[g]u/ 'share'

11. /S/

/s/ The normal retroflex fricative has one allophone.

(i) /s/ – Apico-domal voiceless groove fricative. It occurs at all positions.

/u[s]aa/ 'a personal name'

/u[s]nam/ 'heat'

/atir[s]tam/ 'luck'

/ka [s] tam/ 'difficult'

12./m/

The labial nasal has four allophones.

(i) ~ Nasalization is a co-occurring feature of the word final vowel but marked as a segment.

/pan[o]/ 'money'

/vant[oo]/ 'came-we'

(ii) [ft*] – Dorsovelar palatalized voiced nasal. It occurs before the velar plosives, followed by /i/.

/ititaa[ny]ki/ 'lightning conductor'

/vii[n^]ki/ 'having swollen'

(iii) [n] – Dorso-velar voiced nasal occurs before velar plosives, which is not followed by /i/.

/ta[n]kam/ 'gold'

/sa[h]kam/ 'association'

(iv) [m]: Bilabial voiced nasally. It occurs elsewhere.

/[m]aram/ 'tree'

/a[mm]aa/ 'mother'

/puspa[m]/ 'flower'

13. /n/

The dental/alveolar nasal cavity has three allophones.

(i) [~] – Nasalization, a co-occurring feature found with the word final vowel, but marked as a segment.

/av[a]/ 'that-he'

/vant[aa]/ 'came-he'

(ii) [n] – Apicodental-voiced nasal. It occurs when it is followed by a dental plosive.

/pa[n]tu/ 'ball'

/sa[n]tanam/ 'sandal'

(iii) [n] – alveolar voiced nasal. It occurs elsewhere.

/ma[n]am/ 'heart'

/vanta[n]am/ 'a wishing'

14. /n/

The domal/retroflex nasal had one allophone.

(i) [n] – Apicodomal retroflex voiced nasal. This occurs in the medial and final positions.

/pa[n]am/ 'money'
/ka[n]/ 'eye'

15. /n/

The palatal nasal cavity had one allophone.

(i) [n] – Fronto-palatal voiced nasally. This occurred at the initial and medial positions.
/[n]aanam/ 'wisdom'
/ma[n]cal/ 'yellow'

16. /!/

/I/ The dental/alveolar lateral has one allophone.

(i) [1] – Apicoalveolar voiced laterally. This occurred in all three positions.
/[l]aapam/ 'profit'
/nuu[l]akam/ 'library'
/paa[1]/ 'milk'

17. /l/

/!/The domal-retroflex lateral has an allophone.

(i) [1] – The apicodomal voiced retroflex lateral. This occurs in the medial and final positions.
/ta[l]am/ 'platform'
/pa[ll]i/ 'school'
/tee[l]/ 'scorpion'

18. /l/

/!/The dominal-retroflex continuant has one allophone.

(i) [1] – Apicodomal lateralized retroflex continuant. This occurs in the medial and final positions.
/pa[l]am/ 'fruit'
/tami[l]/ 'Tamil'

19. /r/

The alveolar flap had two allophones.

(i) [r] – Apicoalveolar voiced flap. It occurs initially.
/[r]ampam/ 'saw'

(ii) [r*] – Apicoalveolar voiced flap with one tap. It occurs elsewhere.
/ka[r']uppu/ 'black'

20. /r/

/r/ The alveolar trill had one allophone.

(i) [r] ~ Apicoalveolar voiced trill. It occurs in the medial, inter-vocally, and final positions.

/a[r]am/ 'saw'

/a[r]ai/ 'room'

21. /v/

The labial semivowel has three allophones.

(i) [u] – High back-rounded non-syllabic vocoid. It occurs before the high-back vowel.

/tancaaCy]uuru/ 'a place name'

/kata[u]ul/ 'god'

(ii) [tf] – Labio dental tense continuant. It occurs when preceded by labio-dental continuance.

/av[v]ay/ 'personal name'

/cev[\/]aay/ 'Tuesday'

(iii) [v] – The labio-dental voiced continuant occurs elsewhere.

/[v]ayiru/ 'stomach'

/paa[v]am/ 'sin'

/paa[v]ai/ 'woman'

22. /y/

/y/ The palatal semi-vowel has two allophones.

(i) [i] – High-front unrounded tense non-syllabic vocoid. It occurs when preceded by palatal continuity.

/tay[i]al/ 'stitch'

[i] – High-front unrounded non-syllabic vocoid. It occurs elsewhere.

/[i]aanai/ 'elephant'

/va[i]al/ 'paddy field'

4.4.5 Nasalization

The position of the velum determines two major consonant categories: stops and nasals. When oral sounds are produced, the uvula closes the nasal tract so that air passes through the oral tract. When nasals are produced, the uvula closes its oral tract.

Sometimes, when nasal sounds follow vowels, the air escapes through the nasal and oral tracts simultaneously. In that case, those vowels are nasalized, and this kind of articulation is called salization. The same situation was also found in Tamil. The present study concentrates on the occurrence of nasalization, not in all positions, but in the final position and in the different contexts selected for the study.

4.4.6 Voice

The state of the glottis determines the voice of the segmental sound. In Tamil, voiced plosives were not used until modern times. The use of Sanskrit words and other foreign words in Tamil brought voiced plosives to Tamil. Voiced and voiceless plosives produced with identical points of articulation and articulators are used in identical environments, especially in articulating words, and thereby occur in contrast.

/paavam/ 'sin'

/baavam/ 'expression'

At the same time, there is another situation in which they are non-contrastive and do not signal meaning differences between words.

1. /pantu/ 'ball'
   /bantu/ 'ball'
2. /tantam/ 'tusk'
   /dantam/ 'tusk'

In the Tamil writing system, the voicing of plosives are not made explicit using a graphical representation. The voice is understood and interpreted either as contrastive or not, depending on the context. Therefore, children learning the modem Tamil must use voiced plosives carefully. If so, further questions, such as the following, arise:

1. Is it maintained both in oral language use context and in reading contexts.
2. Whether the variation in voiced plosive is socio-linguistically significant?

This study examines the context and social significance of voicing; because of this, the occurrence of voice in plosives in the initial, intervocalic, and postnasal positions within the units of word level was observed.

4.5 TAMIL MORPHOLOGY

Linguistic study of structure and formation of words in a language is called Morphology. Tamil morphology involves how the words are constructed, their relationships between their smallest units of meaning (morphemes) and how these morphemes are contributed to create meaningful words.

The morphological complexity of Tamil arises from its prosodies for person, gender, and number, as well as the incorporation of auxiliaries. These auxiliaries play a important role in conveying aspects, moods, causation, and attitudes within verbs.

4.5.1 Word Classes

Parts of speech is also known as Word classes, are categories into which words that are traditionally classified bases on grammatical and syntactic functions within language. Each word class has specific role to construct sentences and convey meaning.

Applying both morphological and syntactic criteria, it categorized into eight parts of speech in Modern Tamil: nouns, verbs, postpositions, adjectives, adverbs, quantifiers, determiners, and conjunctions. All lexical or root morphemes in modern Tamil fall into four types, comprising two major groups of nominal and verbal roots, along with two minor groups of adjectival and adverbial roots. All words in Tamil are based on their forms, can be regarded as either inflected or uninflected versions of noun, verb, adjective, or adverb roots. Nouns consist of noun roots, and verbs contain verb roots. However, postpositions, many adverbs, quantifiers, and conjunctions can be seen as inflected and uninflected forms of nominal or verbal roots.

4.6 TAMIL MORPHOLOGICAL CLASSES AND CATEGORIES

Morphological classes and categories refer to the various groups and types of linguistic elements that contribute to the structure of words. These classes and categories include different types of morphemes, affixes, and their combinations. Here are some key morphological classes and categories in Tamil.

4.6.1 Nouns

Nouns are fundamental elements of speech that symbolize places, things, people, or abstract concepts. Nouns serve as the building blocks of sentences and play essential roles in communication.

Example: "பாடகன்" (singer), "வீடு" (house).

Characteristics of Nouns in Tamil

Typically, nouns undergo inflections to indicate number and case categories. The language recognizes two numbers: Singular and Plural.

Noun Roots

Noun roots are the basic, uninflected forms of nouns. They convey the core meaning and serve as the basic for building more complex nouns through inflections and modifications.

Example

"மகன்" (son)
"கடல்" (sea)
"பாடல்" (song)

Nominal Inflections

Nouns in Tamil can undergo inflections, which are modifies the basic form of the noun root. These inflections shall provide crucial grammatical information such as case, number, and gender.

Example

"பழம்" (fruit) → "பழங்கள்" (fruits)
"கோடி" (crore) → "கோடிகள்" (crores)

Gender

Tamil nouns are not implicitly marked for gender. Gender is usually not explicitly expressed in the noun itself but can be inferred from the context or specified through the use of gender-specific words.

Number

Nouns in Tamil can be inflected for number to indicate whether they are singular or plural. This is an essential feature for conveying the quantity or count of objects or entities.

Example

"படம்" (picture) → "படங்கள்" (pictures)
"பழம்" (fruit) → "பழங்கள்" (fruits)

Functions of Nouns in Tamil Sentences

Subject and Object

Noun plays important roles as the subject or object of a sentence. The subject is the one performing the action, while the object is the entity receiving the action.

Example

"அவன் ஒரு விளக்கு ஏற்றுபவன்" (He is a lamp-lighter.)
"அவன் ஒரு புத்தகம் படித்து கொண்டிருக்கிறான்" (He is reading a book)

Possession

Nouns are used to indicate possession or ownership. Possessive constructions involve combining a noun with a possessive marker to express relationships.

Example

"அவன் வீடு" (his house)
"அவளுடைய கருத்து" (her opinion)

Modifiers

Nouns can be modified by adjectives or other nouns to provide additional information or to specify particular qualities. This helps in creating more detailed and descriptive expressions.

Example:

"அழகான மரம்" (beautiful tree)
"குழந்தைகளின் பெயர்கள்" (names of children)

Case Marking

Noun in Tamil can be marked for case, indicating their syntactic function in a sentence. Different cases convey the role of the noun in relation to other elements in the sentence.

Example

"விளக்கு" (the lamp) – nominative case
"விளக்குக்கு" (to the lamp) – dative case

4.6.2 Pronouns

Pronouns in Tamil serve as essential linguistic elements that replace nouns and contribute to clarity and conciseness in communication. Here's an elaboration on pronouns in Tamil:

Types of Pronouns in Tamil

Personal Pronouns

Personal pronouns in Tamil are used to replace specific persons or things in a sentence. They can vary based on person, gender, and number.

Example

"அவன்" (avan) – he
"அவள்" (aval) – she
"அது" (adhu) – it
"நான்" (nān̲) – I
"நீ" (nī) – you
"நாம்" (nām) – we

Demonstrative Pronouns

Demonstrative pronouns in Tamil are used to indicate specific entities in relation to the speaker. They include words for "this," "that," "these," and "those."

Example

"இந்த" (indha) – this
"அந்த" (antha) – that
"இவர்கள்" (ivarkaḷ) – they are
"அவர்கள்" (avarkaḷ) – they are

Interrogative Pronouns

Interrogative pronouns in Tamil are used to form questions and inquire about specific entities. Common interrogative pronouns include "who," "what," "which," and "whose."

Example

"யார்" (yār) – who
"என்ன" (eṉṉa) – what
"எந்த" (enda) – which
"யாராவது" (yārāvatu) – whose

Relative Pronouns

Relative pronouns in Tamil are used to introduce relative clauses that provide additional information about a noun. The most common relative pronoun is "யாருக்கு" (yāruku), which means "who" or "to whom."

Example

"கதை சொல்ல விரும்பும் சிறுவன்" (Āṇ makan, yāruku oru kathai solla virumbukiṟāṉ) – The boy who wants to tell a story.

Indefinite Pronouns

Indefinite pronouns in Tamil refer to nonspecific or unidentified entities. They include words like "யாரோ," "எதாவது," and "எவருமே."

Example

"யாரோ அவர் எங்கே போனார்?" (Yārō avar eṅkē pōṉār?) – Whoever went, where did he go?

Functions of Pronouns in Tamil Sentences

Avoiding Repetition

Pronouns replace nouns to avoid redundancy and repetition in speech or writing, making the language more concise.

Expressing Relationships

Pronouns help convey relationships between entities in a sentence, such as indicating the speaker, the listener, or specific objects.

Forming Questions

Interrogative pronouns play a crucial role in forming questions, seeking information, and initiating conversations.

Connecting Clauses

Relative pronouns introduce relative clauses, connecting and providing additional information about a noun in the main clause.

4.6.3 Verbs

Verbs in Tamil are important components of speech, playing a central role in expressing actions, states, or occurrences within sentences.

Characteristics of Verbs in Tamil

Verb Roots

Verb roots in Tamil are the basic forms that convey the core meaning of an action or state. Examples include:

"படி" (paḍu – to read)

"செல்" (cel – to go)

"உழை" (uḻai – to work)

Verb Inflections

Verbs in Tamil undergo inflections to convey information about various grammatical features, including tense, aspect, mood, person, and number.

Example

"படிக்க" (paḍikka – to read) – infinitive form
"படிக்கின்ற" (paḍikkiṉṟa – reading) – present continuous tense

Tense

Tamil verbs can be inflected for different tenses to indicate the timing of an action or state. Common tenses include present, past, and future.

Example

"படிக்கின்ற" (paḍikkiṉṟa – reading) – present continuous

"படித்தேன்" (paḍittēṉ – I read) – past tense
"படிக்கும்" (paḍikkuṁ – will read) – future tense

Aspect

Aspect refers to the temporal quality of an action. Tamil verbs can be marked to indicate aspects such as ongoing, completed, or habitual actions.

Example

"படிக்கின்ற" (paḍikkiṉṟa – reading) – ongoing aspect
"படித்தேன்" (paḍittēṉ – I read) – completed aspect

Mood

Verbs in Tamil can express different moods, such as indicative, imperative, subjunctive, and potential, through various inflections.

Example

"படிக்க" (paḍikka – read) – indicative mood
"படி" (paḍi – read!) – imperative mood

Person and Number

Tamil verbs agree with the person and number of the subject. The verb form changes based on whether the subject is first person, second person, or third person, and whether it is singular or plural.

Example

"நான் படிக்கிறேன்" (Nāṉ paḍikkiṟēṉ – I am reading)
"நீ படிக்கிறாய்" (Nī paḍikkiṟāy – You are reading)
"அவன் படிக்கிறான்" (Avaṉ paḍikkiṟāṉ – He is reading)

4.6.4 Adjectives

Adjectives in Tamil provides additional information about nouns or pronouns. They modify or describe the qualities, attributes, or characteristics of the entities they accompany, enriching the language with descriptive details.

Characteristics of Adjectives in Tamil

Adjective Roots

Adjective roots in Tamil are the basic, uninflected forms that convey the essential meaning of a quality or attribute.

Examples

"அழகான" (a̲lagā̲n – beautiful)
"புதிய" (putiya – new)
"மிகவும்" (mikavum – very)

Adjective Inflections

Adjectives in Tamil can undergo inflections to match the gender, number, and case of the noun or pronoun they modify. This ensures agreement between the adjective and the modified entity.

Example

"அழகான காட்சி" (a̲lagā̲n parvai – beautiful view)
"அழகான காட்சிகள்" (a̲lagā̲n parvaikaḷ – beautiful views)

Functions of Adjectives in Tamil Sentences

Describing Qualities

Adjectives in Tamil are used to describe the qualities, characteristics, or features of nouns or pronouns. They answer questions like "What kind?" or "Which one?"

Example

"முகம் அழகான" (mukam a̲lagā̲n – beautiful face)
"புதிய புத்தகம்" (putiya pu̲t̲takam – new book)

Providing Details

Adjectives add specificity and details to the entities they modify, and enhance the precision of communication.

Example

"மிகவும் விரைவில்" (mikavum virai vil – very quickly)
"உயரமான கடமை" (uyaramāṉ kaṭamai – high responsibility)

Expressing Quantity

Some adjectives in Tamil are used to indicate quantity or degree, providing information about the intensity or extent of a quality.

Example

"மிகவும் பெரிய" (mikavum periya – very big)
"குறைவான செலவு" (kuṟaivāṉ celavu – minimal expense)

Agreement with Nouns

Adjectives agree with the gender, number, and case of the noun or pronoun they modify. This ensures grammatical concordance within the sentence.

Example

"அழகான பர்வை" (aḻagāṉ parvai – beautiful view)
"அழகான பர்வைகள்" (aḻagāṉ parvaikaḷ – beautiful views)

4.6.5 Numerals

Numerals in Tamil are used to represent numbers and quantify various entities. Tamil numerals have a distinct script and a unique set of symbols, which are different from the numerals used in the Western numeral system.

Number System

Script

Tamil numerals are written in the Tamil script. The script has its own characters for numbers, distinct from the numerals used in other scripts.

Example

"௧" (1), "௨" (2), "௩" (3), "௪" (4), "௫" (5), "௬" (6), "௭" (7), "௮" (8), "௯" (9), "௰" (10), and so on.

Decimal System

Tamil uses a decimal number system, similar to the Western system. It is based on powers of 10, with place values increasing from right to left.

Example

"௧0" (10), "௧00" (100), "௧000" (1000), and so forth.

Cardinal and Ordinal Numerals

Cardinal Numerals

Cardinal numerals represent the quantity or count of objects. They are used for counting and indicating the number of items.

Example

"௩ பதிவுகள்" (3 articles)
"௨௫ பேர்" (25 people)

Ordinal Numerals

Ordinal numerals indicate the position or order of items in a sequence. They are used to express the rank or order of something.

Example

"௧◌ாம்" (first), "௨◌ாம்" (second), "௩◌ாம்" (third), and so on.

Use in Daily Life

Counting

Tamil numerals are used for counting objects, money, and various quantities in everyday life.

Example

"௨ ரூபாய்" (2 rupees)
"௫ கடல்" (5 apples)

Time and Dates

Numerals are used to represent time, dates, and ages in Tamil.

Example

"௯ மணிக்கு" (9 o'clock)
"௧௯௯௮ ஆண்டு" (the year 1998)

Mathematics and Science

Tamil numerals are employed in mathematical calculations, scientific notations, and other technical contexts.

Example

"௪ + ௩ = ௭" (4 + 3 = 7)
"௨.௫ என்பது ஒரு பின்னத்தை குறிக்கிறது" (2.5 represents a fraction)

4.7 LEXICOGRAPHY

Lexicography in Tamil language involves the systematic study, compilation, and documentation of the vocabulary. Lexicographers create dictionaries that serve as authoritative references for the Tamil-speaking community.

4.7.1 Characteristics of Lexicography

Word Collection

Lexicographers gather words from different sources such as classical literature, modern writings, spoken language, and specialized domains. This process ensures that the dictionary have the richness and evolution of the Tamil language.

Defining Meanings

Defining meanings in Tamil lexicography involves to provide clear, accurate, and culturally relevant explanations for each word. Lexicographers aim to capture the significances of word usage in different contexts.

Phonetic Representation

Tamil lexicographers pay attention to the phonetic representation of words, as Tamil has a unique script. Accurate representation helps users pronounce words correctly and enhances the overall usability of the dictionary.

Etymology

It provides information about the origin and historical development of words, known as etymology. Understanding the roots of words adds depth to the user's knowledge and appreciation of the language.

Grammar and Usage

Lexicographers include information about the grammatical aspects of words, including their part of speech and usage in different grammatical structures. This helps users understand how words fit into the overall structure of the language.

Cultural and Regional Variations

To recognize cultural and regional variations in the use of words is crucial in Tamil lexicography. Lexicographers take into account the diverse linguistic practices across different Tamil-speaking communities and regions.

Inclusion of New Words

Lexicographers continually update dictionaries to include new words that emerge due to technological advancements, social changes, or evolving trends. This ensures that dictionaries remain relevant and reflective of contemporary language use.

Bilingual and Specialized Dictionaries

In addition to general dictionaries, lexicographers also work on bilingual dictionaries, translating words between Tamil and other languages. They may also create specialized dictionaries for specific domains such as science, technology, law, or literature.

Digital Lexicography

With the advent of digital technology, lexicographers engage in digital lexicography, creating online dictionaries, mobile applications, and electronic databases. These platforms enhance accessibility and provide dynamic updates.

4.8 SYNTAX

Syntax is the deals with the arrangements of words in a sentence. The word order is important and strict for the languages like English but for agglutinative languages like Tamil the word order is not strict and important. Tamil follows SOV pattern but it need not to be strict for both in spoken and written form. It deals with combination words, arrangements and structure of them. For the below example all the statement gives the same meaning.

1. Kayal pazattai caappiTTaaL (Kayal ate fruit)
   கயல் பழத்தை சாப்பிட்டாள்
2. Pazattai Kayal caappiTTaaL (Kayal ate fruit)
   பழத்தை கயல் சாப்பிட்டாள்
3. Kayal caappiTTaal pazattai (Kayal ate fruit)
   கயல் சாப்பிட்டாள் பழத்தை
4. Pazattai caappiTTaal Kayal (Kayal ate fruit)
   பழத்தை சாப்பிட்டாள் கயல்

In the above statement the word order is SOV, OSV, SVO and OVS respectively. Even though the word order is changed the meaning of the statements are not changed. Here the SVO and OVS are not very common. In Tamil the phrases in the sentence and words within a phrase are freely movable. That is the reason says Thambi Jose. F.S. (2007) states that "Tamil is not free word ordered language, but it is free phrase order language".

4.9 SEMANTICS

Semantics is important in inguistiscts that study the meaning of words, phrases, sentences and how these meanings are understood in a language. For any language semantics covers various aspects like sentence semantics (meaning of sentences) and lexical semantics (meaning of individual words), and the relationships between different linguistic expressions.

1. Lexical Semantics

(a) *Polysemy*

Example: The word "ஆட்டம்" (āṭṭam) in Tamil can mean both "dance" and "game" depending on the context.

"அவன் அழகாக ஆட்டம் பார்க்கின்றான்" – avan̲ al̲agāka āṭṭam pārkkin̲r̲ān̲. – he is watching beatutiful dance

"உங்கள் குழந்தைகள் அருகிலுள்ள பூங்காவில் ஆட்டம் போடுகின்றனர்." – Uṅkaḷ kuḻantaikaḷ arukiluḷḷa pūṅkāvil viḷaiyāṭukiṟārkaḷ. – Your children are playing a game in the nearby park.

(b) *Synonyms*

Example: Synonyms for "happy" include "மகிழ்ச்சி" (makilcci) and "இனிய" (Iṉiya).

"நான் மகிழ்ச்சியாக இருக்கிறேன்" (Nāṉ makilcci-yāka irukiṟēṉ) – "I am happy."

2. Sentence Semantics

(a) *Ambiguity*

Example: The sentence "அவன் குறைந்துவிட்டான்" (Avaṉ kuṟaintu viṭṭāṉ) can be ambiguous without context. It could mean "He reduced" or "He decreased."

"எப்பொழுதும் உடல் எடையை குறைத்துக்கொண் டார்" (Eppoḻutum uṭal eṭaiyai kuṟaittukkoṇṭār) – "He always reduced weight."

(b) *Presupposition*

Example: The sentence "அவன் படிக்கின்றான்" (Avaṉ paḍikkiṉṟāṉ) presupposes that he is currently reading.

"அவன் படிக்கும் போது" (Avaṉ paḍikkuṁ pōtu) – "While he is reading."

3. Pragmatic Semantics

(a) *Speech Acts*

Example: "உன்னை உறுதிசெய்" (Uṉṉai uṟuticey) – "Assert yourself"

This sentence carries literal meaning and also conveys the speaker's intention for the listener to take a specific action.

(b) *Politeness*

Example: "தயவுசெய்து எனக்கு உதவுங்கள்" (Tayavuceytu eṉakku utavuṅkaḷ) – "Please help me."

The use of "தயவு செய்து" (Tayavu ceytu) adds a polite request to the sentence.

4.10 PRAGMATICS

Pragmatics in linguistics branch studies the use of language in context, and consider how context influences communication's interpretation. It involves to understand speaker's intentions, the implied meaning to achieve communication goals. The pragmatics plays a key role in non-compositional (atomic) meanings of words along with syntax and established communication units.

Some of key concepts in pragmatics:

Speech Acts

Example: In Tamil, the way a request is framed can vary based on politeness.

"உதவு" (utavu) is a polite way of saying "help," while "உதவி" (utavi) is more direct.

Politeness Levels

Example: The use of honorifics like "அவர்" (avar) for respectful address and "உன்" (uṉ) for informal address that reflects the politeness level in Tamil communication.

Implicit Meaning

Example: Tamil often uses indirect expressions for politeness.
Saying "ஒரு பை வாங்கு" (Oru pai vāṅgu), literally "buy a bag," might imply "buy a bag for me" depending on context.

Conversational Implicature

Example: If someone says, "நான் உங்களுக்காக கொஞ்சம் உழைக்கிறேன் (Nāṉ uṅkaḷukkāka koñcam uḻaikkiṟēṉ), meaning "I am working a bit for you," it might imply that they are doing a favor for you.

Context-Dependent Meanings

Example: The Tamil word "அப்படி" (appaṭi) might mean "like that" in a general sense but could convey annoyance or disagreement depending on intonation and context.

Direct vs. Indirect Communication

Example: Tamil speakers might use indirect expressions to soften requests or convey information, relying on shared cultural understandings to interpret the intended meaning.

Cultural Nuances

Example: Expressions of respect, such as "கூடியே" (kūṭiyē) or "எங்களுக்கு அனுமதி செய்யுங்கள்" (eṅkaḷukku anumati ceyuṅkaḷ), are culturally embedded ways of seeking permission or showing deference.

Deixis

Example: Tamil uses deixis, where words like "இது" (itu – this) and "அந்த" (anta – that) depend on the physical or conversational context for their meaning.

4.11 CONCLUSION

This section describes Tamil's computational linguistics approach. It includes fundamentals of computational linguistics, Problems of Tamil Linguistic Computation, Phonology, Morphology, Lexicography, Syntax, Semantics, and Pragmatics.Tamil is a good representation of diglossic and dialectal variety in a language. The phonological framework of Tamil presented by Tolkappiyar differs from that of current Tamil in a few ways. The sounds are now divided into vowels, diphthongs, and consonants in phonology. Nouns, Verbs, Adjectives, Pronouns, and Numerals have been recognized as the common morphological classes in Tamil, based on certain morphosyntactic criteria that help identify morphological classes. Pronouns and Numerals are recognized as unique word classes that could not theoretically be classified as subclasses of Nouns, and Nouns, Verbs, and Adjectives are considered as three major classes. Each word class was described in detail, providing information regarding changes to produce different sounds. It also presents the details of syntax, semantics and pragmatics with simple examples.

CHAPTER 5

Tamil Computing Tools and Resources

5.1 INTRODUCTION

NLP serves as a linguistic bridge, facilitating easy communication between speakers of various languages. This technological marvel improves machine translation systems in the Tamil domain by translating text to and from Tamil with ease. This encourages intercultural cooperation in addition to facilitating global communication. Additionally, NLP's specially designed sentiment analysis for Tamil offers a sophisticated comprehension of the feelings and viewpoints conveyed in text, providing businesses and organizations wishing to interact with the Tamil-speaking community with priceless insights. When we consider the importance of NLP, its contribution to improving Tamil language processing becomes evident, demonstrating its transformative power in removing barriers between languages and promoting inclusive communication.

NLP Processing Tools and resources for Tamil

A number of resources and tools have arisen in the field of Tamil Natural Language Processing (NLP) to help Tamil language text processing and analysis. These technologies span the gamut of natural language processing (NLP), from simple text processing to sophisticated tasks like sentiment analysis and machine translation. Tamil text processing is a complicated procedure that includes several components like Tokenizer, Part-of-Speech Tagging, Named Entity Recognition, Sentiment Analysis, Speech Processing, Corpora for Training Models, Linguistic Resources, Morphological Analyzers, Text Summarization, Stemmers and Lemmatizers, Tamil Dependency Parsers, Tamil Language Generation Models, Tamil Text Classification Libraries, Tamil Language Preservation, Collaborative Translation and Cross-Language Information Retrieval.

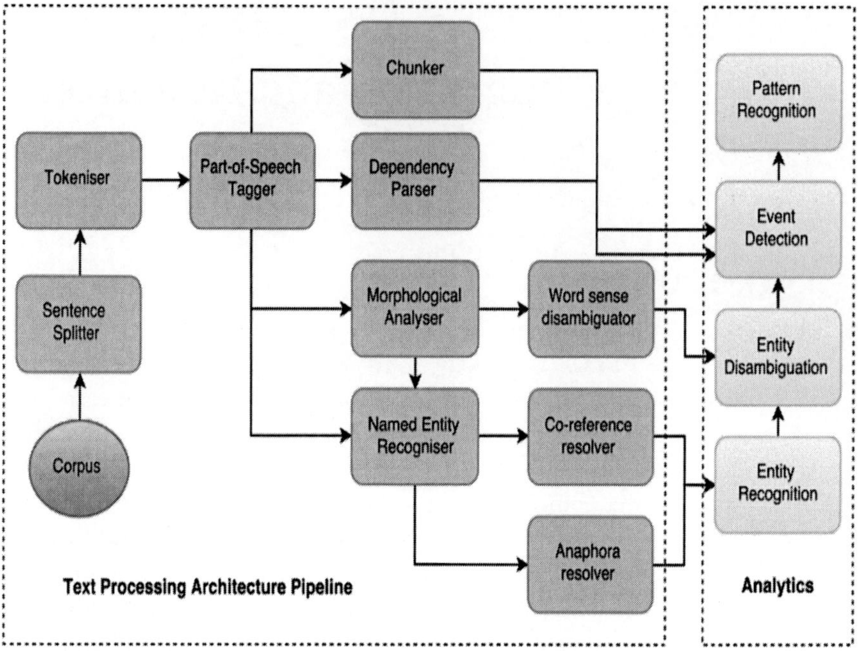

Figure 5.1: Text Processing Architecture Pipeline (Credit: CTNLPR)

5.2 SENTENCE SPLITTER

The task of sentence splitting is crucial in NLP tasks like machine translation, speech recognition, and language modelling. Typically, for several causes, the NLP tools need their input separated into sentences. The sentence boundary disambiguation (SBD), also called sentence breaking. The important issue in NLP is to determine the point where the sentences start and end. However, sentence boundary identification is difficult due to lack of clarity in punctuation marks. For example, the full-stop can be used to denote a decimal point, an abbreviation, an email address and an ellipsis, so such cases can not be treated like end of a sentence. Same way the exclamation and question marks can be in emoticons, slang and embedded quotes.

The following python program would aim to build an efficient sentence splitter module that could break down Tamil text into meaningful sentence.

```
import nltk

nltk.download ('punkt')

from nltk.tokenize import sent_tokenize

def tamil_sentence_splitter_nltk(text):
sentences = sent_tokenize(text, language='tamil')
return sentences

# Example usage with the provided Tamil text:
tamil_text = "நான் இன்று காலை நேரம் சென்று எழுந்தேன். அவன்
நன்கு ஓய்வு எடுக்கட்டும். நீங்கள் வருகைதந்தமைக்கு மிக்க நன்றி."
sentences = tamil_sentence_splitter_nltk(tamil_text)

for index, sentence in enumerate(sentences, start=1):
 print(f'Sentence {index}: {sentence}')
```

The program output can be:

```
Sentence 1: நான் இன்று காலை நேரம் சென்று எழுந்தேன்.
Sentence 2: அவன் நன்கு ஓய்வு எடுக்கட்டும்.
Sentence 3: நீங்கள் வருகைதந்தமைக்கு மிக்க நன்றி.
```

5.3 TOKENIZER

The Tokenization process involves the systematic segmentation of provided textual content into discrete components, encompassing words, notations, phrases, or other meaningful segments known as tokens. These tokens may encompass a spectrum of linguistic elements, ranging from numerical entities to words and punctuation marks.

Within the linguistic context of Tamil, an agglutinative structure prevails, wherein a minimum of two words conjoins. This agglutinative nature of Tamil word forms a nuanced approach to Tokenization, allowing dissection of amalgamated lexical units into distinct tokens. Tokenization is expert to accomplish this task through demarcation of word boundaries, delineating the conclusion of one word and the inception of the subsequent one. The terminology "word segmentation" is interchangeable with Tokenization to describe this linguistic approach.

The linguistic nature of Tamil is characterized by its reliance on white spaces as separators between words, rendering it a space-delimited language.

This spatial demarcation is graphically elucidated in Figure 5.2, illustrating the systematic arrangement of words separated by whitespace.

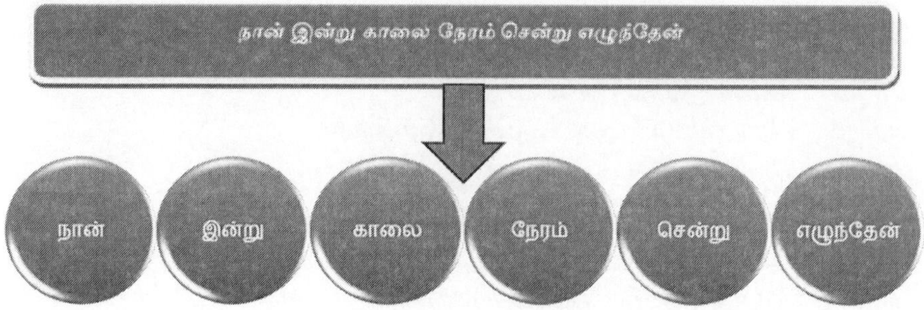

Figure 5.2: Tokenization for Tamil

Tokenization serves as a pivotal tool for executing sophisticated information processing tasks, including the development of intelligent chatbots, sentiment analysis, language translation, spam filtering, and text mining. In the case of Tamil, word boundaries are traditionally denoted by spaces. However, the objective of this module is to construct a module specifically designed to dissect Tamil sentences into individual words. This involves a meticulous examination of the diverse word forms present in sentences. To illustrate, let's contemplate the following textual segments.

நான் இன்று காலை நேரம் சென்று எழுந்தேன்

அவன் நன்கு ஓய்வு எடுக்கட்டும்

நீங்கள் வருகை தந்தமைக்கு மிக்க நன்றி

Consider the above Tamil sentences; the tokenizer will divide the sentence into the following tokens.

Table 5.1: The Tokenizer will Divide the Sentence into the Following Tokens

(1)	*(2)*	*(3)*	*(4)*	*(5)*	*(6)*
நான்	இன்று	காலை	நேரம்	சென்று	எழுந்தேன்
(7)	*(8)*	*(9)*	*(10)*		
அவன்	நன்கு	ஓய்வு	எடுக்கட்டும்		
(11)	*(12)*	*(13)*	*(14)*	*(15)*	
நீங்கள்	வருகை	தந்தமைக்கு	மிக்க	நன்றி	

The Natural Language Toolkit (NLTK) stands as a comprehensive assembly of libraries and tools designed for symbolic and statistical natural language processing (NLP) in Python, primarily tailored for the English language. Established by Steven Bird and Edward Loper within the Department of Computer and Information Science at the University of Pennsylvania, NLTK encompasses model data and graphical demonstrations. A corresponding book elaborates on the fundamental concepts underpinning language processing tasks.

NLTK provides distinct methods for tokenization in Python, including simple token splitting, word tokenization, and sentence tokenization. The ensuing Python program serves as a practical demonstration of tokenization methods.

```
# Tamil Computing First Edition
# Program for Tokenization
import nltk
from nltk.tokenize import word_tokenize, sent_tokenize
if __name__ == '__main__':
# A Complete sentence
    text = "\nநான் இன்று காலை நேரம் சென்று எழுந்தேன். அவன்
நன்கு ஓய்வு எடுக்கட்டும். நீங்கள் வருகை தந்தமைக்கு மிக்க நன்றி."
    print("The given paragraph is :")
    print(text)

# Simple token splitting method for splitting the tokens using text.split() Method.
    tokens = text.split()
    print("\nSplit the given text into individual units:")
    for tok in tokens:
        print(tok)
# Word splitting method for tokenize the tokens using word_tokenize() function
    Words = word_tokenize(text)
    print("\nSplit the given text into individual words:")
    for wd in Words:
        print(wd)
```

The given input paragraph is:

நான் இன்று காலை நேரம் சென்று எழுந்தேன்.

அவன் நன்கு ஓய்வு எடுக்கட்டும்.

நீங்கள் வருகை தந்தமைக்கு மிக்க நன்றி.

Split the given text into individual units:

நான்

இன்று

காலை

நேரம்

சென்று

எழுந்தேன்.

அவன்

நன்கு

ஓய்வு

எடுக்கட்டும்.

நீங்கள்

வருகை

தந்தமைக்கு

மிக்க

நன்றி.

Split the given text into individual words:

நான்

இன்று

காலை

நேரம்

சென்று

எழுந்தேன்

.

அவன்

நன்கு

ஓய்வு

எடுக்கட்டும்

.

நீங்கள்

வருகை

தந்தமைக்கு

மிக்க

நன்றி

.

Two of the common functions in Python are utilized for text tokenization. Word splitting is done using the **split**() method in the first technique while the **word_tokenize**() function is used in the latter one. The simplest way of implementing text tokenization would be to split up the document using a white space as an extra row or tab. This is achieved by passing the embedded string through a **split**() function in Python. The alternative is NLTK's **word_tokenize**() function, which is meant to split strings into tokens, typically equated to words. In this implementation, whitespace and alphanumeric difference will be used, while time stamp, for instance, is a special symbol.

5.4 STEMMING AND LEMMATIZATION

Stemming

Stemming is Text Normalization, or Word Normalization approaches in the NLP applied for preparing the text, words, and documents for more processing. Stemming and lemmatization both aim to decrease variational and occasionally derivationally related word forms to a mutual base form. Though, both words have different tastes. Stemming typically denotes a basic experiential method of cutting off the ends of words to accomplish the aim accurately and, most of the time involves eliminating derivational fixes. The design model of the stemmer is shown in the following Figure 5.3.

Stemming and lemmatization are linguistic normalization processes that aim to reduce words to their base or root forms. Both aim to simplify words and make easier to analyze and compare them in text-based applications. In stemming, suffixes are removed from words to obtain their root or base form, which is known as the 'stem.' The stemmer simple model can be denoted as below Figure 5.3.

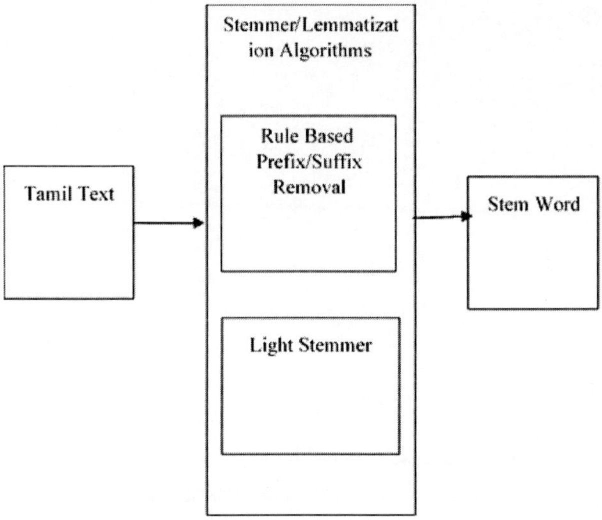

Figure 5.3: Design Model of Tamil Stemmer/Lemmatization

The example of stemming as below table.

Table 5.2: Example of Stemming

Word	*Stem*
கதைகள்	கதை
இக்கதையின்	கதை
அவனால்	அவன்
அவனிலா	அவன்
கரையின்	கரை
அக்கரையில்	கரை

Lemmatization

In lemmatization, words are reduced to their base form or dictionary form, called a lemma. Lemmatization considers the context and employs morphological analysis to obtain the appropriate base form. The objective of both stemming and lemmatization is to reduce structural differences. This is in contrast to a more common procedure known as 'term conflation', which address lexico-semantic, orthographic, and syntactical disparities.

The actual difference between stemming and lemmatization are as follows:

1. Stemming decreases word forms to branches, while lemmatization decreases the word forms to lingually recognized lemmas. These alterations are evident in languages with complex structures but unsuitable for many information retrieval (IR) applications.
2. Stemming can handle derivational differences and lemmatization deals inflectional differences.
3. Stemming can be accomplished by relatively easy rule-based methods but lemmatization needs extra sophisticated and needs dictionary. Lemmatization is for structurally complicated languages.

Lemmatization backed up through a part-of-speech tagging program to clarify homophones.

The word "சிறந்த" has "நல்ல" as its lemma. Stemming lacks this association since it needs to consult a lexicon. The "நட" is the base form of the word "நடைபயிற்சி," and thus it is similar in both stemming and lemmatization.

The word "சந்தித்தல்" might be the base form of a noun or a form of a verb ("சந்திக்க") relying on the framework, i.e., "in our last meeting" or "நாளை மீண்டும் சந்திப்போம்." In contrast to stemming, lemmatization may, technically, choose the suitable lemma reliant on the context.

5.5 PART-OF-SPEECH TAGGER

The part of speech (POS) a basic step for processing any language. POS tagging is the process of automatically assigning labels or syntactic categories to each word in a given corpus, facilitating the annotation of grammatical elements within the text. POS tagging is a NLP task in which each word in a sentence is assigned to a specific part of speech (such as noun, verb, verb, etc.). In POS tagging, a computer program analyzes the sequence of words in a text to determine the syntactic category (part of speech) to which each word belongs. This is an important step in many NLP applications, because syntactic structures are important for language processing tasks in Tamil, including machine translation, text retrieval and text analysis.

As Tamil language has vibrant morphological construction and agglutinative nature it has many grammatical categories that leads to ambiguity. So, this lexical ambiguity taken into account while developing the efficient POS Tagger. The automatic POS tagging can be classified as, statistical tagging, rule-based tagging and hybrid tagging.

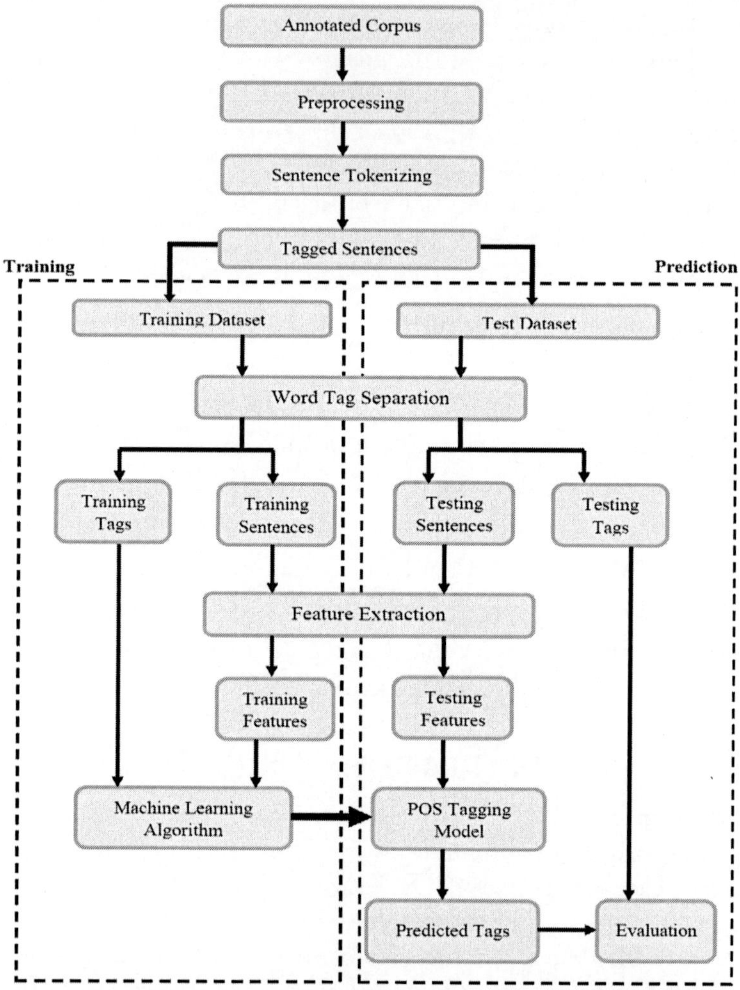

Figure 5.4: Architecture of the Classifier-Based POS Tagger

To POS tagger has multiple components to support tagging as shown in the Figure 5.4. The architecture contains functional components like annotated corpus, pre-processor, sentence tokenizer, machine learning algorithm. The details of these components are given below.

5.5.1 Annotated Corpus

Building the POS tagger involves to create or obtain the annotated corpus where each word is tagged with its corresponding part-of speech.

For example, a sentence in the annotated corpus can be as below:

> "அவன் (he) வீடுக்கு (to home) சென்றான் (went)"
> Each Tamil word is tagged with its POS such as,
> அவன் (he) – tagged as a pronoun
> "வீடுக்கு (to home)" tagged as a preposition,
> "சென்றான் (went)" tagged as a verb.

After the annotated data is created, a POS tagging framework, such as NLTK or SpaCy, can be used to train a machine learning model on this corpus. The trained model can be applied to new Tamil text to automatically assign parts of speech to each word, facilitating more advanced natural language processing tasks in Tamil.

5.5.2 Tag-Set

An annotated tag set refers to a predefined set of tags or labels used to annotate words or tokens in a corpus. They used to indicate their grammatical categories or other linguistic features. For part-of-speech tagging, an annotated tag set consists of labels that represent different parts of speech.

Tamil Part-of-Speech Annotated Tag Set:

> NN (பெயர் – Noun): பூ (flower), கடல் (sea)
>
> VB (வினை – Verb): ஓடு (run), சாப்பிடு (eat)
>
> JJ (விளக்கமான – Adjective): மகிழ்ச்சி (happy), உயரமான (tall)
>
> RB (வினைச்சொல் - Adverb): விரைவில் (quickly), மெதுவாக (softly)
>
> PRP (தனிப்பட்ட பெயர் – Personal pronoun): நான் (I), நீ (you), அவன் (he/she)
>
> PSP (பொருள் சேர்க்கும் சொல் – Postposition): கையில் (in the hand), பிறகு (after)
>
> DET (உருபுருஷம் – Determiner): அந்த (that), இந்த (this)
>
> CC (இணைப்புச்சொல் – Coordinating conjunction): மற்றும் (and), அல்லது (or)

Here, each tag corresponds to a specific part of speech or linguistic category. The actual tag set may vary depending on the specific requirements of the language and the linguistic features being considered. These annotated tag sets are crucial for training and evaluating part-of-speech taggers, as they provide a standardized way to represent the grammatical characteristics of words in a corpus.

5.5.3 Preprocessing

Preprocessing the corpus for Tamil, or any other language, involves a series of steps to clean and structure the raw text data in preparation for further natural language processing tasks, such as part-of-speech tagging. The Mozhi Trust in Chennai has compiled a corpus consisting of approximately 3 million words in modern written Tamil. Currently, the Central Institute of Indian Languages (CIIL) is expanding the existing corpora of Tamil texts and developing a corpus specifically for spoken Tamil.

Organization of Tamil Corpus

The data in the CIPIL corpus are collected from multiple resources like Government documents, books, magazines, textbooks and newspapers. The collected data are like organized as below:

1. major category
2. sub category
3. title of the text
4. author name
5. source
6. publishers
7. year of publication
8. page numbers

This organization assists users in efficiently retrieve and manage data easily.

It also possible to represent the volume number of the book, chapter number of the volume, sentence number in the chapter, word number in the sentence, word, and the POS tag, respectively.

An ordered dictionary is used to store the word-tag pair as the value and combination of volume number, chapter number, and the sentence number as the dictionary's key. This combination is used as the key to identifying the sentences in the corpus uniquely. The output format of this pre-processing module is given in Table 5.3.

Input Data:

1	1	1	1	முதலாவது	QT_QTO
1	1	1	2	அத்தியாயம்	N_NN
1	1	2	1	ஆடித்திருநாள்	N_NN
1	1	3	1	ஆதி	N_NN
1	1	3	2	அந்தமில்லாத	RP_NEG
1	1	3	3	கால	N_NN
1	1	3	4	வெள்ளத்தில்	N_NN

Table 5.3: The Output Format of the Preprocessed Data

Sentence	Key of the Dictionary	Value of the Dictionary
1	1-1-1	முதலாவது QT_QTO
	1-1-1	அத்தியாயம் N_NN
2	1-1-2	ஆடித்திருநாள் N_NN
3	1-1-3	ஆதி N_NN
	1-1-3	அந்தமில்லாத RP_NEG
	1-1-3	கால N_NN
	1-1-3	வெள்ளத்தில் N_NN

Here are the typical preprocessing steps for a Tamil corpus:

5.5.3.1 *Sentence Tokenization*

Sentence tokenization is a process that breaks a text into separate sentences. This task is often direct, as the sentences are typically separated by punctuation marks like exclamation points, question marks and periods. Sentence tokenization for Tamil is challenging due to a difference in punctuation conventions.

5.5.3.2 *Word Tokenization*

This module is responsible for isolating the words from the tags and organizing them into a matrix while maintaining sentence boundaries and store the tags in separately. In a tagged sentence each sentence is accompanied by its corresponding target tag. Therefore, it is essential to separate them before inputting the data into feature extraction module, as features are derived from words. This procedure is important for training and testing sentences.

5.5.3.3 *Feature Extraction*

The feature extraction process contains series of essential steps to transform raw data into a format suitable for machine algorithm. The listed feature is employed for linguistic analysis and machine language applications tailored to unique characteristics of Tamil.

- Target Word (இலக்கு வார்த்தை): This is the word of interest, which undergo analysis.
- Previous Word of the Selected Term (தேர்ந்தெடுத்த முந்தைய சொல்): Refers to the word immediately preceding the target word in the text.
- Next Word of the Selected Term (தேர்ந்தெடுத்த அடுத்த சொல்): The word that follows the target word.
- Last Suffix of the Selected Term (தேர்ந்தெடுத்த சொல்லின் கடைசி பகுதி): Focuses on the grammatical or morphological ending of the target word.
- Last Two Suffixes of the Selected Term (தேர்ந்தெடுத்த சொல்லின் கடைசி இரு பகுதிகள்): Similar to the previous feature, but considers the last two segments of the target word.
- Last Three Suffixes of the Selected Term (தேர்ந்தெடுத்த சொல்லின் கடைசி மூன்று பகுதிகள்): Extends the analysis to the last three segments of the target word.

These features enable a machine learning model to understand the syntactic and morphological aspects of Tamil text.

5.5.3.4 *Machine Learning Algorithm*

Once the features are extracted from training data set, these features will be given to the classification-based machine learning algorithm. The popular algorithms are like Decision Tree, Naïve Bayes, and Support Vector Machine (SVM are used in natural language processing tasks. During the training phase feature vector and the corresponding target POS tag are given as input to model. After completing the training, the model is ready to the classification task, which is POS tagging. The trained model with over-refined parameter shall be used as POS Tagger in prediction module to decide the POS tags for given words.

5.5.3.5 *POS Tagging Model*

A POS Tagging Model is design to assign a specific POS tag to the individual words in a given text. The model is trained with machine learning algorithms on annotated datasets, where words are labeled with their corresponding POS tags. The trained POS model can analyze the new unseen text and predict the POS tag for each word and helps other NLP tasks like text analysis, information retrieval, and machine translation. The accuracy and efficient of POS Tagging model are depend on selection of algorithms, the quality and diversity of the training data, and the feature extraction methods applied during training.

5.5.4 Tagging Approaches

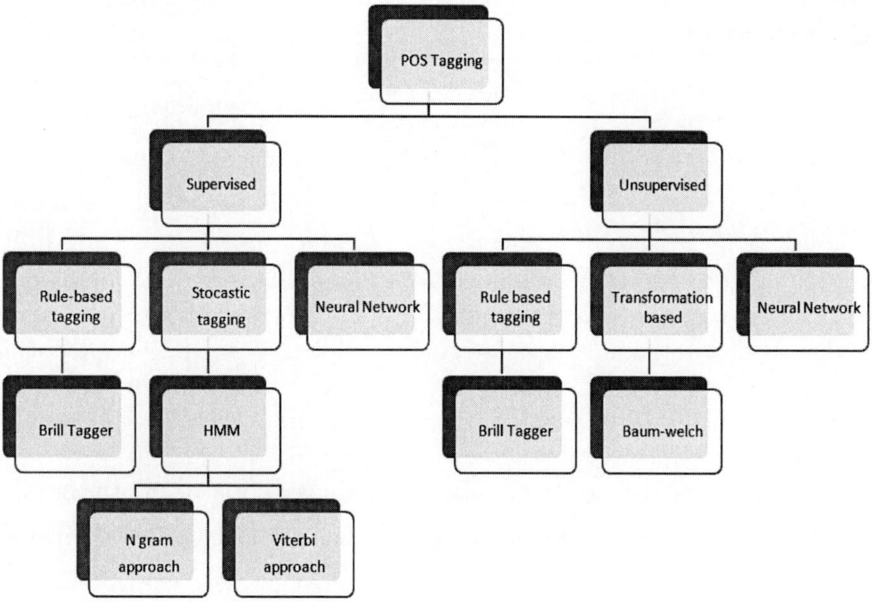

Figure 5.5: POS Tagging Approaches

POS tagging is a fundamental task in natural language processing, and various approaches are used to tackle this problem. The main category is supervised tagging and unsupervised tagging and these are further dived into three categories like rule-based tagging, statistical tagging and hybrid tagging.

5.5.4.1 *Supervised Tagging*

The supervised part-of-speech tagging models require pre-tagged datasets used for training to acquire information regarding the tag set, word-tag frequencies, rule sets, etc. The model's performance usually improves with an increase in the size of this corpus. To increase the size of the performance of the model the size of the corpora needs to be increased. The supervised learning can be subdivided into Rule based, stochastic and Neural Network.

Training Data

பால்/NN குடிக்க/VB போகிறான்/VB மூன்று/NN கடனை /NN விவரிக்க/VB தேவை/NN அவன்/PRP புதிய/NN படங்கள்/NN பார்க்க/VB போகிறான்/VB

Test Data

அவன்/PRP மூன்று/NN புதிய/NN படங்களை/NN பார்க்க/VB போகிறான்/VB

In supervised tagging, annotated corpus is used for training the models, so accuracy is depending on annotated corpus accuracy.

(A) *Rule-Based Approach*

Rule-based semi-speech marking in Tamil consists of developing grammatical rules that specify relationships and structures between words to classify them into grammatical categories. While the rule-based approaches may not be feasible as machine learning methods still can be used in well-defined grammatical structured languages like Tamil.

Text: சூழல் காக்கும் சுற்றுச்சூழல் சார்ந்த செயல்பாடுகள் காரணமாக வெளிநாட்டு அரசாங்கங்கள் செய்யும் திட்டங்களை அவர்கள் கொண்டு செல்ல வேண்டும்.

Rule-Based POS Tagging:

சூழல் (Noun) காக்கும் (Verb) சுற்றுச்சூழல் (Noun) சார்ந்த (Adjective) செயல்பாடுகள் (Noun) காரணமாக (Postposition) வெளிநாட்டு (Adjective) அரசாங்கங்கள் (Noun) செய்யும் (Verb)

திட்டங்களை (Noun) அவர்கள் (Pronoun) கொண்டு (Verb) செல்ல (Verb) வேண்டும் (Verb).

The rule-based tagging depends on particularity and coverage of the rules. The more advanced rules can be framed by considering linguistic features, such as word endings, prefixes, suffixes, and syntactic structures.

(B) *Stochastic based Approach*

Probabilistic models are used in statistical models for part-of-speech tagging in Tamil. These models learn the likelihood of speech features by observing progress in annotated training data. The Hidden Markov Models (HMMs), Maximum Entropy Markov Models (MEMMs), and neural network-based models like Conditional Random Fields (CRF) and transformer models, are commonly used for statistical POS tagging.

Training Data

1. மகன் பள்ளியில் படித்துக்கொண்டு வந்தான்.
2. அவனுக்கு வீடு அருகில் உள்ளது.
3. பல குழந்தைகள் படிக்கின்றனர்.

Annotated Corpus

1. மகன் (Noun) பள்ளியில் (Postposition) படித்துக்கொண்டு (Verb) வந்தான் (Verb).
2. அவனுக்கு (Pronoun) வீடு (Noun) அருகில் (Noun) உள்ளது (Verb).
3. பல (Adjective) குழந்தைகள் (Noun) படிக்கின்றனர் (Verb).

Statistical Model

The statistical model analyzes the annotated training data and learns the statistical distribution for transitions between different parts of speech.

Test Sentence

அவன் அருகிலுள்ள காரில் உள்ளது.

Predicted Tags

அவன் (Pronoun) அருகிலுள்ள (Adjective) காரில் (Noun) உள்ளது (Verb).

The statistical model, learn from training data and predict most of POS tags for each word in the last sentence.

The model predicts that "அவன்" is a pronoun, "அருகிலுள்ள" is an adjective, "காரில்" is a noun, and "உள்ளது" is a verb based on the patterns observed in the training data.

The accuracy of the model depends on quality and diversity of the data. The larger and more distinct annotated corpora can be used to train statistical POS tagging models.

(C) *Machine Learning Models*

Machine learning models provide algorithms to learn patterns and relationship from annotated data to predict part-of-speech tags for words in a given context. In practice, various algorithms and architectures like Support Vector Machines (SVM), Conditional Random Fields (CRF), or neural networks (e.g., LSTM, GRU, or transformer models) can be used.

Consider example with fictional dataset.

Training Data

1. பள்ளி வந்தது.
2. பூமியில் உயிர் உள்ளது.
3. பதில் கேட்டான்.

Annotated Corpus

1. பள்ளி (Noun) வந்தது (Verb).
2. பூமியில் (Noun) உயிர் (Noun) உள்ளது (Verb).
3. பதில் (Noun) கேட்டான் (Verb).

Machine Learning Model (Theoretical):

Let's assume we're using a simple machine learning algorithm like a Naive Bayes Classifier for this example.

```
from sklearn.feature_extraction.text import CountVectorizer
from sklearn.naive_bayes import MultinomialNB
from sklearn.pipeline import make_pipeline
# Training Data
sentences = ["பள்ளி வந்தது.", " பூமியில் உயிர் உள்ளது.", "பதில் கேட்டான்."]
labels = ["Noun Verb", "Noun Noun Verb", "Noun Verb"]

# Create a pipeline with a bag-of-words model and Naive Bayes Classifier
model = make_pipeline(CountVectorizer(), MultinomialNB())

# Train the model
model.fit(sentences, labels)

# Test Sentence
test_sentence = ["பள்ளி உள்ளது."]

# Predict POS tags for the test sentence
predicted_tags = model.predict(test_sentence)
print("Predicted Tags:", predicted_tags)
```

Output

```
Predicted Tags: ["Noun Verb"]
```

In this example, the model can predict the test sentence based on the learning done in the training. In the real-world scenario, more advanced models and preprocessing steps would be used for parts of speech.

5.5.4.2 *Unsupervised Tagging*

The unsupervised part-of-speech tagging model does not require a pre-tagged corpus. Instead, it uses innovative computational approaches, like the Baum-Welch algorithm, to generate alteration rules and tag sets automatically. Based on the data, it either develops the contextual rules needed through rule-based or transformation-based systems or estimates the probabilistic information that the stochastic taggers require.

Unsupervised tagging does not depend on any labeled data and it uses algorithms like clustering algorithms or probabilistic models to identify the patterns or clusters in the data to assign the POS Tags.

The unlabeled data can be:

உள்ளது/UNK வீடு/UNK இருக்கிறது/UNK முன்பு/UNK சென்ற/UNK அவன்/UNK
கூடு/UNK இருக்கும்/UNK இடத்தில்/UNK அவன்/UNK வேலை/UNK செய்யும்/UNK

The "UNK" label represents that the actual POS tags are unknown in this case, as it's part of the unsupervised learning process. As we have the unlabeled data set, need to apply the unsupervised tagging methods to discover patterns and assign potential POS tags.

5.5.4.3 *Transformation-based Parts-of-Speech Tagging*

Transformation-based part-of-speech (POS) tagging is an approach that demands iteratively refine and improve the accuracy of POS tags by using set of transformation rules. This approach was spread by Eric Brill, and Brill's tagger is a familiar example of a transformation-based POS tagging system.

Let's take this example,

Initial Sentence: அந்த பக்கம் விரிவாக இருக்கின்றது.
Initial POS Tags:
அந்த (Determiner)
பக்கம் (Noun)
விரிவாக (Adverb)
இருக்கின்றது (Verb)

Iteration 1: Identify an error, for example, the incorrect tagging of "விரிவாக" as an adverb.

Rule Generation: Create a transformation rule that considers the context, like the presence of specific words before or after, or the suffix of the word.
Rule: If the word ends with "ாக" and is not preceded by a verb, change the tag to Adjective.
Rule Application: Apply the rule to update the POS tag of "விரிவாக" to Adjective.

Updated POS Tags:
அந்த (Determiner)
பக்கம் (Noun)
விரிவாக (Adjective)
இருக்கின்றது (Verb)

Iteration 2: Identify another error and repeat the process.

This iterative cycle continues, with the model learns from its mistakes and adjust the POS tags accordingly. The rules generated capture linguistic patterns in the data and improve the accuracy of the tagging model over multiple iterations.

5.5.4.4 *More Approaches*

Other than these, some other methods of labelling have also been established:

- **Support Vector Machines:** It is an efficient machine learning process employed for several applications in natural language processing and more fields such as bioinformatics.
- **Neural Networks:** These are possible applicants for the categorizing mission as they learn concepts through instances.
- **Decision Trees:** These are categorization tools formed on ordered collections of queries. They are employed for NLP, i.e., parts-of-speech tagging.
- **Maximum Entropy Models:** They prevent specific issues of arithmetical inter dependency and are confirmed effective for works like analyzing and parts-of-speech labelling.
- **Example-Based approaches:** Such approaches discover the training example most identical to the existing issue example and assume a similar category for the novel issue instance as for the identical one.

5.5.5 Transliteration

Transliteration is a represent a text from one script to another script. The transliteration is often used to represent Tamil words using the Latin alphabet. Various transliteration systems present, commonly known is the ISO 15919 standard

Tamil Script:

இனிய நாள்

Transliteration (ISO 15919):

iṉiya nāḷ

In this example, the Tamil phrase "இனிய நாள்" (pronounced iṉ iya nāḷ) is transliterated into the Latin alphabet as "iṉiya nāḷ" which follows the ISO 15919 standard. Each Tamil character is represented with its corresponding Latin character or combination of characters, showing the pronunciation in a way that is accessible to those familiar with the Latin script.

5.5.6 Chunking

Chunking is an efficient and strong way of recognizing brief phrases in the text, or "chunks". It is determined a centre stage to complete analysis. Chunks are normally taken to be a non-recursive correlated group of words. A typical chunk consists of a single content word surrounded by a constellation of function words. Chunking might segment a sentence into its significant non-overlying phrases and assign a tag to all chunks. Later than parts-of-speech tagging, the subsequent stage is chunking, which segments sentences into non-recursive attached phrases. A Chunker finds adjacent, non-overlapping spans of related tokens and groups them together into chunks. Chunker often operates on tagged texts and uses the tags to make chunking decisions. A subsequent step after tagging focuses on the identification of fundamental structural relations between groups of words. This is usually referred to as phrase chunking.

5.5.6.1 *Chunking in Tamil*

Tamil being an agglutinative language, have a complex morphological and syntactical structure. It is a relatively free word order language, but it behaves like a fixed word order language in the phrasal and clausal construction. So, the process of chunking in Tamil is less complex compared to the process of POS tagging. In the Tamil language, transformation-based learning and Machine learning techniques have been used to build a Chunker. Chunker could be based on Noun phrases, Verb Phrases, Adjectival Phrases, Adverbial Phrases, Conjunctions, and Complementizers. The following table shows the sample chunk tag set. Chunking is comparatively easier for Indian languages than POS tagging. The output of the POS tagger is the input to the Chunker.

Besides simplifying the process of full parsing, chunking has many applications in problems like speech processing and information retrieval. Chunking has been traditionally defined as the process of forming a group of words based on local information.

Table 5.4

S. No.	*Chunk Tag*	*Tag Name*	*Possible POS Tags*
1.	NP	Noun Phrase	NN, NNP, NNPC, NNC, NNQ, PRP, QTF, DET, CRD, ORD, ADJ, INT
2.	AJP	Adjectival Phrase	CRD, ADJ
3.	AVP	Adverbial Phrase	ADV, INT, CRD
4.	VFP	Verb Finite Phrase	VF, VAX
5.	VNP	Verb Nonfinite Phrase	VNAJ, VNAV, VINT, CVB
6.	VGP	Verb Gerund Phrase	VBG
7.	CJP	Conjunctional	CNJ
8.	COMP	Complementizer	COM
9.	?	Symbols	O

IOB Tag:

The IOB labels are applied for representing the borderlines of all chunks:

- **I** – the present word is within a chunk.
- **O** – Shows the limit of the sentence.
- **B** – The present word is the starting of a chunk that might be followed by another chunk.

(A) *Explanation of Tagset*

Noun Phrase

Noun Chunks would be labelled as NP. It contains non-recurrent noun phrases and postpositional phrases. The noun chunk's central will be a noun.

Noun qualifiers such as the adjective, quantifiers, determinatives would make the left side border for a noun chunk, and the head noun would mark the right-side borderline for it.

Example for NP chunk is given below:

அவள்	<PRP>	<B-NP>
ஒரு	<DET>	<B-NP>
அழகான	<ADJ>	<I-NP>
பெண்	<NN>	<I-NP>
.	<DOT>	<O>

Adjectival Phrase

An adjective chunk is labelled as AJP. Such chunk would comprise each adjectival chunk, in addition to the predicative adjective. However, adjectives existing earlier than a noun would be clustered with the noun chunk. It can be seen from the example for the noun phrase.

Example for ADJ Phrase is given below:

பல்வேறு	<ADJ>	<B-AJP>
ஆராய்ச்சிகளுக்காக	<ADV>	<B-AVP>
நாடுகள்	<NN>	<B-NP>
செயற்கைக்கோள்களை	<NN>	<B-NP>
விண்ணுக்கு	<NN>	<I-NP>
அனுப்புகின்றன	<VF>	<B-VFP>
.	<DOT>	<O>

Adverbial Phrase

Adverbial chunk is labelled according to the labels employed for parts-of-speech labelling. It is tagged as AVP. Some examples for ADV Phrase is given below:

நான்	<PRP>	<B-NP>
இன்று	<ADV>	<B-AVP>
சென்னை	<NNP>	<B-NP>
செல்கிறேன்	<VF>	<B-VFP>
.	<DOT>	<O>

Conjunction

The words that are used for connecting single words, phrases, and independent clauses are called Conjunction. The conjunctions are labelled as CJP.

ஷைனி	<NNP>	<B-NP>
1	<CRD>	<B-NP>
தங்கம்	<NN>	<I-NP>
மற்றும்	<CNJ>	<B-CJP>
6	<CRD>	<B-NP>
வெள்ளிப்	<NN>	<I-NP>
பதக்கங்களைப்	<NN>	<I-NP>
பெற்றார்	<VF>	<B-VFP>
.	<DOT>	<O>

Complementizer

Complementizers are the words corresponding to the term subordinative conjunction in old-style grammar. Such as the word '*that*' is usually referred to as Complementizer in the English language. The complementizer is labelled as per the tags used for parts-of-speech labelling. It is labelled as COMP.

தீர்ப்பை	<NN>	<B-NP>
ஒத்திவைக்க	<VINT>	<B-VNP>
முடியாது	<VAX>	<B-VFP>
என	<COM>	<B-COMP>
நீதிமன்றம்	<NN>	<B-NP>
கூறியுள்ளது	<VF>	<B-VFP>
.	<DOT>	<O>

Verb Phrase

There are two major categories of verb chunks, namely, Verb limited chunks and verb non-limited chunks. Verb limited chunk comprises the basic verb and its auxiliaries. It is labelled as VFP. Some instances of verb limited chunks are provided under.

பேரணி	<NN>	<B-NP>
நடத்த	<VINT>	<B-VNP>
அவர்	<PRP>	<B-NP>
அழைப்பு	<NN>	<B-NP>
விடுத்திருந்தார்	<VF>	<B-VFP>
.	<DOT>	<O>

Verb Non-finite Phrase

Non-finite verbs contain each non-finite verb's form. Tamil comprises four non-finite forms: relative participle, adverbial participle, conditional verb, and infinitive verb. It is labelled as VNP. Some instances of non-finite verb chunks are provided under.

58	<CRD>	<I-NP>
வினாடிகளில்	<NN>	<I-NP>
ஓடிக்	<VNAV>	<B-VNP>
கடந்து	<VNAJ>	<I-VNP>
சாதனை	<NN>	<B-NP>
படைத்தார்	<VF>	<B-VFP>
.	<DOT>	<O>

Verb Gerundial Phrase

Gerundial forms are represented through a separate chunk. It is labelled as VGP. Following are some examples of a gerundial chunk.

அவர்	<NN>	<I-NP>
வரைவதில்	<VBG>	<B-VGP>
நிறைய	<ADJ>	<B-NP>
ஆர்வம்	<NN>	<I-NP>
உள்ளவர்	<VF>	<B-VFP>
	<DOT>	<O>

Symbols

Special characters such as Question mark (?) and Dot (.) are tagged as O. Whereas, the preceding tag tags Comma (,).

அறைக்கு	<NN>	<I-NP>
இடைகளில்	<NN>	<B-NP>
சுவர்களோ	<NN>	<B-NP>
,	<COMM>	<I-NP>

மறிப்புகளோ	<NN>	<B-NP>
இல்லாமல்	<VNAV>	<B-VNP>
பெரிதாக	<ADV>	<B-AVP>
அமைந்திருந்தது	<VF>	<B-VFP>
.	<DOT>	<O>

5.6 TAMIL MORPHOLOGY AND LANGUAGE

Tamil is an agglutinative language, which means that words are built upon linguistic roots attached to single or multiple affixes, and both are altogether referred to as morphemes. The Tamil works are built by linking the morphemes together. In a sequence. The fundamental element is always a linguistic root or vocabulary morpheme which may or mayn't followed by additional operational or linguistic morpheme.

Let's break down the example "புத்தகங்கள்" (puththakangkaL)

- **புத்தகம் (puththakam):** This is the vocabulary morpheme or linguistic root, representing "book" in Tamil.
- **கள் (kaL):** This is an affix that indicates plurality. It is added to the root புத்தகம் (puththakam) to make it plural, resulting in "புத்தகங்கள்" (puththakangkaL), meaning "books."

In this example, the root புத்தகம் (puththakam) is combined with the affix கள் (kaL) to create a new word which conveys the idea of multiple books. This agglutinative nature allows complex word formation by combining morphemes in a systematic manner.

5.6.1 Syntax of Tamil Morphology

The Tamil language is constantly centre-final and has free word order. It has an SOV pattern. Owing to the language's free word-order feature, the noun phrase arguments earlier than the last verb might occur in any variation, still it produces a similar meaning for a sentence. Demonstratives and convertors antecede the noun in the noun phrase. Secondary clauses antecede the matrix clause's verb. The Tamil language is null subjective, meaning that most of the sentences do not have subjects, verbs, and objects. However, making a correct sentence just using the verb is still conceivable. For instance

For instance, the phrase "முடிவு ஆகின்றது" (mudi-ākiṉṟatu, meaning "Completed") represents a sentence with just a verb. Alternatively, sentences can consist of only a subject and object without a verb, as seen in "அது என் வீடு" (athu en vīṭu, meaning "That, my house").

5.6.2 Word Formation Rules (WFR) in Tamil

Every novel word formed by Word Formation Rules (WFR) should be included in a significant vocabulary class. It considers the class of the rule's output. In Tamil, the linguistic class might or might not vary after the WFR's process. The list of inputs and outputs of various word formation rules in Tamil origin of simple words.

1. Noun → Noun

[[vElai $]_N$ + kAran $]_{suf}$ $]_N$ 'servant'

[[வேலை $]_N$ + காரன் $]_{suf}$ $]_N$ வேலைக்காரன்

[[thozil]N + ALi]suf]N 'laborer'

[தொழில் $]_N$ + ஆளி $]_{suf}$ $]_N$ தொழிலாளி

2. Verb → Noun

[[padi]V + ppu]suf]N 'education'

[[படி$]_V$ + ப்பு $]_{suf}$ $]_N$ படிப்பு

[[ezuthu-$]_V$ + thu $]_{suf}$ $]_N$ 'letter'

[[எழுது$]_V$ + து $]_{suf}$] எழுத்து

[[kEL $]_V$ + vi $]_{suf}]$ $_N$ 'question'

[[கேள் $]_V$ + வி $]_{suf}]$ $_N$ கேள்வி

3. Adjective → Noun

[[walla $]_{adj}$ + thanam $]_{suf}$ $]_N$ 'good quality'

[[நல்ல $]_{adj}$ + தனம் $]_{suf}$] நல்ல தனம்

[[periya$]_{adj}$ + tu $]_{suf}$ $]_N$ 'big'

[[பெரிய $]_{adj}$ + து $]_{suf}$ $]_N$ பெரியது

4. Noun → Verb

[[uyir $]_N$ + ppi $]_{suf}$ $]_V$ 'to give life'

[[உயிர் $]_N$ + ப்பி $]_{suf}$ $]_V$ உயிர்ப்பி

5. Adjective → Verb

[[veLLai $]_{adj}$ + aakku $]_{suf}$ $]_V$ 'to make (something) white'

[[வெள்ளை $]_{adj}$ + ஆக்கு $]_{suf}$ $]_V$ வெள்ளையாக்கு

[[karuppu $]_{adj}$ + aakku $]_{suf}$ $]_V$ 'to make (something) black'

[[கருப்பு $]_{adj}$ + ஆக்கு $]_{suf}$ $]_V$ கருப்பாக்கு

6. Verb → Verb

[[cey $]_V$ + vi $]_{suf}$ $]_V$ 'cause to do'

[[செய் $]_V$ + வி $]_{suf}$ $]_V$ செய்வி

[[wada $]_V$ -thth$]_{suf}$ - u] $]_V$ 'cause to walk'

[[நட $]_V$ -த்து] suf $]_V$ நடத்து

[[vidu $]_V$ + vi $]_{suf}$ $]_V$ 'to liberate'

[[விடு $]_V$ + வி $]_{suf}$ $]_V$ விடுவி

7. Noun → Adjective

[[uyaram]$_{N}$ + Ana]$_{suf}$]$_{adj}$ 'high'

[[உயரம்]$_{N}$ + ஆன]$_{suf}$]$_{adj}$ உயரமான

[[azaku]$_{N}$ + Ana]$_{suf}$]$_{adj}$ 'beautiful'

[[அழகு]$_{N}$ + ஆன]$_{suf}$]$_{adj}$ அழகான

[[nErmai]$_{N}$ + Ana]$_{suf}$]$_{adj}$ 'honest'

[[நேர்மை]$_{N}$ + ஆன]$_{suf}$]$_{adj}$ நேர்மையான

8. Verb → Adverb

[[cey]$_{V}$ + tu]$_{suf}$]$_{adv}$ 'having done'

[[செய்]$_{V}$ + து]$_{suf}$]$_{adv}$ 'having done' செய்து

[[ezuth-]$_{V}$ + i]$_{suf}$]$_{adv}$ 'having written'

[[எழுது-]$_{V}$ + இ]$_{suf}$]$_{adv}$ எழுதி

[[padi]$_{V}$ + ththu]$_{suf}$]$_{adv}$ 'having read'

[[படி]$_{V}$ + த்து]$_{suf}$]$_{adv}$ படித்து

Table 5.5: Compound Word-forms Formation

No.	*Surface Form*	*Inflection*	*Compound Form*
1	Noun	Noun	Noun
2	Noun	Verb	Verb
3	Verb	Noun	Noun
4	Adjective	Noun	Noun
5	Adverb	Noun	Noun

5.6.3 Morphology of Tamil Verb

Tamil verbs are tweaked through postfixes. They could be limited or non-limited structures. Limited action word structures emerge in the sentence's fundamental proviso, while the non-limited structures emerge as a base of optional or fixed conditions. Limited action word structures are basically regulated for mind-set, include, individual, gender, and so forth

Table 5.6 contains the basic limited action word structures. The PNG (individual number-sex) Tag is displayed in the principal segment, while the others show the past and future tenses. In Table 5.6, numerous straightforward limited affectation structures with tense markers and PNG markers are accommodated "படி" padi (study).

PNG postfix is a mix morpheme that encodes the individual, number, and sexual orientation together. Limited action words take the structure, Verb_stem + Tense + person_number_sexual orientation. Four kinds of non-limited action words are distinguished by Tamil: infinitive, verbal participle,

Table 5.6: Simple Verb Finite Forms

PNG	Root-Pres-PNG	Root-Past-PNG	Root-Fut-PNG
3SE	*padi-kinR-Ar*	*padi-thth-Ar*	*padi-pp-Ar*
3SM	*padi-kinR-An*	*padi-thth-An*	*padi-pp-An*
3SF	*padi-kinR-AL*	*padi-thth-AL*	*padi-pp-AL*
2S	*padi-kinR-Ay*	*padi-thth-Ay*	*padi-pp-Ay*
1P	*padi-kinR-Om*	*padi-thth-Om*	*padi-pp-Om*
1S	*padi-kinR-En*	*padi-thth-En*	*padi-pp-En*
2SE	*padi-kinR-Ir*	*padi-thth-Ir*	*padi-pp-Ir*
3SN	*padi-kinR-athu*	*padi-thth-athu*	*padi-pp-athu*
2PE	*padi-kinR-IrkaL*	*padi-thth-IrkaL*	*padi-pp-IrkaL*
3PE	*padi-kinR-ArkaL*	*padi-thth-ArkaL*	*padi-pp-ArkaL*
3PN	*padi-kinR-ana*	*padi-thth-ana*	*padi-pp-ana*

descriptive participle, and restrictive. They take the given requesting limitations set up.

Verb_stem + infinitive_suffix (infinitive)

Verb_stem + vp_suffix (verbal participle)

Verb_stem + tense + rp_suffix (adjectival participle)

Verb_stem + conditional_suffix (conditional)

Modal verbs might be imperfect as they could not take further inflectional suffixes, or they might be regular verbs capable of getting changed for tense and PNG suffixes.

Verb_stem + infinitive_suffix modal_verb

Verb_stem + infinitive_suffix modal_stem + tense + png_suffix

5.6.4 Morphology of Tamil Noun

There are two super-classifications in which the Tamil nouns (and pronouns) are sorted, specifically "judicious" and "unreasonable," which contain absolute five classifications. The "sane" class incorporates people and divinities though, the "unreasonable" comprises of the relative multitude of different things, i.e., articles, natural life, and theoretical things. Level headed things and pronouns are related with any of the three classes: ladylike solitary, manly particular, and sane plural. Then again, unreasonable things and pronouns are related with any of the accompanying two classifications: nonsensical particular and silly plural. The plural structure for objective things can be utilized as an honorific, unbiased, particular structure.

For playing out the tasks of cases or postpositions, postfixes are utilized. Old logisticians endeavoured to characterize the few postfixes into 8 cases like the Sanskrit cases. The cases included nominative, accusative, dative, sociative, genitive, instrumental, locative, and ablative. Table 5.7 contains a few types of the thing, and it likewise shows the particular and plural types of "எலி" eli (rodent) with the case markers.

Table 5.7: Noun Case Markers

Case	Singular	Plural
Nominative	*eli*	*eli-kaL*
Accusative	*eli-ai*	*eli-kaL-ai*
Dative	*eli-uku*	*eli-kaL-uku*
Benfefactive	*eli-ukk-Aka*	*eli-kaL-ukk-Aka*
Instrumental	*eli-Al*	*eli-kaL-Al*
Sociative-Odu	*eli-Odu*	*eli-kaL-Odu*
Sociative-udan	*eli-udan*	*eli-kaL-udan*
Locative	*eli-il*	*eli-kaL-il*
Ablative	*eli-il-iruwthu*	*eli-kaL-il-iruwthu*
Genitive	*eli-in-athu*	*eli-kaL-in-athu*

Noun form with no modulations is known as noun stem and are singular.

aciriyarkaL = aaciriyar (teacher) + kaL (pl.marker)

ஆசிரியர்கள் = ஆசிரியர் + கள்

eenaakkaL = peenaa (pen) + kaL (pl.marker)

பேனாக்கள்= பேனா+கள்

uththakangkaL = puththakam (book) + kaL (pl.marker)

புத்தகங்கள்= புத்தகம் + கள்

The models displayed above are a couple of occurrences of plural balance. Making a plural type of a noun isn't just about connecting *'kaL.'* Similarly, in *"puththakangkaL,"* the stem (*puththakam*) is bent to *puththakangkaL* (*'am'* in the stem is supplanted by 'ang,' trailed by *'kaL')*. These distinctions are because of the *'Sandhi'* changes that happen when the thing stem is linked to the *'kaL'* morpheme.

5.7 MORPHOLOGICAL ANALYZER FRAMEWORK

The Tamil language is morphologically rich, and this type of language requires an in-depth examination at the word level to apprehend the word's meaning from its morphemes and classes. All roots are attached to various morphemes for producing a word. Tamil is postpositionally modified to the root word. More than ten thousand modified word forms might be taken by every root word. Tamil takes linguistic as well as modulational morphology. Linguistic morphology alters the meaning and category of the word by attaching the derivational and combining morphemes to the root. Modulational morphology varies the word's form and attaches further info by adding the modulational morphemes to the root.

Morphologically analyzing a word involves sectioning it into component morphemes and allotting the accurate morphosyntactic info. A morphological analyzer (MA) would return its root word as well as the word category accompanied by further grammatical data relying on its word-class for an assumed term. Tamil is a verb-final, comparatively free word order language having a rich inflectional and derivational morphology. Therefore, building an efficient morphological analyzer is challenging. Finite-state automata and SVM-based approaches have been used in the past to build Tamil morphological analyzers.

The morphological analyzers are employed in search engines in order to recover the documents using the key phrases and enhance the memory of search engines. They are also employed in lemmatization, speech identifier, data extraction/recovery, summarization, grammar and spell check, as well as machine translation.

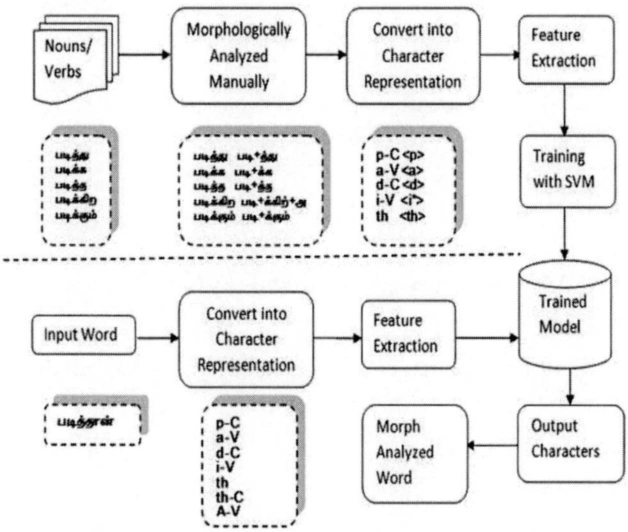

Figure 5.6: Morphological Analyzer Framework

Word can be defined as an order of characters surrounded by spaces, punctuation symbols, and so on in writing. A simple word comprises a stem or root, including prefaces or suffixes whereas, a compound word, also known as a conjoined word, could be split into two or more independent words. Every component word in a compound word is a compound or simple word and might be used individually.

The thorough lingual examination of a word might be essential for natural language processing. However, many natural language processing investigators have focused on some further factors such as semantic interpretation, grammatical analysis, and so on. Consequently, natural language processing systems employ relatively easy morphological analyzers. In contrast, an originator does the total opposite. An originator produces a word accordingly to the root and its characteristics or associations. Correspondingly, a *sandhi* originator might use the output of a structural originator and assemble simple words into compound words wherever feasible.

Examples for Morphological Analysis;

books	=	*book+Noun+PluraL(or)book+Verb+Pres+3SG.*
stopping	=	*stop+Verb+Cont*
happiest	=	*happy+Adj+Superlative*
went	=	*go+Verb+Past*

Examples for Morphological Generator;

book+Noun+Plural	=	*books*
stop+Verb+Cont	=	*stopping*
happy+Adj+Superlative	=	*happiest*
go+Verb+Past	=	*went*

5.7.1 Role of Morphological Analyzer in NLP

The morphological analyzer performs a important part in the sphere of NLP. Figure 5.7 highlights the role of the Morphological analyzer in natural language processing. Some of its features are:

- Spell checker
- Search Engines
- Data extraction and recovery
- Machine Translation system

- Grammar checker
- Content scrutiny
- Question Answering system
- Automatic sentence Analyzer
- Dialogue system
- Knowledge presentation in learning
- Language Teaching
- Language-based educational exercises

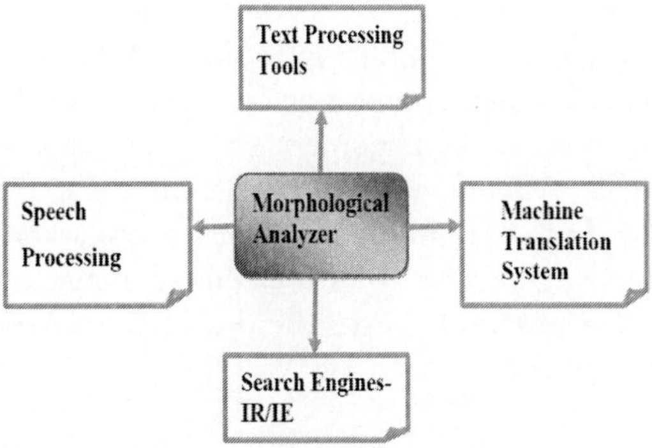

Figure 5.7: Role Morphological Analyzer in NLP

5.7.2 Challenges in Tamil Morphological Analyzer

Tamil's structural build-up is pretty complicated as it varies to gender, person, and number markings and also attaches with auxiliaries representing mood, feature, action, behaviour, etc., in the verb. An individual verb root is capable of inflecting over ten-thousand-word forms along with the auxiliaries. A noun root varies with plural, case, postpositions, clitics, and oblique, and an individual noun root is capable of inflecting over five hundred words forms in addition to postpositions. The root and morphemes require to be tagged and recognized for more language processing at the word level.

5.8 MORPHOLOGICAL GENERATION

The Morphological Generator takes lemma and a Morpho-lexical portrayal as information and gives a word-structure as yield. It is a converse course of Morphological Analyzer. A morphological generator is a fundamental tool in Natural Language Processing (NLP) applications and designed to produce fully-formed final words from root and a set of morphological properties. This tool is essential in the process of generating sentences in the target language within Machine Translation (MT) systems. Additionally, it finds application in Information Retrieval (IR) systems, particularly in the front-end for query construction.

5.8.1 Challenges in Tamil Morphological Generator

Tamil, characterized by its morphological richness, stands as an agglutinative language with each verb exhibiting over 10,000 forms, encompassing auxiliaries and clitics. Conjugations couple descriptive, conditional forms, finite & infinite and verb-modifying, and, these inflections vary across verb categories, adding a layer of complexity to the translation and generation of Tamil verbs. The rule-based approaches are used to develop morphological generator systems. the paradigm number of a given root word is identified using a lookup table containing word-class lemmas and their corresponding paradigm numbers. Still, to frame comprehensive lookup table with all lexical entries proves challenging due to the extensive range of formal entities, places, things, and compound word structures that may not be exhaustively included in the dictionary.

Table 5.8: Morpho-phonemic Changes

Word+ Inflection	Morpho-phonemic Change	Word-form
பூ+கள் (*pU+kaL)*	பூ+க்+கள் *(pUkkaL)*	பூக்கள்(*pUkkaL*)
கத்தி+ஆல்(*kaththi+Al*)	கத்தி+ய்+ஆல் (*kaththiyAl*)	கத்தியால் (*kaththiyAl*)
படம்+ஐ (*padatm+ai*)	பட+த்+ஐ (*padaththai*)	படத்தை (*padaththai*)

To overcome this challenge, the system needs to automate the identification of the paradigm number for dictionary words. When the lemma is provided as input, the system autonomously determines the paradigm number based on its terminal characters.

Another significant challenge in Tamil word generation involves managing morphophonemic changes, reflecting alterations occurring when an affix is appended to a root word. The morphological generator system addresses this challenge through the application of stemming rules and suffixes, as outlined in Table 5.8. Postfixes play essential role in Tamil morphological generator system, and the creation of these postfixes for all word forms lays an impressive task.

5.8.2 Simplified Part-of-Speech Categories

The morphological generator framework contributes significantly to the sentence produced by Statistical Machine Translation (SMT). The specific Tamil sentence is categorized using an enhanced POS tag. The refined POS tag-set is outlined in Table 5.9.

Table 5.9: Simplified POS Tagset

S.No	Minimized POS Tag	POS Tagset
1	**<N> Noun**	<NN>,<NNC>,<NNQ>,<VBG>
2	**<V> Verb**	<VNAJ>,<VNAV>,<VINT>,<CVB>,<VF>
3	**<PN> Pronoun**	<PRP>,<PRIN>,<PRID>
4	**<NP> Proper Noun**	<NNP>,<NNPC>
5	**<O> Others**	CNJ>,<VAX>,<RDW>,<INT>,<EMP>,<ECH>,<COM>,<A DV,<ADJ>,<ORD>,<CRD>,<PPO>,<QW>,<QTF>,<QW>,< COMM>
6	**<S> End of Sentence**	<DOT>,<QM>

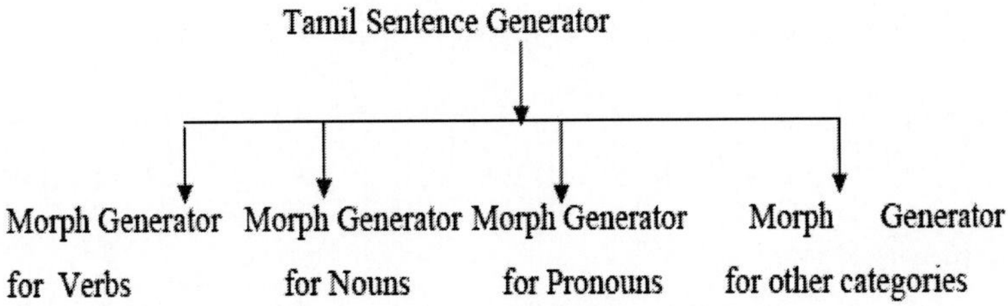

Figure 5.8: Tamil Sentence Generation

The Figure 5.8 shows Tamil sentence generation framework structure, which has five distinct modules. Morphological generators for Tamil nouns and verbs are developed using a postfix-based approach. Pronouns in Tamil are classified under the 'closed word-class category. Therefore, a pattern-matching method is applied to generate pronominal word structures.

5.8.3 Morphological Generator for Tamil Nouns and Verbs

Typically, morphological generator tools are developed using a rule-based approach, depending on a set of morpho-phonemic (spelling) rules and a morpheme dictionary. The algorithm requires an insertion table and the code for paradigm classification. By giving the lemma, POS class, and Morpho-Lexical Inflection (MLI), the proposed algorithm generates the intended word structure.

The morphological generator takes input in the form of lemma+ word_class+Morpho-lexical Information, where the lemma specifies the root expression of the word structure need to be generated, word_class indicates the syntactic category (POS category), and Morpho-lexical Information denotes the type of expression. Word class information is used to determine whether the given word is a noun or a verb. The Morpho-lexical Information (MLI) is derived from the morphological analyzer tool for Tamil. An example of the Tamil morphological generator framework is provided below.

Lemma + WC+ MLI = WORD FORM

ஓடு + V + FT_3SM = ஓடுவான்

Odu + V + FT_3SM = OduvAn (Run)

காடு + N + ACC = காட்டை

kAdu + N + ACC = kAddai (Forest)

"V" addresses action word and "FT_3SM" addresses future tense with the third-individual singular masculine. "N" represents a thing, and ACC implies the accusative case. FT_3SM and ACC are called Morpho-lexical Information (MLI).

Three distinct modules are utilized to assemble the noun and action word generator framework. The main module takes the lemma and POS class as information and gives the lemma's worldview number and word's stem as yield. The subsequent module takes morpho-lexical data as an information and gives its record number as a yield. In the third module, a postfix table produces the word structure with the data from the over two modules.

5.8.4 Algorithm for Noun and Verb Morphological Generator

This subsection outlines the newly developed algorithm for the morphological generator framework, implemented using the Java programming language. The algorithm is depicted in Figure 5.9.

```
Input = (Lemma +word class + morpho-lexical Information)

lemma,wc,morph =SPLIT(Input)

roman_lemma=ROMAN(lemma)

parnum=PARNUM(roman_lemma,wc)

col-index=parnum

row-index=INDEX(morph,wc)

suff=SUFFIX-TABLE[row-index][col-index]

stem=STEM(roman_lemma,wc,parnum)

word=JOIN(stem,suff)

output=UNICODE(word)
```

Figure 5.9: Algorithm for Morphological Generator

The variable "lemma" shows the root expression of the word structure, "wc" signifies the word class, and "transform" denotes morpho-lexical information. The input is segmented into lemma, word class, and morpho-lexical information using the SPLIT function. The lemma or root word in Unicode format is Romanized using the ROMAN function, which result "roman_lemma.".

The "parnum" variable represents the paradigm number of lemmas, and the PARNUM function identifies the paradigm number for the given lemma using the trailing postfixes. The romanized lemma and the paradigm number are then provided as input to the STEM function, along with the word class. The STEM function is utilized to discover the stem of the root word.

The given morpho-lexical information is matched with the morpho-lexical information table, and its corresponding table number is retrieved, referred to as the "row-index." The paradigm number of the input lemma is denoted as "col-index." Using the row and column indices, the insertion component is retrieved from the postfix table. The stem and the retrieved insertion are combined to generate the word structure. Finally, this word structure is converted to Tamil Unicode format.

5.8.5 Word-forms Handled in Morphological Generator

Tamil action word morphological generator is cultivated for producing in excess of 10,000 types of a solitary Tamil action word. A portion of the word structures are displayed in Table 5.10; Thing morphological generator framework handles almost 300-word structures, including postpositions.

Table 5.10: Verb and Noun Word-forms

Verb Word forms	**Noun Word forms**
படி.	நரம்பு.
படித்தான்.	நரம்பை.
படித்தாள்.	நரம்பினை.
படித்தார்.	நரம்பினத்தை.
படித்தார்கள்.	நரம்போடு.
படித்தது.	நரம்பினோடு.
படித்தன.	நரம்பினத்தோடு.
படித்தாய்.	நரம்பினால்.
படித்தீர்.	நரம்பால்.
படித்தீர்கள்.	நரம்புக்கு.

படித்தேன்.	நரம்பிற்கு.
படித்தோம்.	நரம்பின்.
படிக்கிறான்.	நரம்பது.
படிக்கிறாள்.	நரம்பினது.
படிக்கிறார்.	நரம்பின்கண்.
படிக்கிறார்கள்.	நரம்பதுகண்.
படிக்கின்றது.	நரம்புக்காக.
படிக்கின்றன.	நரம்பாலான.
படிக்கின்றாய்.	நரம்புடைய.
படிக்கின்றீர்.	நரம்பினுடைய.
படிக்கின்றீர்கள்.	நரம்பில்.
படிக்கின்றீர்கள்.	நரம்பினில்.

5.8.6 Required Data for the Algorithm

The Tamil morphologic producer for nouns and verb necessitates the below mentioned sources to produce a word form.

- Morpho Lexical Information (MLI)
- Paradigm categorization rules
- Suffix table
- Stemming algorithm

Morpho-Lexical Information File

Morpho-lexical data is the morphological provisions of a word structure. For example, Morpho-lexical information of a word **படித்தான்** (*padiththAn*) is PAST_3SM. The MLI document is a gathering of plausible morphological examples of a particular word. Thing and action word require an individual MLI document.

Table 5.11 shows a case of the Morpho-lexical data record. A postfix table is shaped as per the different MLI designs.

Table 5.11: MLI File for Tamil Verbs

PT+3SM	PRT+1P
PT+3SF	FT+3SM
PT+3SE	FT+3SF
PT+3SE+PL	FT+3SE
PT+3SN	FT+3SE+PL
PT+NOM_athu	FT+3SN
PT+RP+3SN	FT+RP+3SN
PT+3PN	FT+NOM_athu
PT+RP+3PN	FT+3PN
PT+NOM_ana	FT+RP+3PN
PT+2S	FT+NOM_ana
PT+2EH	FT+2S
PT+2EH+PL	FT+2EH
PT+1S	FT+2EH+PL
PT+1P	FT+1S
PRT+3SM	FT+1P
PRT+3SF	FT_3SN
PRT+3SE	RP_UM
PRT+3SE+PL	PT+RP
PRT+3SN	PRT+RP
PRT+RP+3SN	NM+RP
PRT+NOM_athu	PT+RP+3SM
PRT+3PN	PT+RP+3SF
PRT+RP+3PN	PT+RP+3SE
PRT+NOM_ana	PRT+RP+3SM
PRT+2S	PRT+RP+3SF
PRT+2EH	PRT+RP+3SE
PRT+2EH+PL	PRT+3SN
PRT+1S	PRT+3SN

Paradigm Classification Rules

Paradigm classification rules in Tamil are sets of linguistic guidelines that help to determine the paradigm or conjugation class to which a verb belongs based on its root form. These rules are essential for understanding and categorizing verbs into different groups, each associated with specific morphological patterns. Figure 5.10 shows the calculation for worldview grouping. Look into table is utilized for just the worldview 25 (படி, padi) and 26 (நட, wada), as the end postfixes can't be summed up for these two standards.

padi (படி) (read) படித்தான், படிந்தான்,

படிக்க, படிய,

படித்து, படிந்து.

thIr (தீர்) (finish) தீர்த்தான்.தீர்ந்தான்

தீர,தீர்க்க

தீர்ந்து,தீர்த்து

```
Root word is Romanized
For all End Suffix
    If End Suffix is matched with root word
        Then , Paradigm number is identified
    End if
End for
```

Figure 5.10: Pseudo Code for Paradigm Classification

Figure 5.11 shows the pseudo-code for worldview order. End additions with relating worldview numbers are given in Table 5.13. For instance, the action word **பயில்** (*payil*), is coordinated with the consummation postfix '**ல்**' (il). Accordingly, the primary worldview is 11, and there are no opportunities for the subsequent worldview (N). At times, the word might have two ideal models. For instance, the words like (**படி**, *padi*) (**தீர்**, *thIr*) have two ideal models. On account of the word's sense, *padi* has two ideal models, and intransitive structure makes the word *thIr* fall under two standards. An illustration of different word structures is given underneath.

Table 5.12: Look-up Table for Paradigm Classification

End Suffix	*1st P-Num*	*IInd P-Num*
A	10	N
O	17	N
ey	1	N
Ey	1	N
oy	1	N
uy	1	N
ozu	2	N
uzu	2	N
azu	2	N
idu	4	N
sAku	3	N
wOku	9	N
padu	25	4
wadu	4	N
kedu	25	4
sudu	4	N
odu	4	N
pOdu	4	N
eRu	5	N
uRu	5	N
RRu	30	15
Ru	29	N
Ez	6	N
Az	6	N
iz	6	N
az	6	N
Uz	6	N
Ay	6	N
Iy	6	N
vizu	7	N
izu	25	N
ezu	7	N
i	8	N

Table 5.13: Worldview Numbers

ai	8	N
akal	11	N
kal	18	N
al	11	18
AL	12	N
aL	12	N
uL	12	N
kEL	19	N
sol	16	N
ol	13	N
el	13	N
oL	14	N
Ul	18	N
Ol	18	N
vil	18	N
El	19	N
UL	19	N
IL	19	12

UN	20	N
uN	21	N
AN	22	N
in	23	N
wil	24	N
il	11	N
en	27	N
In	28	N
Aku	31	N
puku	32	N
Nuku	15	N
uku	32	N
iku	32	N
u	15	N
r	6	N

Table 5.12 presents the lookup table for the Tamil verb paradigm and end suffixes. Such as the first paradigm isெ◌சய் (*sey*), few more words included in the model are ெ◌பய் (*pey*),ெ◌மய் (*mey*), உய் (*uy*). Thus, the generalized end suffixes are எய் (*ey*), ஏய் (*Ey*), உய்(*uy*).

Suffix Table

The suffix table is a two-dimensional (2D) table in which the row parallels the morpho-lexical info, and the column parallels the paradigm number. Nouns and verbs have their individual suffix table. The noun suffix table has 325 rows (word-forms) and 25 columns (paradigms). There are two sub-suffix tables in the Verb suffix table, the first one is designed for without auxiliaries, and the other is made for with auxiliary. There are 164 rows in the first and 67 rows in the second table, whereas there are 32 columns (paradigms) in both. The number of paradigms and modulations of managed verbs and nouns are given in Table 5.14. The total shows the total number of modulations the producer system manages.

Table 5.14: Paradigms and Inflections

	Paradigms	Word forms			
		Inflections	Auxiliaries	Postpositions	Total
Verb	32	164	67	--	10988
Noun	25	30	--	290	320

Table 5.15: Stemming End Characters

Paradigm Number	End Characters
1	*
2	Zu
3	sAku
4	Du
5	Ru
6	wOku
7	Zu
8	*
9	wOku
10	A
11	L
12	L
13	L
14	L
15	U
16	L
17	*
18	L
19	L
20	*
21	*
22	kAN
23	*
24	L
25	*
26	*
27	*
28	*
29	U
30	Ru
31	U
32	U

For all paradigms, a word is chosen, named as head word; all the modulated word forms are formed.

Stemming Algorithm

The procedure of Stemming involves decreasing the word-form to their stem. The stem requires to be dissimilar to the word's structural root. In search engines and data retrieval, it is an essential procedure. Table 5.15 represents the recognized characters for stemming in accordance with their paradigm. The following characters are eliminated from the root word in stemming. Such as the stemming character for the second paradigm, "azu" is "zu". Hence, the end character "zu" would be eliminated for the words falling under the second paradigm. In case the paradigm number contains an end character "*" it means none of the characters would be eliminated from the word.

5.8.7 Morphological Generator for Tamil Pronouns

Tamil pronouns fall within the closed word-class category and play a vital role in relative pronouns (connecting parts of sentences), indefinite pronouns, everyday conversations, encompassing personal pronouns (indicating the person speaking, being addressed, or spoken about), and reciprocal or reflexive pronouns (where the subject of the verb acts on the verb's object). Given their significance, special attention is required in both analysis and generation processes.

The morphological generation of Tamil pronouns is accomplished individually using the pattern matching method. This method has many advantages like, handling closed-category words. The generation process employs the opposite approach of the pronoun structural analyzer, utilizing the information from the analyzer for production purposes. Figure 5.12 illustrates the morphology of pronoun word forms, and an example of a pronoun structure is provided below.

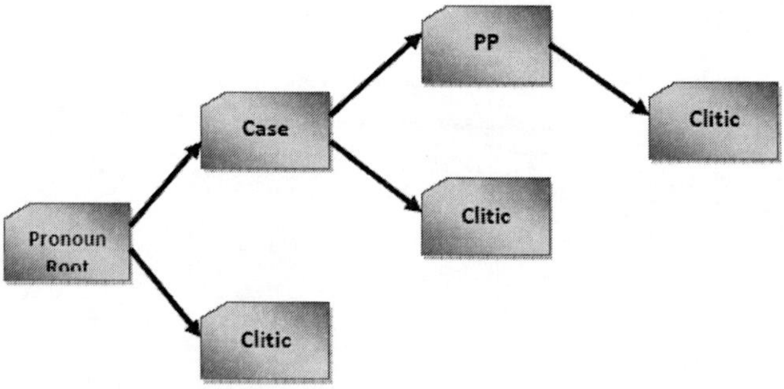

Figure 5.12: Structure of Pronoun Word-form

The below figure shows the structure of pronoun

Example for the Structure of Pronoun

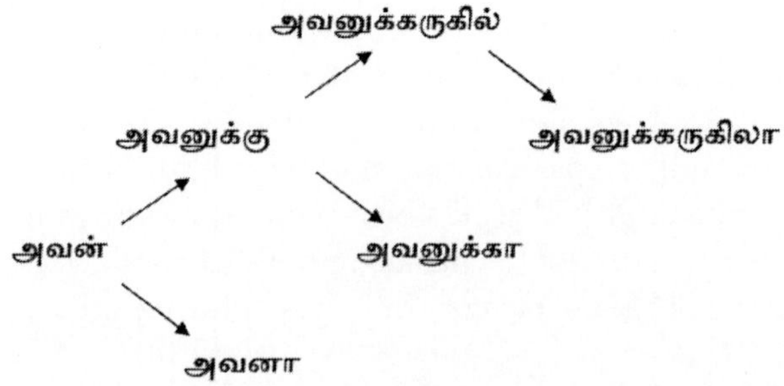

To generate pronoun word form, a pattern matching-based algorithm is used.

5.9 NAMED ENTITY RECOGNITION (NER)

Named Entity Recognition is the method involved with distinguishing and perceiving named elements like an individual, association, area, date, time and cash in the text reports. Named Entity Recognition is a subtask of Information Extraction and Information Extraction is the most common way of extricating important data from information. There is no understanding of capital letters in Tamil, and thus no upper casing data is accessible for named elements in Tamil. All named substances are things and subsequently are Noun Phrases, however not all Noun Phrases are Named Entities. Restrictive irregular fields and secret Markova models have been utilized in the past for named substance acknowledgment, yet it has been done on a really limited scale. This book intends to fabricate a Named Entity recognizer module for Tamil, which could distinguish, and label named elements in every text.

The Named Entity Recognition (NER) alludes to naturally distinguishing named substances in a given text report. NER alludes to the acknowledgment and order of formal people, places or things in the given report. NER can be seen as a naming undertaking. Given a text record, named substances, for example, Person names, Organization names, Location names, Product names are distinguished and labeled. Distinguishing named substances is fundamental in a few higher language innovation frameworks, for example, data extraction frameworks, machine interpretation frameworks, and cross-lingual data access frameworks.

5.9.1 NER System Using CRFs

To create a commonsense NER framework that can be utilized dependably on web information. For a programmed framework to be utilized continuously, it ought to be powerful. In HMM, as the current mark relies upon the past one, it experiences a reliance issue. It likewise needs a huge preparing corpus. Else, it has an information sparsity issue. MEMM have a marking inclination issue in light of the fact that the likelihood progress from some random state should aggregate to one, and consequently it has a predisposition towards states with active changes. Here we have picked CRFs as a result of their benefits over HMM and MEMM. CRFs are one most appropriate method for grouping marking assignments.

5.9.2 NER Tagset

This 106 different evened out label set involves fundamentally three classes Entity Names (ENAMEX), Numerical and Time articulations (NUMEX,

TIMEX). In the execution part, we had required 22 second-level marks from the reformist label set. Components may be alluded to in a message by their name, shown by something regular or thing phrase or tended to by a pronoun. Individual, Organization, Location, Facilities, Cuisines, Locomotives, Artifact, Entertainment, Organisms, Plants and Diseases are the eleven sorts of Named components. Numerical explanations are masterminded as Distance, Money, Quantity and Count. Time, Year, Month, Date, Day, Period and Special day are seen as Time explanations. This is the standard label set used commonly in the Indian Language research neighborhood public undertakings like CLIA and IL-IL MT.

5.9.3 Our NER Engine

Capitalization, postfix, prefix, word reference designs, first word, regular word, digit are the broadly utilized components for NE distinguishing proof. These provisions differ for every language. Word reference examples and gazetteer list changes for each language, and it contains just the continuous named substances. The primary objective of our motor is to recognize NEs with just essential components like word, pos and chunk. The current word joined with POS of going before two words and current word joined with succeeding two words are taken as provisions. The components utilized are semantically enlivened. Components utilized in our framework are as per the following.

- Word – individual words
- Part of speech tag – pos tag of words
- Combination of word and POS
- Chunk – noun phrase, verb phrase
- Combination of the word, POS and chunk

The standards for the element choice are clarified as follows: POS tag assumes an essential part in the errand of NE ID, and it means whether the substances are appropriate or normal things or cardinal numbers. The grammatical form data assists with distinguishing the connection between the current, going before and succeeding words. Phrase chunking is utilized to discover the noun phrases where the named elements have happened. A mix of provisions like word, POS and chunk in the window of five lifts the NER engine to gain proficiency with the setting of the named substance.

5.9.4 Challenges in NER

Indian languages have a place with a few language families, the significant ones being the Indo-Aryan languages, Indo-Aryan and the Dravidian languages. Tamil has a place with the Dravidian Language family. The difficulties in NER emerge because of a few components.

Agglutination

All Dravidian languages, including Tamil, have agglutinative nature. Case Markers attach as postpositions to proper or common nouns to form a single word.

1. Ta: Koyilil vituthi ullathu
   En: Temple -NN+PSP hostel -NN be-VM
   (there is a hostel in the temple)
   The case marker "il" is suffixed to the common noun "koyil" in the above example.

2. Ta: Kerala king marthandavarmanukku therivikkappattathu
   En: Kerala-NN king- NN marthandavarman- NNP+PSP
   therivikkappattathu
   informed-VM
   (informed to the king marthandavarman of kerela)
   Where the case marker "kku" is attached to the proper noun 'marthanda-varman'.

   As the case markers suffixed to the noun increase, the number of NEs in the training corpus also increases. So, it is difficult for the machine to learn distinct NE patterns.

Ambiguity

In the corpus, we discover a ton of equivocalness among normal and formal people, places or things. For instance, the normal names, for example, roja (rose) in Tamil, thamarai (lotus), malar (blossom) in word references can likewise be the names of the individual, and in such cases, it ought to be considered as NE. From the model sentences given underneath, the issue of vagueness can be seen without any problem.

3. Ta: 'Thiya sakthi thaiva sakthiyai vella mudiyathu'
   En: Evil power god power+acc conquer cannot
   (Evil power cannot overcome the power of god):

'Sakthi thanathu tholigalutan koyilukku cenral.'

En: Sakthi her with friend's temple go+past

(Sakthi went to the temple with her friends)

In this example, 'Sakthi" is an ambiguous word having two meanings: a person name and power or energy.

4. Ta: 'velli suriyak kudumbathil irandavathaka amainthulla oru kolakum'

   En: Venus solar family second place be-form one planet

   (In the solar system, Venus is the second planet from the sun) Ta: 'velli vilai thidirena kuraiththathu'

   En: Silver rate suddenly reduced (silver rate suddenly declined)

   Here "velli" has two meanings, one name of the planet and the other as "silver".

5. Ta: 'anbu sakalathaiyum thankum'

   En: love all bear

   (Love bears all things)

   Ta: 'anbu pattap patipai mudithan'

   En: Anbu graduation study complete+past

   (Anbu completed graduation)

   Here "anbu" has two meanings "love" and as the name of a person.

   In example 4, the word "velli" is an interesting example, where both types are NEs, but belonging to different categories. The first one belongs to the category "celestial", and the second belongs to "artifact". Similarly, words such as "thamarai" belong to different NE categories "flower" and "person name".

Nested Entities

In some cases, if the proper noun is considered separately, it belongs to one NE type, but if we consider the same NE as a nested entity, it belongs to another NE type. For instance,

6. Ta: Kanchi sankaracharyar

   En: kanchi sankaracharya

"kanchi" refers to a location individually, in the case of a nested entity, it refers to the person "sankaracharyar" who lives in "kanchi".

Ta: andal sannathi En: andal temple

In general, we observe that more extended length entities are formed by combining two or more individual named entities.

7. Ta: indira ganthi palkalaikallagam – Organization
   En: Indira Gandhi University
   Ta: indira ganthi - Person name
   En: Indira Gandhi
8. Ta: krishna jeyanthi – Special day
   En: Krishna jayanthi (birthday)
   Ta: krishna – Person name
   En: (Krishna)
9. Ta: chithirai ther thiruvilla – Entertainment event
   En: Chithirai boat festival
   Ta: chithirai – Month name
   En: Chithirai

5.10 SENTENCE PARSER

The parser is the primary apparatus in regular language handling like language interpretation measure, syntax checker, and multilingual data extraction. It is utilized to comprehend the linguistic structure and semantics of a characteristic language sentence restricted to syntax. It is utilized to distinguish the syntactic constituents of a sentence as a tree structure. Parser for the Tamil language is a perplexing cycle in view of the free word request component of the language because of the tight coupling between the morphological and syntactic levels. The parser is a computational framework that cycles input sentences as indicated by the language creations and assembles at least one constituent construction called parse trees that adjust to the syntax. A parser allows a language to be thought about in contrast to a possibly enormous assortment of test sentences, assisting the etymologist with distinguishing deficiencies in their examination.

A morphologically broke down sentence is contribution to the real parsing measure. The morphological analyzer can't examine all words. This might be on the grounds that the specific word is absent in the word reference, or the word might be related with more than one syntactic classification. These unidentified words can be distinguished utilizing etymological based heuristic guidelines.

Ex. 7: இராமன் நான்றாகப்பாடுவான்

TF: iraaman n'anRaakap paaTuvaan

EF: Raman well sing

In this sentence, if the verb dictionary doesn't contain the verb பாடுவான் (TF: paaTuvaan, EF: sing), it can be identified as a verb by the heuristic rule that it is the last word of the sentence and its preceding word is an adverb.

For the simple sentence, adjectives and adverbs are attached with their corresponding words irrespective of the presence of adverb anywhere in the sentence before its verb. Then the NC (noun constituent) and VC (verb constituent) are attached to the tree's root.

Ex. Consider the above example sentences 4 & 5.

The tree structure of these two sentences given by the parser is shown below.

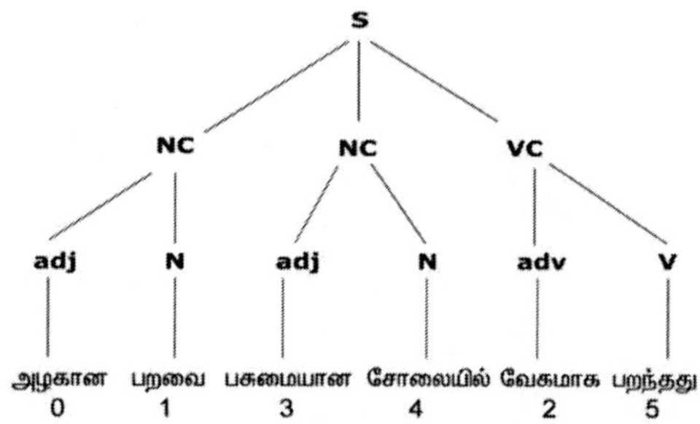

Figure 5.13: Parser Tree, for Example, Sentence 3

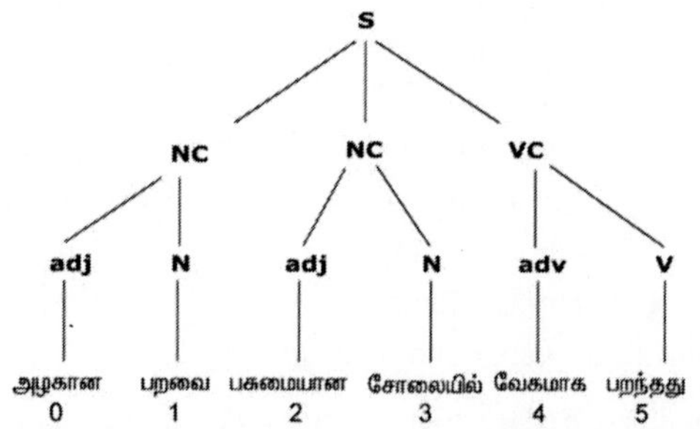

Figure 5.14: Parser Tree, for Example, Sentence 4

Note that these two tree structures are the same except for the word positions.

PNG marker of the verb performs a vital role in identifying the subject of a sentence. A noun is a subject if it first matches the sentence's verb in the following three ways while processing from left to right.

- The person of the noun must be the same as the person of the verb.
- The number of the noun must be the same as the number of the verb.
- The gender of the noun must be the same as the gender of the verb.

The third condition is simple in the case of pronouns. But in other words, the problem is not trivial. To perform subject classification, the gender, animate and inanimate information of a noun is required. Thus, semantic information may have to be associated with noun words in the dictionary.

Ex. 8. *இராமன் படம் பார்த்தான்*

TF: iraaman paTam paarttaan

EF: Raman picture saw

In this sentence, the verb contains the third person, singular and masculine gender. At present, the information about the two nouns is third person and singular. In this example, Roman and Padam are both nominatives, and the position does not indicate the subject in Tamil. Here information about Raman and fruit are required to identify subject and object.

5.10.1 Simple Sentence

For the simple sentence, adjectives and adverbs are attached with their corresponding words irrespective of the presence of adverb anywhere in the sentence before its verb. Then the NC (noun constituent) and VC (verb constituent) are attached to the tree's root.

Ex. Consider the above example sentences 4 & 5.

The tree structure of these two sentences given by the parser is shown below.

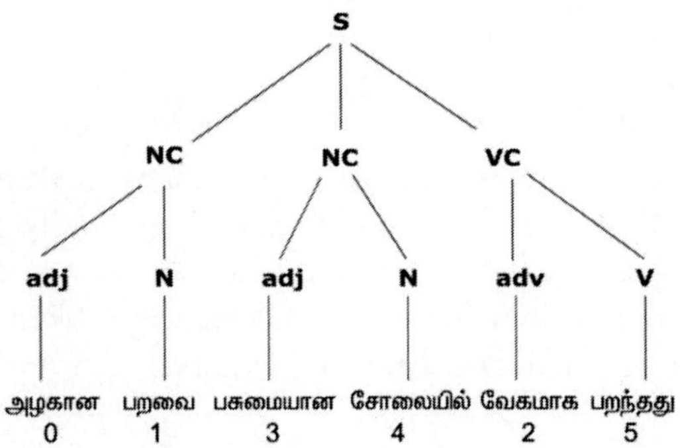

Figure 5.15: Parser Tree, for Example, Sentence 3

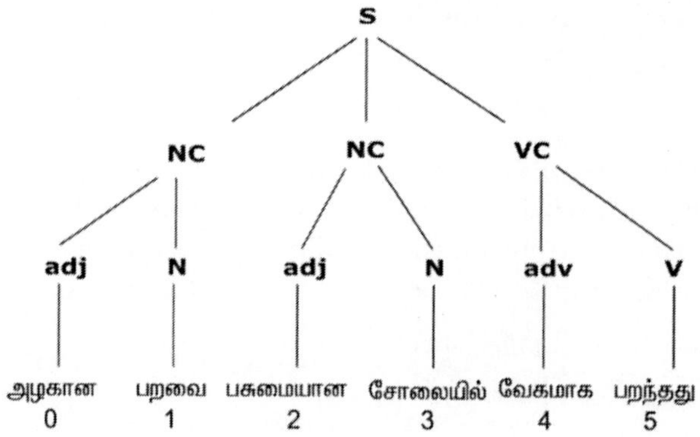

Figure 5.16: Parser Tree, for Example, Sentence 4

Note that these two tree structures are the same except for the word positions.

PNG marker of the verb performs a vital role in identifying the subject of a sentence. A noun is a subject if it first matches the sentence's verb in the following three ways while processing from left to right.

- The person of the noun must be the same as the person of the verb.
- The number of the noun must be the same as the number of the verb.
- The gender of the noun must be the same as the gender of the verb.

The third condition is simple in the case of pronouns. But in other words, the problem is not trivial. To perform subject classification, the gender, animate and inanimate information of a noun is required. Thus, semantic information may have to be associated with noun words in the dictionary.

Ex. 8. இராமன் படம் பார்த்தான்

TF: iraaman paTam paarttaan

EF: Raman picture saw

In this sentence, the verb contains the third person, singular and masculine gender. At present, the information about the two nouns is third person and singular. In this example, Roman and Padam are both nominatives, and the position does not indicate the subject in Tamil. Here information about Raman and fruit are required to identify subject and object.

5.10.2 Complex Sentences

Complex sentences with noun clauses, adjective clauses, and adverb clauses are considered. The following two steps parse these complex sentences.

- Converting the complex sentence into a simple sentence by grouping the three clauses with corresponding words and forming NC and VC.
- Parsing the simple sentence can be done as mentioned earlier.

Grouping the clauses is the main process of the parser. The clauses are generally indicated by special cue suffixes/cue phrases. Grouping is done by the position of the cues and linguistic-based heuristic rules.

Ex. Consider the sentence with all three clauses.

5. இராமன் நான்றாகப்பாடுவான் என்று வகுப்பிலேயே முதன்முதலாக வந்த பாலலுக்கு அவனுடைய பாடலைக்கேட்டு தெரிந்தது

TF: iraaman n'anRaakap paaTuvaan enRu vakuppileeyee mutalaavataaka van'ta paaluviRku avanuTaiya paaTalaik keeTTu terin'tatu

EF: Raman well sing that class first-come Balu his song hear know.

After step 1:

NC பாலுவுக்கு (TF: paaluviRku, EF: Balu)(with its adjective clause) தெரிந்தது (TF: terin'tatu)(with its adverb clause)

After step 2: The result of step 1 will give the tree structure as shown below in Figure 5.17.

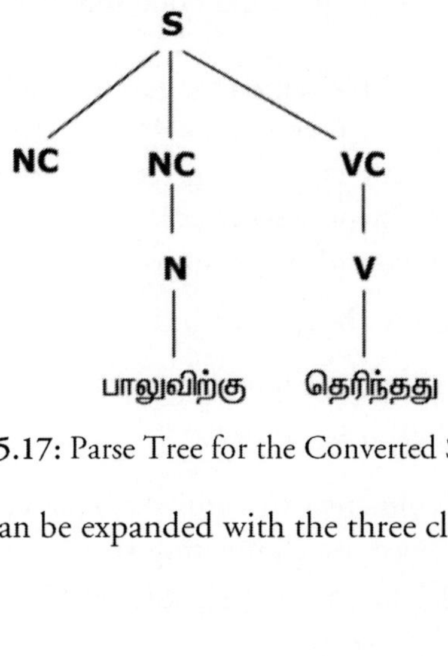

Figure 5.17: Parse Tree for the Converted Sentence

This simple tree can be expanded with the three clauses, as shown below.

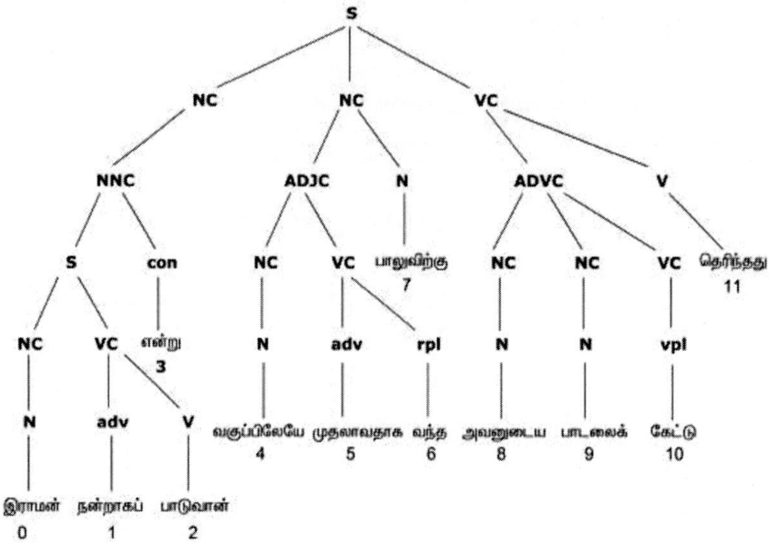

Figure 5.18: Parser Tree for a Sentence with Three Clauses

The tree structure of the example sentence 6 is similar to the above tree structure except for the word position. The parser takes care of the positional mixing of adverbial clauses. In a complex sentence, the subject can be identified in the simple converted sentence, as mentioned earlier.

The following steps can parse complex sentences with more than one verb with a conjunction

- Resolve the sentence into more than one simple sentence by eliminating the conjunctions.
- If any one of these simple sentences doesn't have the subject, consider the subject of the previous sentence.
- Parse these simple sentences as sub sentences of the main sentence separately and join these parsed sub sentences with conjunctions to form the syntactic constituents of the main sentence.

Ex. *நான் பாடம் படித்தேன் மேலும் அவன் படம் பார்த்தான்*

TF: n'aan paaTam paTitteen meelum avan paTam paarttaan

EF: I read lesson and he saw picture

This example sentence contains two verbs and conjunction. If this sentence is divided into two sentences by eliminating the conjunction '**மேலும்**' (TF: meelum, EF: and), there exists a noun '**அவன்**' (TF: avan, EF: he) which matches with the second verb 'பார் • த்தான்' • (TF: paarttaan, EF: saw) and so act as a noun of the second sentence. So, these two sentences can be parsed separately and joined with the conjunction as sub sentences of the main sentence.

10. நான் படம் பார்த்தேன் மேலும் பாடம் படித்தேன்

TF: n'aan paaTam paTitteen meelum paTam paartteen
EF: I read lesson and saw picture

This sentence also contains two verbs and conjunction. If this is divided, the second part will not have the subject. So, the subject of the first sentence can be considered as its subject and can do the further process.

5.10.3 Features of Tamil Language

The syntax of the Tamil language is agglutinative. Postfixes are utilized to check noun class, number, and case. Tamil words comprise of a lexical root to which at least one appends are joined. The majority of the Tamil attaches are additions that can be derivational or inflectional. The length and degree of agglutination are longer in Tamil, bringing about long words with many additions.

In Tamil, nouns are characterized into reasonable and unreasonable structures. People go under the sane structure, though any remaining things are named silly. Rational nouns and pronouns have a place with one of the three classes: manly solitary, female particular, and normal plural. Nonsensical things have a place with one of two classes: unreasonable solitary and silly plural. Postfixes are utilized to play out the elements of cases or post positions. Tamil action words are additionally curved using postfixes. The addition of the action word will show individual, number, state of mind, tense, and voice.

Tamil is reliably head-last language. The action word comes toward the finish of the provision with an average word request of Subject Object Verb (SOV). Notwithstanding, the Tamil language permits word request to be changed, making it a relative word request free language. Other Tamil language highlights are utilizing plural for honorific things, continuous reverberation words, and invalid subject element, i.e., not all sentences have subject-action word and article. To oblige these difficult requirements, LSP utilizes a cross breed language model created from state organized Treebank. Expression organized Treebank is created with Part of Speech (POS) label set of Tamil language needs more fantastic inclusion for all things, action words, different POS, and their enunciations. Since Treebank development is work concentrated, something like a medium-sized jargon Treebank will be utilized to prepare the language model.

5.11 SPELL CHECKER

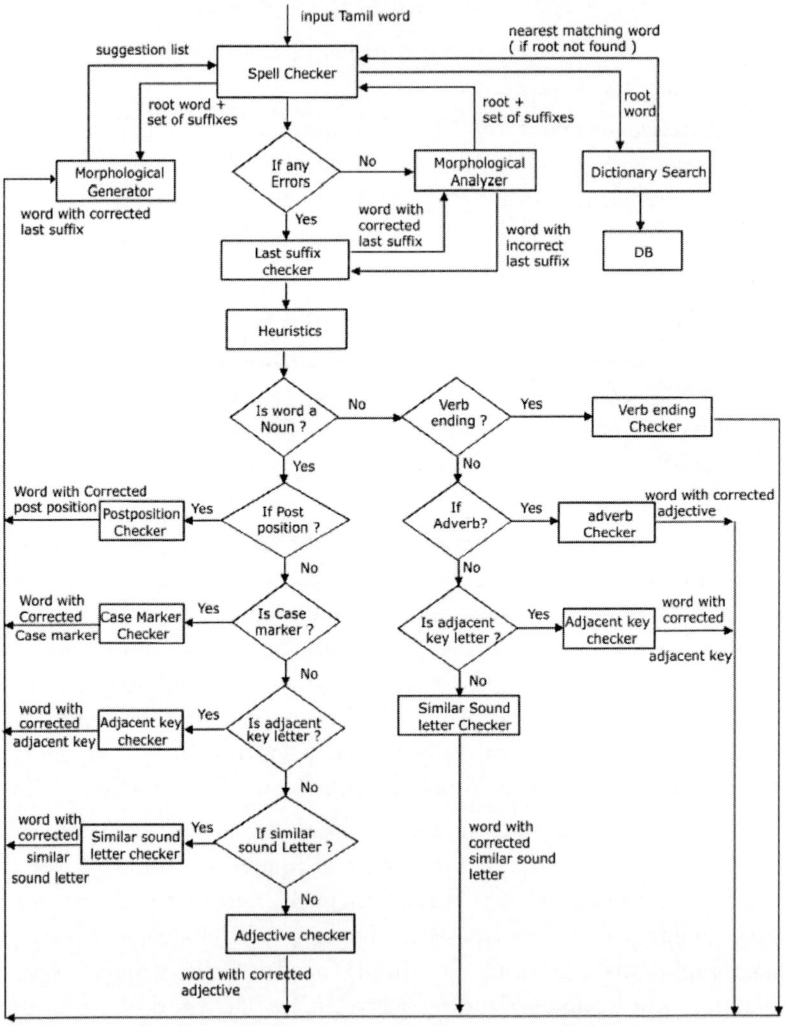

Figure 5.19: General Flow of Tamil Spell Checker

Lexicons with morphological and syntactic data are required for the improvement of spell checkers, morphological and syntactic analyzers. Tamil is a morphologically rich language where most morphemes arrange with the root words as postfixes. Individual, sensual orientation, and number markings join with root words and regularly match with an individual, gender, and number of markings of the sentence's subject. Spell checking applications present legitimate ideas to the client dependent on each error they experience in the client's archive. The instrument gives an office to modify the spell checker's word reference with the goal that the words like Company's name, specialized words identified with a specific area and formal people, places or things and so forth, can be affixed according to the client's need.

5.11.1 Difficulty in Tamil Spell Checking

In Tamil Spell-checker, the following issues must be tackled.

1. Handling the case endings (Suffixes).

   In the English language, the prepositions come as a separate word before the noun. But in the Tamil language, these prepositions come as case endings or postpositions.

   Ex.

   Ram went to Delhi.

   Ram Delhiikku cenRaan.

   Here the preposition 'to' comes as a separate word in English. But in Tamil, that comes as a case ending ('kku') and is attached to the noun.

   - Raman tells about Krishnan
   - Raman krishnanaip patRi solkiRaan

   Here the preposition 'about' comes as above. But in Tamil, it comes as a postposition ('paRRi').
2. Classification of the root word as noun or verb by the case endings.
3. Handling the short vowel and long vowel errors.

   E.g. 'kiNaRu' can be misspelled as 'keeNaRu'
4. Handling the Sandhi letter between two words.

   E.g. 'avanukkup piRaku' Here, the sandhi letter 'p' joins the two words.

5.11.2 The Modules of the Tamil Spell Checker

The Spell Checker peruses extricated words from the record, each in turn. The word reference then, at that point looks at the extricated words are gotten. The spell checker comprises of the accompanying stages: text parsing, spelling confirmation and rectification, and age of the idea list. To support these stages, the spell checker utilizes the following.

- Morphological analyzer for analyzing the given word.
- Morphological generator for generating the suggestions

Text parsing isolates a word appropriate for spell checking from its encompassing text in the information archive. This word is taken for spelling check. On the off chance that the word found is mistaken, it is additionally gone to the spelling amendment and idea age stages.

Subsequent to parsing the report into a rundown of words, each word is passed to the morphological analyzer. The morphological analyzer first attempts to part the postfix. It is planned so that it can dissect just the right words. At the point when it can't part the postfix because of a spelling botch, it passes the word to the spelling confirmation and adjustment stage to address the misstep. Subsequent to parting the word into the root word and a bunch of postfixes, the root word is checked for its legitimacy by contrasting it against the word reference. In the event that the word is absent in the word reference, the closest coordinating with words is picked as the ideas.

5.11.3 Co-reference Resolution

Co-reference analysis is also referred to as identity uncertainty or record linkage. It is a complex but significant issue in NLP. This examination discovers the nouns and phrases denoting the similar unit, allowing the mining of relationships between units and even complicated proposals.

Co-referring units perform an essential role in binding discourse intra and inter sentential. The co-referring units form a thread in the script. The current work is for recognizing the co-reference threads in Tamil text through recognizing the co-referring units, comprising pronominal, definite descriptions, reflexives, reciprocal, distributives, and noun-noun anaphora and their antecedents. Co-reference threads are crucial to constructing cutting edge NLP tools like the entity-based summary generator, profile building, entity-specific sentiment analyzer, and so on. Determine the given example.

Ex. 1.a
raaju$_{1,2}$ ***avanutaiya***$_{1}$ *naNpan* ***baaluvin***$_{2}$
Ramu(N) he(PN)+gen friend(N) Balu(N)-gen
viittiRku *cenRaan.*
house(N)+dat go(V)+past+3sm
(Raju went to his friend Baalu's house.)

5.12 ANAPHORA RESOLUTION

Anaphora is a relation of interpretational dependency between an antecedent referring expression and an anaphoric referring expression. In general, one considers that the referent of the latter is determined by knowledge inferred from the former. Tamil pronominal phrases include 'avan,' 'aval', and 'atu'. The 'atu' is the third person singular neuter pronoun. The inter-linkage among a pronoun and its precursor assists in offering extra info that might be taken out. Conditional random fields as well as Decision tree learning have been used before in building an automatic anaphora resolution system for Tamil.

Anaphora Resolution is the problem of resolving what a pronoun or a noun phrase in a sentence refers to. Anaphora resolution is vital for machine translation, summarization, question-answering systems, and so on. Anaphora, involving pronouns, is the most common phenomenon in which the pronouns are substituted with previously mentioned entities. There are four types of pronouns. They are as follows:

Table 5.16: Types of Tamil Pronouns Anaphora Classification

Pronoun Type	*Example*
Nominative and Objective	avaN 'he', avaL 'she', athu 'it', avai 'they', avarkaL 'they'
Reflexive	thaNakku 'himself', thaNakku 'herself', thaNakku 'itself', thaNkalukku 'themselves'
Possessive	avaNutaiya 'his', avaLutaiya 'her', athaNutaiya 'its', avaRkalutaiya 'their', avaikaLutaiya 'their'
Expletive (Not referring to any item mentioned before)	athu 'it'

They are intra-sentential anaphora and Inter-sentential anaphora. Intra-sentential anaphora implies that the anaphor and its relating pronoun happen in a similar sentence. Between sentential anaphora is the place where the pronoun shows up in the past sentence of the sentence with the anaphor.

5.12.1 Methodology

Resolving anaphora is crucial for understanding the cohesive structure of a text. Here's a general methodology for anaphora resolution.

- The given sentences are tokenized. The constituent words in the main sentence are exposed to shallow morphological parsing, morpheme naming, and word-class labeling.
- Person, number, gender, tense markers, and case markers are recovered.
- The constituent words are labeled with their comparing POS labels.
- Sub-order highlights are added to the constituent words utilizing wordnet, including cosmology and OntNet (Explained in ensuing segments).
- All potential implications of the constituent words are extricated from the Linguistically Annotated Database.
- The pronoun in the subsequent sentence is separated. VPs in the two sentences are found utilizing a standard based syntactic parser.
- If there is a vague word in the principal sentence, then, at that point utilizing the semantic components of the words in the VP, right word sense is discovered.

5.12.2 Anaphora Resolution Using Ontnet

Anaphora Resolution is imperative for machine interpretation, outline, question-noting frameworks, etc. In this part, a mix of wordnet and metaphysics is utilized for anaphora goal. Sub arrangement highlights are added to the constituent pronoun, nouns, and action words in the given sentences utilizing WordNet and OntNet.

5.12.2.1 *OntNet – Establishing Relationship between Noun Ontology and Verb Ontology*

OntNet is an extra semantic organization set up between the Ontology tree of Noun elements and the Ontology tree of Verb substances. In a WordNet, a word's semantic connection as a hypernym (superordinate), hyponym (subordinate), equivalent, antonym to different words will be portrayed. For the most part these relations are set up between expressions of a similar classification, i.e., an equivalent or antonym of a thing will likewise be a thing. A semantic relationship that can exist between a word having a place with the Noun classification and that to a Verb class isn't set up on account of WordNet.

OntNet centers around building up the semantic connection between the Noun cosmology tree and Verb Ontology tree. An assortment of Ontsets structures an OntNet of Tamil. Typically, a Synset in WordNet establishes interchangeable words. In any case, in the OntNet that will be produced for Tamil, expressions of a similar semantic classification can be gathered to frame an Ontset. Figure shows the verb and noun Ontset.

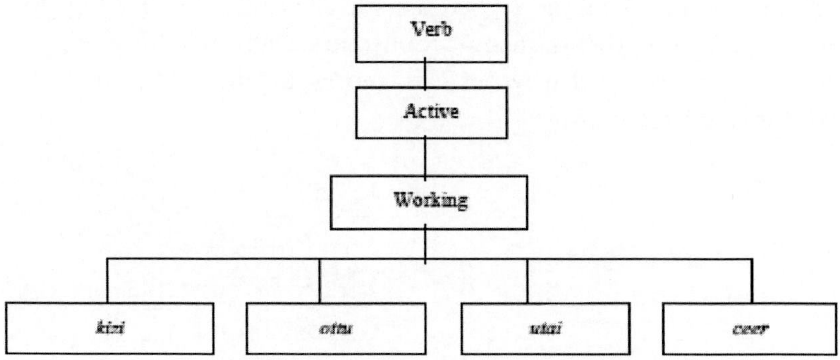

Figure 5.20: Example for Noun Ontset

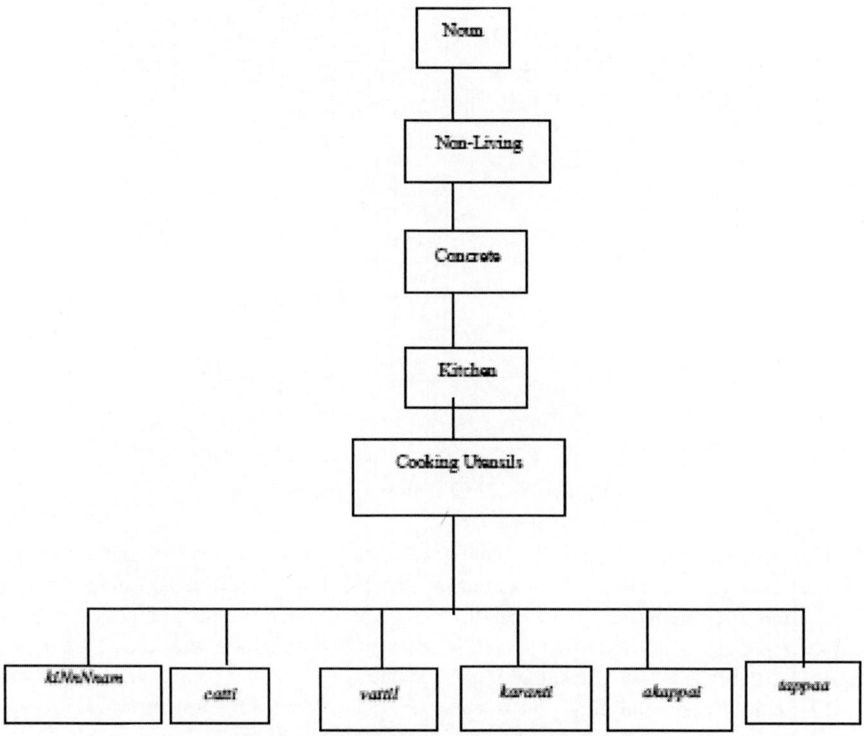

Figure 5.21: Example for Noun Ontset

5.12.2.2 Semantic Network between Noun and Verb Ontology Trees

When the metaphysics trees are shown up at, the planning of the classifications inside nouns and mapping of the classes among things and action words are done dependent on their semantic connections. This planning brings about a semantic organization that works with setting up the relevant importance of a word in a given sentence.

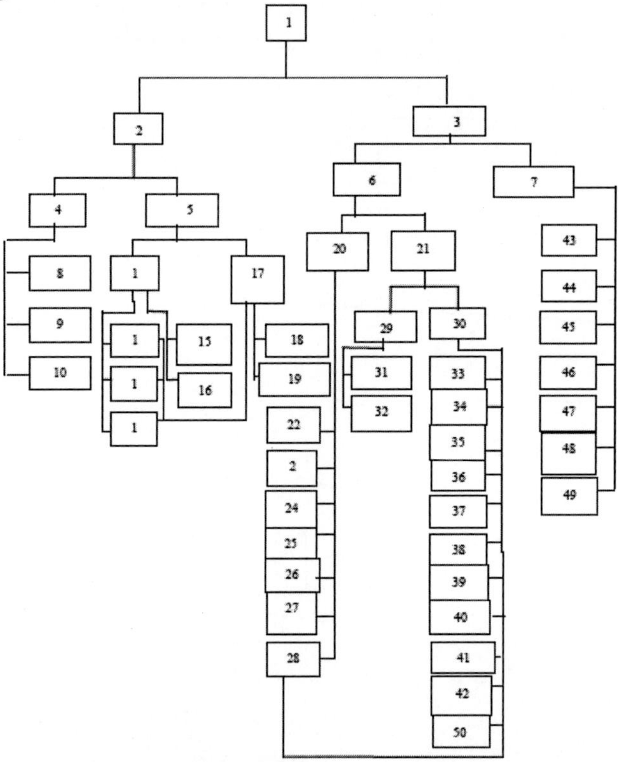

Figure 5.22: Ontology Tree of Nouns

1-Noun, 2-Living, 3-Non-Living, 4-Human, 5-Non-human, 6-Concrete, 7-Abstract, 8-Profession, 9-Relation, 10-Character, 11-Plants,12-Land, 13-Water, 14-Desert, 15-Edible, 16-Inedible, 17-Animals/Birds, 18-Vertebrae, 19-invertebrate, 20-Natural, 21-Man-Made, 22-Bodyparts, 23-Seasons, 24-Places, 25-Objects, 26-Diseases, 27-Supernaturals, 28-Consumables, 29-Mobile, 30- Immobile, 31-Vehicles, 32-Machinery, 33-Building, 34-Jewellery, 35-Cutleries, 36-Furniture, 37-Weapons, 38-Instruments, 39-Clothes, 40-Appliances & Gadgets, 41-Religious Materials, 42-Entertainment, 43-Emotion, 44-Time,45-Event, 46-Act, 47-Festivals, 48-Senses, 49-Shapes, 50-Medicine

It tends to be investigated how the between sentential anaphora in the sentences can be settled utilizing ontsets for Tamil. The accompanying sentences can be thought of.

1. *"kuzanthaip paalaik kutiththathu. athu kiNnNnaththil irunthathu"*. 'The child drank the milk. It was in the bowl'. Here, the pronoun *athu* 'it' alludes to *paal* 'milk.'
2. *"kuzanthaip paalaik kutiththathu. athu paciyaaka irunthathu"*. 'The child drank the milk. It was ravenous'. Here, the pronoun *athu* 'it' alludes to *kuzanthai* 'baby.'

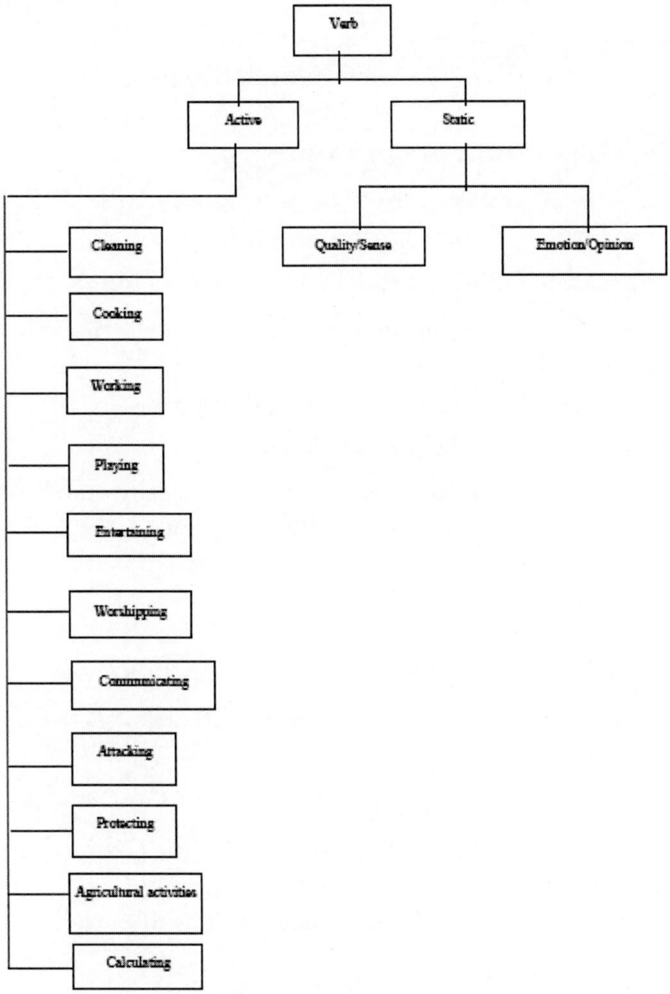

Figure 5.23: Ontology Tree of Verbs

5.12.2.3 *Ontsets*

O1: paal 'milk,' thayir 'curd,' moor 'buttermilk,' sarpath 'shorbet,' pazaccaaRu 'fruit juice' – Edibles

O2: paaNai 'pot,' thattu 'plate,' cempu 'tumbler,' catti 'vessel,' kiNnam 'small vessel' – Utensils

O3: paci 'hunger,' thaakam 'thirst,' vali 'pain,' koopam 'anger,' makilchi 'happy,' cirippu 'laugh,' azukai 'cry,' cookam 'sad' – Senses.

O4: *kuzanthai* 'baby,' *aaNn* 'man,' *peNn* 'lady,' *maNithaN* 'human' – Human beings.

The categories of the above seen ontsets O1, O2, O3, and O4 are derived from the Noun and Verb entity Ontology trees. (Figures 5.22 & 5.23)

5.12.2.4 *Sub Categorization Features Tagging*

Using the above-seen ontology trees of nouns and verbs, the constituent words are tagged with their semantic features as follows.

"kuzanthaip paalaik kutiththathu. athu kiNnNnaththil irunthathu"

kiNNam 'Bowl – [Noun][+Non-living] [+Concrete] [+Man-made] [+Immobile] [+Utensils]

paal 'Milk – [Noun][+Non-living][+Concrete][+Edible]

kuzanthai 'baby' – [Noun][+Living][+Human]

Then from the Semantic network, i.e., the Ontnet shown in Figure 5.24, it can be clearly established that [+Edible] is related to [Utensils] and [+Human] is not related to any of the other two categories. Thus it is evident that the pronoun *athu* refers to *paal.*

"kuzanthaip paalaik kutiththathu. athu paciyaaka irunthathu"

paal 'Milk – [Noun][+Non-living][+Concrete][+Edible]

kuzanthai 'baby' – [Noun][+Living][+Human]

paci – [+Verb][+Static][+Senses]

Referring to Figure 5.24, [+Human] is related to [+Senses] and not to [+Edible]. Thus here, the pronoun *athu* refers to *kuzanthai,* which falls under the category [+Human]. Thus OntNet plays a vital role in disambiguating ambiguous words.

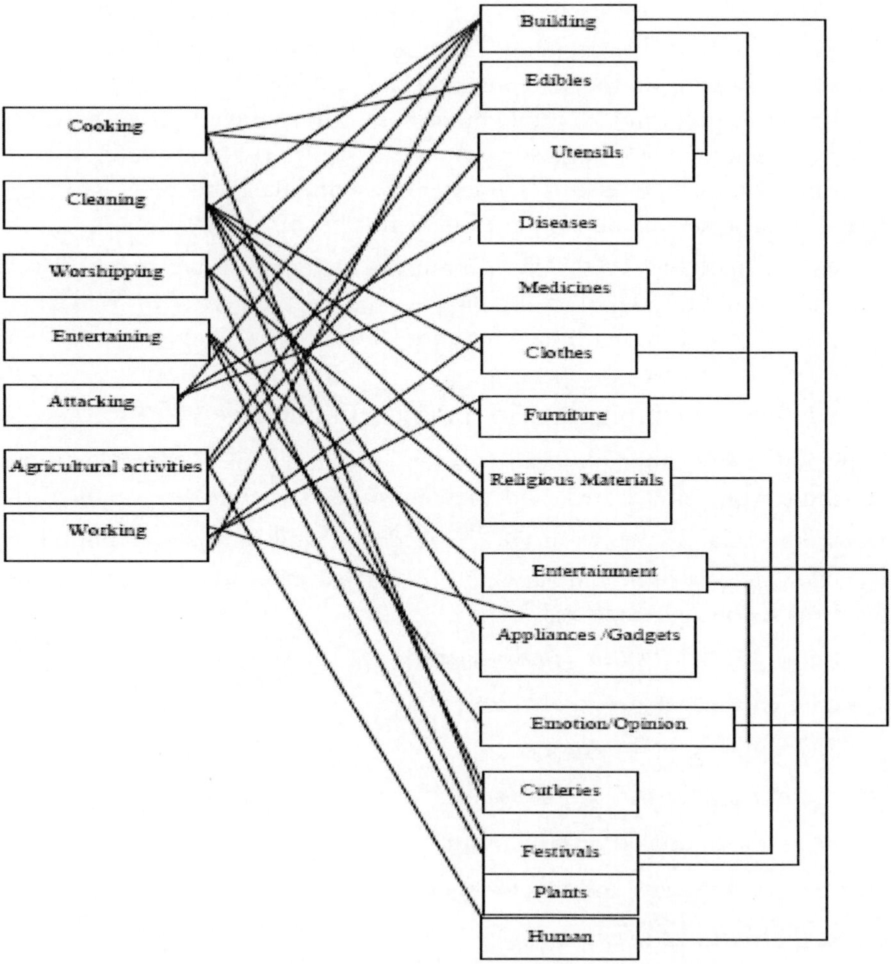

Figure 5.24: OntNet of Verb and Noun Ontologies

5.13 WORD SENSE DISAMBIGUATION

The word sense disambiguation (WSD) the process to determine the correct meaning of a word in the context of a sentence, particularly when the word has multiple meanings. This task is essential for various NLP applications, like information retrieval, machine translation and question answering. Addressing the challenge of disambiguating the ambiguous words is a key concern in NLP activities, and support vector machines prove effective in classifying contexts to select the most appropriate sense for the target word. Unsupervised approaches, leveraging clustering methods, have also been explored.

The goal is to accurately identify the intended sense of words from a piece of Tamil text. Lexical items introduce the challenges for translators and translation systems, as they often exhibit homophony (same sound, different meanings) or polysemy (multiple meanings). The ambiguity from polysemy and homophony in the linguistic system can lead to confusion to in order to determine the correct sense of lexical items. Tamil, like many other languages, faces lexical ambiguity due to these linguistic phenomena.

As far back as 1960, the Automatic Language Processing Advisory Committee (ALPAC) report highlighted the lack of effective WSD as a significant obstacle in machine translation.

5.13.1 Lexical Ambiguities in the Tamil Language

Polysemy and homography lead to ambiguity in Tamil. Polysemous words are those which are related, and they are called semantic extensions of the word. For example, the word ஓடு (*ooTu*) in Tamil can denote running by legs, flowing of a river, and running of a cinema in a theatre, as can be seen from the following sentences.

அவன் மைதானத்தில் **ஓடி**க்கொண்டிருக்கிறான்

avan maitaanattil **ooTi**kkoNTirukkiRaan

'He is ***run***ning in the ground.'

ஆறு கிழக்கு நோக்கி **ஓடு**கிறது.

aaRu kizakku nookki **ooTu**kinRatu

'The river is ***flow***ing towards the south.'

அந்த தியேட்டரில் படம் **ஓடு**கின்றது.

anata tiyeeTTaril cinimaa **ooTu**kinRatu

'A cinema is ***run***ning/going on in that theatre.'

If two different words have the same spelling, they are considered homographs. For example, அறை (*aRai*) 'room' and அறை (*aRai*) 'slap' as we found in the following sentences are homographs.

அவன் அந்த ***அறை***யில் வசிக்கிறான்.

avan anta **aRai**yil vacikkiRaan

'He is staying in that ***room.***'

அவன் கன்னத்தில் ஒரு ***அறை***கொடுத்தான்.

avan kannattil oru **aRai** koTuttaan

'He gave a ***slap*** on the face.'

If two different words have different spelling but have the same pronunciation, they are considered homophones. Homophones are not found in Tamil, but English has several homophones. For example, the words *read,* and *reed* is homophones. Homophones are not our concern here as we are working on written text and not on spoken text. As for machine translation or, for that matter, for any NLP application, the resolution of polysemy and homography is treated alike as both involve disambiguation only by context.

It is difficult to find out a monosemous word in the dictionary. Words are mostly polysemous, denoting various senses. Comparatively, verbs are more polysemous than nouns. We will find out the number of senses listed below each verb. We will find out many verbs have parallel nominal forms with the same graphic forms, thus showing categorical ambiguity. For example, the verb குடி (*kuTi*) 'to drink' has the nominal equivalent குடி (*kuTi*) 'drinking habit,' the verb கடி (*kaTi*) 'to bite' has the nominal equivalent கடி (*kaTi*) 'bite' and so on. Almost all nominal forms can function as adjectival forms. For example சிவப்பு (*civappu*) 'redness'/red' function as a noun as well as an adjective, மரம் (*maram*) 'wood/wooden' functions as a noun as well as an adjective and so on. Categorical ambiguity can be resolved by parts-of-speech tagging.

5.13.2 Resolution of Lexical Ambiguity

Context is the only way to select the meaning of a polysemous word. Due to that cause, nearly every attempt at sense disambiguation depends on the context of the target word. Data from micro-context, topical context, and domain contributes to sense selection. Most WSD approaches use the local context of word occurrence as a primary source of information for WSD. Local or micro context is usually determined as a small window of words nearby the target word. The nearest word may contribute to the sense selection than the distant word. Collocation is used for WSD in various ways. In many WSD systems, syntactic info is used in combination with other data. Verbs derive more disambiguating info from their object than from their subjects, adjectives derive nearly all disambiguating information from the nouns altered by them, and adjacent adjectives or nouns disambiguate nouns.

5.13.3 Word Sense Disambiguation for Tamil

There exist two types of methods for WSD; they are supervised WSD and unsupervised WSD. The supervised WDS makes use of annotated text, whereas unsupervised approaches do not make use of the annotated information. The supervised disambiguation includes Decision Lists, Decision Trees, Naive Bayes, Neural Networks, Exemplar-Based or Instance-Based Learning, Support Vector Machines (SVMs), Ensemble Methods, Minimally and Semi-supervised Disambiguation. The unsupervised method includes Word Clustering, Context Clustering, and Co-occurrence Graphs. It can be further differentiated between knowledge-based (or knowledge-rich, or dictionary-based) and corpus-based (or knowledge-poor) methods.

To make use of the unstructured text for the implementation of WSD, the text needs to be transformed into a structured format. The structuring of text involves the following steps

- **Tokenization:** It portions the text into tokens (generally words)
- **POS tagging:** It involves allotting a linguistic class to all words.
- **Lemmatization:** It is the process of finding out the base form from the inflected words.
- **Chunking:** It involves the division of the textual sentences into syntactically correlated parts (for example, into noun phrases and verb phrases)
- **Parsing:** It involves identifying the syntactic construction of the textual sentences (usually in a phrase-structure tree's shape).

5.13.4 Architecture of the Proposed WSD System

The proposed WSD system for the Tamil language makes use of a Support Vector Machine. Generally, WSD is a two-stage process. The first stage determines the set of applicable meanings of a word for a particular context, and the second stage determines the most appropriate sense. Figure 5.25 portrays the structure of the projected SVM-based WSD system for the Tamil language.

Here WSD problem is formulated as a classification task. The SVM classifier has to predict the correct sense of a target word using a given set of feature values describing the context.

The WSD of Tamil proposed here involves two phases as any machine learning approach: the training and testing phases. The text having the uncertain target word will be POS-tagged and lemmatized first before feeding into the WSD-system; a portion of text with the target ambiguous word will be annotated with English gloss (sense labels) and allow the machine to learn the disambiguating contexts. The SVM system will do the categorizing procedure of discriminating the contexts, thereby discriminating the ambiguous senses of the target word. Here the monitored approach is applied to a certain number of ambiguous words. All the occurrences of the limited number of words are manually annotated, and this data is used to implement the SVM-based supervised sense disambiguation system. Features are extracted, and a classifier is trained for each ambiguous target word.

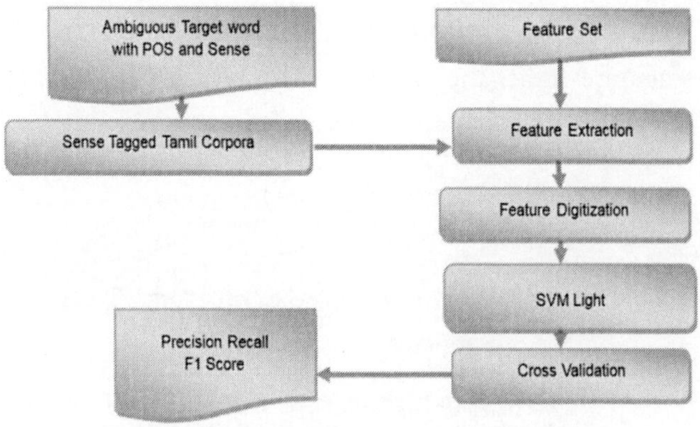

Figure 5.25: WSD Framework for Tamil

5.13.5 Support Vector Machines

A Support Vector Machine is a supervised machine learning algorithm primarily designed for binary classification, but it can be extended to handle regression and multi-class classification tasks. Recently, SVM has found successful applications in addressing practical issues, particularly in the region of NLP. SVM have proven to be an effective learning algorithm in the context WSD. Additionally, SVMs have demonstrated successful implementations in various Indian language applications, including POS tagging, morphological analyzers, transliteration, and dependency parsing. The adaptability and performance of SVMs make them a valuable tool in tackling diverse challenges within the field of NLP.

5.13.6 Features for Support Vector Machines

Feature set and the architecture are suited for any machine learning-based classifier to solve the word disambiguation problem. Semantic information is drawn from the surrounding text using morpho-syntactic information like lemma and the POS tag. Three major categories of features of the sense ambiguous word are used in this WSD framework. They are,

- Bag-of-Words
- Collocations
- Part-of-Speech and Word class

For example, consider the Tamil sentence

"நீதிமன்றத்திற்கு திருடன் கையில் விலங்கு மாட்டி போலிஸ்காரர் அழைத்து வந்தார்".

Let us assume that the target word *w* is "விலங்கு", and the corresponding features of the sentence are explained in Table 5.17.

Table 5.17: Feature and Examples

Features	*Example*
Bag-of-Words	{நீதிமன்றம்,திருடன்,கை,மாட்டு, போலிஸ், அழை, வா}
Collocations	{R_திருடன், R_கை, L_மாட்டு, L_போலிஸ்}
POS	{NN,NN,VNAV,NN,VNAV}
POS-Right and Left	{R_NN,R_NN,L_NN,L_NN}
Lemma with Position	{திருடன்_-2,கை_-1,மாட்டு_+1, போலிஸ்_+2}
POS with Position	{NN_-2,NN_-1,VNAV_+1, NN_-2 }
Lemma_WC	{{நீதிமன்றம்_N,திருடன்_N, கை_N,மாட்டு_V, போலிஸ்_N, அழை_V, வா_V}

Bag-of-Words (BoW)

The bag-of-Words feature considers all the neighboring context words of the target ambiguous word in a sentence. Here, the exact position of the word is not used. To avoid the data sparseness problem in feature vector space, words in the sentences are lemmatized using an existing machine learning-based Tamil morphological a analyzing tool. These BoW features have an important effect on system performance in WSD. It is used to represent the presence or absence of words within a sentence of a target word. Here fixed window size is not considered because each sentence contains a different number of words, so it is not sensible to represent a fixed window size for extracting the features of the given target word.

Collocations

For the Collocation feature, the window size is set to five/seven words, i.e., two/three words to the right and two/three words to the left. The experiments are conducted for different sizes of the context window. Similar to the BoW feature, the collocation feature also considers the lemma instead of a word. The main difference between collocation and BoW feature is that the former includes the additional position information in each word/lemma, whereas the later does not consider it.

Part-of-Speech and Word class

The effectiveness of a WSD system is strongly influenced by the POS of the target word and the nearby words. Tamil POS tagger is used for POS tagging the Tamil sentences. Word-class information is also extracted from it. Here we called coarse-grained POS tag information as Word-class. This Word class information is contained within the feature set. This feature considers the Word class of all neighboring words of the uncertain target word in a sentence. Additionally, the POS tag of each word along with the side (either right or left) in a window size of five and seven is also considered a feature. In addition to the features mentioned above, the POS tag of each word, the position information and Word class of each word, and the lemma in a window size of five and seven are also considered.

5.14 CONCLUSION

In this chapter, multiple Tamil computing tools and their functions are discussed along with issues discussed. The complexity of Tamil text processing and its components like tokenizer, Sentence Splitter, Stemmer, Lemmatization, Chunker, Part-of-Speech, Tagger, Dependency Parser, Morphological Analysis, Morphological Generation, Co-reference Resolution, Word sense disambiguation, Named Entity Recognition, and Anaphora Resolution, all are explained here along with the examples. It has been found that due to the agglutinative nature of Tamil, it is relatively complicated to perform several operations.

CHAPTER 6

Tamil Information System Applications

6.1 INFORMATION EXTRACTION

Information extraction is a procedure to extract organized evidence from disorganized text sources. The organized proof can include a document's concepts, entities, relations, and significances. The enriched document corpus can be developed from various websites, cleaned as a text document, and utilized to accomplish semantic knowledge. This semantic information can be used in the semantic information extraction process. No specific and appropriate techniques are available in Tamil to semantically analyze and conceptually get a clear idea of documents.

The semantic analysis consists of three stages: extracting concepts, entities, and relation of concepts and entities. In concept extraction, thematic ideas are identified. In the entity extraction process, entities are identified and classified as predefined categories. At last, the relation between concepts and entities is determined. It helps to present a graph called Semantic Relationship Graph (SRG).

6.1.1 Semantic Information Extraction

The style of the semantic extraction procedure is represented in Figure 6.1. The extraction process is classified into two stages teaching and testing phases. The domain-specific documents are semi-automatically interpreted for concepts, entities, and relations during the teaching stage. The interpreted document helps learn clues and attributes for the entity and concept extraction process. In the testing phase, the information learned in the training phase is utilized to extract the information from input documents that are not involved in the training process, and their performance is also analyzed.

This information extracted can extract the relations, entailment, and facts or events. The entire information provides the semantic knowledge of input documents. The knowledge can be used for several Tamil text processing.

Tamil is a morphologically rich language. Nearly 2000 morpheme components are present in Tamil, from which a new word can be framed by adding 0–13 morpheme components into the root word. The framed nouns can be,

Root Noun + [Plural Marker] + [Oblique] + [Case Marker]

Example: மாணவர்களுடன் [ManavarkaLutan] (with students).

The usual morphological derivative of Tamil Verb is like,

Root Verb + [Tense Marker] + [Verbal Participle Suffix] + [Auxiliary verb]1 to 4 + [Tense Marker] + [Person, Number, Gender]

Example: செய்திருக்கிறார்கள் [ceythirukkiRarkaL] (They have done)

Adjective = Abstract noun + [adjectival suffix]

Example: அழகான [azhakAna] (beautiful)

Adverb = Abstract noun + [adjectival suffix]

Example: வேகமாக [vEkamAka] (fastly).

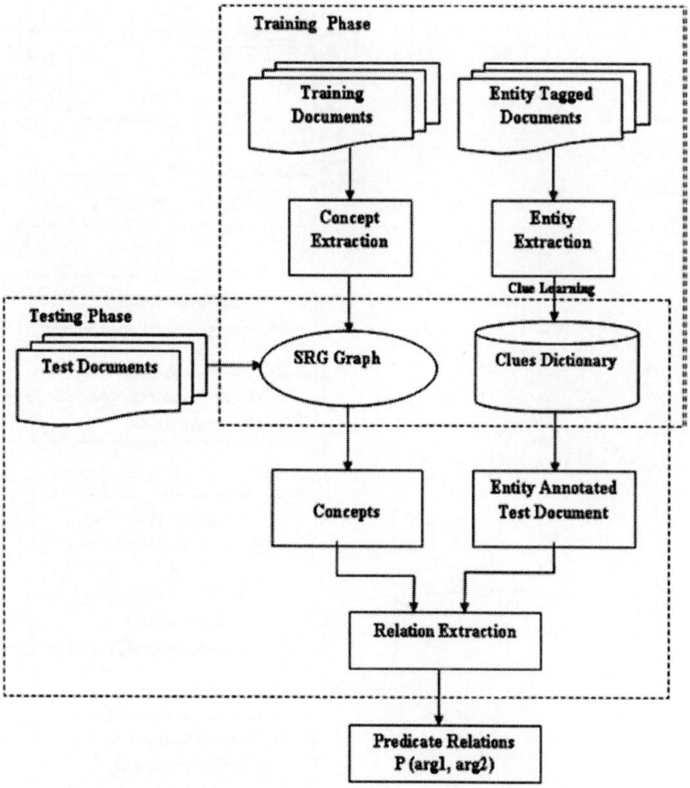

Figure 6.1: Semantic Information Extraction

6.1.2 Design and Implementation

Three phases, concept, entity, and relation extraction are developed for the information extraction process.

6.1.2.1 *Concept Extraction*

Concept extraction is a process of identifying theme words and extracting the semantic relationship between those words. The bag of word approach is followed to process every unique word in the document, and they will be semantically tied to make a significant concept. Figure 6.2 illustrates the formation of the concept extraction system, which has six steps to be followed.

- *Preprocessing:* An adroit document will be the output of this process, which will not have any punctuation from the training document.
- *Tokenization:* The tokenization system will split the preprocessed document to create tokens, and stop words will be removed from the list of tokens.

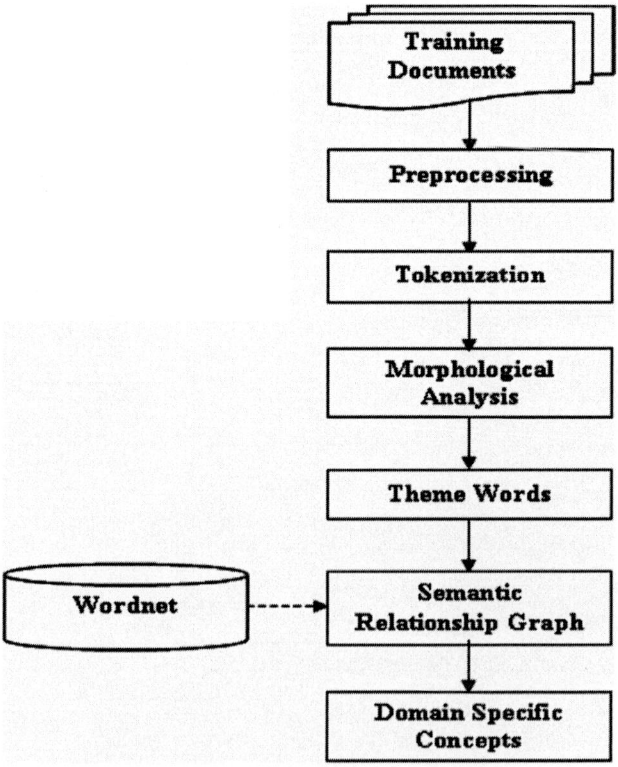

Figure 6.2: Concept Extraction System

- ***Morphological Analyzer:*** The morphological analyzer Atcharam, developed by RCILTS, Chennai, is rule-based and takes Tamil text documents as input and outputs Parts of Speech (POS) tag. Morphological components like case-markers for every word of a document. From the word list, unique words will be identified, and word frequency will be maintained to determine the theme words. The tokens will be analyzed to figure out root and POS.
- ***Theme Word Identification:*** The weightage will be given to identify the theme words on the frequency of each word and occurrence. The comment which does not provide the relevant information will be removed from the words list. The weight of each word is calculated as,

  $$\text{Weight (X)} = \frac{\text{(Frequency of the documents)} + \text{(No. of docs in which present)}}{2}$$

  The higher weight value words are treated as theme words, and they form the initial words list.
- ***Construct SRG:*** From the initial words, the list identifies the hypernym, hyponym, and synonym relationship between the words using a lexical database like Wordnet. Figure 6.3 shows the semantic relationship graph, the relation of these words can be identified using Wordnet, which will have hypernym, hyponym, and synonym for every word.

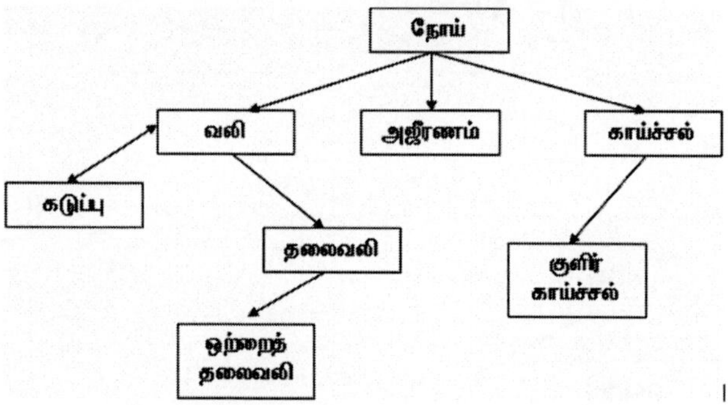

Figure 6.3: Semantic Relationship Graph

SRG can be developed using an algorithm; empty SRG is the initial step of the algorithm. Input is domain-specific Tamil documents, and output is SRG.

Step 1: Clean the documents.

Step 2: Tokenize and morphologically analyze to find the root and POS of each word.

Step 3: From the root wordlist, form *wordlookuplist.*

Step 4: Set depth = 0 and set *wordlookuplist* to be the core word.

Step 5: Lookup hypernym, hyponym, and synonym of all words in *wordlookuplist* and keep track of the sense and parent of the word.

Step 6: If a new core word is found, add components of the path which are already present in the graph.

Step 7: Set *wordlookuplist* to new words which are present in the lookup list of old *wordlookuplist.*

Step 8: Increment depth and repeat from step 5 until it reaches the cut-off.

Figure 6.3 shows a sample SRG; this single-ended arrow shows hypernym, hyponym relationship, and a double-sided arrow shows the synonym relationship of words.

6.1.2.2 *Entity Extraction*

Entity extraction is the process of identifying the proper names of a document and classifying them into a person, location, date, time, money and organization.

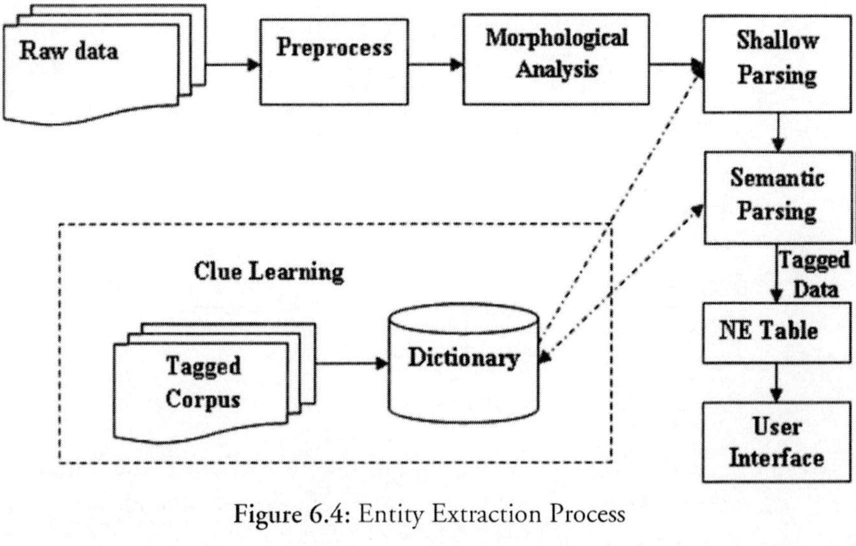

Figure 6.4: Entity Extraction Process

The entity extraction process is depicted in Figure 6.4, which takes raw Tamil documents as input and provides named entity-tagged documents as output. The system also provides a named entity table with a list of entities found in the document, attributes, and the probability vector for names entity types. The explanation of the components is as follows.

- *Preprocessing:* The preprocessor scans Tamil text documents and indexes all sentences into a data structure for easy access with comma-separated. Date and time were also considered, and a proper probability assignment was made.
- *Morphological Analyzer and Clue Extractor:* Input data is passed through an extractor module with two primary functions.
  - Morphological analyses.
  - *Clue Extraction:* The extraction of attributes, clues, verbs, and prepositions from the dictionary.

Figure 6.5 shows clues, attributes, and verbs from the dictionary.

Word Internal Evidence (Intra Clues): Words that appear as part of an NE eg. இல்
Word External Evidence (Inter Clues): Words that appear as separate words near an NE eg. நகரம்
Conjunctions: Words joining two or more entities of the same time eg. ஆகிய, ஆகியோர்
Substring clues – Words forming part of other clues (அமைச்சர்) or words that form part of an NE and help identify the type (மலை)
Attributes – Words used to indicate possession by an NE (சகோதரர்) or emotions/states of an NE (துன்பம்)
Numbers in words like ஒன்பது, நாற்பது, etc.
Postpositions and word case markers like அடுத்த and உக்கு, within a word or outside it provide semantic and case information
Verbs: A list of verbs like செய் and உள்ளது with information on their PNG markers and arguments

Figure 6.5: Clues, Attributes and Verbs

- *Dictionary:* The main analytical component of the NER system is a dictionary, which comprises text files in permanent storage with rules to perform shallow and semantic parsing.
- *Shallow Parser:* POS-tagged inputs are entered into a shallow parser responsible for checking context clues and assigning initial probabilities to entity check. This system outputs an entity chunk and an initial probability vector. Two levels of contextual clues are utilized.

- *Clues:* From the dictionary, it represents word-internal (morphological components) and word external evidence ('naming words') with heuristic values.
- *Attributes:* Represent possession or emotion of entity type.

  So, the output of the shallow parser module is the NE table which comprises entities, probability vectors, clues, and its vectors.
- *Semantic Parsing:* In this phase, verbs identify the subjects/objects in a sentence. Verbs are helped to identify and classify the entities present in the NE table accurately. Verb information is learned from the training corpus, as shown in Figure 6.6.

```
விரும்பு    ஆள் start sub PER 6.0 obj PER 3.0 LOC 2.0 ORG 1.0 end
விரும்பு    ஆள் start sub PER 6.0 obj PER 3.0 LOC 2.0 ORG 1.0 end
விரும்பு    ஆளர் start sub PER 6.0 obj PER 3.0 LOC 3.0 end

வா    start sub PER 6.0 obj LOC 6.0 end
செல்  start sub PER 6.0 obj LOC 6.0 end
படி   start sub PER 6.0 obj LOC 3.0 ORG 3.0 end
```

Figure 6.6: Probability Information and Verb Information

Probability information is learned and maintained based on its semantic meaning and is used to update the probability array that prevailed in the shallow parsing stage. Unknown words which do not have clues will be tagged based on the semantic parsing. Figure 6.7 shows the NER system of Tamil.

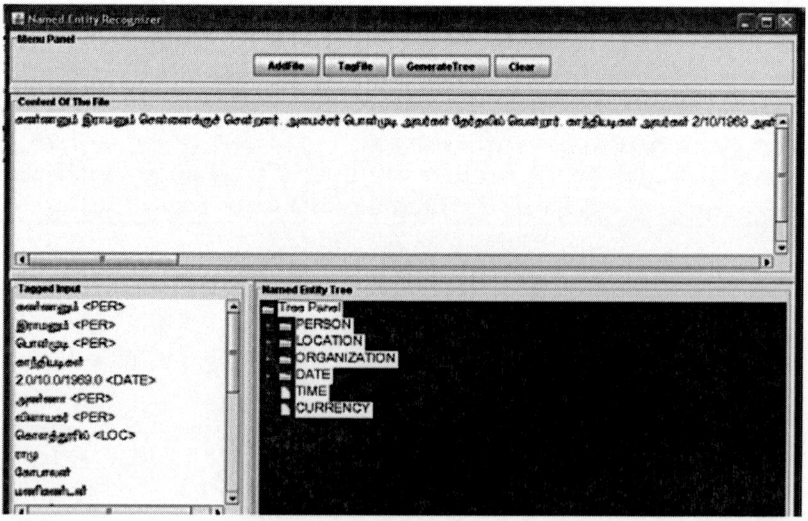

Figure 6.7: Screenshot for NER

6.1.2.3 *Relation Extraction*

Relation extraction is a process of extracting predicate relationships between concepts and entities in each sentence. Learning rules from the training corpus generate these predicates, and each sentence's Verb term is set as a predicate. The Subjects and Objects in the sentence are identified using the Predicate of a sentence. It is helpful for probabilistic learning. Figure 6.8 explains the relation extraction process.

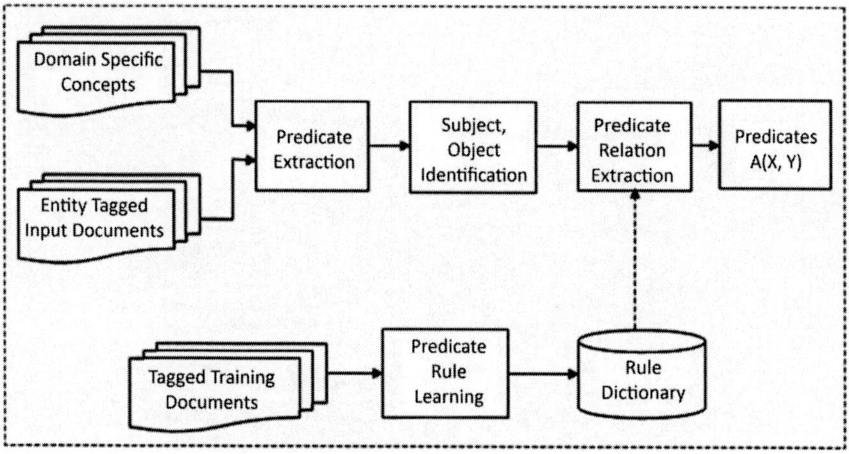

Figure 6.8: Relation Extraction Process

Predicate Extraction

The morphological analyzer identifies the verb in a sentence and is set as a predicate. Verbs are categorized based on the argument type and several arguments using manually tagged training documents.

Argument Extraction

For each predicate, the argument is identified based on the verb category and has a combination of arguments. The arguments are specified with the help of PNG markers. Some arguments are SRC, DEST, SUB, DOBJ, and IOBJ.

Predicate Relation Extraction

Nouns are identified as subjects or objects matched for appropriate concepts with a concept list. Predicate relation can be extracted after identifying arguments in a sentence. Figure 6.9 Prediction Relation.

Predicate Rule Learning

Rules are necessary to predicate relations learned from the tagged training corpus and stored as a rule dictionary.

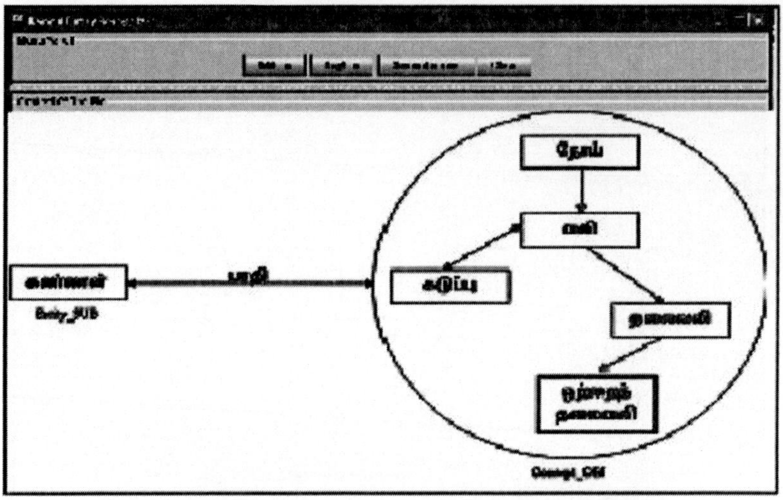

Sl. No	*Tamil word*	*Transliterated*	*English*
1	கண்ணன்	kannan	kannan
2	பாதி	pAthi	pathi
3	கடுப்பு	katuppu	
4	நோய்	nOi	disease
5	தலைவலி	thalaivali	Head ache
6	ஒற்றைத்தலைவலி	otRRaithavali	sinus

Figure 6.9: Prediction Relation

Figure 6.9 thick-lined rectangular node shows the word found as a concept and object in the given input. Entity_SUBand Concept_OBJ are tagged with the predicate that relate subject and object.

6.2 INFORMATION RETRIEVAL SYSTEM

It is essential to archive and retrieve information when needed. In this computer era, storing and retrieving a considerable amount of data is accessible. Information retrieval (IR) system is growing to fulfill the various users' needs. The requirement for Tamil literary information retrieval of different documents is increased and helps to share on the internet. Most Tamil IR systems read the text, identify whether the word is a verb or noun, and find the word from the database. It is time-consuming because the search is done after the entire word is entered. So, to start searching when the first word is entered is always the best.

The IR system of the Tamil system was complicated due to the old period Tamil was in poetry format. Usually, the IR system returns the comprehensive directory of papers per worker inquiry and consumes processing time, memory, and disk space. Getting a high precision quality result with less searching turnaround time is critical. The vector space model is used for analysis for data extraction of Tamil documents.

6.2.1 System Architecture

The system architecture is displayed in Figure 6.10; in these 3 phases are present: i) Classification and Indexing, (ii) Text Processor, and (iii) Retrieval Unit.

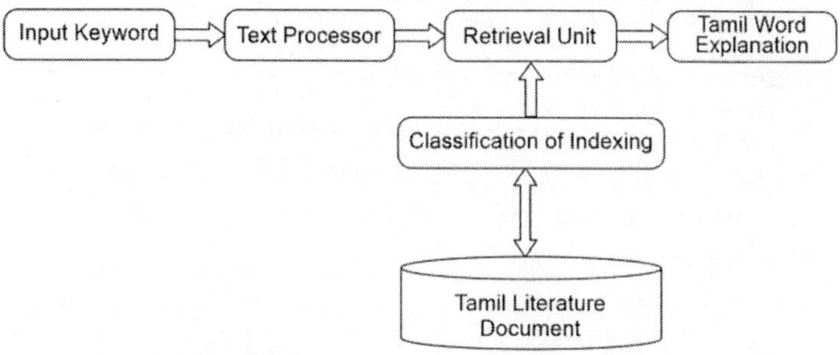

Figure 6.10: System Architecture of IR

Classification and Indexing

It has the following set of tasks.

- Identify the significant groups and classify them into various categories.
- Identify the main topics that is heading the groups.

Tamil letters	**Vowels (V)**	**Short (V-S)**	அ	இ	உ	எ	ஒ	ஐ
		Long (V-L)	ஆ	ஈ	ஊ	ஏ	ஓ	ஔ
	Consonants (C)	**Hard (C-H)**	க்	ச்	ட்	த்	ப்	ற்
		Medium (C-M)	ய்	ர்	ள்	வ்	ழ்	ல்
		Soft (C-S)	ங்	ஞ்	ண்	ந்	ம்	ன்

Figure 6.11: Tamil Vowel-Consonant Table

- Issues are arranged gradually with subtitles.
- All keywords placed with topics and subtitles.

A database table is classified into five components like Vowel-Short (V-S), Vowel-Long (V-L), Consonant-Hard (C-H), Consonant-Medium (C-M), Consonant-Soft (C-S) as displayed in Figure 6.11 table. Segregation is done as given below.

- Choose the number of papers to include in the query.
- Go over each paper word by word.
- Conduct a CV assessment to identify the first letter of the term as vowel and consonant. If it is a vowel, place it as long or short and update the word with type in a database table.
- Check if the first letter of the term is consonant; check type as hard, medium, and soft. Update the time in the database table based on the style.

Text Processor

Text processors process and evaluate every letter based on the phonemes of Tamil. The system will detect the Tamil virtual keyboard if the key is pressed as a vowel or consonant, as displayed in Figure 6.12.

முதல் ==>மு = ம் + உ
(CV) = (C-M) (V-S)
த = த் + அ
(CV) = (C-M) (V-S)
ல் = (C-S)

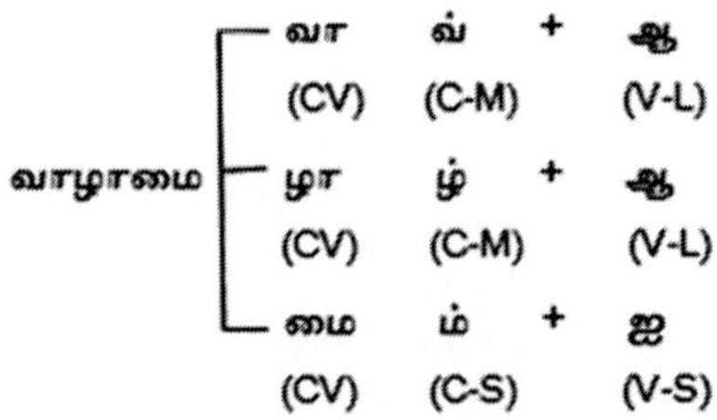

Figure 6.12: Input Keywords

After the letter is recognized, trace the letter from the record. The index level must update for each successive letter until the entire word has been scanned. The procedure will continue till all letters are processed.

Retrieval Unit

The Retrieval unit is responsible for retrieving the contents from the Tamil documents through the vector space model. The search performance could be increased when splitting the search as per 1) Main topic search, 2) Subtitle search 3) Keyword search. For example, if the search word is given in Subtitle search other two places, the search can be skipped, which increases efficiency in searching.

Spell Checker

The spell checker identifies errors and provides recommendations to assist the user in repairing the spelling mistake. In general, the user does not enter the first letter wrongly; mainly, the spelling mistakes are expected more in letters like

1) ர ற 2) ல ள ழ 3) ன ண ந

So, the spell checker can be designed to skip the first letter and do the spell check for the rest of the word.

Case 1: If the single combination is available in DB, get the word and replace it.

Case 2: If there is more than one combination, list all possible combinations to select.

Case 1: கள்வி → கல்வி புகல், புகள் → புகழ்

அரிதல் → அறிதல்

Case 2: பளம் → பலம் , பழம்

6.2.2 Vector Space Model

The information retrieval process can be done through three classic models.

1. *Boolean Model:* It is a set-theoretic. Document and query are characterized as a set of index terms.
2. *Probabilistic Model:* Modelling documents and inquiry representation is dependent on probability theory.
3. *Vector Space Model:* Model and query are demonstrated as vectors in t-dimensional space. It is based on the term weighing.

6.2.2.1 *Term Weighing*

Term weighing is a prominent feature of the text retrieval system. The terms can be words, phrases, or other indexing factors that can be utilized to recognize the text's contents. As the diverse terms can associate with the various standing of text, a weightage must be provided. Term weight is assigned for each term,

$$\begin{pmatrix} & T_1 & T_2 & \cdots & T_t \\ D_1 & w_{11} & w_{21} & \cdots & w_{t1} \\ D_2 & w_{12} & w_{22} & \cdots & w_{t2} \\ \vdots & \vdots & \vdots & & \vdots \\ \vdots & \vdots & \vdots & & \vdots \\ D_n & w_{1n} & w_{2n} & \cdots & w_{tn} \end{pmatrix}$$

Term Frequency

A term may occurred several time in the document. A score value can be calculated using query term *t*, document *d*, and based on the weight of *t* in *d*. Assign a weight equal to the number of occurrences of term *t* in document *d*. This weighing scheme is referred to as term frequency and denoted as tf_t, d, in which the superscript represents the term and document accordingly.

Document Frequency

It is known as several papers in the assortment containing a term *t* and is denoted as df_t.

Inverse Document Frequency

It is a measurement of the universal position of the term. Divide the total number of documents by several documents containing the term, then take the logarithm of that quotient.

$$idf_t = \log \frac{N}{df_t}$$

Where, *N*: Total number of documents in a collection, df_t: Document frequency.

6.2.2.2 *T_f–id_f Weighing*

To generate the combined weight of each document's term, combine the term frequency definition with inverse document frequency. The t_f–id_f weighing scheme assigns to term *t*, and weight of document this given as,

$$t_f\text{–}idf_t, d = tf_t, d \times idf_t$$

$tf\text{-}idf_{t,}d$ assigned as per the below statements.

1. When the highest *t* occurs many times within a small number of documents.
2. When the lower term occurs a fewer times in a document or many times in a document.
3. When the lowest term occurs a virtually in all the documents.

The effectiveness of searching needs to be completed. The critical property of search effectiveness is recall (Portion of the relevant document retrieved by the system) and precision (a portion of the retrieved document which is appropriate).

6.3 TEXT SUMMARIZATION

In general, text summarization is a text summary produced from one or more texts with a significant portion of the original text. Users like men and machines generate and consume a massive amount of data. So, we need an automated system for text summarization for producing high-quality content at an unpredicted speed. Summarization is classified as extractive and abstractive. Extractive methods aim to collect prominent features, sentences, or elements from the text. But abstractive process generates the summary from scratch without the enforcement to use the original text.

6.3.1 Types of Summarization

Several types are available based on the function of summary, kind of summary, the genre of the document, target audience, number of documents, and supported media type.

Summarization categories based on the type of generated summary.

- *Extractive Summarization:* It mainly focuses on selecting a subset of the existing text units (word/phrase/sentence) in the original text by assigning a weightage to each textual unit and picking the most informative unit to create a summary.
- *Abstractive Summarization:* This method uses a semantic representation of text and NLP techniques to create a summary from scratch. There can be grammatical correctness and more coherence. But in practical due to poor performance, extractive summaries are preferred.

Summarization categories based on several documents.

- *Single-Document Summarization:* The system takes one document as input and produces a summary of the input document. Sentence ranking is essential.
- *Multi-Document Summarization:* The system takes multiple documents referring the same theme/cluster and produces a single summary of the original multi-document text. It supports two-fold approaches.
    (a) *Sentence Ranking:* Based on their informativeness, scoring is done.
    (b) *Sentence Selection:* Selecting top *k*-sentences based on a ranking score the selected sentences should not be redundant.

Summarization categories based on the content of the summary.

- *Indicative Summarization:* This mainly concentrates on reducing the length of the original text by 90% but fails to provide factual information. It helps the user to read the document.

- *Informative Summarization:* Content is a little longer with a reducing length of 70–80%. It includes facts and information which can replace the original text.
- *Evaluative Summarization:* It aims to capture the opinion or views of the author on a given subject. It is also referred to as opinion-based summarization.

Summarization categories based on the target audience.

- *Generic Summarization*: It focuses on a general audience and is independent of the document domain and the intended user's purpose.
- *Query-focused Summarization:* It is based on the user's query. The system generates the summary based on the user's query, a phrase, keyword, or question. Search engines are based on this summarization.
- *Update Summarization:* It is a special summarization where the user looks for the content which is new/novel. Detecting the novelty after the summary of the content is a crucial step.

Summarization categories based on the type of summarizer.

- *Author Summarization:* It reflects the author's point of view and is a non-technical document in an understandable format.
- *Expert Summarization:* It is produced by domain experts but not skilled in summarization.
- *Professional Summarization:* It is produced by professional summarizers but not domain experts.

The summarization categories are based on input and output language:

- *Monolingual Summarization:* The input text and summary are in the same language.
- *Multilingual Summarization:* The system still functions in multiple languages; the input and summarization follow the same vocabulary.
- *Cross-lingual Summarization:* It can process several languages; input text and summary are in different languages.

6.3.2 Single Document Extractive Summarization

This section discusses the single document extractive summarization. The convolutional bidirectional extended short-term memory network is used to capture better document summarization. Based on the deep networks, data-driven and end-to-end enhanced encoders and decoders can summarize news articles. The hybrid MemNet model can be used for summarization which consists of a document reader (encoder) and sentence extractor (decoder).

6.3.2.1 *Hybrid MemNet Model*

The architecture of this model is represented in Figure 6.13. This model has two main blocks like.

- ***Document Encoder:*** Responsible for capturing local information (n-grams) and global information (Sentence level) and the notion of summary-worthy sentences.
- ***Decoder:*** Attention-based sequence to sequence decoder.

Document Encoder

The document encoder is responsible for incorporating m-gram features and sentence-level information with the notion of prominence and redundancy of sentences. The Hybrid MemNet model is represented with Convolutional Long Short-Term Memory (Conv-LSTM; for hierarchical encoding) and MemNet (for capturing salience and redundancy).

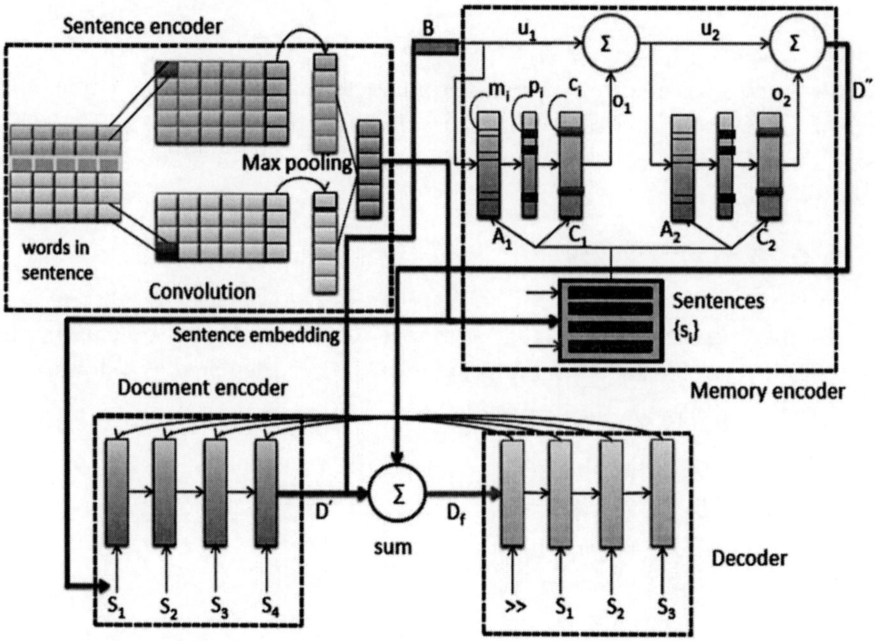

Figure 6.13: Architecture of Hybrid MemNet Model

Convolutional LSTM Document Encoder

The recurrent neural network has a vanishing gradient problem on the long sequence of the LSTM network. To obtain the hierarchical document encoding, a sentence vector can be found from the convolutional sentence encoder fed to LSTM, which is responsible for capturing both local and global sentential information.

MemNet Based Document Encoder: This model uses attention and captures the temporal context. For a document D from the sentence, the encoder gets input sentence vectors set as $s_1, s_2, \ldots, s_i$.

Let D' be the document representation of D obtained from the Conv-LSTM model, and D'' is the document embedding from the MemNet model. The entire set of $\{s_i\}$ is transformed into memory vectors $\{m_i\}$ of dimension d in continuous space, using a learned weight matrix A (of size $d \times v$; where v is the embedding size of a sentence). Similarly, an input document embedding $D0$ is transformed via a learned weight matrix B with the same dimension as A to obtain internal state u. We then compute the match between u and each memory m_i by taking the inner product followed by softmax.

$$p_i = \text{softmax}\,(u^T m_i)$$

where softmax $(z_i) = e^{z_i} / \sum_j e^{z_j}$ and p is the probability vector over the inputs. Each s_i has a corresponding output vector c_i (using another embedding matrix C). The output vector from memory o is computed as the sum over the transformed inputs c_i, weighed by the probability vector from the input as follows.

$$o = \sum_i p_i c_i$$

In the case of a multiple-layer model to handle K hop operation, the memory layer is stacked, and input to layer $k + 1$ is calculated as follows,

$$u^{k+1} = u^k + o^k$$

D'' obtained from the last memory unit o^k. Final unified document representation D_f. It is calculated as the summation of output from the Conv-BLSTM (D') and output of MemNet (D'').

$$D_f = D' + D''$$

D_f captures the hierarchical information and notion of the worthiness of a sentence.

Decoder

The decoder uses LSTM to label sentences sequentially by taking care of individual relevance and mutual redundancy. Labeling the following sentence is done by considering the document encoding and the previously labeled sentences. If encoder hidden states are $(h_1, h_2, h_3 \dots . h_m)$ and decoder hidden states are $(\hat{h}_1, \hat{h}_2, \hat{h}_3 \dots . \hat{h}_m)$ at time step *t*, then for t^{th} sentence, the decoder equations are as follows.

$$\hat{h}_t = LSTM\ p_{t-1}s_{t-1}, \hat{h}_{t-1}$$

$$p(yL(t) = 1 \mid (D) = \sigma\ (MLP)(\hat{h}: h_t))$$

Where, p_{t-1} is the degree to which the decoder assumes the previous sentence that is a part of the summary and memorized.

6.3.3 Neural Sentence Ranking of Multiple Documents

To improvise the sentence scoring task, the notion of sentence saliency depends on incorporating document-dependent and independent features. The document relied on features are position and term frequency. The independent document features include length, stop-word ratio, and word polarity. The independent document feature allows for deciding the summary-worthy document.

For the neural data-driven model Convolutional Sentence Tree Indexer (CSTI) is used to capture a semantic and compositional aspect of a sentence.

6.3.3.1 *HNet Model Architecture*

The system architecture is displayed in Figure 6.14. This model architecture allows measuring the sentence summary worthiness by combining document having dependent and independent features. It has two major components.

CSTI: Captures local and global information and the notion of sentence saliency.

Extractor: Extracts document-dependent features from the given sentence.

Convolutional Sentence Tree Indexer

This method is used to get the sentence information with minimum loss of information. So global information is discovered and local information is preserved.

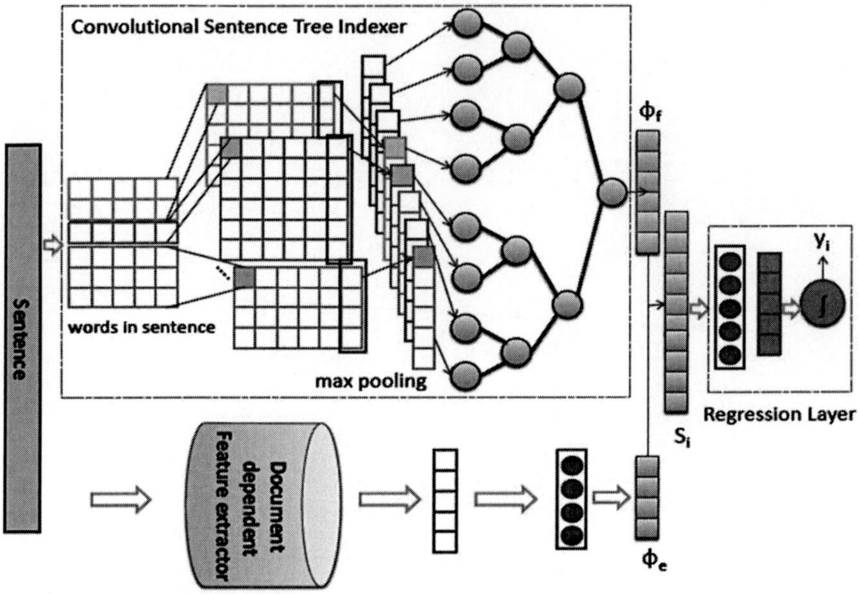

Figure 6.14: Architecture of HNet

CSTI has Convolutional Encoder and Bidirectional Long Short Term Memory Tree Indexer (BLSTM Tree Indexer).

Convolutional Encoder

A convolutional neural network (CNN) with multiple filters automatically captures a set of phrases (n-grams) based on features, followed by pooling operations to ger a set of feature vectors. The CNN can be easily trained without long-term dependency. It also handles variable sentence length and learns n-grams effectively. It is used successfully in sentence-level classification and sentiment analysis.

Bidirectional Long Short Term Memory Tree Indexer

BLSTM is used to obtain the independent document feature by combining semantic and compositional aspects in a sentence. It captures the semantic and compositional elements of the document. The Bi-LSTM provides the sequential power of LSTMs and the compositional power of the recursive model without a parse tree. This model constructs a binary tree to process the input sequences with a node function in a bottom-up approach. It creates a single vector of root nodes for all information.

Extractor

Apart from the document-independent features, the document-dependent features are also required for better sentence salient estimation. Consider the position of the sentence, average clustered frequency values of words in a sentence, average term frequency values of words in the sentence, average word IDF values in a sentence, divided by sentence length, and maximal word IDF score in a sentence.

6.3.4 Neural Sentence Selection for Multi-Document

Sentence ranking and sentence selection are essential in extracting multiple document text summarization. Handling redundancy in numerous documents is challenging. In order to select the right sentence the sentence ranking approach is used.

This system has two main components as below.

- *CSTI Base Network:* It incorporates document-independent features with document-dependent features, which are then forwarded to the regression layer to obtain the salient sentence score.
- *Distance Metric Layer:* Predicts the similarity; thus, it helps identify the redundant sentence.

6.4 MACHINE TRANSLATION SYSTEM

Machine translation is an automatic translation process of one language to another language using Natural Language Processing. The translation is not a word replacement. It must interpret and analyze all the words. It requires an in-depth knowledge of grammar, sentence structure, idioms and phrases, and the origin of different cultures. Cross-culture understanding is challenging to address to achieve better translation records. Many types of research exist for syntax, semantics, pragmatics and discourse.

It is a great challenge to design an automatic machine translation system by considering all the required information. Two individual human translators cannot produce identical translations for the same text in the same language pair. So, designing a fully automated translator with high-quality translation is difficult. Machine translation is an essential module in speech translation systems—machine translation in language learning is unfamiliar due to poor output. A sound machine translation system can help students to improve students writing and translation skill.

Rule approaches are used to develop a machine translation system, in which rules are fed into the machine using appropriate representations. It is challenging to provide all linguistics information to a machine. But in the statistical translation model, it learns translation patterns directly from data and generalize them to translate a new text. SMT approach is a language-approach. SMT can be coupled with new models for re-ordering and decoding. It has to learn parallel corpora for generating a translation system.

6.4.1 Statistical Machine Translation

Statistical Machine Translation (SMT) works well for translating a specific domain with the engine trained with a bilingual corpus. An SMT system needs high computing hardware resources to train the model, and billions of calculations are required to train the machine. SMT automatically generates statistical patterns. SMT can generate more natural or closer to the literal translation. As long as the model is set up, the SMT model will automatically study the algorithm for parameter estimation.

This section deals with morphology-based prototype factored SMT system for English to Tamil translation system by integrating several linguistic tools. Monolingual corpora of Tamil were collected and factored in using the Tamil POS tagger and morphological analyzer. After preprocessing, the bi-lingual sentences are created and transformed into bi-lingual sentences. These sentences will be used for training the factored SMT.

6.4.1.1 *Architecture of the SMT System*

Tamil morphology rich language is free word order of Subject-Object-Verb pattern while English has Subject-Verb-Object pattern. The base SMT will not perform well for a language with heterogeneous morphological order and which is having different word order. The factored model, a subtype of the SMT system, will allow multiple levels of words from specific levels to general forms of analysis like lemma, POS, and morphological features. Figure 6.15 displays the system architecture for the English to Tamil translation system. This module covers bi-lingual corpora into factored SMT systems using morphology-based linguistic tools and re-ordering rules. The preprocessing model is attached externally to factored SMT system. After the preprocessing, the source language syntax closely matches the target language and decreases the alignment complexity, which is a critical problem in baseline SMT.

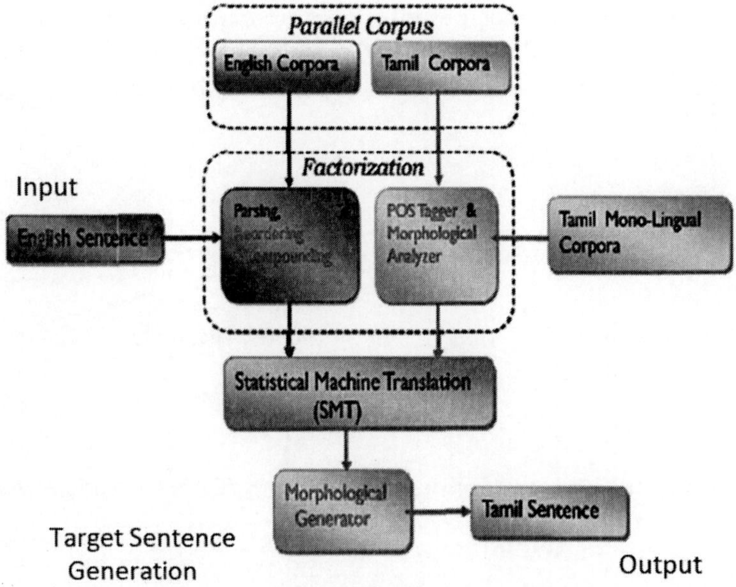

Figure 6.15: SMT System Architecture

Parallel corpora are used to train statistical translation models. The preprocessing technique creates parallel corpora and converts them into factored parallel corpora. POS Tagger and Morphological analyzer are used for the English Stanford Parser tool and the Tamil language. Monolingual corpus is collected and factored using Tamil linguistic tools. In post-processing, a Tamil morphological generator generates a surface word from output factors.

6.4.1.2 *Pre-Processing English Language Sentence*

Pre-processing is performed on the raw source language sentence to translate into a language sentence. English language sentence consists of re-ordering, factorization, and compounding.

Re-ordering English Language Sentence

Rearrange the source language's word order into word order closer to the target language sentence. Tamil and English word orders are different. So the syntactic structure must be processed. Tamil follows SOV word order, and English follows SVO word order. English syntactic relation is retrieved from the Standford Parser tool, and its sentence is re-order based on re-ordering rules. One hundred eighty re-ordering rules are framed based on the sentence structure of Tamil and English, and 80% of English sentences are re-ordered correctly according to the rules developed. Sample re-ordering is done as below Figure 6.16.

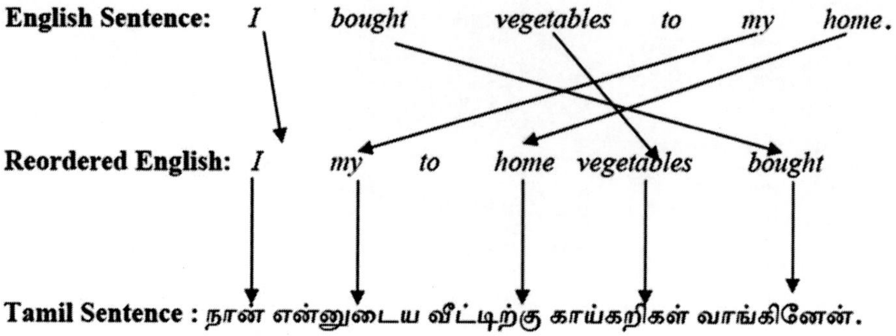

Figure 6.16: Re-ordered English Sentence

Factorization of English Language Sentence

Factored models are used in morphologically rich language to reduce the amount of bi-lingual data. Factorization refers to splitting the word into linguistic factors and integrating it as a vector. Standford parser is used to parse the English sentence and create the parsed tree, linguistic information like lemma, POS tags, and syntactic and syntactic information are retrieved. This linguistic information is integrated as factors in the original word.

Compounding for English Language Sentence is Collected

Additional morphological information is collected like function word, subject information, dependency relations, auxiliary verbs, and modal verb translated into the morphological factor of the source language words. The function words are identified from English corpora in the compounding phase using dependency identification. Specified function words were removed from factored sentences and attached with morphological factors to the corresponding content word. Compounding reduces the length of English sentences by removing functional words, auxiliary verbs, and modal verbs also removed and attached to the morphological factor of the source language words. After this, the morphological representation of English sentences will be similar to Tamil language sentences. Table 6.17A and Table 6.17B show the factored and compounded sentences, respectively.

Table 6.17A: Factored English Sentences

I | *i* | *PN* | *prn*
my | my | *PN* | *PRP$*
home | home | *N* | *NN*
to | *to* | *TO* | *TO*
vegetables | vegetable | *N* | *NNS*
bought | buy | *V* | *VBD.*

Table 6.17B: Compounded English Sentences

I | *i* | *PN* | *prn_i*
my | my | *PN* | *PRP$*
home | home | *N* |*NN_to*
vegetables | vegetable | *N* | *NNS*
bought | buy | *V* | *VBD_1S.*

6.4.1.3 *Factored SMT System for English to the Tamil Language*

Factored translation integrates additional morphological and lexical information like lemma, word class, gender, number, etc., at the word level on the source and the target languages. An efficient search algorithm quickly finds the highest probability translation among an exponential number of choices. In the SMT system, three different toolkits are implemented using GIZA++, SRILM, and Moses. Figure 6.18 explains the mapping of English and Tamil factors in Factored SMT System.

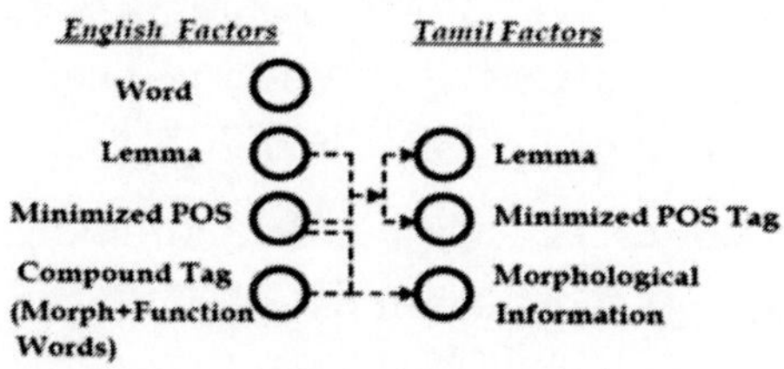

Figure 6.18: Mapping English Word Factors to Tamil Word Factors

Morphological, syntactic, and semantic information can be integrated as factors in factored translation models during training. English factors "Lemma" and "Minimized-POS" are aligned to Tamil factors "Lemma" and "M-POS" then "Minimized-POS" and "Compound-Tag" factors of English word aligned to "Morphological information" factor Tamil word. Elements are generated from the SMT system, and surface word is generated in the post-processing stage. The system is evaluated with sentence patterns like simple, continuous, and modal auxiliaries and 85% of the sentences are translated correctly.

6.4.2 Factored SMT System for English to Tamil

The integration of linguistic knowledge in factored translation models and the development of factored corpora.

6.4.2.1 *Statistical Machine Translation*

The noise channel model is used in speech recognition and machine translation. Suppose you must translate sentence f in the source language F to a sentence e in the target language E. In that case, the noisy channel model describes the situation as the sentence f to be translated initially conceived in language E as some sentence*s*. During the process, sentence e was corrupted by the channel to sentence *f*. Each sentence in E is a translation of the sentence with some probability, and the sentence chose the translation ($\widehat{e}$) is the one that has the highest probability,

$$\hat{e} = arg_e \max \frac{P(e)P(f|e)}{p(f)}$$

Since f is permanently fixed, P*(f)* is omitted in the maximization step in the above equation.

$$\hat{e} = arg_e \max (P(e)P(f|e))$$

$P(f|e)$ is split into $P(e)$ and $P(e|f)$ according to Bayes rule. When the words in *f* are translations of words is e. When the English sentence "He will come tomorrow" is translated into Tamil, both $P(e|f)$ and $P(f|e)$ are same.

ஆவன் நாளை வருவான் – (avan nALaai varuvAn)

ஆவன் வருவான் நாளை – (avan varuvvAn nALai)

The second sentence will be removed as the first sentence has a higher value of *P*(*e*).

Components of SMT

The main element of SMT is,

1. Translation model
2. Language model
3. The Statistical Machine Translation Decoder.

Translation Model

The system can produce the words that retrieve the original meaning and arrange those words in sequences of the target language. The role of the translation model is to find $P(f|e)$. The training corpus for the translation model is a sentence-aligned parallel corpus of the languages and E. The parallel corpus can support only the sentence alignments and does not provide the word alignment. The probability of given source sentence *f* translated into sentence *e*.

The word alignment in sentences can tell how the sentence *f* is translated into e. **Expectation-Maximization** (EM) algorithm is used to identify the word alignment probabilities of the training corpus, which is sentence aligned.

Expectation-Maximization Algorithm

Expectation-Maximization: When the number of times a word aligns with the corpus is identified, it is easy to calculate word translation probabilities. If a uniform word translation probability is started, calculate alignment probabilities and use these alignment probabilities to get better translation probabilities. This iterative procedure is called Expectation Maximization.

Language Model

The language model is used to estimate the fluency of translated sentences. The best fluent sentence with a high value of $P(e)$among all possible generations of $P(f|e)$. The high value is assigned to fluent sentences and the low value for the least fluent sentence.

For example, consider

"The pen is on the table."

Which can be translated into

"**எழுதுகோல் மேஜையின் மேல் உள்ளது**"
"**எழுதுகோல் மேல் மேஜையின் உள்ளது**"
"**மேஜையின் மேல் எழுதுகோல் உள்ளது**"

The language model assigns the probability more significant in the first sentence than in the other two sentences.

The Statistical Machine Translation Decoder

The Statistical Machine Translation Decoder finds a target translated sentence for the source sentence using the translation model and language model. This decoder uses the best-first search based on heuristics. The decoder constructs the possible translation and looks for the most probable. Greedy decoders and beam search decoders are essential decoders available for the statistical machine translation decoders. In greedy decoders, the initial hypothesis is done using word to word and later refined iteratively using hill-climbing heuristics. Beam decoders use a heuristic search algorithm to explore graphs by expanding the most promising node in a limited set.

Tools Used in SMT System

Moses

It is an open-source tool kit for SMT. It has an efficient data structure that allows memory-intensive translation and language models using considerable data resources with limited hardware. It uses a beam search algorithm that quickly finds the highest probability translation among the exponential number of choices. Two types of translation models are present in Moses.

1. Phrase-based translation models
2. Tree-based translation models

Moses allows decoding the confusion network and word lattices to integrate ambiguous upstream tools like automatic speech recognizers.

GIZA++ and MKCLS

GIZA++ is an SMT tool kit used by IBM model 1–5 and an HMM word alignment model. It is an extension of GIZA. It implements HMM alignment model and various smoothing techniques for fertility, distortion, or alignment parameters. It uses the Mkcls tool for unsupervised classification, which helps the model.

SRILM

SRILM is for language modeling used in speech recognition, statistical tagging and segmentation, and statistical machine translation. It is a collection of C++ libraries, executable programs, and supporting scripts. It implements smoothing algorithms like Good-Turing, Absolute discounting, Written-Bell, and modified newer-Ney.

6.5 QUESTION AND ANSWERING SYSTEM

Question and answering systems (QAS) are a combination of information retrieval and natural language processing involving building systems that automatically answer the questions presented by humans in natural language. QAS requires more complex Natural Language Process (NLP) techniques due to an extensive search of answer matching rules and answer types. In the QA, questions can be classified as yes or no, factoid, list, and definitional. The answer complexity depends on the question type, and the current QA system depends on the question classifier module. After the questions are analyzed, the complex NLP techniques are applied to obtain accurate and concise answers. Developing a QAS system for Tamil is a thought-provoking task due to its partially free-word order nature with no capitalization of proper nouns and rich in morphology. In this chapter, we discuss the design and implementation of the factoid-type QAS.

The significant components of Tamil QAS are shown in Figure 6.19. This system consists of information retrieval, information extraction, and

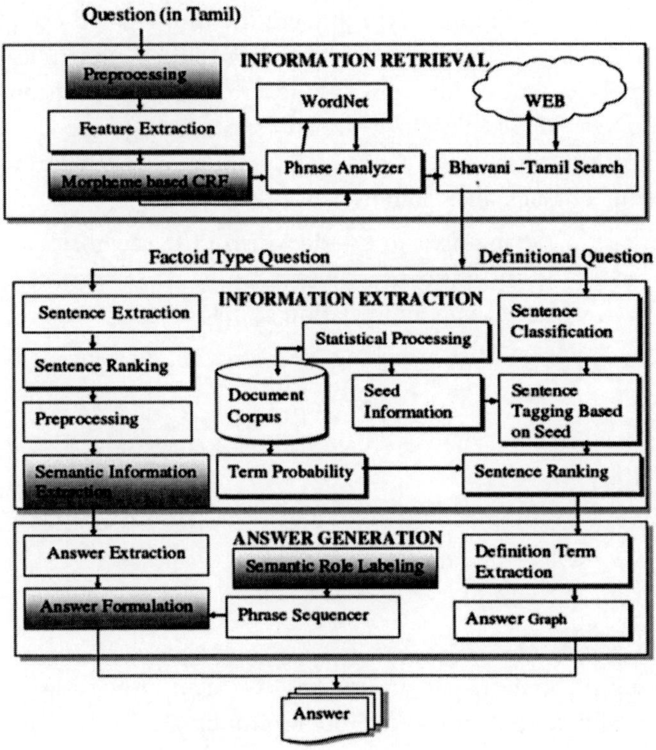

Figure 6.19: Tamil QAS

answer generation. The information retrieval component accepts user queries and gets a relevant document from the web. The information extraction component is responsible for extracting semantic and seed-based information for factoid and pertinent definitional questions from the documents. The answer generation component formulates factoid questions and makes a ranked system for definitional who-type questions.

6.5.1 Information Retrieval

Natural Language Processing (NLP) is significant in text corpus analysis. The information retrieval system consists of preprocessing, feature extraction, morpheme-based CRF model, and phrase analyzer. Part of speech (POS) tagging and chunking are necessary for the question and answering system. The design of POS tagging is based on the sequence of morphological sub-components proceeding and uses its context for processing. Chunking is based on the morphological sub-components of the preceding, current, and succeeding words that are considered for handling the unique characteristics of Tamil. The corpus linguists typically use the fine-grained classifications of the word, and they are referred to as POS tags. These tags indicate syntactic categories, such as noun, verb, adjective, adverb, etc., and occasionally include number and verb tense. The first task of POS tagging is to decide the tags from various POS tag sets. A probabilistic model is suited for a partial free word ordering language like Tamil.

The task of POS tagging is to decide which POS categories are associated with the word in the current context. For example, POS tags are appended at the end of each word with an abbreviation as below sentence.

Children NNS are VBP watching VBG some DTprograms NNS on IN television NN.

where, NNS – Noun Singular
VBP – Verbal Part
VBG – Verbing
DT – Determinant
IN – Preposition
NN – Noun

Chunking or Shallow parsing is a task to identify and segment the text into syntactically related, non-overlapping groups of words. For a sentence, there are three chunk types (NP – Noun Phrase, VP – Verb Phrase, and

PP – Prepositional Phrase). The chunk tags can vary depending on the information to be captured. The below example shows the chunking process.

[NP Children NNS] (VP are VBP watching VBG) [NP some DT programs NNS] [PP on IN television NN]

6.5.1.1 *Tamil POS Tagging Method*

To decide the Tamil POS tags, the morphological components of a word play a vital role. The morpheme parts and root of a word are used to determine the POS tag and can be statiscally analyzed. Integrating morpheme-based probabilistic models and the Conditional Random Fields (CRF) models provide better results for POStagging. It can be done in two stages. The first stage is preliminary POS tagging on morpheme components of words, which the Naive Bayesprobabilistic model performs. In the second stage, it resolves the conflict through the position and context of the word, which occurs during the first stage.

A tagged corpus can be obtained using the various Tamil web page categories by considering named entity recognition and the question and answering system. The corpus can be tagged with a tag-set of thirty-four POS categories shown in Table 6.1. Use an available morphological analyzer to separate the root word and the associated morpheme components, and they can provide the type of the root word. Thus, the tagged corpus can be obtained, which will be the base of the morpheme component-based probabilistic model.

Table 6.1: List of Tamil Tags and Description

Sl. No.	*Tag*	*Description*	*Example*
1.	N	Noun	Ellai – limit
2.	NI	Noun Inflected	Ellaiai – in limit
3.	NN	Noun + Noun	Mathiya unavu – noon meal
4.	NNI	Noun + Noun Inflected	Paalnilavil – in milk moon
5.	IN	Interrogative Noun	Yaar – who
6.	INI	Interrogative Noun Inflected	Yaaritam – whom
7.	PN	Pronominal Noun	Vanthavar – the person who came
8.	PNI	Pronominal Noun Inflated	Vanthavarai – call the person who came

Sl. No.	*Tag*	*Description*	*Example*
9.	VN	Verbal Noun	Nataththal – walking
10.	VNI	Verbal Noun Inflected	Nataththalal – by walking
11.	Pn	Pronoun	Avan – he
12.	PnI	Pronoun Inflected	Avanukku – him
13.	Nn	Nominal Noun	Varuvathu – thing that coming
14.	NnI	Nominal Noun Inflected	Varuvathai – thing that coming
15.	V	Verb	Vaa – come
16.	VI	Verbal Inflected	Varum – will come
17.	Vinf	Verb Infinitive	Varukira – coming
18.	Vvp	Verb Verbal Participle	Kotukka – to give
19.	Vrp	Verbal Relative Participle	Vantha – [b oy] who came
20.	AV	Auxiliary Verb	Natanthu kontiru – is walking
21.	FV	Finite Verb	varukiRathu – come
22.	NFV	Negative Finite Verb	vaRathu – will not come
23.	adv	Adverb	Veekamaaka – fast
24.	SI	Sub-ordinate Clause Conjunction Inflected	AppoluthE – when itself
25.	SCC	Sub-ordinate Clause Conjunction	Appoluthu – when
26.	Par	Particle	Pinnar, poothu, maRRum – after, when, and
27.	adj	Adjective	Azhakiya – beautiful
28.	Iadj	Interrogative Adjective	Entha, evvalavu – which, how
29.	Dadj	Demonstrative Adjective	Intha, antha, ithan athan – this, that, its, that's
30.	Inter	Interjection	Aha, oho, waw, yov – oh!
31.	Int	Intensifier	Caala, athi, caRRu – very good, very old
32.	CNum	Character Number	naaRpathu, nallaaliram – forty
33.	Num	Number	42, 432
34.	DT	Date Time	Naalai, maalai – tomorrow, evening

Naive Bayes Probabilistic Model

To determine the word's POS tag, this model considers the lexical category of the root word along with morphological components. If a word is a root, then the POS category is the same as the root word's lexical category. Suppose a word is a combination of root and a single morphological component. In that case, the probabilistic model is designed to consider the lexical category of the root word and the morphological element. It is explained in equation 5.1.

$$arg \max_{i\in\{T\}} P\ (\text{pos}_i/\text{word}) = \alpha_1 p\ (\text{pos}_i/\text{root\_type(word)}) + \alpha_2 p\ (\text{pos}_i/e_1(\text{word})) \quad \ldots (5.1)$$

where $i \in \{T\}$ Represents ith POS tag belongs to POS tag set T in Table 6.1. α_1 and α_2 determine the importance of contributing factors, always $\alpha_1 + \alpha_2 = 1$, and this is estimated using the evidence in the corpus. The probability of a given word belonging to a particular POS tag category is $P\ (\text{pos}_i/\text{word})$. The given word has a root and morphological ending e_1. The prior probability of POS tag can be mentioned using a particular root type and a morphological ending as $p\ (\text{pos}_i/\text{root\_type (word)})$ and $p\ (\text{pos}_i/e_1(\text{word}))$ respectively. The prior probability can be calculated as below equation 5.2,

$$p\ (\text{pos}_i/e_1(\text{word})) = \frac{P\ (\text{pos}_i)p(e_1(\text{word})/\text{pos}_i)}{P(e_1(\text{word}))} \quad \ldots (5.2)$$

with the below constraints,

$$\sum_{i=1}^{34} P\ (pos_i) = 1$$

$$\sum_{i=1}^{34} p\ (e_1(\text{word})/\text{pos}_i) = 1$$

pos_i= In the given corpus, posterior independent probability of the particular POS i.

$p\ (e_1(\text{word})/\text{pos}_i)$ = the posterior probability of the final morphological component, which gives the POS tag from the tagged corpus.

$P\ (e_1(\text{word}))$ = the posterior independent probability of the final morphological component, computed from the tagged corpus. It is calculated as below equation 5.3.

$$P\ (e_1(\text{word})) = \sum_{i=1}^{k} p(\text{pos}_i)p(e_1(\text{word})/\text{pos}_i) \quad \ldots (5.3)$$

In the last, the probability is calculated as,

$$P\ (e_{1-1}(\text{word})) = \sum_{i=1}^{k} p(\text{pos}_i)p(e_{1-1}(\text{word})/\text{pos}_i)$$

Where, $P\ (e_{1-1}(\text{word}))$ calculated as the summation of all possible POS types k.

$P(e_{1-1}(\text{word}))$, the product of $p(\text{pos}_i)$, the posterior probability of the given post type I in corpus and $P(e_{1-1}(\text{word}))$. The posterior probability of the final morpheme component.

The coarse step finds the optimal value of the parameter up to one decimal point.

Performance Evaluation of POS

The performance can be evaluated using precision, recall, and f-measure, generally used in assessing an information retrieval system.

$$\text{Precision (p)} = \frac{\text{No. of items tagged correctly}}{\text{Total No of items tagged}}$$

A recall is defined as the portion of the target item that the system is meant to tag,

$$\text{Recall (R)} = \frac{\text{No. of items tagged by system}}{\text{Total No. of items to be tagged}}$$

Single measure (F) evaluates the overall performance,

$$F = \frac{1}{\alpha\frac{1}{P}+(1-\alpha)\frac{1}{R}} \text{ and simplified as } F = \frac{2PR}{P+R}$$

Where α is a factor, P and Rare precision and recall, respectively.

The Perplexity factor is helpful to judge the probabilistic model to match with the test corpus, and it is measured as,

$$H(\text{tag\_type}) = -\frac{1}{n}\sum_{i=1}^{n} \log(p\ (\text{tag}(w_i)))$$

$$\text{perplexity (tag\_type)} = 2^{H(\text{tag\_type})}$$

This model is evaluated using a test corpus with 43,678 words, in which 36,128 words are morphologically analyzed from a tag set. The following graph depicts results obtained by the probabilistic models for determining the tags.

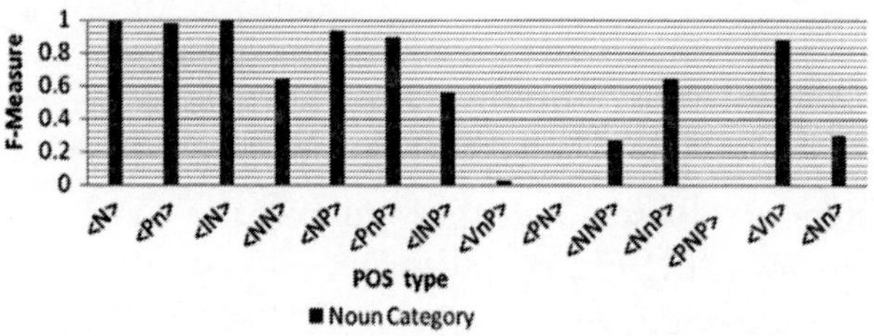

Figure 6.20: F-Measure for the Pos Tag of the Noun Category

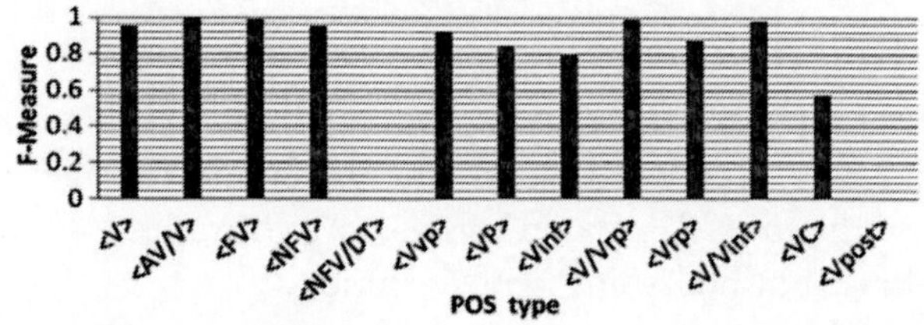

Figure 6.21: F-Measure for the Pos Tag of the Verb Category

Conditional Random Fields for Ambiguity Resolution

Tamil is a partially free word order language; it allows words to be present in any order. So conditional random fields are suitable for representing a pattern. CRF is an undirected graphical model $p(x|z)$, the conditional distribution over the hidden variables x for the given observations z.

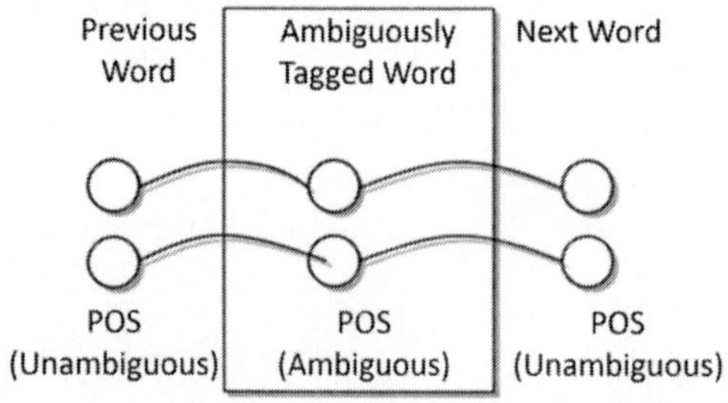

Figure 6.22: CRF Models to Disambiguate the Ambiguous Tag

The selection of features is an essential part of the CRF model. Its context resolves the ambiguity of a language. So the model is framed by focusing on the ambiguity-tagged word, its previous and next term. The patterns are collected from the last phase POS tagged, the initial corpus disambiguates them, and the model has to be trained. Figure 6.22 shows the CRF model to disambiguate.

The state feature can be current, previous, following words, and POS of recent, prior and subsequent words.

The transition features are

- POS (current word)/Root type (previous word)
- POS (Next word)/POS (current word)
- Current word/previous word
- Next word/previous word

6.5.1.2 *Chunking for Tamil*

Chunking depends on morpheme endings and their root type—the morpheme end part of a word allows for predicting the next and previous words. The modified CRF model works on the selected features that is inherent for phrase boundary and type detection.

Morpheme Feature-Based CRF Model

The selected features to design a CRF are POS type, last end morpheme component (E_l), and previous to the end morpheme component (E_{l-1}). A morpheme component of a word can be predicted using previous and following features. So now the window size is set as 3. From left to right, the sequence is set as –1, 0, 1. The zeroth position is considered for chunking to be tagged as *B, I*, or *O*.

So, the state features are: *POS* (–1), *POS* (0), *POS* (1), *E* l–1(–1), *E* l–1 (0), *E* l–1 (1), *E* l (–1), *E* l (0), *E* l (1).

The transition features are: *POS* (–1)/*POS* (0), *POS* (0)/*POS* (1), *E* l–1 (–1)/*E* l–1 (0), *E* l–1 (0)/*E* l–1 (1), *E* l(–1)/*E* l (0), *E* l (0)/*E* l (1), *POS* (–1)/ *POS* (0)/*POS* (1), *E* l–1 (–1)/*E* l–1 (0)/*E* l–1 (1) and *E* l (–1)/*E* l (0))/P (*E* l (1)).

6.5.2 Information Extraction

The information extraction component attempts to classify the question, formulate the queries and retrieve the information. The search engines result in a massive amount of relevant documents based on the user queries. So, the QA system must first classify the questions and process the information. The QA system has two parts: Question Classification (QC) and information Retrieval (IR).

QC is responsible for analyzing the question and formulating a suitable query for the search engine. It assigns the label accurately to the question based on the expected answer type. To determine the types of the expected answers, analyze the question using POS, chunking, and NER. QC is responsible for filtering the irrelevant answer using query and expected answer types. A good QC system should improve the overall performance of the QA system.

6.5.2.1 *The Morpheme-Based CRF Model for QC*

QC has two approaches: Regular expression and handwritten grammar rules to analyze answer types. And another method uses probabilistic techniques, including machine learning and language modelling approach.

Question Taxonomy

It has to decide the exact class for determining the classification problem. The taxonomy using the QA system is classified into two types based on the structure: the flat and the hierarchy type taxonomies. And another is based on size.

Table 6.2: Expected Answer Type Categories Derived from TREC Corpus

Coarse Category	*Fine Category*
Abbreviation	Abb, exp
Entity	Animal, body, color, creative, currency, dis.med., event, food, instrument, lang, letter, other, plant, continued, evaluation, class product, religion, sport, substance, symbol, technique, term, vehicle, word.
Description	Definition, description, manner, reason…
Human	Group, ind, title, description.
Location	City, country, mountain, other, state.
Numeric	Date, count, money, period. volsize, other, speed, perc. code, dist. temp, ordinal, weight, class, order, other, period, size, height, length.

- *Small Taxonomies:* Flat and usually consist of 6–12 different categories.
- *Medium-sized taxonomies:* Either flat or hierarchical and consist of 15–30 different types.
- *Large taxonomies:* Are hierarchical and consist of 50–150 categories.

Two-level hierarchy answer type taxonomy is used in question classification. The 50 answer type classes are chosen to mark the questions, which document entities can recognize. This answer type classification is used to train the model for QC. Tamil questions have been derived by translating the TREC question corpus of 5500 questions. Table 6.2 shows the expected answer type derived from the TREC question corpus.

Morpheme Feature-Based CRF Models

Question statements are initially processed and arranged; the features recognize the expected answer type information regarding the question term's position. The preprocessed question is applied to the CRF model to identify the question in the former position. Figure 6.23 shows the CRF model's features and function in the question. The word is a lexeme corresponding to the position of the previous word with respect to the question word and next word to the question word. The root is the root type of the corresponding word. The M_end denotes the final morpheme part of the corresponding word.

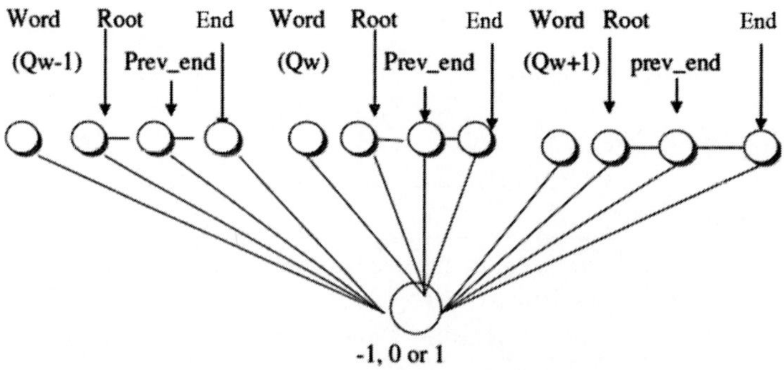

Figure 6.23: Morpheme-Based CRF Models for QC

Table 6.3 shows the transient features in the cliques (denoted transition in the graphical model) considered for the CRF.

Table 6.3: The Transient Features for CRF

M_end(Qw–1)/Root(Qw–1)	M_prev_end(Qw–1)/M_end(Qw–1)
M_end(Qw)/Root(Qw)	M_prev_end(Qw)/M_end(Qw)
M_end(Qw+1)/Root(Qw+1)	M_prev_end(Qw+1)/M_end(Qw+1)

Where M_end (Qw–1)/Root(Qw–1) denotes the transient feature of the Root part of a word at position Qw–1 and the final morpheme part of the same word.

The CRF model analyses the question using the defined model and gives the position considered for the expected answer type (EAT) labelled as –1, 0, 1. Label –1 denotes the last term of the question term, and +1 refers to the term next to the question term. 0 refers to the position of the question term as a reference.

Phrase Analyzer

The phrase analyzer analyzes phrase chunks containing EAT and question words about computing the excellent category of EAT. The hyponym of the headword in a phrase chunk can be using TamilWordNet.

6.5.3 Answer Generation

Selecting the content and generating the sentences is essential to form the absolute answer in the Natural Language Process. Sentence formation of factoid type question answer is based on the answer along with the semantic roles and for who type question is based on the answer graph.

6.5.3.1 *Sentence Formation for Factoid Type*

The answer for factoid type is a single sentence, and a set of phrases that belong to the answer which is collected from the question and extracted information. The phrases are rearranged to form a realistic answer. The procedure for a learner is the ability to realize a sentence from the content of semantic role information. It is a statistical model developed and trained from a preprocessed corpus of sentences. The preprocessing of sentence corpus is POS tagging, chunking, and semantic roles like subject, action, agent, co-agent, location, time, manner, direction, cause, extent, purpose, and modal occurrence in a sentence are tagged. The collective information is statistically analyzed, and the memory-based learner is called the bi-gram model.

The phrase generator generates a sequence of phrases for sentence realization. The memory-based learner is the kernel part, and the model obtained can produce the appropriate sequence for a given input with its semantic role. Figure 6.24 shows the Tamil sentence formation.

The semantic role sequencer is a model that learns sequence from a given corpus containing a collection of sentences. These sentences can be labelled by another model called semantic role labeller. The phrase generator uses information like a person, number, gender, PNG identifier and data set containing rules that generate sentences.

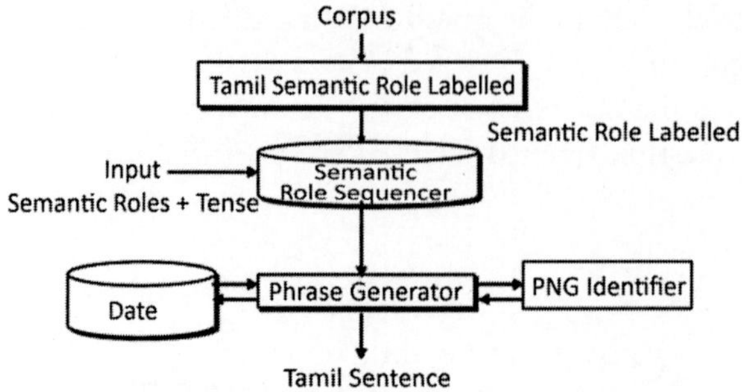

Figure 6.24: Tamil Sentence Formation

Semantic Role Labeler

Semantic role labelling as analyzing the propositions expressed by some target sentence verbs. The elements for each target verb in a sentence fill the semantic role of the verb. The semantic role labeller considers 16 semantic role tag sets. The tag set is,

1. A0 – Agent
2. A1 – Patient
3. A2 – Other Objects like Beneficiary
4. A3 – Co-Agent
5. AM-TMP – Temporal Entity Identifier
6. AM-LOC – Location Identifier
7. AM-MNR – Manner Identifier
8. AM-PRP – Causal Entity Identifier
9. AM-CAU – Purpose Identifier
10. AM-INS – Instrument Identifier
11. AM-DIR – Directional Entity Identifier
12. AM-SRCLOC – Source Locative Entity Identifier
13. AM-DSTLOC – Destination Locative Entity Identifier
14. AM-SRCVAL – Source Numerical Value Identifier
15. AM-DSTVAL – Destination Numerical Value Identifier
16. VRB-PHR – The Phrase Containing the Target Verb

Semantic Role Labeler Architecture

Semantic Role labeller has two main phases: learning and evaluation. The learning phase contains the Maximum Entropy Model (MEM) learning component and verb-frame component as the architecture in Figure 6.25.

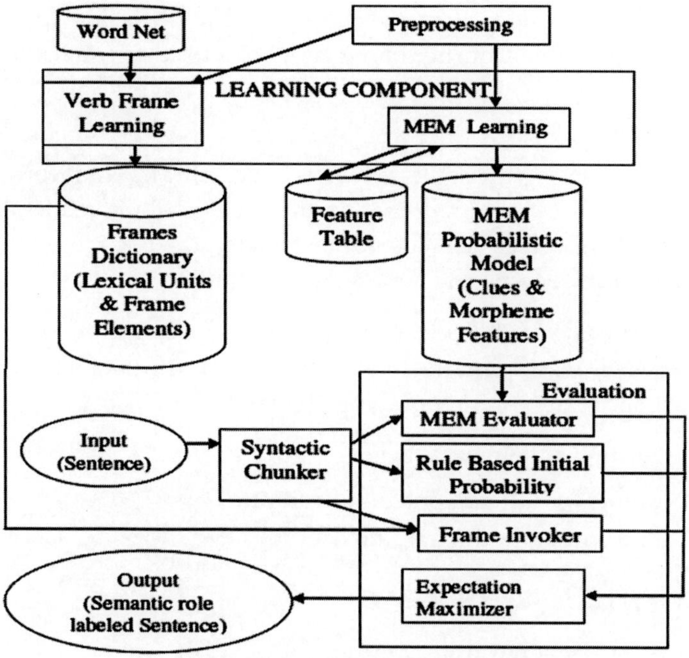

Figure 6.25: The Semantic Role of Labeller

A generalized Iterative Scaling algorithm is used to find MEM and selected for the sematic role classification. The verb-frame component identifies the verb and associated probability of each semantic role that verb can take and encode the information into frames. And frame dictionary was also built.

Evaluation Phase

The evaluation phase contains four main components: the MEM evaluator, the verb-frame invoker, the rule-based probability analyzer, and the EM component.

- *MEM Evaluator:* The probability vector represents the probability of each tag associated with the phrase.
- *Verb Frame Invoker:* The probability of each role associated with the target verb, based on the values in the frame dictionary.
- *The Rule-Based Probability Assigner:* Assign the probability values to tags of phase based on heuristics specific to the Tamil language. The output of these three modules is a tagged sentence with the sematic role labelled, which is then fed into the expectation maximizer component.

- ***Expectation Maximizer Component:*** It uses the EM algorithm to select a maximum probable sequence of semantic roles for the sentence as output.

Learning Phase

This phase consists of a list of sentences with phrases and corresponding semantic roles. It is used to train the semantic role labelling model to identify phrase tags of the given sentence. This phase has two components like Maximum Entropy Model and Verb Frame learning.

Maximum Entropy Model: Generalized Iterative Scaling (GIS) is applied using the <o, s> is set to learn the maximum entropy solution. The assumption made is sequence state for each training observed.

The GIS algorithm is defined as below.

1. N←Number of <phrase, outcome> samples
2. For each feature f_a in the training data

   $f_a \leftarrow (1/N)\sum f_a$ (phrase, outcome)
3. Initialize $\lambda a \leftarrow$ some arbitrary value for each feature
4. The expected frequency of each feature in the model is calculated.

   $E_a = (1/N)\sum\sum P\left(\frac{\text{outcome}}{\text{phrase}}\right) \times f(\text{phrase, outcome})$
5. Update λa to make E_a much closer to F_a

   $\lambda a = \lambda a + \log(F_a) - \log(E_a)$
6. Repeat Steps 4 and 5 until convergence.

Verb Frame Learning Component

Verb frame incurred from the corpus contains verb and probability of semantic roles. Semantic roles depend on the context in which the verb appears. So, the context generator is introduced, which generates the relevant context for the given verb. The headword hypernyms are obtained from WordNet and included in the feature list for a verb-frame.

The pseudo-code is described below.

```
vector learn(Vector sentences)
{
For each verb v in the corpus
```

```
{Add the verb and the list of sentences that have the verb to the
HashMap verb_sentenceList <String, Vector>}
clusterVerbs()
For each Class of verbs c.
{Add the list of sentences containing verbs in c to the vector
cluster_sentences. Build VerbFrame v_f for cluster_sentences using
Maximum Entropy. Add v_f to Vector verbFrames}
Return verb frames;
}
void clusterVerbs()
{
For each verb v in verb_sentenceList
{
Get Troponyms t, Synonyms s of v from WordNet.
If v is already in some Class c{ Add s, t to c }
Else if some verb vInT, in the troponym list t, is in Class c
{Add s, t, v to c }
Else if some verb vInS, in the synonym list s, is in Class c
{Add s, t, v to c }
Else{Create a new Class c Add s, t, v to c }
}
}
```

Semantic Roles Sequencer

The bi-gram module trains the corpus of semantic roles sequence of sentences. It is used to find out the best possible sequence of semantic roles. It is actually a product of probabilities of all the bi-grams in a sequence. The possibility of smoothening distribution generates more accurate statistics of unseen data and integrates conditional probability of individual phrases that appear in the specific slots.

Phrase Generator

This module reads the input from the file and acquires a possible sequence of sematic roles received from the memory biased bi-gram model. Using agent and co-agent identifies person, number, and gender (PNG) used by the verb phrase module. A verb phrase is generated according to the tense and PNG of a noun phrase. The prepositional phrase module generates Prepositional phrases based on semantic roles.

- *Noun Phrase:* The agent is the subject, and it may be a person or group of persons. The person, number, and gender are to be identified.
- *Verb Phrase:* This contains the morphological form of a verb. The expandable verb list has 843 verbs. So the submodule can develop a verbal phrase with a concept of PNG agents.
- *Prepositional Phrase:* Select the appropriate preposition combination according to the semantic role.

6.5.3.2 *Answer for the Definitional Type*

The answer graph is generated through the seed-based pattern matching method, traversed, and the corresponding sentence of the traversed node in the traversing order is arranged as a paragraph. It preserves the coherence of context and avoids the duplication of the sentence.

6.6 TAMIL DICTIONARY

Dictionary, which provides search facilities, allows for identifying a word's meaning and grammatical information. A dictionary provides information like syllables, intonation, and pronunciation of words. The grammatical category is essential to help Natural Language Processing tasks dictionary that represents pronunciation, definition, and etymology. The Universal Networking Language (UNL) is an artificial computer language designed to process information and knowledge.

The UNL is designed to represent semantically language-independent knowledge, concepts, semantic constraint, and relations and has its Universal Word with its vocabulary. The UNL system can represent knowledge language-independent and allow it to move from one language to another easily. UNL has two components: UNL knowledge base or UNL ontology and language-dependent universal-based dictionaries.

Various external Tamil knowledge sources can be used in Tamil dictionary (Agaraadhi), and Tamil WordNet is used to obtain synonyms. Agaraadhi is a Tamil-Tamil-English dictionary that gives the Tamil meaning of a word along with the English meaning. A morphological analyzer extracts the root word POS and specific attributes. The UNL semantic constraints are obtained from the UNLKB. In UNL we can remove redundant and incorrect entries.

6.6.1 The Universal Networking Language

UNL is an artificial language that converts any natural language into a deep semantic representation. UNL is a directed acyclic graph with nodes (represent concept) and edges (relation between the concepts). UNL has 46 semantic relations, which are used to describe the relationship between the concepts. UNL attribute represents mood, tense, and aspects. The process of converting natural language into a UNL equivalent graph is called enconversion, and converting UNL to natural language is called deconversion.

UNL dictionary standard format is given below:

[NLW]{ID} "UW" (ATTR....) < FLG, FRE, PRI > Where,

- *NLW* is the headword of the natural language lexical item.
- *ID* is the unique identifier of the entry.
- *UW* is the Universal word (English word from UNL knowledge base).
- *ATTR* is the list of linguistic features of the NLW; these are set according to the UNL tagset. It also includes the affixation, linear, and sub-categorization rules in the generated dictionary.
- *FLG* is the three-character language code according to ISO 639–33.
- *FRE* is the frequency of NLW in natural texts. It is used in natural language analysis (NL-UNL).
- *PRI* is the priority of the NLW. It is used in natural language generation (UNL-NL).
- *COMMENT* is any comment necessary to clarify the mapping between NL and UNL entries.

Automatic Generation of Tamil—UNL Dictionary

Tamil is a morphologically rich language, so the morphological suffixes express lexical, syntactic, and semantic information, which helps assign semantic constraints quickly and accurately using UNLKB. Figure 6.26 shows the flow diagram of the automatic dictionary. Take a document with infected words run through the morphological analyzer, and then we get the root word, POS, case ending, and other attributes. The root words will be checked against the Tamil-Tamil-English dictionary, and a Tamil WordNet obtains the synonym. These words will be matched with the English WordNet to obtain the equivalent English word. This English word checks in UNLKB/UNL ontology to get the corresponding UWs, and then the UNL entry will be created.

The UNL dictionary has the following steps.

1. Morphological analysis of Tamil words
2. Extraction of Tamil Synonyms

3. Extraction of English meanings and their synonyms
4. Finding UNL semantic constraints
5. Checking semantic similarity of constraints.

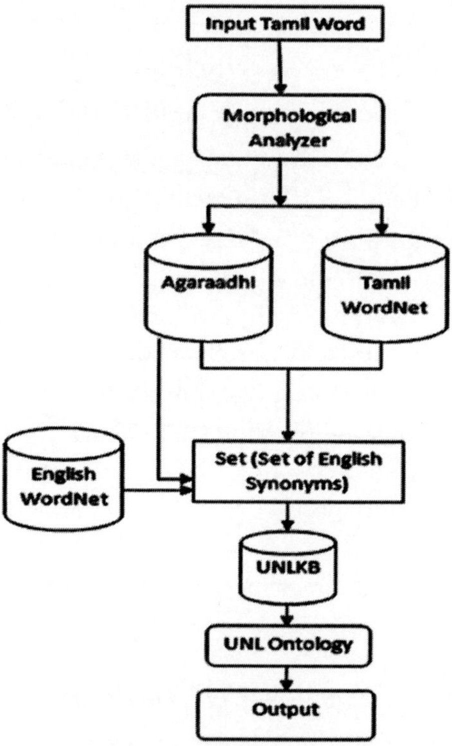

Figure 6.26: Automatic Dictionary

Morphological Analysis of Tamil Words

The extracted Tamil words are given to the Tamil morphological analyzer, root word, and its grammatical information, POS, morphological suffixes, and case markers will be extracted. Three cases can occur in the case of extracting information.

1. Produces correct word as the root word.
2. Unable to handle (unknown words).
3. Produces the incorrect word (root word may or may not be valid).

The root word will be checked in the dictionary; a meaningful word will get the match. Erroneous words will be discarded.

For example:

(a) illathil → illam + noun
<in the house> → house + Noun

(b) ottapanthayam → unknown
<running race> → unknown

(c) vibaritham → vibara + Adjective
<accidental> → details + Adjectives

Extraction of Tamil Synonyms

The morphologically analyzed Tamil root word will be processed in the Agaraadhi dictionary and Tamil WordNet to extract the synonym. Here two sets of synonyms are obtained and intersect to get a new set. This new set of synonyms will have very close meaning and sense.

- *A* → refers to the synonyms which are collected from Agaraadhi.
- *W* → refers to the synonyms which are collected from WordNet.
- *AWi* → refers to the collection of common words from sets *A* and *W*.

For example:

- Agaradhi → illam, thainadu, uttkalam, vittil, mugappu, agam, viidu, oyevidam, iyalidam, mania.
- WordNet → illam, agam, viidu, manai, kappagam.
- *AWi* → (common words) illam, agam, viidu, mania.

Extraction of English Meanings and their Synonyms

Each word in the set *AWi* is given as input to the Agaraadhi dictionary to obtain the English meanings. This English meaning finds the synonyms using English WordNet. Each Tamil word has English words, which have another set of synonyms. Now intersects these two sets to find out common words.

Each word *TWi* is given to Agaraadhi to get all the English meanings. Then for each *TWi* we will get a set consisting of English words.

(i.e.) $S(TW1) = \{EM1, EM2, EM3\}$

$S(TW2) = \{EM1, EM2, EM3, EM4, EM5\}$ $S(TW3)$

$= \{EM1, EM2, EM3, EM4\}$

$S(TW4) = \{EM1, EM2, EM3, EM4, EM5\}$

Now the sets are intersected $[S(TW1) \cap S(TW2) \cap S(TW3) \cap S(TW4)]$ to obtain a single set of common English words for the corresponding Tamil words in the set,

S(EMi).

$S(EMi) = \{EM1, EM2\}$

For Example:

- illam → Home, House, Hostel
- agam → Unit, Home, Subject, House, Heart, chest, inner
- viidu → home, nest, house, building, Bower, heaven
- manai → house, habitat, place, Home, aerie

$S(EMi) = \{\text{Home, House}\}$

Finding UNL Semantic Constraints

The English words obtained in *S*(*EMi*) are passed to UNL Knowledge Base to obtain UNL semantic constraints. UNL semantic constraints have four concepts. (i) Nominal concepts, (ii) Attributive concepts, (iii) Adjectival concepts and (iv) Predicate concepts. The predicate concepts are further divided into be_verbs, do_verbs, and occur_verbs. The constraints can be extracted using two search methods. (a) General search – search is done in the whole UNLKB (b) POS-based search – search is done based on the POS of the word in the respective concepts.

POS-based search example:

- Home → icl > person, icl > place, icl > country
- House → icl > building, icl > person, icl > company

General search example:

- Home → icl > person, icl > place, icl > country
- House → icl > building, icl > person, icl > company, agt > person, agt > person
- obj > thing, agt > thing, obj > person

Semantic Similarity of Constraints

When a single Tamil word maps to more than one constraint, it should be disambiguated. The semantic similarity of the constraints is done through UNL ontology using the parent-child relationship. For each constraint, check for a parent, and count the number of typical constraints. It is called a similarity score.

Similarity Score = Sum (Max. no. of constraints occurring in the parents)

For Example:

Home → icl > place

House → icl > building

UNL Attributes

Classify the UNDL tags concerning POS information received, and some UNDL tags are common to all types of POS tags, such as Nouns, Verbs, Adjectives, Adverbs, Postpositions and Pronouns. The list of UNL tags common to all POS types are POS and LEX. The tag values are assigned automatically for each entry.

6.7 CONCLUSION

This section deals with the Tamil information system applications. Information extraction is a procedure to extract organized evidence from the disorganized text sources. The organized proof can include a document's concepts, entities, relations, and significances. The enriched document corpus can be developed from various websites, cleaned as a text document, and utilized to accomplish semantic knowledge. This semantic information can be used in the semantic information extraction process. Information is learned and maintained based on its semantic meaning and is used to update the probability array that prevailed in the shallow parsing stage. It is essential to archive and retrieves information when needed. In this computer era, storing and retrieving a considerable amount of data is accessible. Information retrieval (IR) system is growing to fulfill the various users' needs. Most Tamil IR systems read the text, identify whether the word is a verb or noun, and find the word from the database. The research reveals that the requirement of Tamil literary information retrieval of different documents is increased and helps to share on the internet.

CHAPTER 7

MS-Office and Google in Tamil

7.1 INTRODUCTION

Tamil Computing supports a few simple programs to help make modern technology accessible to the public. To begin with, one needs to view some applications as being essential while one might wish to have every famous application run in Tamil. At the earliest opportunity, the following set of applications must be offered in common. Whatever Tamil considers on computers, the suggestions must consider the situations and provide realistic, innovative solutions.

7.1.1 Tools for Data Preprocessing

DTP is a type of data entry and printing software used for personal and commercial purposes. It is used for Publishing and preserving newspapers and magazines on a vast scale.

The web is used to broadcast and distribute knowledge. Among the possibilities are generating web content, search engines, archiving programs, and applications for conserving historical documents in their original forms.

7.1.2 Software for Text Processing

Large datasets must be processed, categorized, and searched in software. Database software supports contact in Tamil. Sometimes, it is essential to generate the report in Tamil. It will help maintain accounts in many states and private and commercial organizations. The computing system needs conventional Database systems such as Oracle, Access, Informix, etc.

7.1.3 Technologies in Learning

The Tamil people have to access the teaching contents in the Tamil Language. Similarly, different languages have to be learnt through Tamil. Development of Tamil-language computer-based programs are required to supplement training courses. All the content must be active and accessible via internet.

7.1.4 Advances in Linguistics

Assessment and research of the structure of languages require a vast amount of intelligence. Studying ancient texts from a linguistic angle and Concordance generation is the main objective of the linguistic study of a language. Therefore, sentence analysis, grammar, word count estimations, translation, spoken language analysis, and more techniques are available.

7.1.5 Email Communications

Applications to manage email in Tamil need to provide a better communication facility. It is essential to accommodate such a facility in the real world.

7.1.6 Technologies Precise to the Government and Public Organizations

Text databases, police records, historical data, meeting minutes, and other information are kept for fast and easy accessibility.

7.1.7 Other Possibilities for Customers

Accounting and minor database systems support user interfaces in Tamil. Client-server applications support user interfaces in Tamil to work with usual databases. The significant challenges to Tamil are the non-availability of popular software like Microsoft Applications for the Tamil Language. The users intend to prepare the Tamil documents, and many User Interfaces are unavailable for the Tamil Language. This problem is solved in MS Office 365, where the user can also see the complete interface in Tamil and access Tamil's entire applications. In this version, the user can access Word/text processing, Data Preparation, Educational Applications, Email Applications, Searching applications, Language Applications, Printing documents, and other consumer applications in Tamil. This chapter explains the Microsoft Office for Tamil applications in detail.

7.2 ABOUT MICROSOFT OFFICE

Microsoft Office, or simply Office, is a collection of Microsoft's applications and services. Bill Gates initially broadcast it on August 1, 1988, at COMDEX in Las Vegas. Microsoft Word, Microsoft Excel, and Microsoft PowerPoint were included in the earliest version of Office, which was marketed as a marketing name for an office suite. Microsoft Office applications have grown significantly closer with shared features like a common spell checker, OLE data integration, and the Visual Basic for Apps scripting language. Microsoft presents Office as an application framework for line-of-business applications in the Office Business Applications brand.

Microsoft Office comes in various editions for different customers and operating systems. The desktop edition, accessible for PCs running Windows and macOS, is the initial and most extensively used edition. Microsoft also supports Android and iOS phone applications. Microsoft Office on the Internet is a web-based edition of the software.

Since Office 2013, Microsoft has supported Office 365 as the principal method of acquiring Microsoft Office. It allows users to subscribe to the software and other services, and users receive feature updates to the software for the duration of their subscription, including new features and cloud computing integration that aren't always included in "on-premises" releases.

Microsoft Office on the Web is a free, lightweight web version of Microsoft Office that principally consists of three web services: Word, Excel, and PowerPoint. It also comprises Outlook.com, OneNote, and OneDrive, which are reachable by a combined app switcher. Users can use SharePoint, Microsoft Exchange Server, and Microsoft Lync Server to deploy the on-premises edition of this service, termed Office Online Server, in private clouds.

Word, Excel, and PowerPoint on the web can natively open, edit, and save Office Open XML files (Docx, xlsx, pptx) and OpenDocument files. They can also open the older Office file formats (doc, Xls, ppt) but will be converted to the newer Open XML formats if they wish to edit them online.

Other formats, like CSV in Excel or HTML in Word, and Office files secured with a password, cannot be opened on the web apps.

In this chapter, the following section explains Windows 10 with the MS Office 365 package, which can display, Tamil menus and documents.

7.2.1 Language Configuration

The language configuration has two components: keyboard mapping and the other one is Office Language Enabling. To do the keyboard mapping, one should do the following steps.

The first step is to go to the Windows setting.

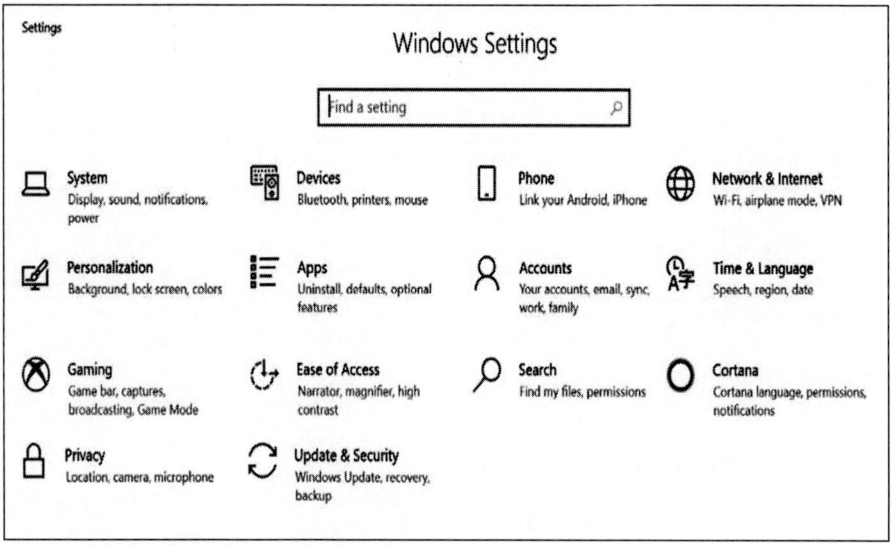

Figure 7.1: Windows Setting

The second step is to select the Time and Language setting.

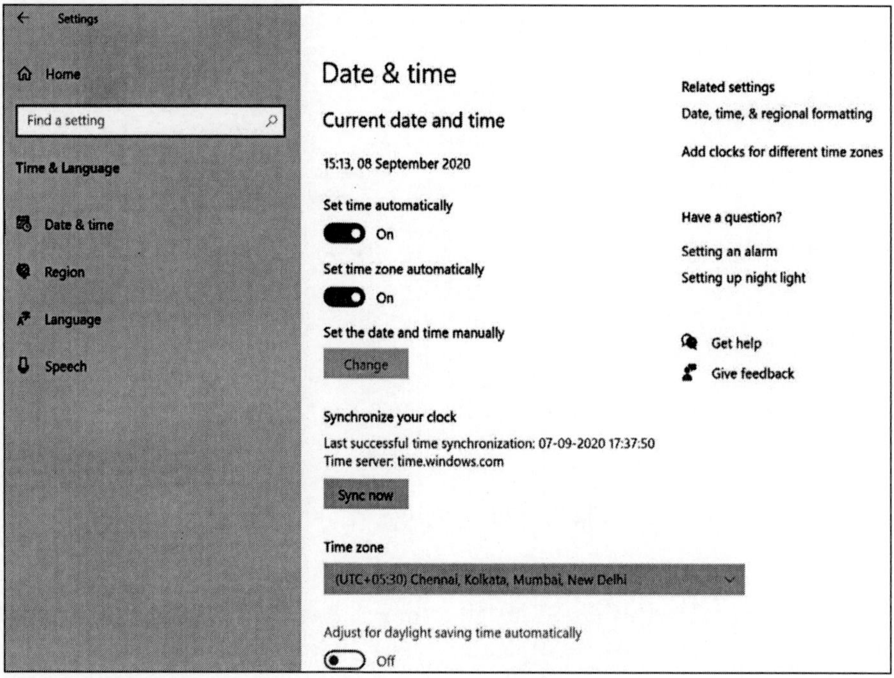

Figure 7.2: Date and Time

Then select the language setting.

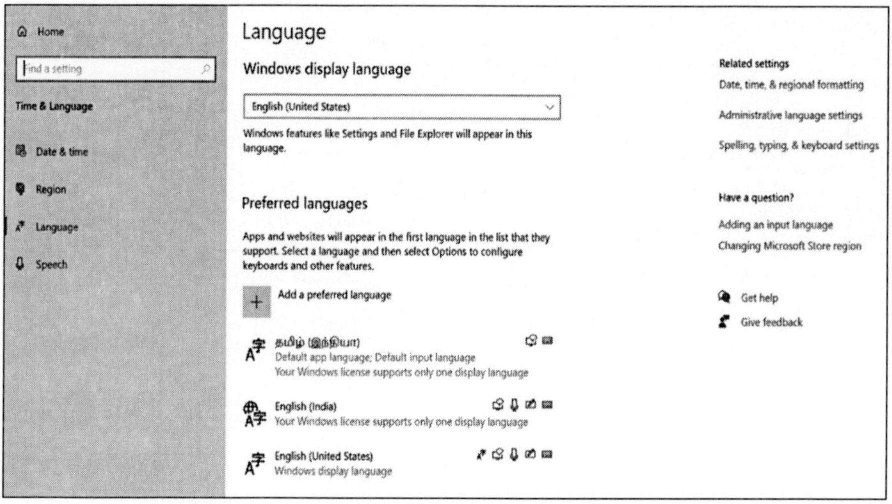

Figure 7.3: Language Setting

In the above screen, select Tamil as the preferred Language.

Language Options: Tamil (India)

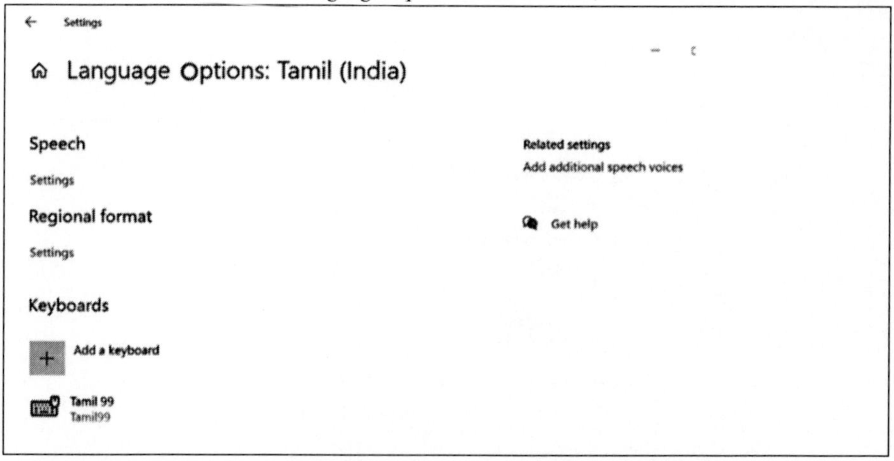

Figure 7.4: Language Options

If the language keyboard is already installed, then one must select the Tamil Language Keyboard and install it, or it has to be installed. It will allow one to install a particular language keyboard mapping in the system. Once installed, one can select the Tamil language keyboard for the language setting from the desktop itself. Typically, two kinds of keyboards are available with Microsoft. One is the language keyboard, and another is the glyph-based keyboard, which permits the user to type contents in Tamil using English voice. If one does the font setting without keyboard mapping, one cannot access the Language for inputting.

Moreover, the second important thing is the language setting in MS Office. To enable the Language in MS Office, one should first go to the software like MS-Word/MS-Excel/MS-Access/MS-PowerPoint and then select the File menu, and on the bottom of the menu, one can find the MS-Office Options. In the MS Office menu options, one must choose the language options. In the language options, there are two language menus available. The Office Display Language indicates the Language for Buttons, menus, and other controls. Another one is the Office authoring Language and Proofing, which manages languages used for creating and editing documents, including proofing and tools such as spelling and grammar checks. In addition, if one wishes to save the paper in a Tamil name, that is also possible. One can also print the document in the respective Language once the Language is enabled.

7.2.1.1 *Microsoft-Word*

First, Microsoft-Word can be used as follows.

Figure 7.5: Microsoft-Word

Open the new document and select the Language by selecting the keyboard language setting option on the right side.

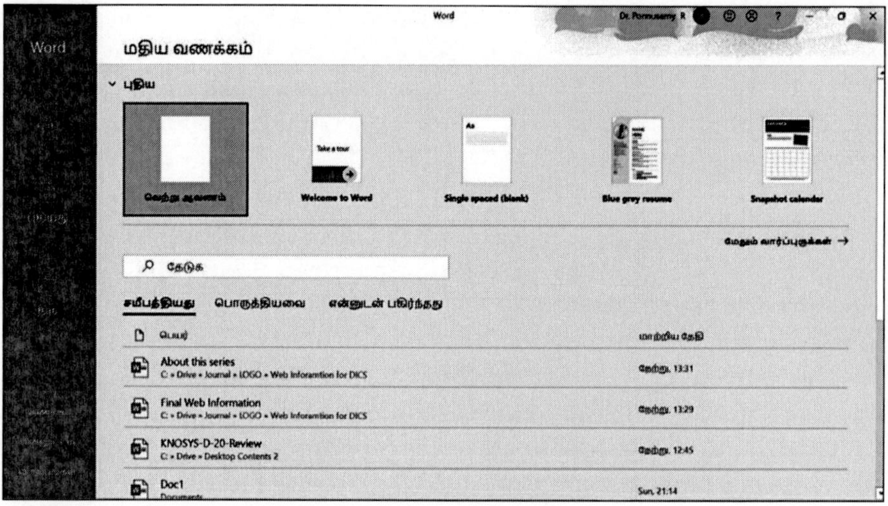

Figure 7.6: Presents Selecting the Keyboard Language Setting Option

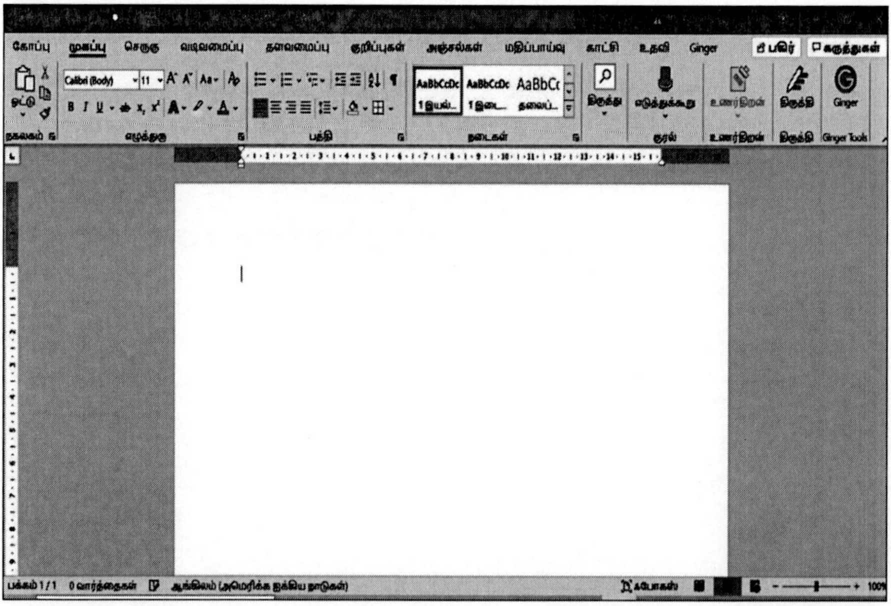

Figure 7.7: MS Word in the Tamil Language

After selecting the Language, one can type it in Tamil. Apart from Language, one can do all operations available in MS Word-like, increasing/decreasing the size of the fonts, formatting the documents, spell checking, etc.

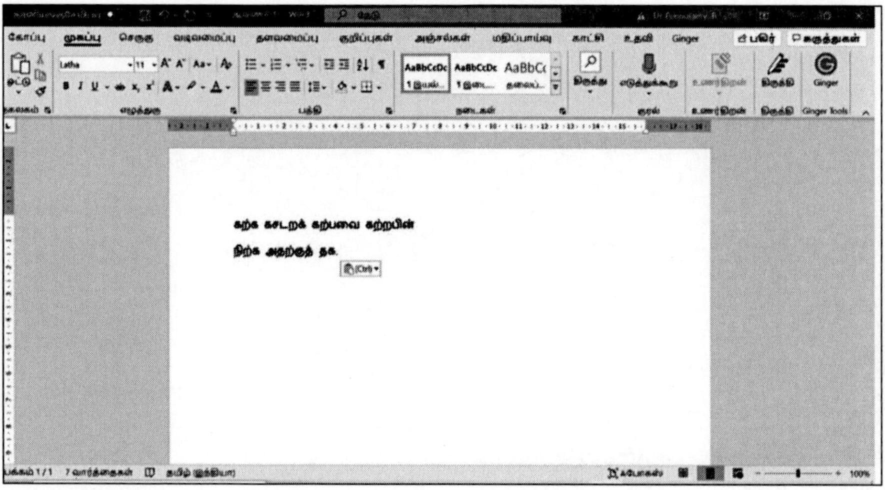

Figure 7.8: Shows the Tamil Writing

7.2.1.2 *MS-Excel*

Entering data, Formatting data, Indexing data, drawing charts, creating animations, etc., are possible through MS Excel. Like earlier MS-Word language settings, in this case, one can also do the language setting and all the operations in Tamil. It is shown on the following screen.

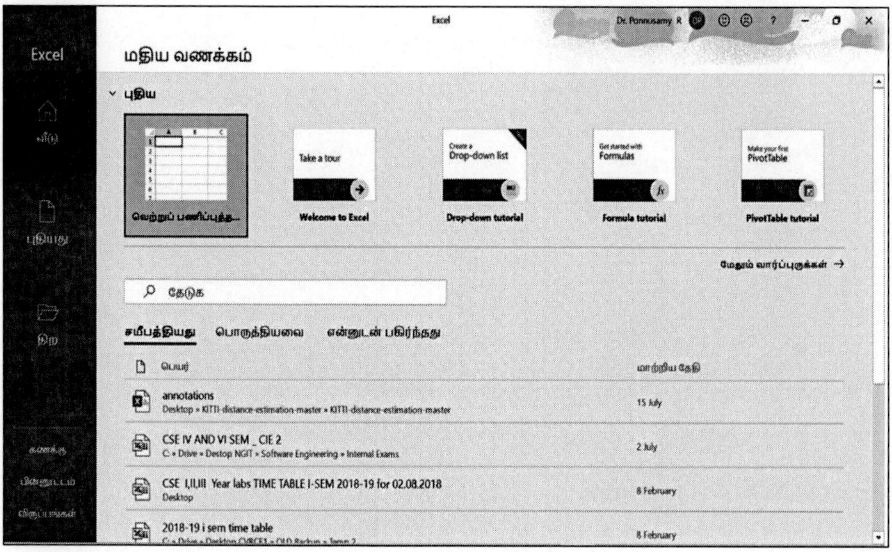

Figure 7.9: MS-Excel

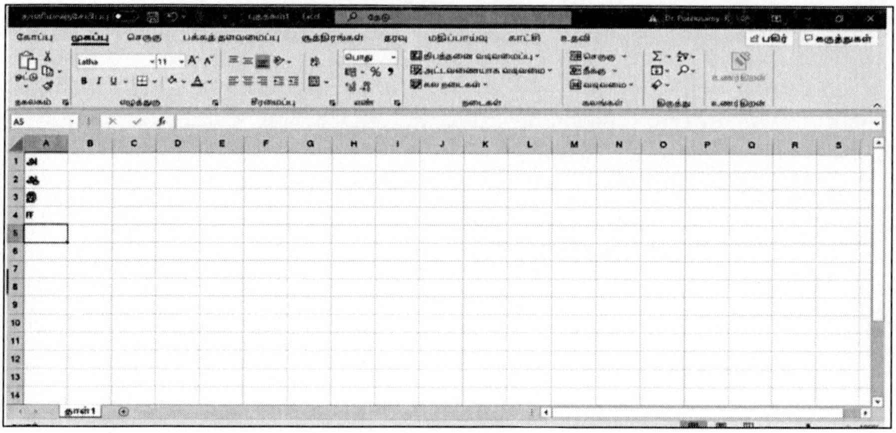

Figure 7.10: MS-Excel is the Tamil Language

7.2.1.3 *MS-Access*

The MS-Access is used to create, update, and save the data; to do that, MS-Access can open the database and enter the data in Tamil. It is shown in the following MS-Access table.

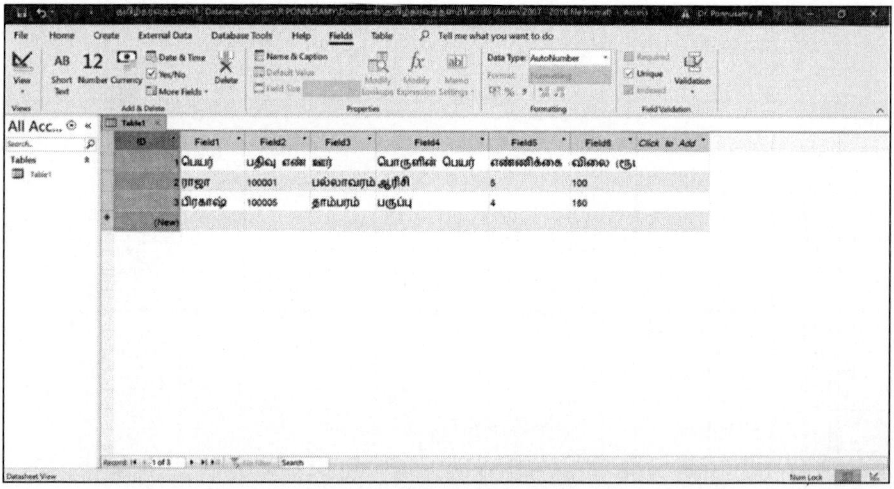

Figure 7.11: MS-Access

7.2.1.4 *MS-PowerPoint*

MS-PowerPoint is used to create presentations, similar to other software, this can be used to create a presentation in Tamil. It is shown in the following presentation screen and the other operations one can perform regularly. One can also type the contents in Tamil, and the exhibition is shown in the following display.

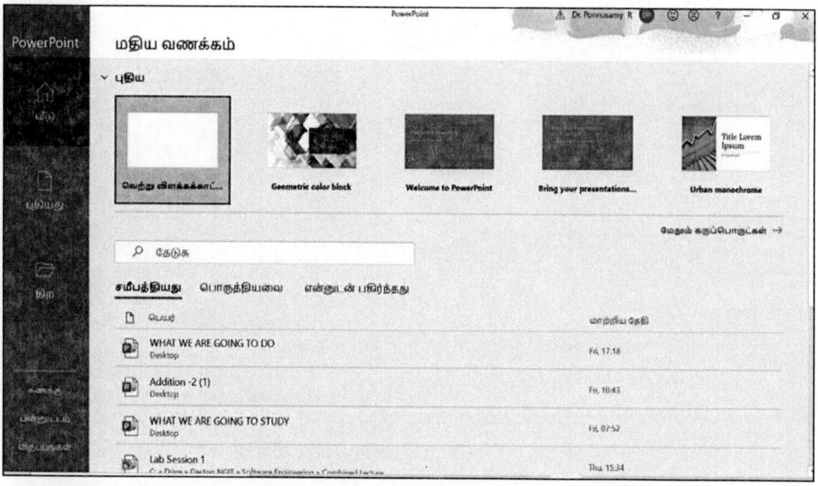

Figure 7.12: MS-PowerPoint

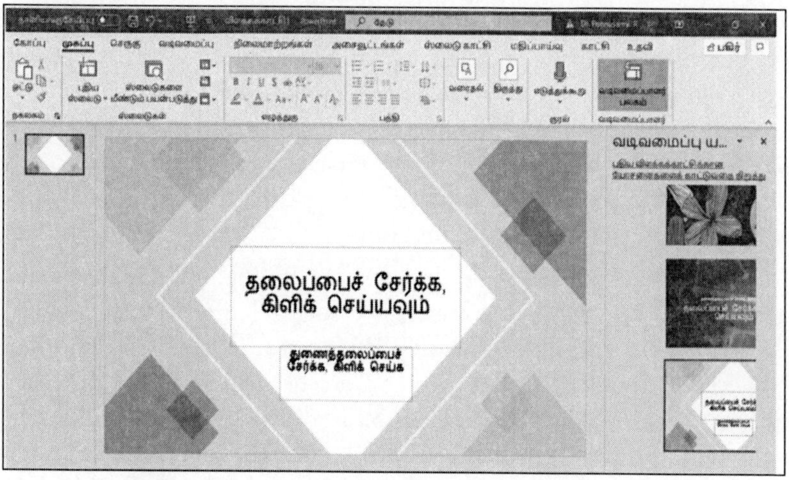

Figure 7.13: MS-PowerPoint Presentation in Tamil

7.2.1.5 *Microsoft Outlook*

Microsoft outlook is used to compose and send an email, as, like other software, this can be used to write and send emails in Tamil. One can also type the email in Tamil; the screen look is shown in the following email.

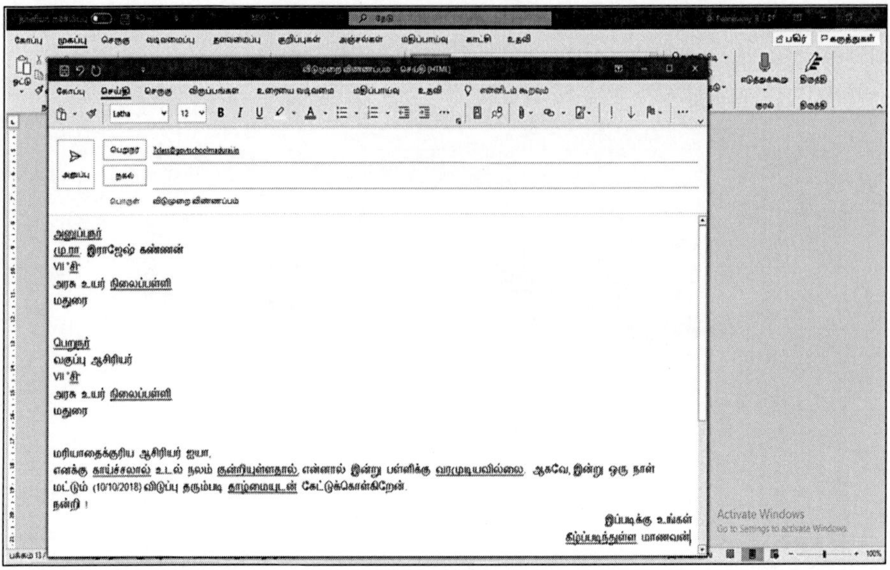

Figure 7.14: Microsoft Outlook

7.2.1.6 *Google Translate*

Google Translate is a free international machine translation tool produced by Google that allows users to translate text and websites into different languages. Google Translate handles 109 languages at multiple levels as of November 2020, and as of April 2016, it had over 500 million cumulative users, translating over 100 billion words daily. It has a website interface, an Android and iOS mobile app, and an application platform that allows developers to create web browsers and software programs.

In November 2016, Google declared that Google Translate would shift to a neural machine translation engine—Google Neural Machine Translation (GNMT)—which translates "whole sentences at a time, rather than just piece by piece. It uses this broader context to help it figure out the most relevant translation; then it rearranges and adjusts to be more like a human speaking with proper grammar". GNMT, initially only allowed for some languages in 2016, is now used in all 109 languages on the Google Translate list as of November 2020, except for the English-Latin language combination. Tamil is also one of the Languages supported in this translation of English to Tamil translation.

Google Translate imitates numerous types of texts and media across languages, including texts, audios, websites, and texts on display is still or live video pictures. Google Translate can make synthesis speech from the text in some languages, and in some combinations, certain related words and phrases between the source and reference text can be emphasized. Supplementary data occasionally accompany the translation box. Still, it isn't a dictionary, and it has been demonstrated to construct translations for terms. It doesn't comprehend in all languages. It is shown in the following figure.

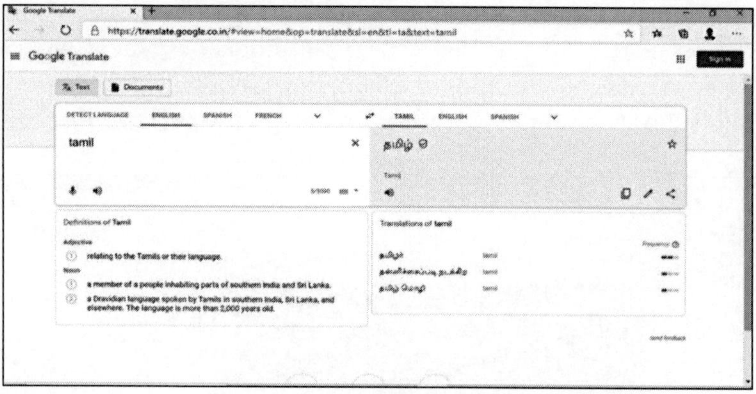

Figure 7.15: Google Translate

7.2.1.7 *Google Searching*

To search documents in Tamil, one has to first go to www.google.com, then select Tamil as the Language for searching. Then you can type the string in Tamil and search in Tamil. The following screenshot shows the same.

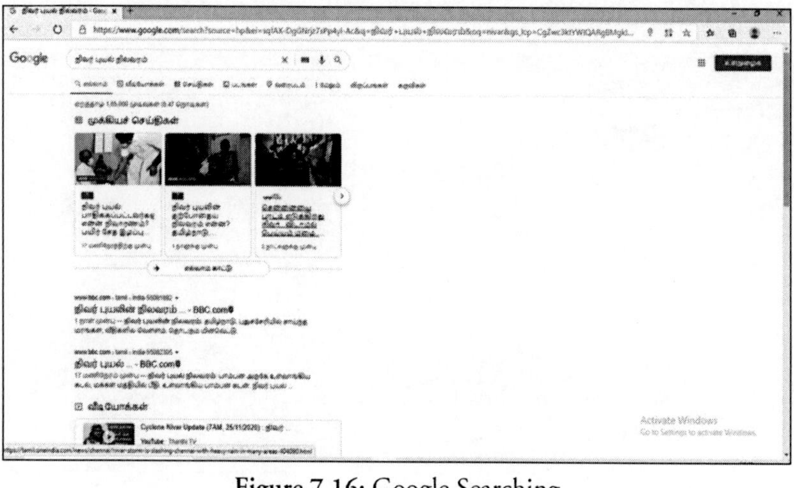

Figure 7.16: Google Searching

If one wants to give the input invoice, that is also possible using search by voice. It will let you retrieve the documents, videos, images, etc.

7.2.1.8 *YouTube*

YouTube is an American online video streaming and social media platform launched by Steve Chen, Chad Hurley and Jawed Karim in February 2005. Its users watch more than one billion hours of videos every day. As of 2019, videos are estimated to be uploaded over 500 hours of content per minute. One can access this tool in different languages; the following figures show the Tamil language setting of YouTube and access the contents in Tamil.

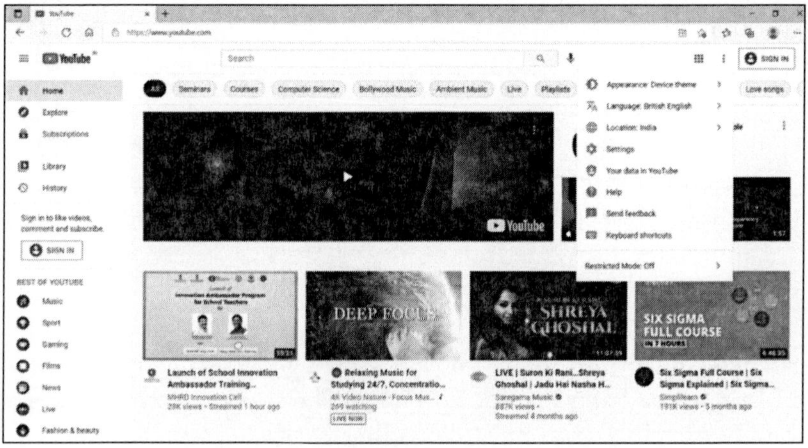

Figure 7.17: YouTube Page in English

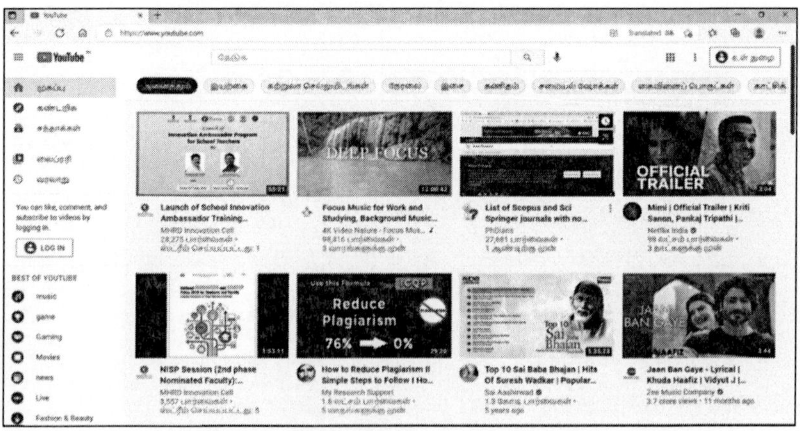

Figure 7.18: YouTube Page in Tamil

7.3 CONCLUSION

In terms of using Tamil on computers on a nationwide scale, information technology must inevitably aspire to reach all people to provide them with the advantages of this new technical marvel. No matter how great the results seem, any method of dealing with the Tamil user interfaces cannot depend on software solutions that serve data entering and printing. It's not a straightforward problem that can be solved using regular keyboard mappings or developing typefaces. These approaches will not provide a detailed, standard, and easy-to-use method of communication for everyone. For the long-term expansion of the Tamil language for electronic processing, it is vital to approach the problem from data processing.

CHAPTER 8

Database Management System in Tamil

8.1 INTRODUCTION OF DBMS (DATABASE MANAGEMENT SYSTEM)

Database: A database is an assortment of related information which helps in productive recovery, inclusion, and cancellation of information from the data set and sorts out the information as tables, sees, mappings, reports, and so forth. For instance, the college data set arranges the information about understudies, personnel, administrative staff, and so on, which helps in productive recovery, inclusion, and erasure of information.

- *DDL:* is the short name for Data Definition Language, which manages data set constructions and portrayals of how the information should dwell in the data set.
- *CREATE:* Make a data set and items like (table, record, sees, store method, capacity, and triggers).
- *ALTER:* Alters the structure of the existing database.
- *DROP:* Delete objects from the database.
- *TRUNCATE:* Eliminate all records from a table, including all spaces assigned for the forms are taken out.
- *COMMENT:* In the data dictionary, add comments.
- *RENAME:* Rename an object.
- *DML:* Is the short name for Data Manipulation Language, which deals with data manipulation and includes most common SQL statements such as SELECT, INSERT, UPDATE, DELETE, etc., and it is used to store, modify, retrieve, delete and update data in a database.
- *SELECT:* Retrieve data from a database.
- *INSERT:* Insert data into a table.
- *UPDATE:* Updates existing data within a table.
- *DELETE*: Delete all records from a database table.
- *MERGE:* UPSERT operation (insert or update).

- *CALL:* Call a PL/SQL or Java subprogram
- *EXPLAIN PLAN:* Interpretation of the data access path
- *LOCK TABLE:* Concurrency Control
- ***Database Management System:*** Database Management System (DBMS) manages the database. For Example, MySQL, Oracle, etc., are popular commercial DBMS used in different applications. DBMS allows the users the following tasks.
- ***Data Definition:*** It helps create, modify, and remove definitions that define data organization in the database.
- ***Data Updating:*** It helps insert, modify, and delete the actual data in the database.
- ***Data Retrieval:*** It helps retrieve data from the database and that applications can be used for various purposes.
- ***User Administration:*** It helps in registering and monitoring users, enforcing data security, monitoring performance, maintaining data integrity, dealing with concurrency control, and recovering information corrupted by unexpected failure.

8.2 DATABASE MANAGEMENT SYSTEMS IN TAMIL

In the modern world, people's needs are changing daily, and business intelligence is also changing according to the market requirements. Tamil is one of the crucial communities that needs a Tamil Database Management System to meet the market requirements. Most modern databases support multilingual databases. The help for Multilingualism is problematic with suggestions for information stockroom plan and announcing execution. This section discusses how Tamil can be kept in the different databases for the operations mentioned above and demonstrated using the python program.

8.3 TAMIL DATABASE MANAGEMENT SYSTEM USING MS-EXCEL

Microsoft Excel is an accounting page created by Microsoft for Windows, macOS, Android, and iOS. It highlights computation, diagramming devices, turn tables, and a large-scale Visual Basic for Applications (VBA) programming language. It has been a generally applied accounting page for these stages, mainly since adaptation 5 of 1993, and it has supplanted Lotus 1-2-3 as the business standard for bookkeeping pages. This type of database permits the manipulation of the data through the direct method and programming method. This programming method is used to manipulate the data in Tamil using the XlsxWriter method. In chapter 8, Tamil's direct form of data manipulation is explained in detail.

XlsxWriter is a python module for composing documents in the XLSX record design. It tends to contain text, numbers, and equations for different worksheets. Additionally, it upholds elements like organizing, pictures, outlines, page arrangement, auto channels, restrictive designing and numerous others.

Use this command to install the xlsxwriter module.

pip install xlsxwriter

Note: Throughout XlsxWriter, rows and columns are zero-indexed. The first cell in a worksheet, A1 is (0, 0), B1 is (0, 1), A2 is (1, 0), and B2 is (1, 1) similarly for all cells.

Let's see how to create and write to an excel-sheet using Python.

Code #1: Using A1 notation (cell name) to write data in Tamil's specific cells.

```
# import xlsxwriter module
import xlsxwriter
 # Workbook() takes one, non-optional, argument
# which is the filename that we want to create.
workbook = xlsxwriter. Workbook('hello.xlsx')
# The workbook object is then used to add new
# worksheet via the add_worksheet() method.
worksheet = workbook.add_worksheet()
# Use the worksheet object to write
# data via the write() method.
worksheet. Write('A1', 'வரிசைஎண்')
worksheet. Write('B1', 'தமிழ்')
worksheet. Write('C1', 'பெயர்')
worksheet. Write('D1', 'ஊர்')
# Finally, close the Excel file
# via the close() method.
workbook. Close()
```

Output

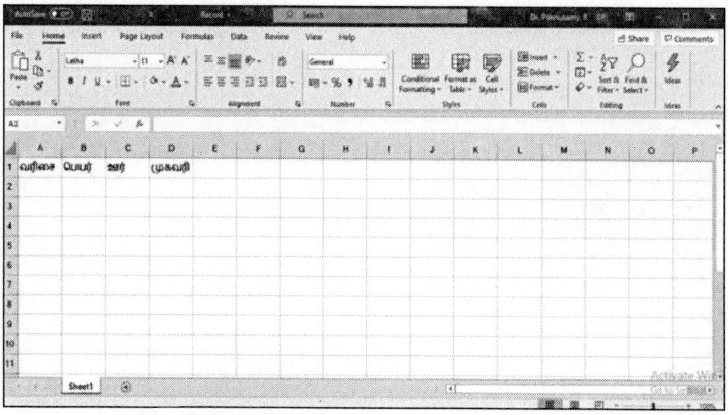

Figure 8.1: Using the Row-Column Notation (indexing value) for Writing Data in the Specific Cells

Code #2: Using the row-column notation (indexing value) for writing data in the specific cells.

```
# import xlsxwriter module
import xlsxwriter
workbook = xlsxwriter.Workbook('Table2.xlsx')
worksheet = workbook.add_worksheet()
# Start from the first cell.
# Rows and columns are zero indexed.
row = 0
column = 0
content = ["அன்கித்", "ராகுல்", "பிரியா", "கர்ஷிதா",
          "சுமித்", "நீரஜ்", "சிவம்"]
# iterating through content list
for item in content:
 # write operation perform
Worksheet.write(row, column, item)
# incrementing the value of row by one
# with each iteratons.
row +=
workbook. Close()
```

Output

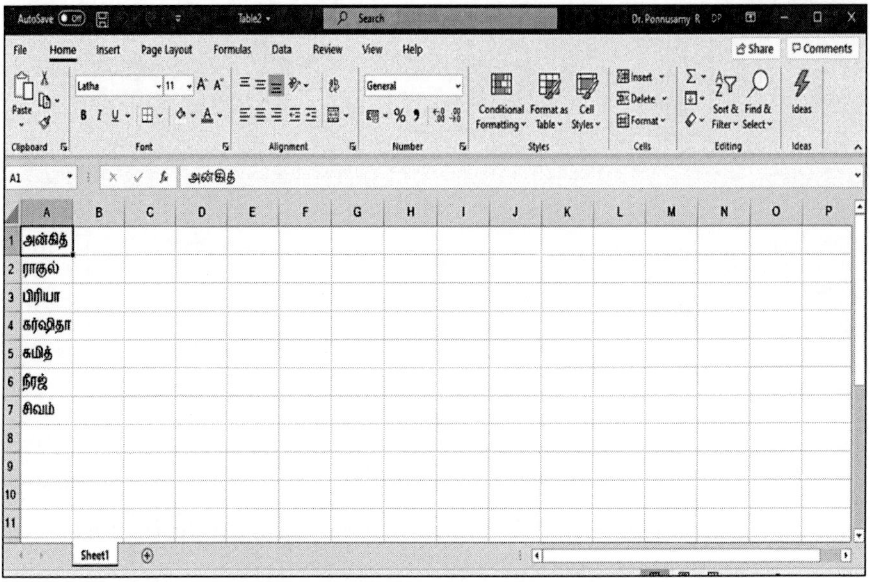

Figure 8.2: Creating a New Sheet with the Specific Name

Code #3: Creating a new sheet with the specific name

```
# import xlsxwriter module
import xlsxwriter
workbook = xlsxwriter.Workbook('Table3.xlsx')
# By default, worksheet names in the spreadsheet will be
# Sheet1, Sheet2 etc., but we can also specify a name.
worksheet = workbook.add_worksheet("என்னுடையதமிழ்தாள்")
# Some data we want to write to the worksheet.
scores = (
   ['அன்கித்', 1000],
   ['ராகுல்', 100],
   ['பிரியா', 300],
   ['கரிஷதா', 50],
) # Start from the first cell. Rows and
# columns are zero-indexed.
row = 0
```

```
col = 0
# Iterate over the data and write it out row by row.
for name, score in (scores):
worksheet. Write(row, col, name)
worksheet. Write(row, col + 1, score)
row += 1
workbook. Close()
```

8.4 PYTHON TAMIL PLOTTING CHARTS IN EXCEL SHEET WITH DATA TOOLS USING XLSXWRITER MODULE

XlsxWriter is a Python library that can play out the different procedures on dominant records like making, composing, number-crunching tasks, and plot diagrams. How about we perceive how to plot outlines with various kinds of Data Tools utilizing continuous information.

Charts are made of fewer than one Series of at least one information focus. The Series themselves have involved references to cell ranges. To plot the outlines on an excel sheet, first and foremost, make a diagram object of explicit graph type (i.e., Line graph, and so on). After making outline objects, embed information in them, and finally, add that diagram object in the sheet object.

Code #4: Plot a Chart with Trendlines.

For plotting this sort of diagram on an excel sheet, use add Series () technique with the 'trendline' keyword contention of the graph object.

```
#
# An example of creating Excel Line charts with Python and XlsxWriter.
#
# Copyright 2013-2021, John McNamara, jmcnamara@cpan.org
#
import xlsxwriter
workbook = xlsxwriter.Workbook('chart_line.xlsx')
worksheet = workbook.add_worksheet()
bold = workbook.add_format({'bold': 1})
# Add the worksheet data that the charts will refer to.
```

```
headings = ['எண்', 'தொகுதி1', 'தொகுதி2']
data = [
   [2, 3, 4, 5, 6, 7],
   [10, 40, 50, 20, 10, 50],
   [30, 60, 70, 50, 40, 30],]
worksheet.writes_row('A1', headings, bold)
worksheet.write_column('A2', data[0])
worksheet.write_column('B2', data[1])
worksheet.write_column('C2', data[2])
# Create a new chart object. In this case an embedded chart.
chart1 = workbook.add_chart({'type': 'line'})
# Configure the first series.
chart1.add_series ({
   'name':       '=Sheet1! $B$1',
   'categories': '=Sheet1! $A$2: $A$7',
   'values':     '=Sheet1! $B$2: $B$7',
})
# Configure a second series. Note the use of alternative syntax to define ranges.
chart1.add_series ({
   'name': ['Sheet1', 0, 2],
   'categories': ['Sheet1', 1, 0, 6, 0],
   'values': ['Sheet1', 1, 2, 6, 2],
})
# Add a chart title and some axis labels.
chart1.set_title ({'name': 'மாதிரி பகுப்பாய்வின் முடிவுகள்'})
chart1.set_x_axis ({'name': 'சோதனை எண்'})
chart1.set_y_axis ({'name': 'மாதிரி நீளம் (மில்லிமீட்டர்)'})
# Set an Excel chart style. Colours with white outline and shadow.
# Insert the chart into the worksheet (with an offset).
worksheet. Insert_ chart ('D2', chart1, {'x_offset': 25, 'y_offset': 10})
```

 # Create a stacked line chart sub-type.

```
#
chart2 = workbook.add_chart({'type': 'line', 'subtype': 'stacked'})
# Configure the first series.
chart2.add_series({
    'name':       '=Sheet1! $B$1',
    'categories': '=Sheet1! $A$2: $A$7',
    'values':     '=Sheet1! $B$2: $B$7',
})

# Configure second series.
chart2.add_series ({
    'name':       '=Sheet1! $C$1',
    'categories': '=Sheet1! $A$2: $A$7',
    'values':     '=Sheet1! $C$2: $C$7',
})
# Add a chart title and some axis labels.
chart2.set_title ({'name': 'அடுக்கப்பட்ட விளக்கப்படம்'})
chart2.set_x_axis ({'name': 'சோதனை எண்'})
chart2.set_y_axis ({'name': 'மாதிரி நீளம் (மில்லிமீட்டர்)'})
# Set an Excel chart style.
chart2.set_style (12)
# Insert the chart into the worksheet (with an offset).
worksheet.insert_chart('D18', chart2, {'x_offset': 25, 'y_offset': 10})
```

 # Create a percent stacked line chart sub-type.

```
#
chart3 = workbook.add_chart({'type': 'line', 'subtype':
'percent_stacked'})
# Configure the first series.
chart3.add_series({
    'name':       '=Sheet1! $B$1',
    'categories': '=Sheet1! $A$2: $A$7',
```

```
    'values':     '=Sheet1! $B$2: $B$7',
})
# Configure second series.
chart3.add_series ({
    'name':       '=Sheet1! $C$1',
    'categories': '=Sheet1! $A$2: $A$7',
    'values':     '=Sheet1! $C$2: $C$7',
})
# Add a chart title and some axis labels.
chart3.set_title ({'name': 'சதவீதம் அடுக்கப்பட்ட விளக்கப்படம்'})
chart3.set_x_axis ({'name': 'சோதனை எண்'})
chart3.set_y_axis ({'name': 'மாதிரி நீளம் (மில்லிமீட்டர்)'})
```

 # Set an Excel chart style.

```
chart3.set_style (13)
# Insert the chart into the worksheet (with an offset).
Worksheet. insert_ chart ('D34', chart3, {'x_offset': 25, 'y_offset': 10})
workbook. Close()
```

Output

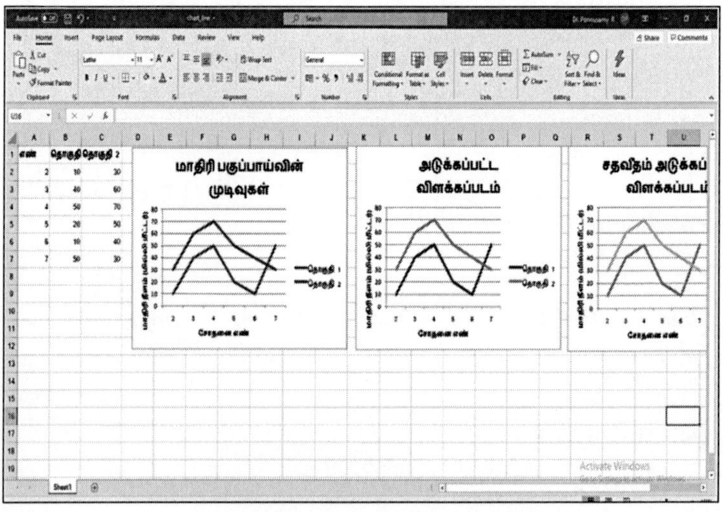

Figure 8.3. Plot the Simple Chart

Code #5: Plot the simple Pie Chart.

For plotting the simple Pie chart on an excel sheet, use add_chart() method with type 'pie' keyword argument of a workbook object in Tamil.

```
# import xlsxwriter module
import xlsxwriter
 # Workbook() takes one, non-optional, argument
# which is the filename that we want to create.
workbook = xlsxwriter.Workbook('chart_pie.xlsx')
# The workbook object is then used to add new
# worksheet via the add_worksheet() method.
worksheet = workbook.add_worksheet()
# Create a new Format object to formats cells
# in worksheets using add_format() method.
# here we create bold format object.
bold = workbook.add_format({'bold': 1})
# create a data list.
headings = ['வகை', 'மதிப்புகள்']
data = [
   ['ஆப்பிள்', 'ஆரஞ்சு', 'மாம்பழம்'],
   [40, 30, 30],
]
 # Write a row of data starting from 'A1'
# with bold format.
worksheet.write_row('A1', headings, bold)
# Write a column of data starting from
# A2, B2, C2 respectively.
worksheet.writ_column('A2', data[0])
worksheet.write_column('B2', data[1])
# Create a chart object that can be added
# to a worksheet using add_chart() method.
# here we create a pie chart object.
chart1 = workbook.add_chart({'type': 'pie'})
 # Add a data series to a chart
```

```
# using add_series method.
# Configure the first series.
#[sheet name, first_row, first_col, last_row, last_col].
chart1.add_series({
    'name':      'பழ விற்பனை தரவு',
    'categories': ['Sheet1', 1, 0, 3, 0],
    'values': ['Sheet1', 1, 1, 3, 1],
})
 # Add a chart title
chart1.set_title({'name': 'பிரபலமான பழவகைகள்'})
# Set an Excel chart style. Colours with white outline and shadow.
chart1.set_style(10)
 # Insert the chart into the worksheet(with an offset).
# the top-left corner of a chart is anchored to cell C2.
Worksheet. Insert _chart('C2', chart1, {'x_offset': 25, 'y_offset': 10})
# Finally, close the Excel file
# via the close() method.
workbook. Close()
```

Output

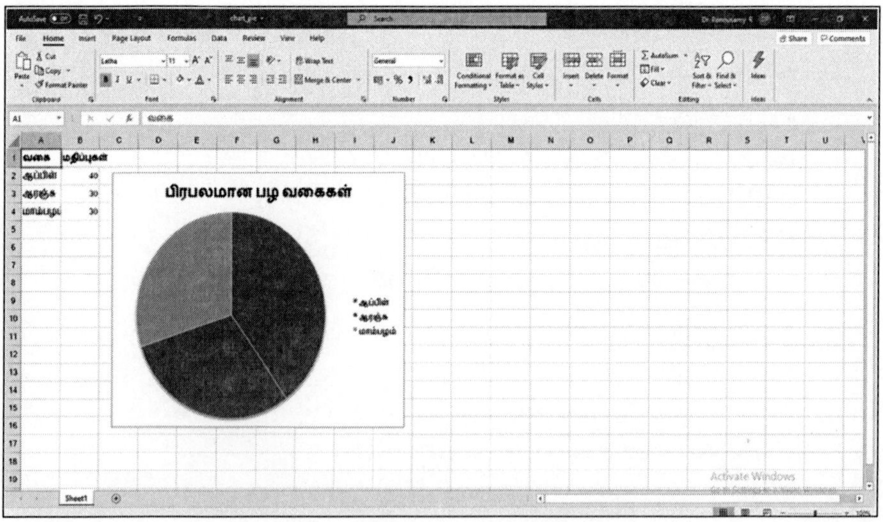

Figure 8.4: Plot the Simple Pie Chart

8.5 TAMIL DATABASE MANAGEMENT SYSTEM USING MYSQL

An information base is a different application that stores an assortment of information. Every information base has at least one explicit API for making, getting to, overseeing, looking at, and reproducing the information it holds.

Different information stores can likewise be utilized, for example, records on the document framework or huge hash tables in memory. However, information bringing and composting would not be quick and straightforward with those frameworks.

These days, we utilize social data set administration frameworks (RDBMS) to store and deal with the massive volume of information. It is known as a social data set since all the information is put away in different tables and relations are established using the primary keys or other keys known as **Foreign Keys.**

A Relational Database Management System (RDBMS) is programming that

- Enables you to carry out a data set with tables, sections, and lists.
- Guarantees the Referential Integrity between lines of different tables.
- Updates the lists naturally.
- Interprets an SQL inquiry and consolidates data from different tables.

RDBMS Terminology

Before we clarify the MySQL data set framework, let us reexamine several definitions identified with the data set.

- ***Database***: the table of the assortment with the connection information.
- ***Table:*** A table is a lattice with information. A table in an information base which resembles a specific accounting page.
- ***Column***: One segment (information component) contains information of a similar kind, for instance, the section postcode.
- ***Row***: A column (= tuple, section, or record) is a gathering of related information, for instance, the knowledge of one membership.
- ***Redundancy***: Storing information twice, repetitively, to make the framework quicker.
- ***Primary Key***: An essential key is exceptional. A fundamental worth can't happen twice in one table. With a key, you can discover one column.
- ***Foreign Key***: A foreign key is a connecting pin between two tables.

- ***Compound Key***: A compound key (composite key) is critical that comprises numerous sections since one segment isn't adequately remarkable.
- ***Index***: A record in a data set takes after a file at the rear of a book.
- ***Referential Integrity***: Referential Integrity ensures that an unfamiliar key worth consistently focuses on a current column.

Despite all these concepts and components common in all database management systems, the primary question raised before us is to implement the Tamil Language Database Creation, Insertion, Updating, Querying and Deleting database is the Challenging one. In all the modern databases, it supports the multilingual database. This subsequent section explains how to perform the above-said operations in Tamil and is described in detail.

8.5.1 Python MySQL—Create Database

Python Database API (Application Program Interface) is the Database interface for the standard Python. Most Python Database interfaces cling to this standard. Python Databases like MySQL uphold different Database workers. We must import the MySQL connector interface from Python to associate with the MySQL information base worker.

Syntax:

8.5.2 Create Database Database_Name

 # importing required libraries

```
import MySQL. Connector
database = MySQL. connector. Connect (
  host = "localhost",
  user = "root",
  passwd = "root"
)
```

 # preparing a cursor object

```
cursor Object = database. Cursor ()
 # creating database
CursorObject.execute ("CREATE DATABASE StudentDatabase")
```

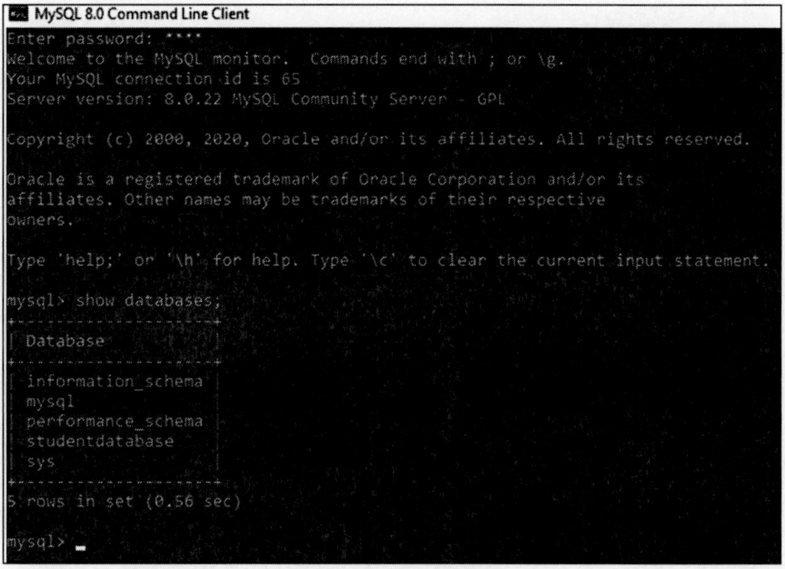

Figure 8.5: MySQL

8.5.3 Python MySQL—Delete Database

Python allows to delete the MySQL database like creation of the following python program will delete the database.

 # importing required libraries

```
import MySQL. Connector
database = MySQL. connector. Connect (
 host = "localhost",
 user = "root",
 passwd = "root"
)
```

 # preparing a cursor object

```
cursor Object = database. Cursor ()
 # creating database
CursorObject. Execute("DROP DATABASE StudentDatabase")
```

After executing the above program, show databases; the result is shown in the following Figure 8.6.

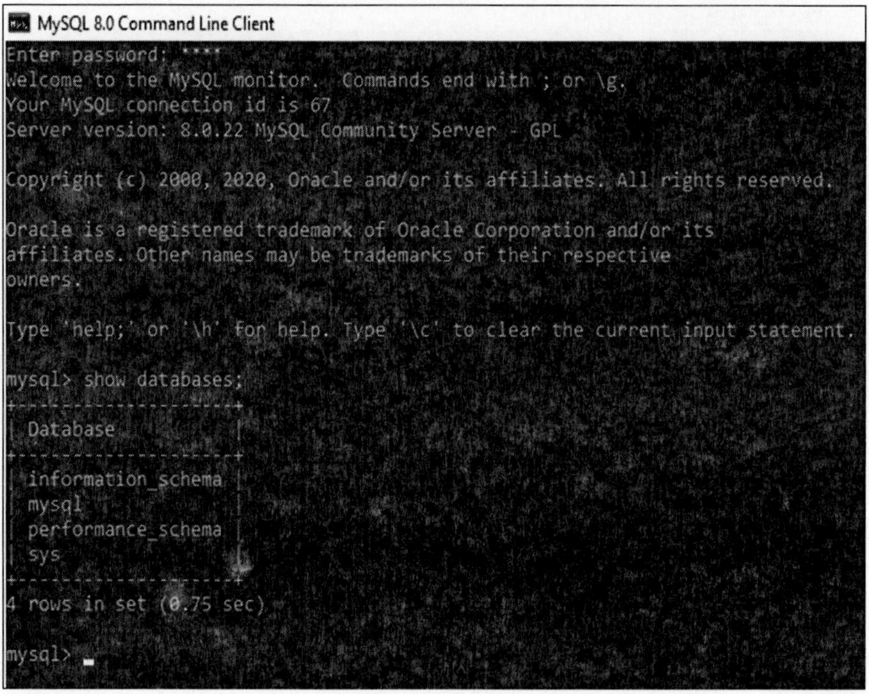

Figure 8.6: MySQL Database Result after Execution

8.5.4 Python MySQL—Create Table

Python allows to create the database table; the following python program will create the database.

```
# importing required library
        import MySQL. Connector
# connecting to the database
        database = MySQL. connector. Connect (
                        host = "localhost",
                        user = "root",
                        passwd = "root",
                        database = "student database")
# preparing a cursor object
        cursor Object = database. Cursor ()
# creating table
```

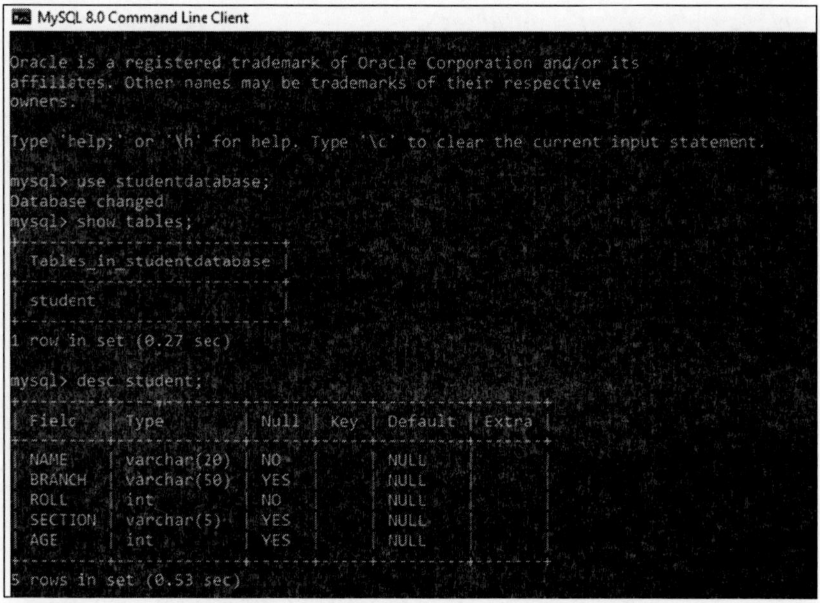

Figure 8.7: Python MySQL – Create Table

```
StudentRecord = """"CREATE TABLE STUDENT (
        NAME  VARCHAR(20) NOT NULL,
        BRANCH VARCHAR(50),
        ROLL INT NOT NULL,
        SECTION VARCHAR(5),
        AGE INT
        )""""
# table created
    CursorObject. Execute(studentRecord)
# disconnecting from server
    database.close()
```

8.5.5 INSERT into MySQL Database Using Python

Python allows to insert the database table; the following python program will insert the record into the database. The important thing is that it allows inserting the records in Tamil. However, it cannot be accessed in the normal MySQL command line. Again, one needs a separate program to display the records in Tamil.

#Insert the record into the database

```
import MySQL. Connector
 my db. = MySQL.Connector. Connect (
  host = 'localhost',
   database = 'student database',
   user = 'root',
   password = 'root'
)
 cs = mydb. Cursor()
statement = "INSERT INTO STUDENT(NAME, BRANCH,ROLL,
SECTION, AGE)VALUES('ராமேஷ்குமார்','சென்னை',1001,'பி',
22)"
cs. Execute(statement)
mydb. Commit()
print(cs. row count, " record(s) added")
print(cs.Lastrowid)
```

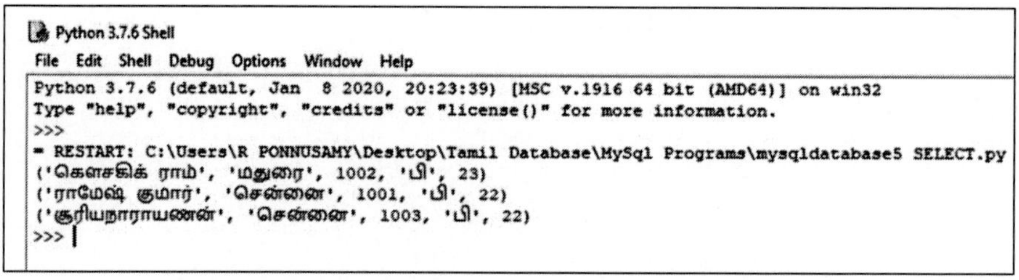

Figure 8.8: Insert into MySQL Database using Python

8.5.6 Select From MySQL Database Using Python

Python allows the database table to be displayed; the following python program will display the record into the database using the SELECT statement.

Approach:

- Import module.
- Make a connection request with the database.
- Create an object for the database cursor.
- Execute the following MySQL query.

```
SELECTselect_list FROM table_name;
# SELECT FROM DATABASE
import MySQL.connector
my db. = MySQL. connector. Connect (
   host = 'localhost',
   database = 'student database',
   user = 'root',
   password = 'root'
)
  cs = mydb. Cursor()
statement = "SELECT * FROM student"
cs. Execute(statement)
## fetching all records from the 'cursor' object
records = cs.Fetchall()
## Showing the data
for record in records:
   print(record)
```

the result of the above program is shown in the following output screen.

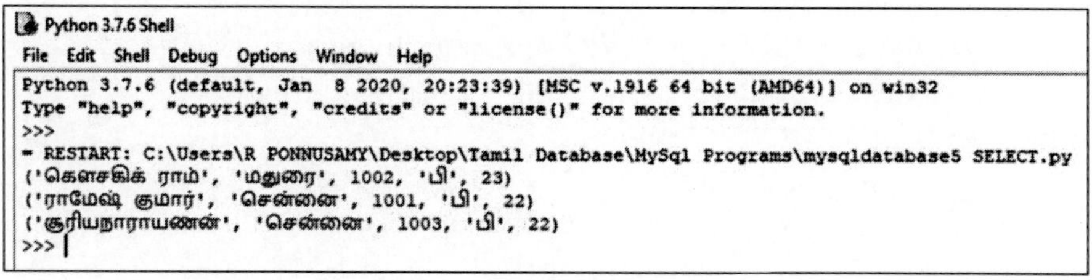

Figure 8.9: Select from MySQL Database Using Python

8.6 DELETING ELEMENT FROM TABLE IN MYSQL USING PYTHON

MySQL Connector—The python module is an API in Python for speaking with a MySQL information base. Python permits the coordination of a broad scope of information base workers with applications. An information-based interface is needed to get to a data set from Python. To erase information from a table, you utilize the MySQL DELETE proclamation. The accompanying represents the language structure of the DELETE explanation.

Approach

- Import module.
- Make a connection request with the database.
- Create an object for the database cursor.
- Execute the following MySQL query:

```
DELETE FROM TABLE_NAME WHERE Name =
'சூரியநாராயணன்';
# DELETE FROM DATABASE
import MySQL. Connector
 mydb.  = MySQL. connector. connect (
  host = 'localhost',
  database = 'student database',
  user = 'root',
  password = 'root'
)
 cs = mydb. Cursor()
statement = "DELETE FROM Student WHERE NAME =
'சூரியநாராயணன்'"
cs. Execute(statement)
statement = "SELECT * FROM  student"
cs. Execute(statement)
## fetching all records from the 'cursor' object
records = cs. Fetch all ()
mydb.commit()
## Showing the data
for record in records:
   print(record)
```

The output of the above program is shown on the following screen.

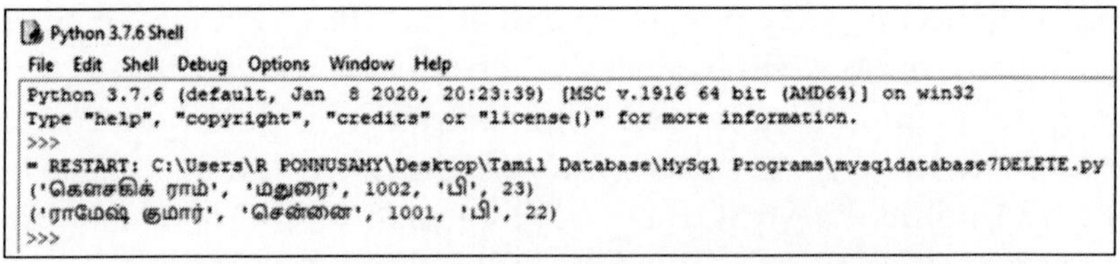

Figure 8.10: Deleting Element from Table in MySQL Using Python

8.6.1 Update Record from MySQL Database Using Python

Python allows to update the database table. The following python program will update the record into the database using an UPDATE statement.

```
UPDATE STUDENT SET  ATTRIBUTE = 'VALUE' WHERE
CONDITION;
# UPDATE THE RECORD DATABASE
import MySQL. Connector
 mydb.  = MySQL.connector.connect(
    host = 'localhost',
    database = 'studentdatabase',
    user = 'root',
    password = 'root'
)
cs = mydb. Cursor()
statement = "UPDATE STUDENT SET NAME =
'சூரியநாராயணன்' WHERE AGE = 23"
cs. Execute(statement)
statement = "SELECT * FROM  student"
cs. Execute(statement)
## fetching all records from the 'cursor' object
records = cs. Fetchall()
## Showing the data
for record in records:
    print(record)
```

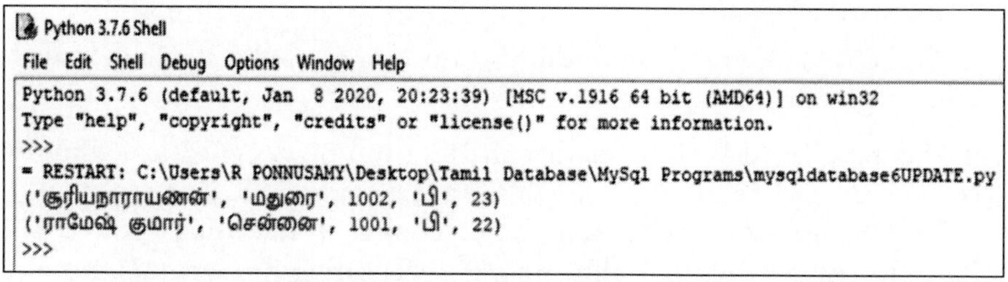

Figure 8.11: Update Record from MySQL Database Using Python

8.7 TAMIL DATABASE MANAGEMENT SYSTEM USING SQLITE

SQLite is an in-measure library that executes an independent, serverless, zero-arrangement, conditional **SQL** data set motor. It is an information base, which is zero-arranged, which means, like different data sets, you don't have to design it in your framework. **SQLite** motor isn't an independent cycle like different data sets; you can interface it statically or progressively according to your prerequisite with your application. **SQLite** gets to its stockpiling documents straightforwardly.

Overall, **SQLite** works incredibly as the information base motor for generally low to medium traffic sites (or, in other words, most locations). The measure of web traffic that **SQLite** can deal with relies upon how vigorously the site utilizes its data set. Any site that gets less than 100K hits/day should turn out great with **SQLite. SQLite** doesn't need a different worker cycle or framework to work (serverless). **SQLite** is independent, which implies no external conditions. **SQLite** is minuscule and lightweight, under 400KiB ultimately arranged or under 250KiB with discretionary provisions discarded.

In this segment, the understudy information base application is illustrated, giving an openness to plan the screens in Tamil. It additionally empowers the client to enter, update, recover and erase the information in Tamil.

If you press,

1. புதியனவற்றைசேர் Button enables the user to add student data into the database.
2. காட்சிபா டுத்து Button displays all the student records right-side student details box.
3. அழி Button allows the user to clear the input boxes.
4. நீக்கு Button enables the user to delete the records from the database.
5. தேடு Button allows the user to search the record from the database.
6. புதுப்பி Button empowers the user to update the record from the database.
7. வெளியேறு Button enables the user to exit from the student database management system.

This program demonstrates that the user can be designed in Python to access the data in Tamil. Also, it will store and retrieve the data in Tamil. It will help the users to develop such applications in Tamil using Python. The prime constraint to running this program is ensuring the system's installed SQLite. The user screen is shown in the following user interface.

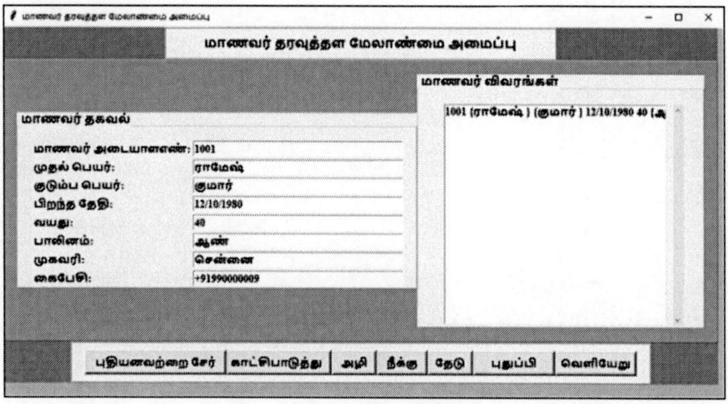

Figure 8.12: Student Database Management System UI

```
# Front End User Interface Screen
from tkinter import *
import tkinter.messagebox
import dbbackend
class Student:
def __init__(self,root):
self.root =root
self.root.title("மாணவர்தரவுத்தள மேலாண்மை அமைப்பு")
self.root.geometry("1080x580+0+0")
      self.root.Config(bg="lightpink")
#cadet blue
StdID = StringVar()
Firstname = StringVar()
      Surname = StringVar()
DoB = StringVar()
      Age = StringVar()
      Gender = StringVar()
      Address = StringVar()
      Mobile = StringVar()
# ---------------------------------Functions--------------------------------
defiExit():
iExit = tkinter.messagebox.askyesno("மாணவர்தரவுத்தள
மேலாண்மை அமைப்புகள்", "நீங்கள் வெளியேறவிரும்பினால்
உறுதிப்படுத்தவும்")
```

```
        if iExit> 0:
root.destroy()
            return
defclearData():
self.txtStdID.delete(0, END)
self.txtfna.delete(0, END)
self.txtSna.delete(0, END)
self.txtDoB.delete(0, END)
self.txtAge.delete(0, END)
self.txtGender.delete(0, END)
self.txtAdr.delete(0, END)
self.txtMobile.delete(0, END)
defaddData():
if(len(StdID.get())!=0):
dbbackend.addStdRec(StdID.get(), Firstname.get(), Surname.get() ,
DoB.get() ,Age.get(), Gender.get(), Address.get(), Mobile.get())
studentlist.delete(0, END)
studentlist.insert(END, (StdID.get(), Firstname.get(), Surname.get(),
DoB.get(), Age.get(), Gender.get(), Address.get(), Mobile.get()))
defDisplayData():
studentlist.delete(0,END)
for row in dbbackend.viewData():
studentlist.insert(END, row, str(" "))
defStudentRec(event):
        global sd
searchStd= studentlist.curselection()[0]
sd = studentlist.get(searchStd)
self.txtStdID.delete(0, END)
self.txtStdID.insert(END, sd[1])
self.txtfna.delete(0, END)
self.txtfna.insert(END, sd[2])
```

```
self.txtSna.delete(0, END)
self.txtSna.insert(END, sd[3])
self.txtDoB.delete(0, END)
self.txtDoB.insert(END, sd[4])
self.txtAge.delete(0, END)
self.txtAge.insert(END, sd[5])
self.txtGender.delete(0, END)
self.txtGender.insert(END, sd[6])
self.txtAdr.delete(0, END)
self.txtAdr.insert(END, sd[7])
self.txtMobile.delete(0, END)
self.txtMobile.insert(END, sd[8])
defDeleteData():
if(len(StdID.get())!=0):
dbbackend.deleteRec(sd[0])
clearData()
DisplayData()
defsearchDatabase():
studentlist.delete(0,END)
        for row in dbbackend.searchData(StdID.get(),
Firstname.get(), Surname.get() , DoB.get() ,Age.get(), Gender.get(),
Address.get(), Mobile.get()):
studentlist.insert(END, row, str(""))
    def update():
if (len(StdID.get()) != 0):
dbbackend.deleteRec(sd[0])
if (len(StdID.get()) != 0):
dbbackend.addStdRec(StdID.get(), Firstname.get(), Surname.get(),
DoB.get(), Age.get(), Gender.get(),Address.get(), Mobile.get())
studentlist.delete(0, END)
studentlist.insert(END, (StdID.get(), Firstname.get(), Surname.get(),
DoB.get(), Age.get(), Gender.get(), Address.get(), Mobile.get()))

#----------------------------------Frames-----------------------------------
```

```
MainFrame = Frame(self.root, bg="orchid")
MainFrame.grid()
TitFrame = Frame(MainFrame, bd=2, padx=54,pady=8, bg="Ghost White", relief=RIDGE)
TitFrame.pack(side=TOP)
self.lblTit = Label(TitFrame ,font=('times new roman',14 ,'bold'),text="மாணவர்தரவுத்தள மேலாண்மை அமைப்பு",bg="Ghost White")
self.lblTit.grid()
ButtonFrame =Frame(MainFrame,bd=2,width=800,height=70,padx=19,pady=10,bg="Ghost White",relief =RIDGE)
ButtonFrame.pack(side=BOTTOM)
DataFrame = Frame(MainFrame, bd=1, width=800, height=400, padx=20, pady=20, relief=RIDGE,bg="plum")
DataFrame.pack(side=BOTTOM)
DataFrameLEFT = LabelFrame(DataFrame, bd=1, width=800, height=600, padx=20,relief=RIDGE,bg="Ghost White", font=('times new roman',13 ,'bold'), text="மாணவர் விவரங்கள்\n")
DataFrameLEFT.pack(side=LEFT)
DataFrameRIGHT = LabelFrame(DataFrame, bd=1, width=450, height=300, padx=31, pady=3, relief=RIDGE,bg="Ghost White",font=('times new roman',13,'bold'),text="மாணவர்விவரங்கள்\n")
DataFrameRIGHT.pack(side=RIGHT)
#-------------------------------entries----------------------------------------
self.lblStdID = Label(DataFrameLEFT, font=('times new roman', 12, 'bold'), text="மாணவர்அடையாளஎண்:",padx=2,pady=2,bg="Ghost White")
self.lblStdID.grid(row=0,column=0,sticky=W)
self.txtStdID = Entry(DataFrameLEFT, font=('times new roman', 12, 'bold'), textvariable=StdID, width=39)
self.txtStdID.grid(row=0, column=1)
```

```
self.lblfna = Label(DataFrameLEFT, font=('times new roman', 12,
'bold'), text= "குடும்ப பெயர்:", padx=2, pady=2,bg= "Ghost White")
self.lblfna.grid(row=1, column=0, sticky=W)
self.txtfna = Entry(DataFrameLEFT, font=('times new roman', 12,
'bold'), textvariable=Firstname, width=39)
self.txtfna.grid(row=1, column=1)

self.lblSna = Label(DataFrameLEFT, font=('times new roman', 12,
'bold'), text= "பிறந்த தேதி:", padx=2, pady=2,bg= "Ghost White")
self.lblSna.grid(row=2, column=0, sticky=W)
self.txtSna = Entry(DataFrameLEFT, font=('times new roman', 12,
'bold'), textvariable=Surname, width=39)
self.txtSna.grid(row=2, column=1)
self.lblDoB = Label(DataFrameLEFT, font=('times new roman', 12,
'bold'), text= "பிறந்ததேதி:", padx=2, pady=2,bg= "Ghost White")
self.lblDoB.grid(row=3, column=0, sticky=W)
self.txtDoB = Entry(DataFrameLEFT, font=('times new roman', 12,
'bold'), textvariable=DoB, width=39)
self.txtDoB.grid(row=3, column=1)

self.lblAge = Label(DataFrameLEFT, font=('times new roman', 12,
'bold'), text= "வயது:", padx=2, pady=2,bg= "Ghost White")
self.lblAge.grid(row=4, column=0, sticky=W)
self.txtAge = Entry(DataFrameLEFT, font=('times new roman', 12,
'bold'), textvariable=Age, width=39)
self.txtAge.grid(row=4, column=1)

self.lblGender = Label(DataFrameLEFT, font=('times new roman', 12,
'bold'), text= "பாலினம்:", padx=2, pady=2,bg= "Ghost White")
self.lblGender.grid(row=5, column=0, sticky=W)
self.txtGender = Entry(DataFrameLEFT, font=('times new roman', 12,
'bold'), textvariable=Gender, width=39)
self.txtGender.grid(row=5, column=1)
```

```
self.lblAdr = Label(DataFrameLEFT, font=('times new roman', 12,
'bold'), text="முகவரி:", padx=2, pady=2,bg="Ghost White")
self.lblAdr.grid(row=6, column=0, sticky=W)
self.txtAdr = Entry(DataFrameLEFT, font=('times new roman', 12,
'bold'), textvariable=Address, width=39)
self.txtAdr.grid(row=6, column=1)
self.lblMobile = Label(DataFrameLEFT, font=('times new roman', 12,
'bold'), text="கைபேசி:", padx=2, pady=2,bg="Ghost White")
self.lblMobile.grid(row=7, column=0, sticky=W)
self.txtMobile = Entry(DataFrameLEFT, font=('times new roman', 12,
'bold'), textvariable=Mobile, width=39)
self.txtMobile.grid(row=7, column=1)
#------------------------------scroll bar and list box------------------------------
scrollbar= Scrollbar(DataFrameRIGHT)
scrollbar.grid(row=0,column=1,sticky='ns')
studentlist = Listbox(DataFrameRIGHT, width=41, height=16,
font=('times new roman', 12, 'bold'),yscrollcommand=scrollbar.set)
studentlist.bind('<<ListboxSelect>>',StudentRec)
studentlist.grid(row=0, column=0, padx=8)
scrollbar.config(command=studentlist.yview)
#------------------------------------buttons------------------------------------
self.btnAddData = Button(ButtonFrame, text="புதியனவற்றை சேர்",
font=('times new roman', 12, 'bold'), height=1, width=22, bd=4,
command=addData)
self.btnAddData.grid(row=0, column =0)
self.btnDisplayData = Button(ButtonFrame, text="காட்சிபாடுத்து ",
font=('times new roman', 12, 'bold'), height=1, width=16, bd=4,
command=DisplayData)
self.btnDisplayData.grid(row=0, column=1)
self.btnClearData = Button(ButtonFrame, text="அழி", font=('times
new roman', 12, 'bold'), height=1, width=6,
bd=4,command=clearData)
self.btnClearData.grid(row=0, column=2)
```

```
self.btnDeleteData = Button(ButtonFrame, text="நீக்கு", font=('times new roman', 12, 'bold'), height=1, width=7, bd=4,command=DeleteData)
self.btnDeleteData.grid(row=0, column=3)
self.btnSearchData = Button(ButtonFrame, text="தேடு", font=('times new roman', 12, 'bold'), height=1, width=6, bd=4,command=searchDatabase)
self.btnSearchData.grid(row=0, column=4)
self.btnUpdateData = Button(ButtonFrame, text="புதுப்பி", font=('times new roman', 12, 'bold'), height=1, width=12, bd=4,command=update)
self.btnUpdateData.grid(row=0, column=5)
self.btnExit = Button(ButtonFrame, text="வெளியேறு", font=('times new roman', 12, 'bold'), height=1, width=12, bd=4, command=iExit)
self.btnExit.grid(row=0, column=6)
if __name__=='__main__':
root = Tk()
   application = Student(root)
root.mainloop()
# Back End Database Manipulation
import sqlite3
defstudentData():
   con=sqlite3.connect("student.db")
cur = con.cursor()
cur.execute("CREATE TABLE IF NOT EXISTS student(id INTEGER PRIMARY KEY,StdID text, Firstname text, Surname text, DoBtext,Age text, Gender text,Addresstext,Mobile text)")
con.commit()
con.close()
defaddStdRec(StdID, Firstname, Surname , DoB ,Age, Gender, Address, Mobile):
   con = sqlite3.connect("student.db")
cur = con.cursor()
cur.execute("INSERT INTO student VALUES (NULL,?,?,?,?,?,?,?,?) ", (StdID, Firstname,Surname,DoB,Age, Gender,Address,Mobile))
```

```
con.commit()
con.close()
defviewData():
   con = sqlite3.connect("student.db")
cur = con.cursor()
cur.execute("SELECT * FROM student")
rows = cur.fetchall()
con.close()
   return rows
defdeleteRec(id):
   con = sqlite3.connect("student.db")
cur = con.cursor()
cur.execute("DELETE FROM student WHERE id=?",(id,))
con.commit()
con.close()
defsearchData(StdID="", Firstname="", Surname="",DoB="",
Age="", Gender="", Address="", Mobile=""):
   con = sqlite3.connect("student.db")
cur = con.cursor()
cur.execute("SELECT * FROM student WHERE StdID=? OR
Firstname=? OR Surname=? OR DoB=? OR Age=? OR Gender=? OR
Address=? OR Mobile=?",(StdID, Firstname,Surname,DoB,Age,
Gender,Address,Mobile))
rows = cur.fetchall()
con.close()
   return rows
defdataUpdate(id,StdID="", Firstname="", Surname="",DoB="",
Age="", Gender="", Address="", Mobile=""):
   con = sqlite3.connect("student.db")
cur = con.cursor()
cur.execute("UPDATE student SET StdID=?, Firstname=?,
DoB=?,Age=?,Address=?Mobile=?,WHERE id=?", (StdID, Firstname,
Surname, DoB, Age, Gender, Address, Mobile, id))
con.commit()
con.close()
studentData()
```

8.8 CONCLUSION

In this section, an outline of the use of Databases in Tamil is clarified comprehensively. It will give a plan to the developers about the fundamental Tamil portrayal and use of the data set administration framework. This section plans to think about storing and utilizing the Tamil Language scripts in the information base. In this way, the requirement of complete information and finding out the nuts and bolts of the data set administration framework. Also, a couple of data set frameworks are introduced here, similar to MS-Excel, MySQL, and SQLite, with python projects to control it.

CHAPTER 9

Open Tamil

9.1 INTRODUCTION

Open-Tamil is a free and open-source Tamil Text/Natural Language Processing library (NLP) written in Python and developed in the early 2010s. This chapter explains the Open-Tamil capabilities and features presented in the Open-Tamil python library. The Open-Tamil Python package is distributed under an MIT license. The package is available at the site https://pypi.org/project/Open-Tamil, and the latest version of this package is 1.0. The users can invoke the particular functions per their needs by using the specific package/sub-packages.

Installation

Installation from the Python Package Index is also recommended, following the commands, *$ pip install open-tamil.*

After installation, the user can invoke the required function from the Open-Tamil package. The functionalities available in the systems are listed in the website www.tamilcomputing.co.in.

S. No.	*Functions (in English)*	*Functions (in Tamil)*
1.	GNU ASpell Spell Checker	GNU ASpell Spell Checker
2.	TamilinayaVaani Spell Checker	TamilinayaVaani Spell Checker
3.	Text to Speech Synthesizer	உரை ஒலி மாற்றி
4.	Classifier	சொல் மொழி பகுப்பாய்வு - செயற்கை நுண்ணறிவு

S. No.	*Functions (in English)*	*Functions (in Tamil)*
5.	Crossword	சொல் தேடல் - குறுக்கெழுத்து
6.	Tamil Number	தமிழ் எண்கள்
7.	Tamil Stemmer	தமிழ் வேர்ச்சொல் பகுப்பாய்வு
8.	Sandhi Checker	தமிழ் சந்திப்பிழை திருத்தி
9.	Tamil Multiplication Tables	பெருக்கல் அட்டவணை
10.	Word Count	சொல் எண்ணி
11.	Transliteration	ஒலிபெயர்ப்பி
12.	Tamil Spell Checker	தமிழ் எழுத்துப் பிழைதிருத்தி
13.	Unicode Converter	ஒறுங்குறி (யுனிகோட்) மாற்றி
14.	Tamil N-gram	தமிழ் N-கிராம்
15.	Tamil Game Minnal	தமிழ் மின்னல் விளையாட்டு
16.	Tamil Unigram	தமிழ் யுனிகிராம்
17.	Tamil Anagram	தமிழ் அனாகிராம்
18.	Reverse Words	சொல்லை திருப்பி எழுது
19.	Text summarizer	தமிழ் உரை சுருக்கி
20.	Tamil Morse Code	தமிழில் மோர்சு குறியீடு (தந்தி)
21.	Open-Tamil Version	ஓப்பன்-தமிழ் வரிசை எண்
22.	Matthirai	மாத்திரை

All these functions are demonstrated through the Tamil Web site http://tamilpesu.us/ta, which is shown in the following section one by one.

9.2 OPENING PAGE OF TAMILPESU.US

It lists all the functionalities available on the website. The user can select the menu options and access the particular demonstration. It demonstrates how a specific functionality will work with a sample example. The learners can understand the same by accessing the website.

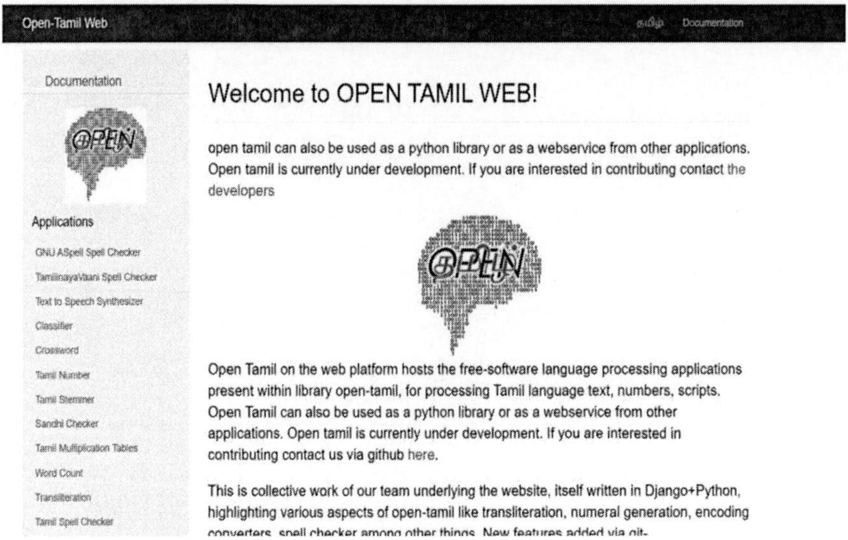

9.3 GNU ASPELL SPELL CHECKER

GNU Aspell, usually called just Aspell, is a free software spell checker designed to replace Ispell. It is the standard spell checker for the GNU operating system. It also compiles for other Unix-like operating systems and Windows. The working nature of GNU ASpell Spell Checker functionality is shown below.

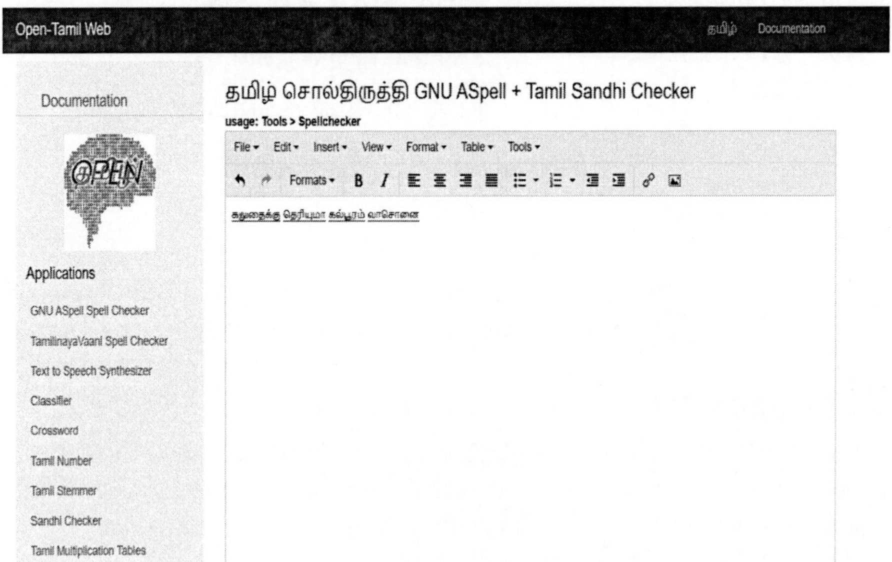

After entering into this spell checker, the user can type the text and access the text editor to type the text. Once the text is organized, the user can correct the text by going to the tool option and the Spellcheck option. Once the option is selected, the system will show the result with red underlining. Then the user can go to the individual words and correct the terms. The correct sentence is shown in the following picture.

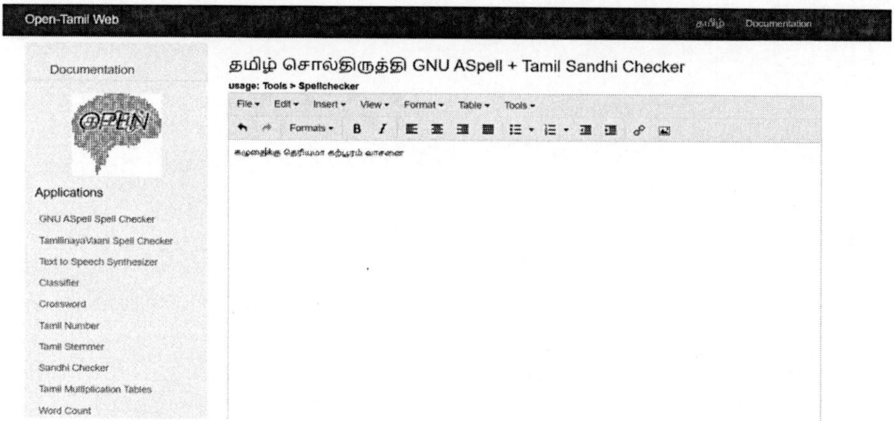

9.4 TAMILINAIYAVAANISPELL CHECKER

It is a spell checker from the Tamil Virtual Academy, used in the python environment. The main technical problem of correcting Tamil spelling errors in the text is due to the discrete infinity of vocabulary generation mechanisms in the morphologically rich agglutinative language and conjugation "sandhi: and free-word order properties of Tamil Language. It prevents us from seeing much success while applying cookie-cutter techniques like Levenshtein-distance search on a fixed wordlist either exhaustively, a poor choice, or via a selective search of edit distance by the Norvig Algorithm. Applying case rules, stemming the words and using a list of commonly occurring errors has shown success in proprietary spelling checkers like Vaani, MenTamizh, etc., which are the current state of the art.

The functioning method of the Tamilinaiyavaani spell checker is demonstrated here. After entering into this spell checker, the user can type the text and access the text editor to type the text. Once the text is organised, the user can correct the text by going to the tool option and the Spellcheck option. Once the option is selected, the system will show the result with red underlining. Then the user can go to the individual words and correct the words correctly. The correct sentence is shown in the following picture.

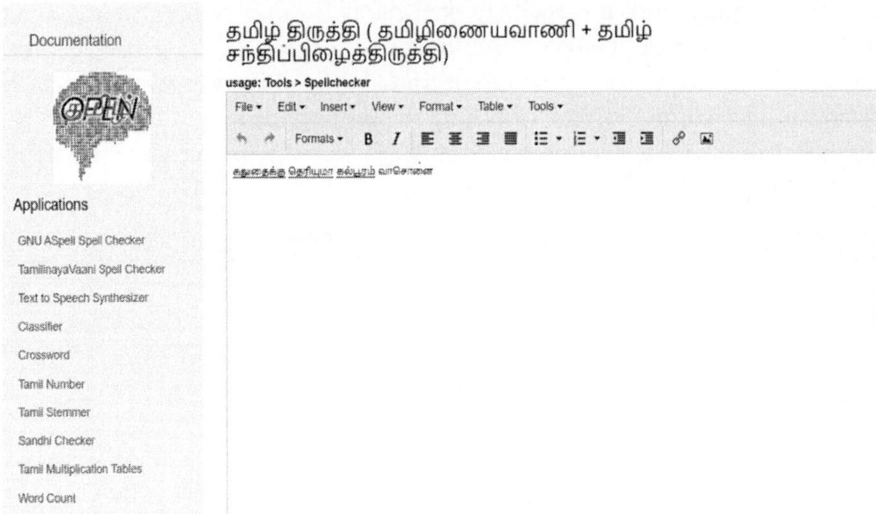

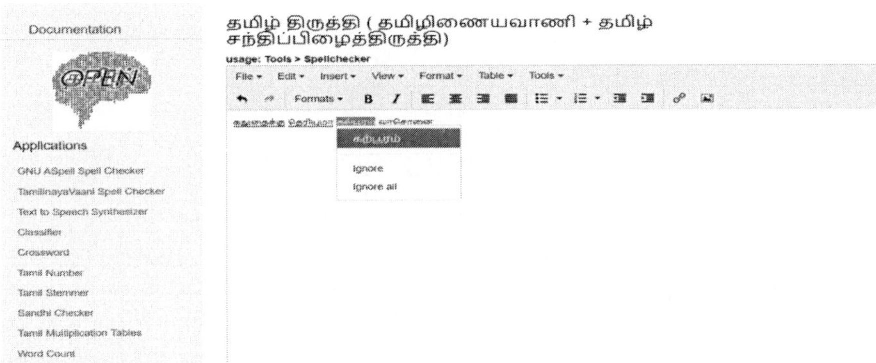

9.5 TEXT TO SPEECH SYNTHESIZER

TTS converts text to speech. It will investigate how Tamil's language structure can be used to find a suitable algorithm; when applied systematically, a set of rules can generate the speech from text. But first, we need to understand what a phonetic language is. The key is to identify that Tamil is a phonetic language; we have some simple ways of doing this. If we write "முத்து" we say it as "மு + த் + து" phonetically. English is not the same, "Muthu" is written as such but pronounced in groupings of "Mu"+ "th"+ "u" as 3-syllables but with five letters. In Tamil, முத்து has 3-letters and three syllables, with the number of letters to syllables mostly remaining the same. It used the voice of Prof. Vasu Renganathan.

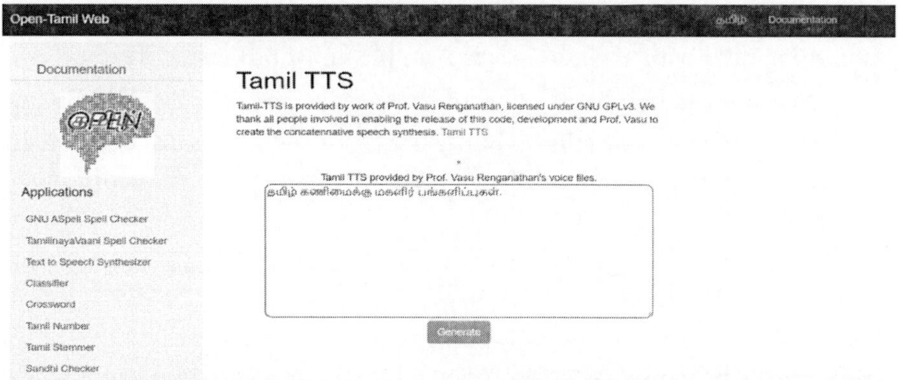

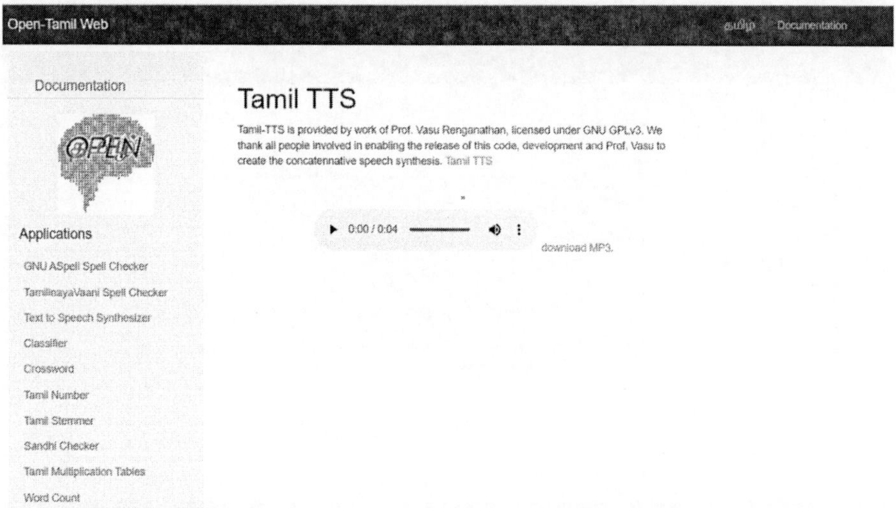

After the generation of the voice, the user can download the voice and play it on their computer. They can also change their playback speed from 0.25 to 2.

Basic Algorithm

I propose a simple-minded algorithm to generate speech from text.

Split the given Tamil text into words and for each word, apply steps 2–5.

Split the word into phonemes (phonemes = syllables) for Tamil.

For each syllable, find the corresponding phoneme (phoneme is pronunciation) in the form of a sound clip. In Tamil, this is called a 'மாத்திரை'.

Concatenate all these phonemes into the word, and apply a linear smoothing filter with a window. It is a simple signal processing theory.

Add a pause or beat based on word spacing or sentence/paragraph spacing.

This algorithm is simplistic, but it does capture the essence of a text-to-speech engine. It could sound mechanical or 'robotic', but the sound needs to be improved.

9.6 CROSSWORD

The word-grid generator application provides simple grids for building word-search games or crossword applications. One can also enter the words in the box and their equivalent English translation. It will generate a set of grids.

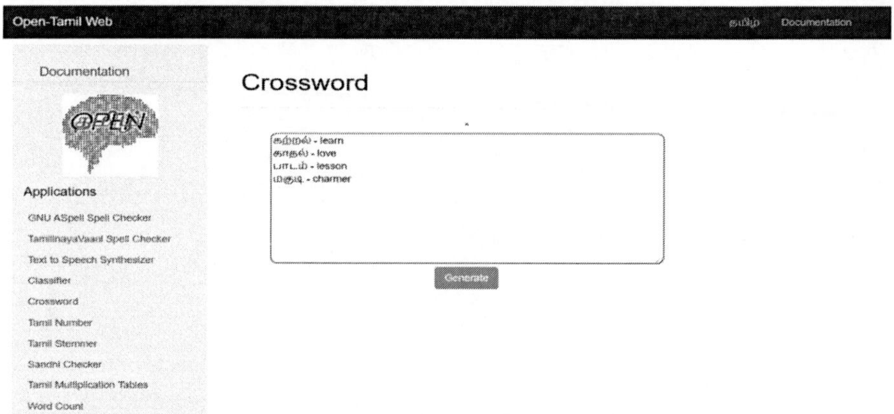

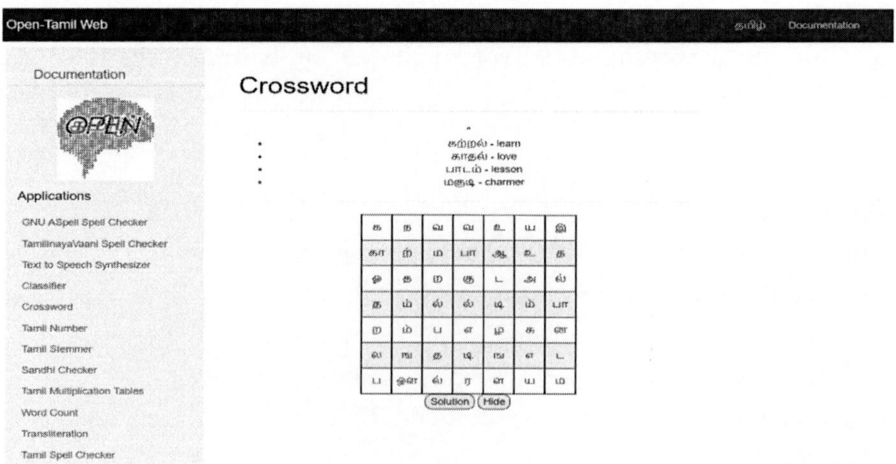

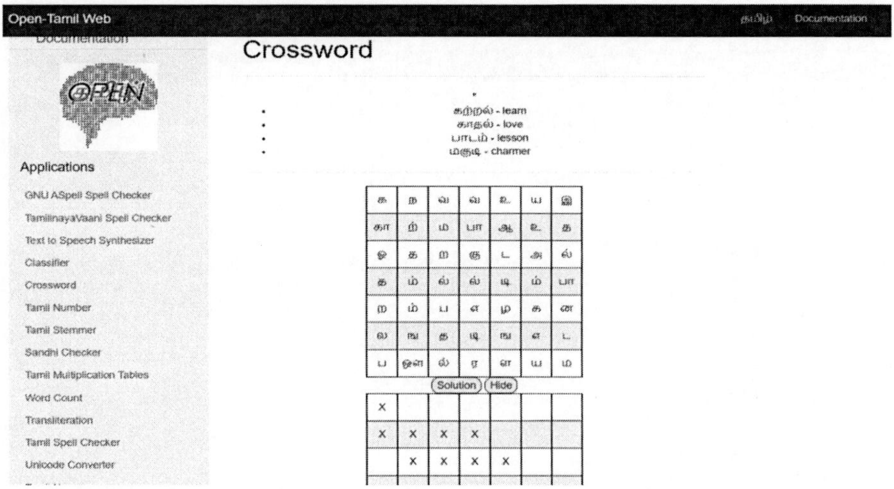

9.7 TAMIL NUMBER

When you type the number in the number option, this will generate the Tamil Number in words. It is demonstrated in the following example. In the following example, the number 100000 is typed in the first box and will display the same at the bottom in words. The user has the option to select two different styles. One is the Indian Standard, and another one is the American Standard. It is shown in the following figures.

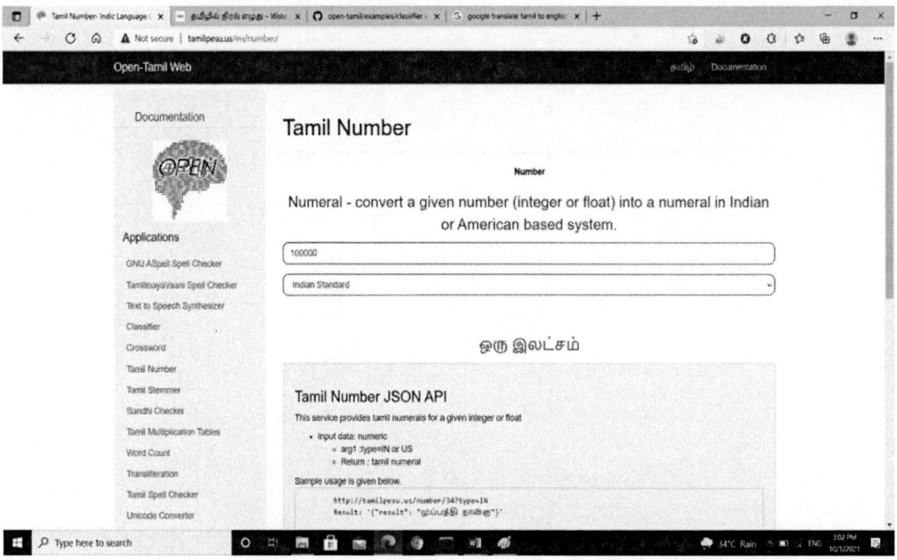

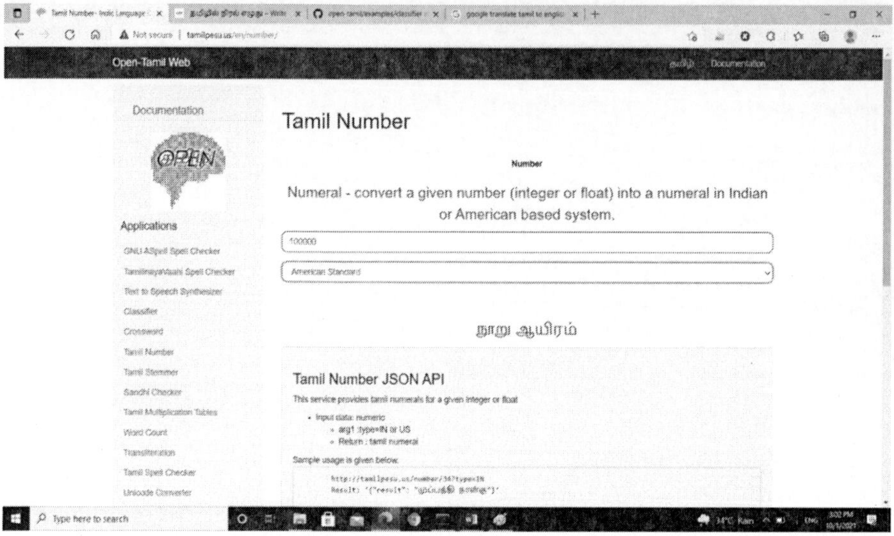

9.8 TAMIL STEMMER

It is a Tamil stemmer; a stemming algorithm is a procedure that attempts to map all the derived forms of a word to a single root, the stem. It is widely used in various applications with the main motive of enhancing the recall factor. In this tool, if you enter the line, it will automatically extract the root stem words and display them, as shown in the following example.

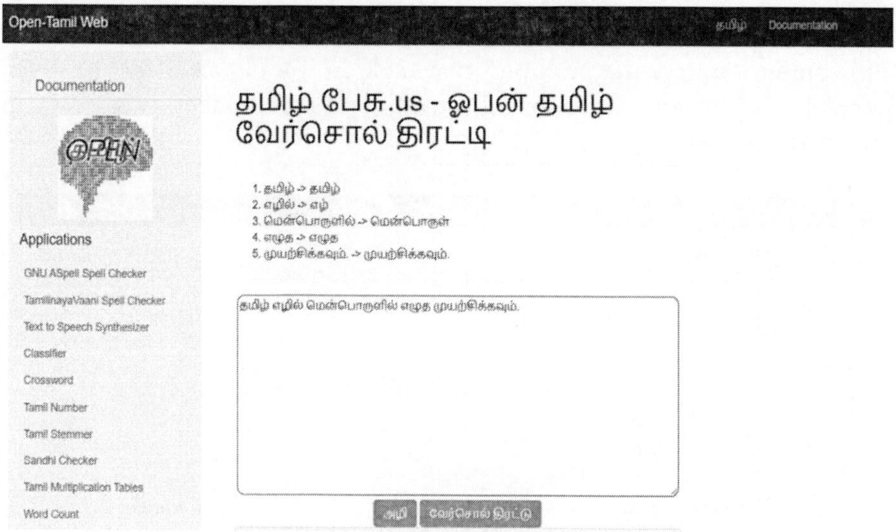

9.9 SANDHI CHECKER

The Sandhi is a cover term for various sound changes at morpheme or word boundaries. The examples include the fusion of sounds across word boundaries and the alteration of one sound depending on the nearby sounds or the grammatical function of the adjacent words. It is an error corrector, which will correct the error based on the morpheme of the Tamil Language. It is shown in the following figure.

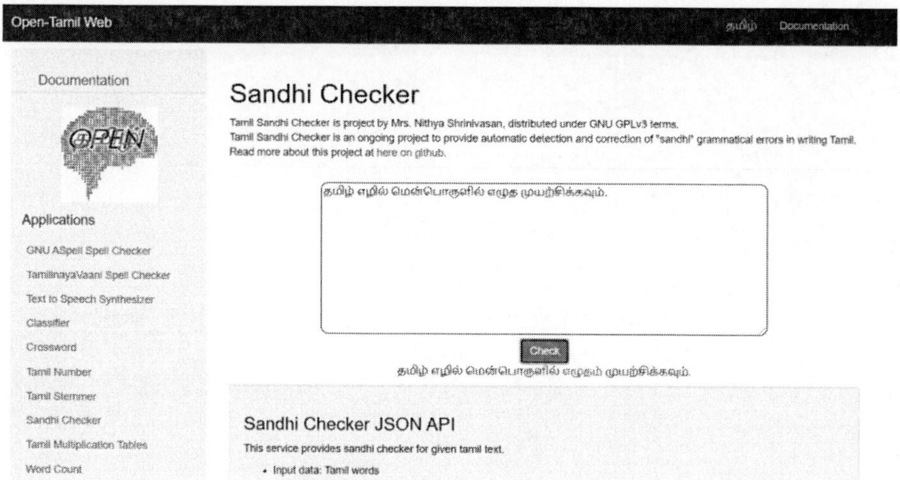

9.10 TAMIL MULTIPLICATION TABLE

This option displays the multiplication table in Tamil words for the given number, and the second option will extend up to that number. It is shown in the following figure.

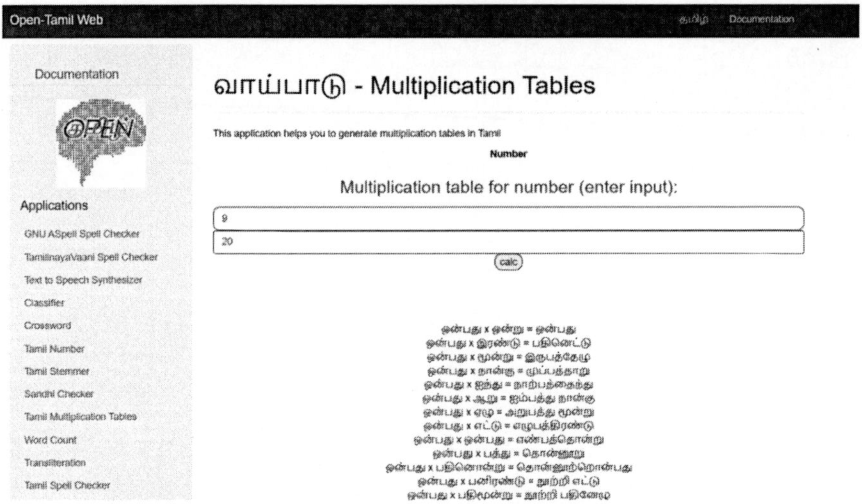

9.11 WORD COUNT

This tool counts several words and letters and displays the same. It is shown in the following figure.

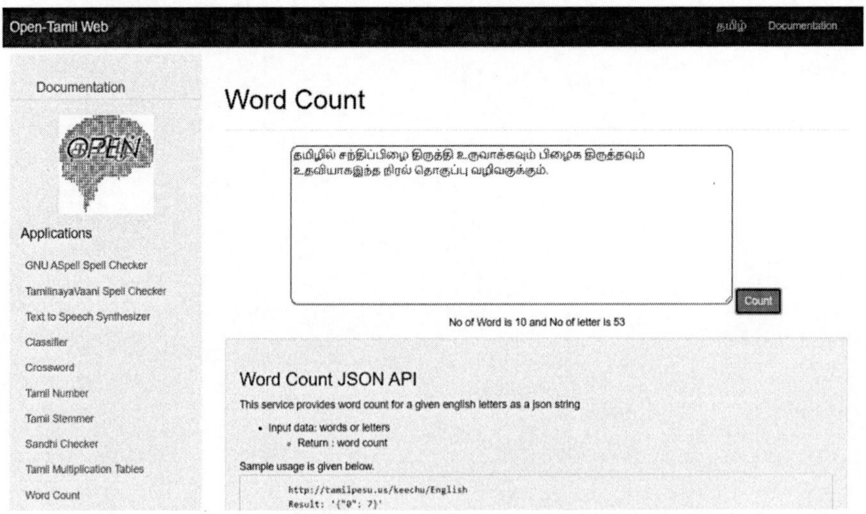

9.12 TRANSLITERATION

It will transliterate the given string English into Tamil. To start typing in Tamil, type a word as it is pronounced in English. It would then be transliterated into Tamil. e.g. if you type "Tamil moliyiltattaccucey yavirumpukiren" then it would be transliterated into "**தமிழ் மொழியில் தட்டச்சு செய்ய விரும்புகிறேன்**". It is shown in the following figure.

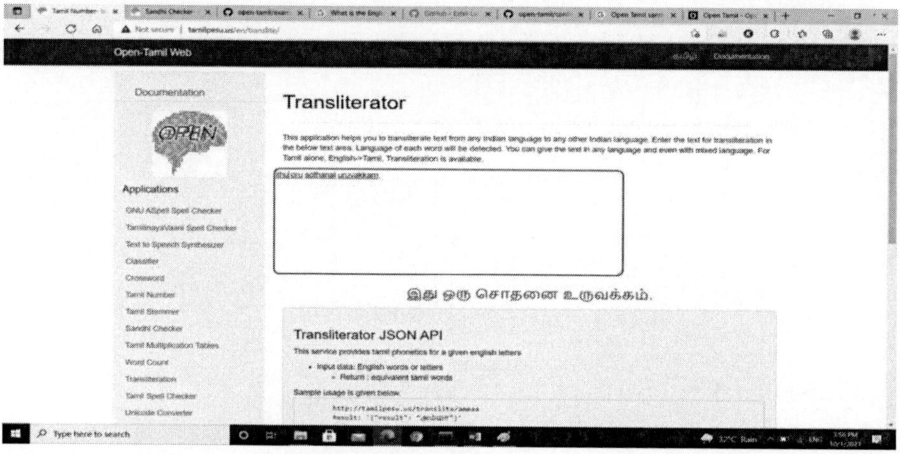

9.13 UNICODE CONVERTER

This code converter will convert other code text into Unicode text and display the same on the screen, which is shown in the following figure.

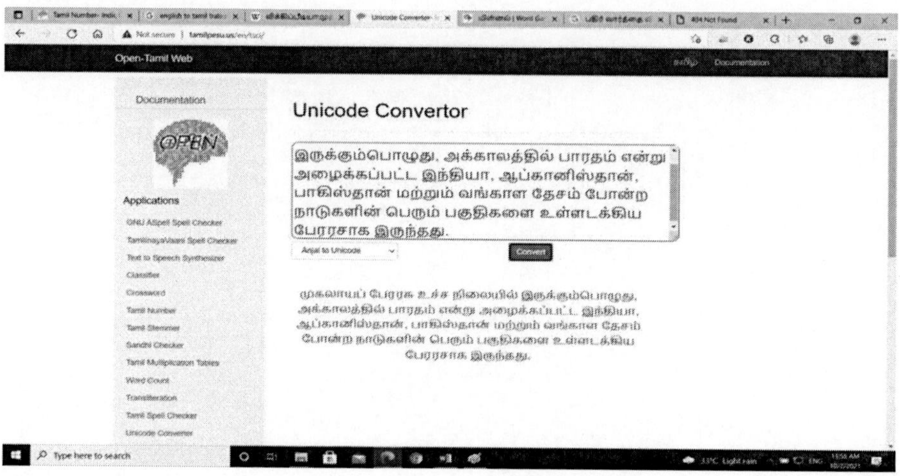

9.14 ANAGRAM

It generates alternate Tamil words using the same letters. It is shown in the following figures.

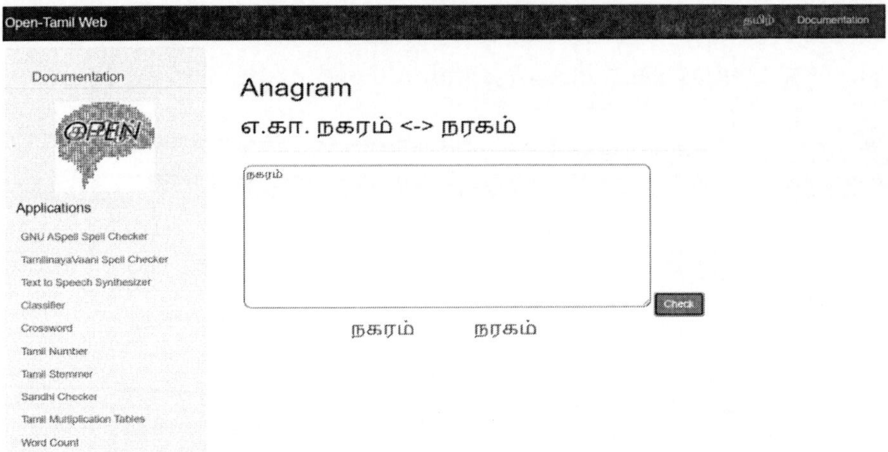

9.15 N-GRAM

In computational linguistics and probability, an n-gram is a contiguous sequence of n items from a given line of text or speech. According to the application, the items can be phonemes, syllables, letters, words, or base pairs. The n-grams are typically collected from a text or speech corpus.

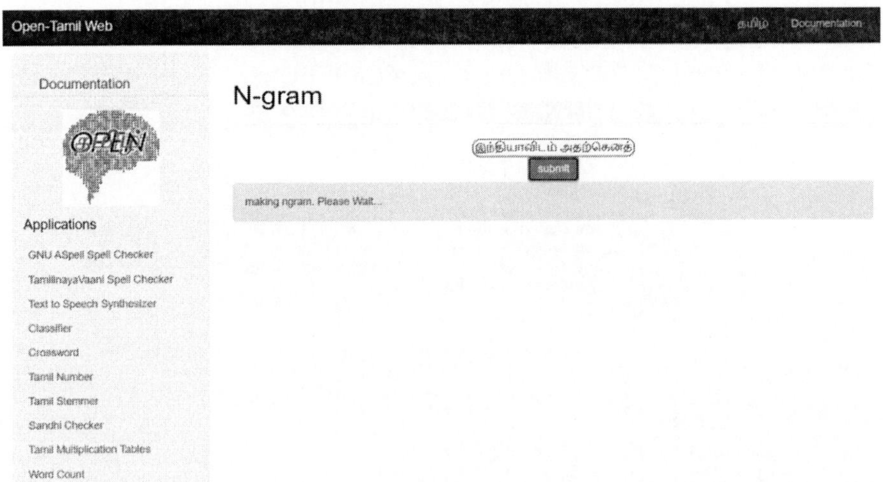

9.16 UNIGRAM

It will generate the possible words for the given numbers, shown below.

9.17 TAMIL GAME MINNAL

It is a game through which they can identify the different words occurring in particular boxes. It is shown in the following figure.

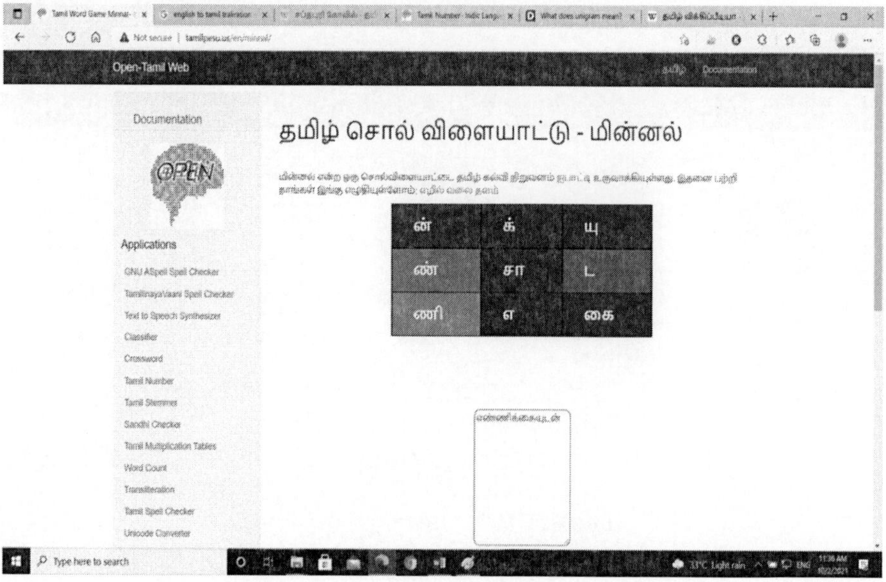

9.18 REVERSE WORDS

These reverse word tools reverse the words in straight reverse order, as shown below.

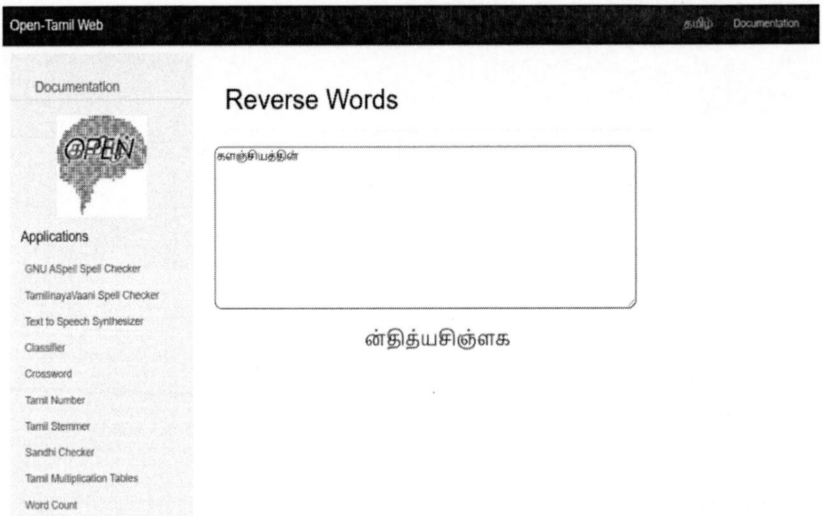

9.19 TEXT SUMMARIZER

The text summarizer summarizes the Tamil text and displays the same on the page. It converts the ten-line statement into two line statement. It is shown in the following figures.

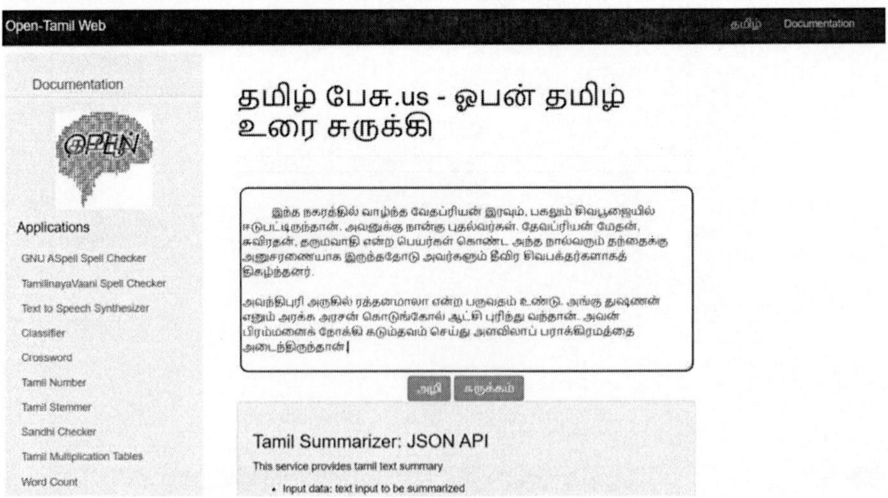

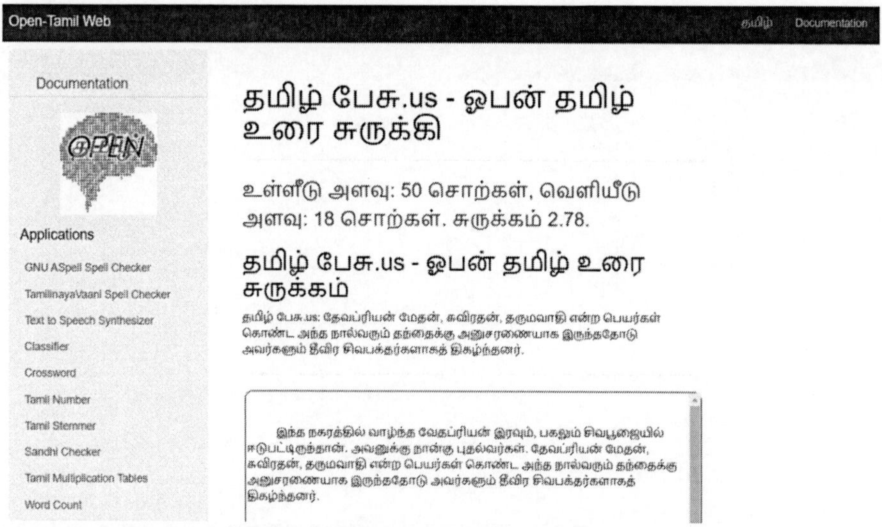

9.20 TAMIL MORSE CODE

Morse code is a method used in telecommunication to encode text characters as standardized sequences of two different signal durations, called dots and dashes, or dits and dahs. Morse code is named after Samuel Morse, one of the inventors of telegraph.

In this open Tamil, one can encode the Tamil text into Morse code, and the reverse is also performed. It is shown in the following figure.

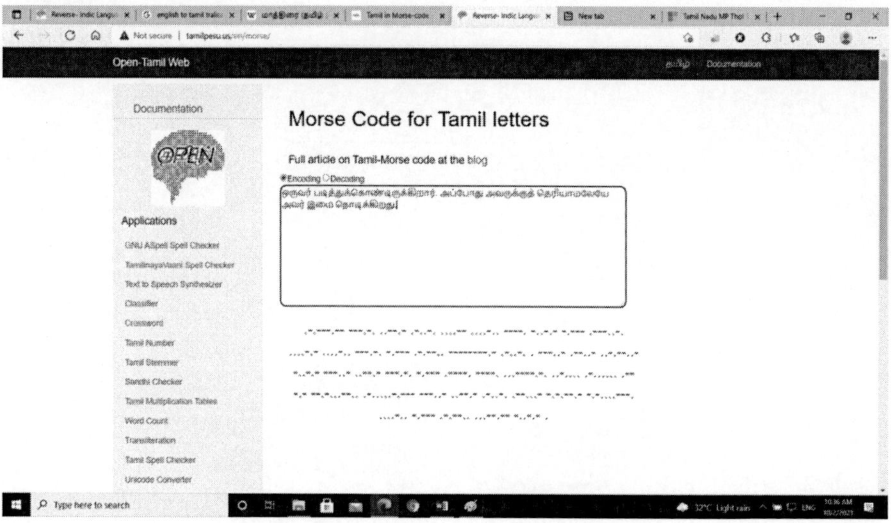

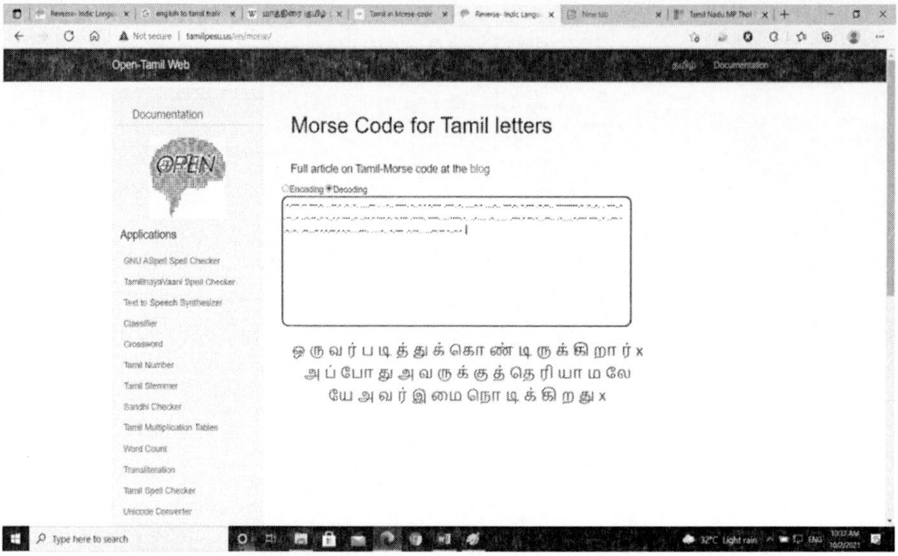

9.21 MATTHIRAI

It is a Tamil word pronunciation, and phonology term also refers to the sound system of any particular language variety. At one time, the study of phonology is only related to studying the systems of phonemes in spoken languages. It counts the number of phonemes in the sentence as per phonology.

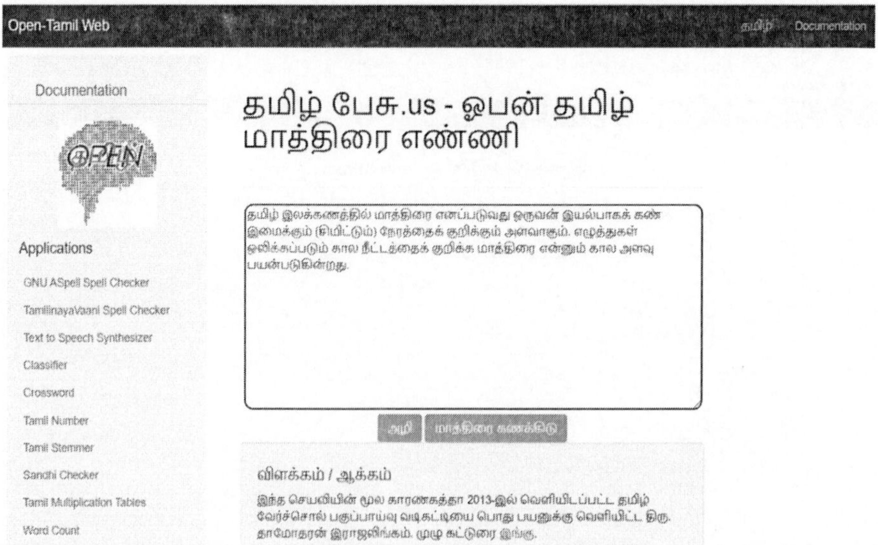

After entering the sentence in Tamil, if you enter, it will give the phoneme value for each word. It is shown in the following figure.

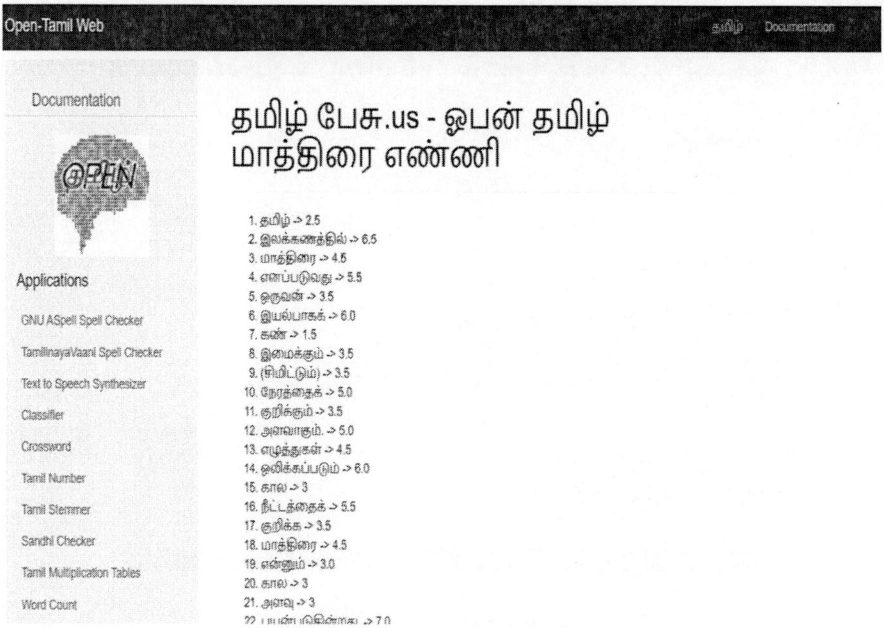

It will also show the rule for phoneme value for each type of letter and is given as follows.

மாத்திரை கணித்தல்: ஒரு தமிழ் சொல்லின் @letters மாத்திரை அளவை கணிக்கும்.

விதிகள்:

நெடில் எழுத்துக்கள் ஒலிக்கும் கால அளவு 2 மாத்திரை.

குறில் எழுத்துக்கள் ஒலிக்கும் கால அளவு 1 மாத்திரை.

மெய் எழுத்துக்கள் ஒலிக்கும் கால அளவு 1/2 மாத்திரை.

ஆய்த எழுத்தை ஒலிக்க ஆகும் கால அளவு 1/2 மாத்திரை.

மகரக் குறுக்கம் “ன்”, “ண்” ஐ தொடர்ந்து வரும் “ம்” ஆனது தன அரை மாத்திரையில் இருந்து கால் மாத்திரையாய் ஒலிக்கும்

ஔகாரக் குறுக்கம் சொல்லின் ஆரம்பத்தில் வரும் ஔ, மௌ, வௌ என்பன 1 மாத்திரையில் ஒலித்தல்

9.22 TEXT-BASED CALCULATOR

A calculator accepts the numbers in text strings and operators and produces the total number. It is shown in the following figures.

After entering the number once, if you enter the "**கணக்கிடு**" button, it will compute the value and return the results.

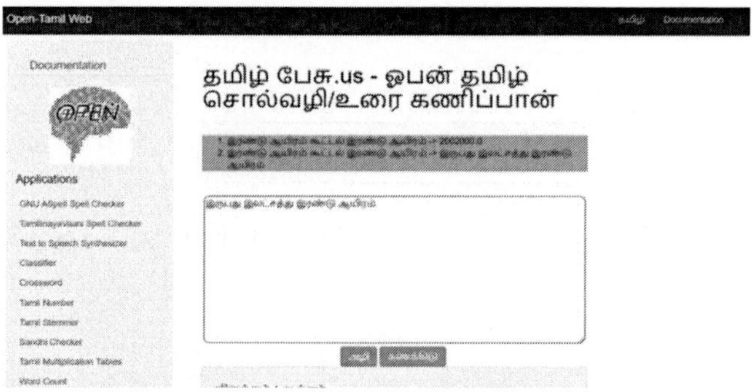

The code for all the above programs are available on the website www.tamilcomputing.com.

9.23 CONCLUSION

Open Tamil is free, open-source software developed by the independent Tamil software developers interested in Tamil Computing. It provides various functionalities, which are demonstrated in the above sections. The package consists of 21 tools and the functionalities shown above. The users can also access the codes of these tools by accessing the open Tamil packages, which are available on the www.tamilcomputing.co.in.

CHAPTER 10

Speech Processing

10.1 SPEECH PROCESSING

The understanding of speech involves collecting the meaning of utterance to carry out the speaker's command. The speech processing technique allows studying the human vocal communication of a language and processing those as signals. The characteristics considered for speech processing are acquiring, manipulating, storing, and transferring the output speech signals. The speech recognition system develops the methodologies and technologies to realize and translate oral communication into text by a computer system. It is widely known as automatic speech recognition (ASR), computer speech recognition, or speech-to-text (STT). The ASR allows transcribing the speech into a text of a language. The ASR is always a challenging research field.

Although the ASR for various foreign languages like English, French, Czech, etc., is still mature, the research is for the Indian languages like Hindi, Telugu, and Tamil. Even though many people are working on the Tamil language for large vocabulary continuous speech recognition (LVCSR), the significant level of Tamil is still not explored. The difficulties of the Tamil language are due to the lack of resources like annotated speech and text corpora for a different domain. Ten million words of text corpus and 30 hours of speech recoding are required to design an authentic statistical ASR language model. But Tamil does not have such a vast data set. Tamil is an agglutinated language, which increases complexity and requires many data sets to train the model to achieve a good result.

10.2 TAMIL: PHONOLOGY

Tamil vowels are classified as a short sound vowel (குறில்), five letters, and long sound vowel (நெடில்), with seven in numbers. The sharp sound vowel has one diphthong, and the long sound vowel has two diphthongs. Similarly, the consonants of Tamil are categorized into three parts, hard, soft, and medium. In addition to the standard 247 characters, Tamil has a unique letter ayutham (ஃ), and six characters are taken from Sanskrit and another language. The Tamil phonology has retroflex consonants, and very few consonant clusters are permitted, which are not permitted as a word's initial letter. Tamil cannot distinguish the aspirated and unaspirated consonants. The plosive voice follows strict rules. Everywhere the plosives are voiced except word-initial or double-dare treated as unvoiced.

10.3 TAMIL: AGGLUTINATIVE NATURE

Tamil follows the agglutinative grammar structure in which the suffixes mark noun class, number and case, verb, tense, and other grammatical forms. These suffixes followed morphotactic rules and allowed to frame many inflectional variants of each word. The STEM of Tamil is followed as given below.

STEM: Negative participle nominalization plural locative ablative inclusive.

In English, maximum of four-word forms for a verb and a noun. But in Tamil, assume only two affixes of each type, at least 2^7 = 128 inflected word forms present for each stem. But in nature, more than two options are current, but there can be gaps. So, for 1,000 lexical vocabularies, the inflected Tamil words can be 1,28,000.

Due to inflections, the Part of Speech has different forms. The morphological inflections of nouns include gender and number. The prepositions can be independent or nouns combined like accusative, dative, instrumental, sociative, locative, ablative, benefactive, genitive, vocative, clitics, and selective. Table 1 shows the possible suffixes in Tamil.

Table 10.1: Noun Case Suffixes in Tamil

Cases	*Suffixes*
Accusative	ஏ, ஐ
Dative	க்கு, ற்கு
Instrumental	ஆல்
Sociative	ஒடு, உடன்
Locative	இல், உள், இடம்
Ablative	இருந்து
Benefactive	க்காக, ற்காக
Genitive	இன், அது, உடைய
Vocative	ஏ
Clitics	ம், ஓ, தான்
Selective	ஆவது
Interrogative	ஆ, ஓ

The verbs in Tamil also take various forms like simple, transitive, intransitive, causative, infinitive, imperative, and reporting. Table 2 shows the verb case suffixes in Tamil.

Table 10.2: Verb Case Suffixes in Tamil

Suffix	*Categories*	*Sub-categories*	*Suffixes*
Tense	Present		கிறு, கின்று, ஆனின்று
	Past		த், ந், ற், இன்
	Future		ப், வ்
Person	First	Singular	ஏன்
		Plural	ஓம்
	Second	Singular	ஆய்
		Plural	ஈர்கள்
		Honorific	ஈர்
	Third	Male Singular	ஆன், அன்
		Female Singular	ஆள்
		Common Plural	ஆர்கள்
		Honorific	ஆர், அர்
		Neutral Singular	அது
		Neutral Plural	அன
Other	Causative		இ
	Verbal Noun Untensed		அல்
	Infinitive		உ
	Imperative	Plural	உங்கள்
		Negative	ஆதே, ஆது
	Passive		படு
	Future	Negative	மாட், இல்லை
	Optative		முடியும், வேண்டும், கூடும், ஆம்
		Negative	முடியாது, கூடாது, வேண்டாம்
	Morphophonology		ந், க், ம், ச், த்
	Plural		கள்

10.4 MORPHOPHONOLOGY

Morphonology is commonly known as *sandhi,* in which the two words can be combined by deletion, insertion, or substitution of phonemes in word boundaries to form a new comment. The below example shows *sandhi.*

அரசு (*government*) + பணி (*service*) → அரசுப்பணி

ஆபரணம் (*ornament*) + தங்கம் (*gold*) → ஆபரணத்தங்கம்

ஒன்று (*first*) + ஆவது (*selective case suffix*) → ஒன்றாவது

In the first example, *ப்* is inserted. In the second example, the last letter of the first word (*ம்*) is replaced by a new letter (*த்*). And in the third example, the first word's final consonant (*று* = *ற்* + *உ*) is merged with the second word's first letter's vowel (*ற்* + *ஆ* = *றா*) and forms a new word.

In Tamil, morphophonology is based on phonotactics. The following rules are included in Tamil.

- '*உ*' removal rule
- '*வ்*' and '*ய்*' removal rule
- Doubling rule
- *க்*, *ச்*, *ட்* and *ப்* insertion rule.

Sometimes, the morphophonology is based on the context; for example, பழக்கூடை and பழங்கூடை (old basket) due to which modeling of morphophonology is difficult in Tamil.

10.5 TAMIL PRONUNCIATION AND PROSODY

The spoken Tamil language has several dialects. People from different parts of Tamilnadu speak in different accents. Tamil is assumed to have no stress or accent at the word level, and all language syllables are pronounced with the same emphasis.

The prosody of Tamil is autochthonal and original. There are six basic elements present. They are, phone (*ellutu*), prosodic syllable (*acai*), metrical foot (*ciir*), linkage (*taLai*), metrical line (*aTi*) and ornamentation (*toTai*). The prosodical prescriptions play a major role in many grammatical formulations and the choices for the poet in the post-classical era.

The prosodic syllable is the primary unit for speech. The prime component of Tamil prosody is the prosodic syllable (acai) which is also known as extreme and forms the metrical foot (ciir). Some prosodic syllables can overlap the phonologically defined syllable. Word boundaries are often merged with morphophonology.

10.6 FEATURES AND HURDLES OF TAMIL

Tamil has the following features, which allow for building a reliable prosodic syllable model for ASR.

- The inflectional morphology, morphophonology, morphotactic and phonotactics are complex, but rule-based.
- The stress and pitch accent is absent.
- Prosodic syllable plays an important role in intonation and duration of the phase.
- Simple and well-defined linguistic rules to identify syllables in a phrase.

As we have many syllables, a sound method to integrate syllables with the phone is much more necessary.

The prominently identified problems for the context variability in the LVCSR system in the prosodic syllable modeling are

- Management of large vocabulary size due to inflectional morphology when transcribing the speech utterance into prosodic syllable units.
- Integrateprosodic syllable information into triphone modeling, which reduces the real triphones to be modeled.
- Use Mel Frequency Cepstral Coefficient (MFCC) or Spectral Sub-band Centroid Histogram (SSCH) to develop a method to adapt to the environment automatically.

10.7 AUTOMATIC SPEECH RECOGNITION

10.7.1 Concepts of ASR

Technology in speech allows many applications like speech recognition, TTS, speaker or language identification, and verification. Usually, speech recognition automatically transcribes the speech into text. In recent years, ASR has been much developed and allows human-computer interaction with or without pointing devices.

ASR involves signal processing, feature extraction, acoustics, information theory, linguistics and computer science. Acoustics provide the necessary understanding of the relationship between speech utterance and phycological processes in speech production and perception. The speech recognition process helps extract discriminate and relevant information called features from speech signals with robustness.

10.7.2 Architecture of ASR

In speech recognition, the acoustic input is treated as a noisy version and decoded to all possible sentences and the probability is computed. The sentence with maximum probability is chosen as output. Figure 10.1 explains this,

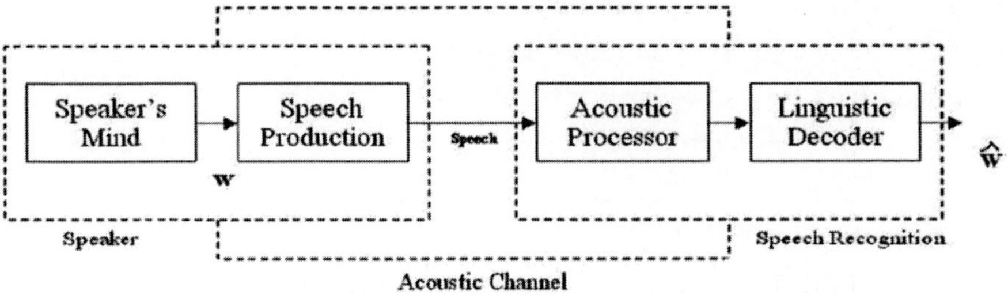

Figure 10.1: Source Channel Model

Source: Frederick Jelinek (1997).

The Hidden Markov Model (HMM) is the preferred structure for the acoustic model because it can normalize time variations of speech signals and characterize statistical speech signals. The state-of-the-art commercial and the most laboratory speech recognition system are based on the HMM model that gives very low WER when tested with standard speech databases.

10.7.3 Issues of Speech Signal Variability

The well-developed ASRs cannot match performance due to some traits like speaker and language dependency, speaking style and apply environmental applicability.

10.7.3.1 *Context Variability*

Languages have the same phonetic sound of the same word with different meanings, depending on the context. So, the physiology of articulators involved in speech production depends on the neighboring phones.

10.7.3.2 *Style Variability*

Discrete speech recognition with a small vocabulary can easily detect the speech as the user pauses between the words. But in continuous speech recognition, it isn't easy to get the perfect accuracy rate for the speech. The higher the speaking rate is the higher the word error rate (WER).

10.7.3.3 *Speaker Variability*

The speaker's vocalization is dependent on many factors like a vocal tract, age, sex, health education, etc. A speaker-independent includes a user enrollment process, which will train the system before using it.

10.7.3.4 *Environment Variability*

The reliability can be less in the acoustic environment, which will be a significant limitation in speech-based interfaces in mobile communication devices. The acoustic model is always unpredictable and cannot be used to train the model.

10.7.4 Speech Signal Acquisition and Feature Extraction

The forepart is the signal processing module in the speech recognizer, which reduces the data rate, removes noise, and extracts salient features required for the speech recognition algorithm. In the case of 8 kHZ bandwidth of the speech, 16 kHZ sampling is enough and for reduced bandwidth like telephone, speech 8 kHz can be used.

The critical issue in speech recognition is the extraction of the reliable feature of the speech signal. The time-domain features computation is more expensive than frequency domain features like Linear Predictive Coding (LPC) and Mel Frequency Cepstral coefficients (MFCC). Moreover, temporal changes in the speech signal are also required to capture. The 16 kHZ sampling rates of the feature vectors are followed.

- 13th order MFCC c_k
- 13th order – 1st order delta MFCC computed as $\Delta c_k = c_{k+2} - c_{k-2}$
- 13th order – 2nd order delta MFCC computed as $\Delta\Delta c_k = c_{k+1} - c_{k-1}$.

The MFCC coefficient can have 39 coefficients the feature vector of x_k is $x_k = \begin{pmatrix} c_k \\ \Delta c_k \\ \Delta\Delta c_k \end{pmatrix}$.

The 13th order MFCC with 1st and 2nd derivates is used; it reduces 20% of WER.

10.7.5 Hidden Markov Models

Hidden Markov Model (HMM) characterizes the detected data sample in a discrete-time frame. It is considered a powerful statistical tool for building an economic parametric model by the dynamic programming model for unified segmentation and classification of patterns like speech utterances. It can characterize speech into a parametric random process. In HMM, there is no one-to-one correspondence, and it is impossible to decide the determinant state sequence for the observed series. The state sequence is hidden here.

The HMM is represented by,

- $O = o_1 o_2 o_3 o_4 \ldots . o_M$ – an output observation alphabet. The output symbols correspond to the system's speech features.
- $\Omega = \{1, 2, 3, 4 \ldots \mathrm{N}\}$ – A HMM state-space set. The state occupancy is denoted as s_t, *t* is time.
- $A = \{a_{ij}\}$ – A transition probability matrix. The a_{ij} is the probability of transition from state i to state *j*. $a_{ij} = P(s_t = j \mid s_{t-1} = i)$.
- $B = \{b_i(k)\}$ – An output probability matrix. When state $i$enters the probability of producing a symbol of o_k is $b_i(k)$. It is given as $b_i(k)$ = $P(X_t = o_k | s_t = i)$'
- $\pi = \{\pi_i\}$ – An initial state distribution in which π_i= $P(\, s_0 = i)$ for 1$\leq$ $i \leq N$'
- The HMM model is represented in Figure 10.2. In this figure, the three stages are displayed. The one state to another state transition is shown with directed edges, and the weight of each transition is probability is a_{ij}. The output $b_i(k)$ of every state is shown in a rectangle box and the initial probability π_i is also shown.

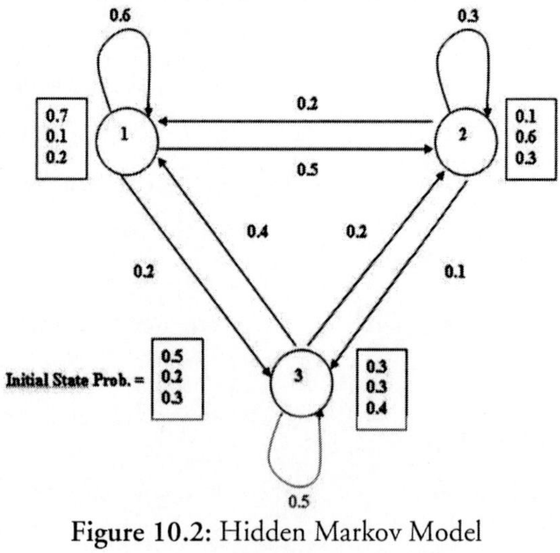

Figure 10.2: Hidden Markov Model

Source: Xuedong Huang *et al.* (2001)

As the $\pi_i, b_i(k)$ and a_{ij} are probabilities they must satisfy the following.

$a_{ij} \geq 0, b_i(k) \geq 0$ and $\pi_i \geq 0$ for all i, j, k

$\sum_{j=1}^{N} a_{ij} = 1$, $\sum_{i=1}^{N} \pi_i = 1$ and $\sum_{k=1}^{N} b_i(k) = 1$

The complete specification of HMM has two constant size parameters, M and N, representing the total number of output symbols and states, respectively, and A, B, π. So the HMM can be framed as,

$\phi = (A, B, \pi)$

The HMM can treat the following problems.

- ***Evaluation:*** When the given model ϕ and observation sequence is $X = (x_1, x_2, x_3 \dots x_T)$, calculate the probability $P(X|\phi)$. A forward algorithm is used to determine the likelihood of the observation sequence.
- ***Decode:*** When the given model ϕ and observation sequence is $X = (x_1, x_2, x_3 \dots x_T)$, then find the most likely state sequence $S = (s_0, s_1, s_2 \dots s_T)$ in the observations. The Viterbi algorithm is used for decoding. It allows unhiding the hidden state sequence.
- ***Learn:*** When the given model ϕ and observation sequence is $X = (x_1, x_2, x_3 \dots x_T)$, then adjust the model to maximize the likelihood $\prod_x P(X|\phi)$. The *BanumWelch* or *Forward-Backward* algorithm is used to train the models.

All these problems are linked with the same probabilistic framework, which can be achieved using the dynamic programming design technique. Left to right HMM model can be used to model speech units. HMM is typically used in the concatenation of phone models to form dictionary words. It represents a word or sub-word of speech vocalization of the Figure 10.3 which shows the 3-state HMM, and the fourth model will be added automatically in HMM.

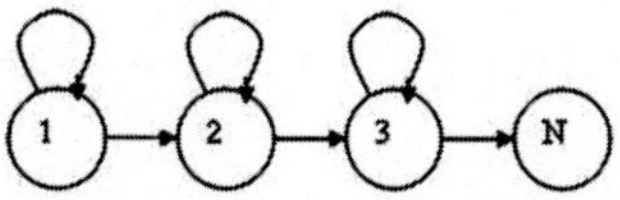

Figure 10.3: 3-State HMM

10.8 TEXT-TO-SPEECH SYNTHESIS

Text to speech as a layman's understanding converts ordinary text language into speech by the speech computer or speech synthesizer. In today's technological world, artificial intelligence, like Natural Language Processing (NLP), treats the natural language text as information extraction, translation into other languages, domain-specific transcriptions, etc. This NLP allows language text into speech-language to help blind people, non-reader of native and non-native speakers. The Text To Speech (TTS) converts the standard text into speech using a speech synthesizer computer system. Generally, the given text needs to be processed based on the linguistics and acoustics.

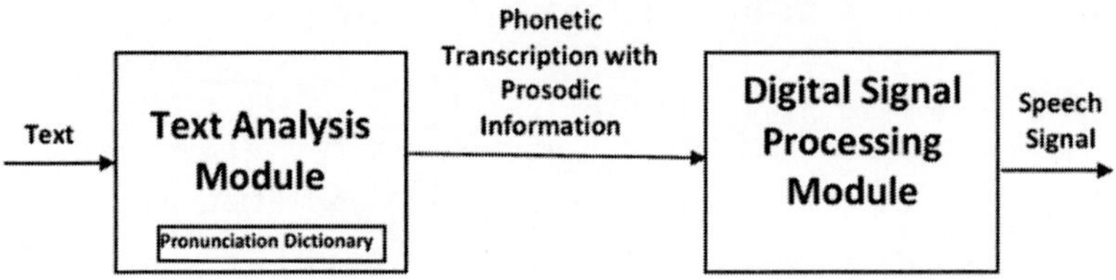

Figure 10.4: Simple Outline of the TTS System

Figure 10.4 shows the basic structure of the TTS system. The text analysis module separates the grammatical units like sentences, phrases, morphemes, and words with initial level tagging. The appropriate sound in digital signal processing will be developed for each word and morphemes. A pronunciation dictionary must be installed in the TTS system, which helps to have all pronunciation of words in single morpheme and allomorphs.

10.8.1 Text to Speech in Tamil

Natural speech depends on prosody, nothing but specific properties like pitch, loudness, intonation, and duration. The prosody is important for synthesized speech which conveys language's aspect of meaning and structure. The acoustic features correspond to variations in the period of speech units, amplitude and frequency. The proper prosody generation for the Tamil language is complex as Tamil has less or no explicit information about prosody and very tricky to deduct the data automatically. The output of the text analysis module is a phonetic transcription of input text along with the output waveform of desired pitch, duration, and intensity.

10.8.2 Prosody Modeling Approaches

The functional aspects of prosody are

- Phrasing
- Duration
- Intonation
- Intensity

Besides the above aspects, it includes focus on grammar, melody, tempo, discourse, emotion, and rhythm. There are two approaches present to model prosodic rule-based and corpus-based systems. The rule-based complex set of rules is used to design the prosodic model by observing the natural speech. And experts can add the new rules after a thorough examination. In the corpus-designed speech, the annotated speech corpus is designed with various levels of prosodic information. When new units are found, they can be appended by the database administrator in the corpus.

10.8.2.1 *Prosodic Phrasing*

Tamil is well structured with the subject-verb-object combination (SOV). The prosodic model is essential to increase the naturalness of the synthesis speech. The prosody variation allows for assigning meanings to certain parts of the synthesized speech, and the Tamil language mainly depends on phrasing and not on punctuation marks. The CART (Classification And Regression Trees decision tree can predict the prosodic phrases based on the features like the length of utterance and the relative position of the word/sub-word.

10.8.2.2 *Pitch Modeling*

When the prosodic boundaries are identified, the prosodic elements like duration, intonation and intensity are applied to each phrase—the main factor of intonation is the word's context and intended meanings.

For example: 'adhaippArththEn'—A single prosodic phrase with SV pattern, in which sometimes the stress given to 'adhai' (seen which) and sometime in verb 'pArththEn' (whether seen or not).

In the above example, we notice the different pitch contours of each sentence with interrogative, declarative, imperative, and exclamatory. The intonation is based on gender, attitude and emotional and physical states.

10.8.2.3 *Duration Modeling*

The duration of speech units can be short of their time when spoken in isolation which is indicated in milliseconds. In Tamil, it is denoted as "maathirai," equivalent to the blink of the human eye. The factors that decide the duration of the speech units are

- Influences of adjacent words
- Number of speech units
- The unique characteristics of speech unit.

The duration modeling is essential to producing natural, synthetic speech units in the TTS system. Many methods are present for the duration model, and the data-driven model of Riley using CARTs is used widely. The CART starts with the root node and builds the tree structure by selecting the binary queries at each node. The sample CART tree is explained in Figure 10.5. It depends on the binary answer to each question. The factors in building the tree are:

- Segment context
- Lexical and phrasing position
- Stress

10.8.2.4 *Intensity Modeling*

Intensity and intonation modeling use Artificial Neural Networks (ANNs) to predict the syllable energy. It cannot be performed at the same time using any perfect algorithm. It needs manual work like phrasing, tagging, and labeling. It requires a large amount of speech data and expert knowledge.

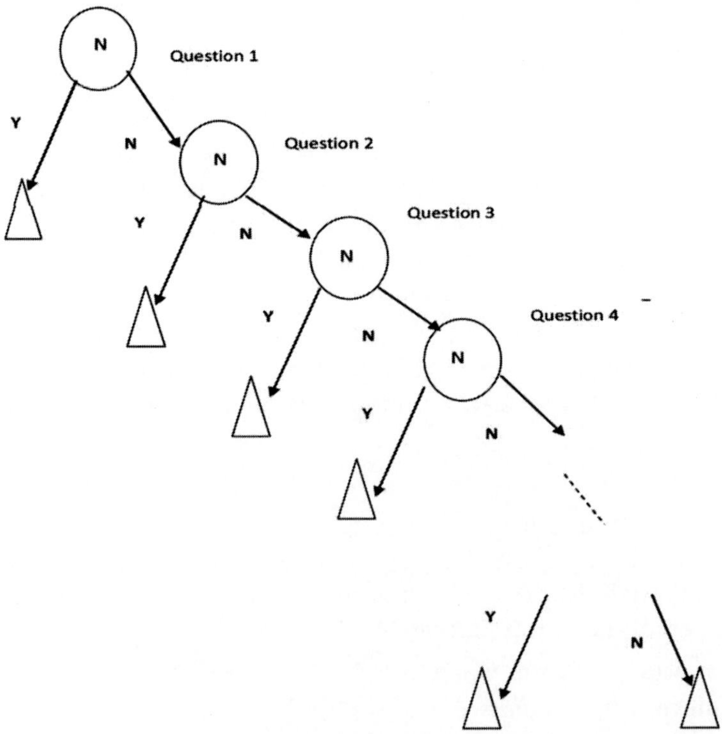

Figure 10.5: CART Model Example

10.8.3 Automatic Speech Unit Generation in TTS Synthesis

This section explains automatic speech unit generation in the Festival TTS framework. Festival is a free, language-independent synthesis engine. It has text-processing, waveform generation, and prosodic/linguistic processing modules and these modules can be rewritten. It supports two synthesis techniques called unit selection synthesis and diphone synthesis.

10.8.3.1 *Diphone Synthesis*

Diphone provides the synthesis between co-articulation effects capturing, minimizing discontinuities at concatenation points, and is relatively small in number. Figure 10.6 shows the architecture of TTS synthesis using the festival synthesis engine. The prosodic model has prosodic phrasing, generating segment duration and F0 contour generation. The unit will be selected from databases and modified based on the models. The diphone synthesis requires identifying-redundant and consistent sets of diphones. The distributed entries need to be cleared from the DB. Regular itemization requires information about whether the diphone has a vowel or consonant, the position and consonant joints, and vowel length. The identified diaphones are embedded in carrier words to pronounce clearly and consistently. The carrier words also are tagged, recorded, and labeled.

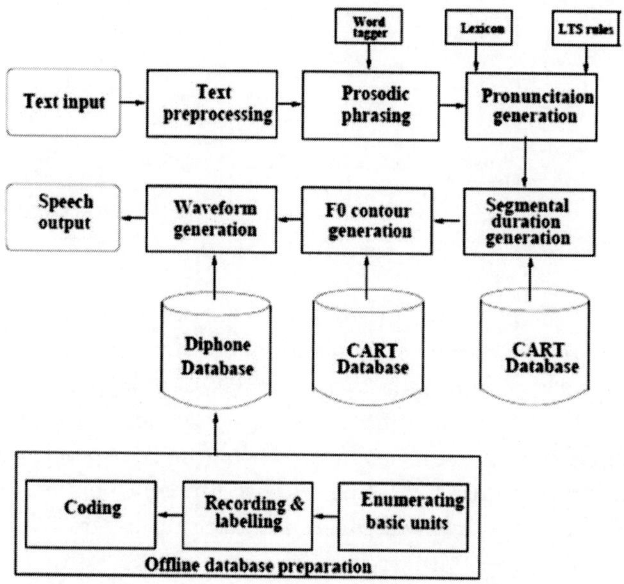

Figure 10.6: TTS System Using Diphone Synthesis

The festival's waveform synthesizers are the UniSyn synthesizers and the OGI diphone synthesizers. The CART-based models are used to segment the duration prediction of Dravidian Languages. The diphone database is coded with the intermediate form required for the waveform synthesizer.

A good database modeling autistic and prosodic information is required for prosodic information. A good prosodic model is needed for the TTS system based on diaphone synthesis to produce a sound speaker system.

10.8.4 Unit Selection Synthesis

To select the best-sequenced speech unit from the speech corpus and generate speech done in the unit selection synthesis technique. This technique should satisfy the following rules.

- It should be the best fit for the target specification given by the text analysis module of linguistic components.
- When concatenated, it should be the best fit that joins smoothly.

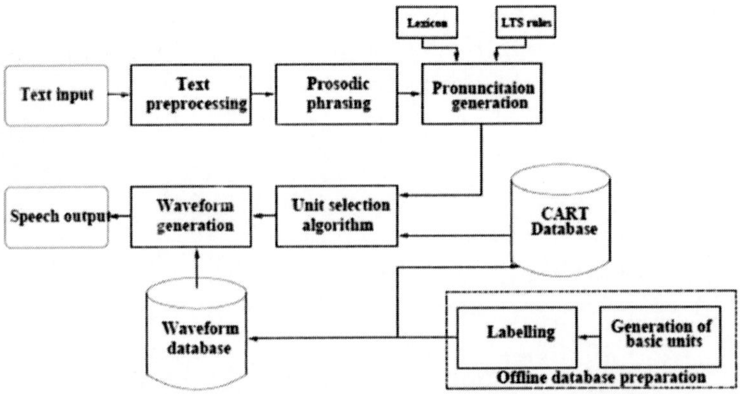

Figure 10.7: TTS System Using Unit Selection Synthesis

Figure 10.7 shows a clear picture of TTS system architecture using unit selection synthesis. It receives the text input and is processed in various phases to produce speech output—the system makes simple speech units. In the synthesis phase, each unit is synthesized, and the decision tree is identified from the speech database. For example, if the /bi/ is a speech unit, then the system algorithm will cluster all instances with different phonetic and prosodic contexts into the same class and makes the decision binary tree. Figure 10.8 shows the decision tree with various examples of the same speech unit. A synthesizer will perform a search starting from the root node and arrive at a leaf node. The queries will be framed based on the target specification of each speech unit at each node. A set of candidate units is formed from the best match of target specification derived at a leaf node.

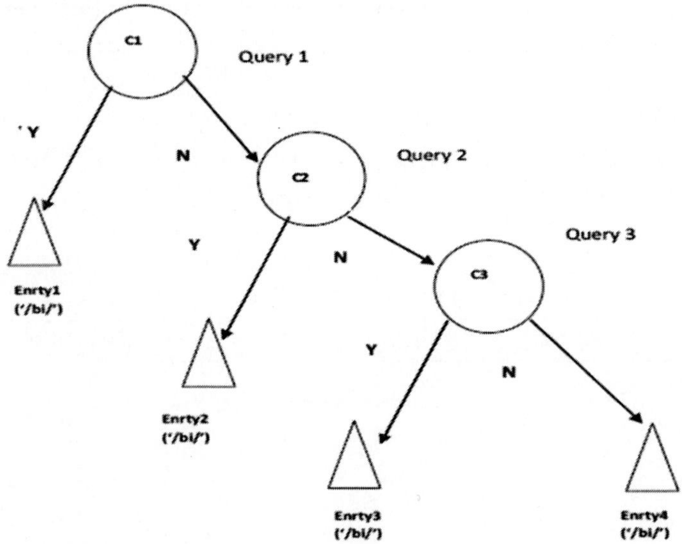

Figure 10.8: A Decision Tree with Various Entries of '*/bi/*'

10.8.4.1 *Manual Extraction of Syllables*

Consider the following example *'/arasAngam/'* for manual extraction of syllables in Tamil words.

'/ar/' '/as/' '/Ang/' '/gam/'

VC VC VC CVC

Table 10.3: Shows How Each Syllable is Divided into Respective Codes and Rhymes Using Manual Syllabification

S. No.	*Syllable*	*Onset*	*Rhyme*
1.	'/tha/'	'/th/'	'/a/'
2.	'/mi/'	'/m/'	'/i/'
3.	'/zha/'	'/zh/'	'/a/'
4.	'/ga/'	'/g/'	'/a/'
5.	'/m/'	–	'/m/.'

Table 3 Shows the Manual Syllabification of the Word 'Arasangam'.

10.8.4.2 *Minimum Phase Group Delay Method*

The nature of speech production is dependent on time-varying amplitude and energy. As the speech is time-varying in the heart, simple time-domain processing and characterizing important features is called Short Term Energy (STE). The STE is specified with high energy at the center and reduced energy at both ends. With these characteristics, the speech signal is segmented in their minimum energy points, which have syllable structure.

Consider the below example ***/peNgaLE nAttin kaNgaL AvArgaL/,*** the boundaries can be /pen/, /ga/, /LE/, /nAt/, /tin/, /kaN/, /gaL/, /Av/, /Ar/, /gaL/

Table 10.4: Assigning Labels Based on CVC Units

S. No.	*CVC Units*	*VC Units*	*CV Units*
1.	/pen/	/Av/	/LE/
2.	/nAt/	/Ar/	/ga/
3.	/kaN/		
4.	/kaL/		
5.	/tin/		

Table 4 shows the label assignment based on the syllabification rules. It indicates that Tamil has more CVC units.

The group delay segmentation algorithm consistently produces acceptable results close to manual segmentation.

10.8.5 The System Architecture of the Tamil Speech Recognition Framework

The development of ASR includes the language model, acoustic model, and speech corpus. To train the acoustic model, the Carnegie Mellon University (CMU) Spinx trainer can be used along with CMU Statistical Language Model to build the language model. The Mysore corpus with Central Institute of Indian Languages of a word-based trigram language model of perplexity with 72. CMU Spinx Decoder can be used with language and acoustic models to test the model.

The CMU Spinx 4.0 is an open-source system programmed in Java with the association of CMU, Sun microsystem, and Mitsubishi Electric Research Laboratories, USA. It is an HMM-based speech recognition system that can be portable to many numbers of computational platforms.

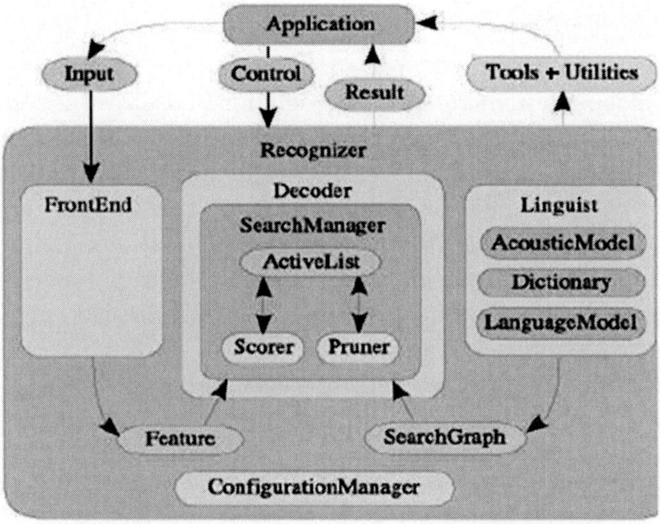

Figure 10.9: CMU Sphinx 4.0 Architecture

Figure 10.9 shows the system's architecture; this has three main independent modules: Front-end, Decoder, and Linguist. As they are separated, one can work on their interested module without touching another, making the system more accessible. The linguist model has three parts: Acoustic, Dictionary and language. Based on the linguist, the configuration manager can secure the different modules.

Speech Corpus and Acoustic Features

Tamil corpus is required to train the model, which can comprise continuous speech recording of both male and female voice recordings. Same way, to test the model, continuous recordings are required. The recording should be done in a noise-free environment. Make a table with the following details for better clarity.

- Hours of Recordings
- Number of speakers (Both male and female)
- Number of utterances
- Training set
- Testing set

The msmav file format can be used for acoustic features with 16 bit depth, mono channel, an estimated window size of 25 ms, and frameshift of 10 ms in MFCC.

10.9 CONCLUSION

This chapter introduced speech recognition technology in Tamil that provides information about automatic speech recognition and text-to-speech processes. Technology in speech allows many applications like speech recognition, TTS, speaker or language identification, and verification. Tamil's difficulties are due to a lack of resources like annotated speech and text corpora for a different domain. Ten million words of text corpus and 30 hours of speech recoding are required to design an authentic statistical ASR language model. But Tamil does not have such a vast data set. Tamil is an agglutinated language, which increases complexity and requires many data sets to train the model to achieve a good result. Tamil speech processing with subword units like phonemes, morphemes and syllables are fundamental components. The speech processing technique allows studying the human vocal communication of a language and processing those as signals. For ASR systems HMM model is the most popular technique to achieve the highest word recognition. HMM characterizes the detected data sample in a discrete-time frame. The HMM can treat the evaluation, decode and learn.

CHAPTER 11

Handwritten Character Recognition

11.1 HANDWRITTEN CHARACTER RECOGNITION

Recognizing handwritten characters using a machine is necessary in today's modern world. A computer system should be intelligent enough to receive and interpret handwritten input. The logic of a complete handwritten character recognition (HCR) system must adopt steps like formatting, correct segmentation of characters and determining possible words. The primary phase of the character recognition system is data acquisition, classified as online and offline character recognition, as presented in Figure 11.1. The online character recognition system captures the pen-up, pen-down, order of the strokes and speed using a digitizer. Offline character recognition is comparatively complex to an online character recognition system. Offline character recognition is further classified as Magnetic Ink Character Recognition (MICR) and Optical Character Recognition (OCR). MICR uses magnetic ink to print and a reading device can recognize the character based on the unique magnetic field of each character. This functionality is typically used in banks to check authentication. But in an OCR system, data in a paper is scanned or photographed as an image and converted as bit patterned text using the optical recognition technique. Again, the OCR system is subdivided into handwritten character recognition and printed character recognition. In printed recognition, images are processed in standard fonts like Times New Roman, Arial, Courier, etc. The printed character recognition accuracy is 99% with minimal constraints. Still, the real challenge is present in handwritten recognition because the writing style of each individual varies with the size, shape, thickness and speed of characters written. And another difficulty is with HCR similarities among the characters and the infinite variety of forms.

Due to limitations and inaccuracy, the offline HCR system opens research in image processing and pattern recognition areas. Offline character recognition is fully developed in English, Chinese, Arabic and Korean. Active research for Indian languages like Devanagari, Bangla, Telugu, Kannada and Tamil are in progress.

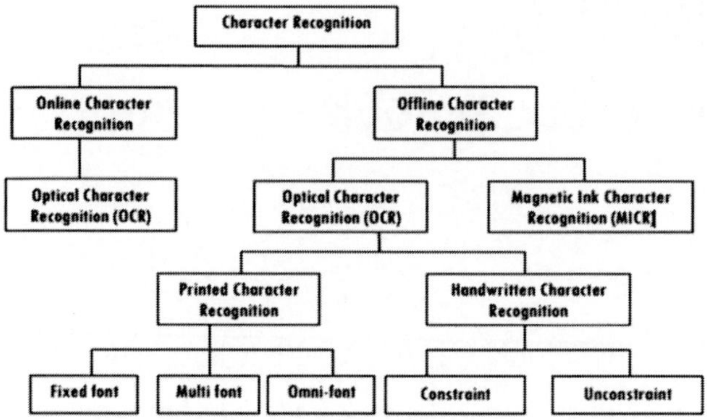

Figure 11.1: Character Recognition System Classification

11.1.1 Steps Involved in HCR System

HCR system has general steps like image acquisition, preprocessing, segmentation, feature extraction, classification and post-processing.

(a) **Image Acquisition:** Gray-level scanning of a handwritten paper document with a typical resolution of 300-1000 dpi.

(b) **Preprocessing:**
- Binarization (two-level thresholding)
- Segmentation to extract individual character
- Conversion for a character template

(c) **Feature Extraction**
- Collecting meaningful features

(d) **Classification**
- Recognition using one or more classifier

(e) **Contextual verification on post-processing**

The Block diagram of Figure 11.2. shows the various general steps involved in the offline HCR system. As an initial step, the HCR is image acquisition, in which the document can be scanned or photographed or directly written on a computer using a stylus or pen. This step is called digitization process. The next step is preprocessing, which involves multiple operations to remove noise, binarization, resize and angle correction. The noise of the document can be removed by applying proper filters like a mean filter, min-max filter and gaussian filter. The binarization process converts the scanned/photographed grayscale or colored image into black and white photos. Binary morphological operations like opening, closing, thinning, hole filling, etc., can be applied to enhance the image quality.

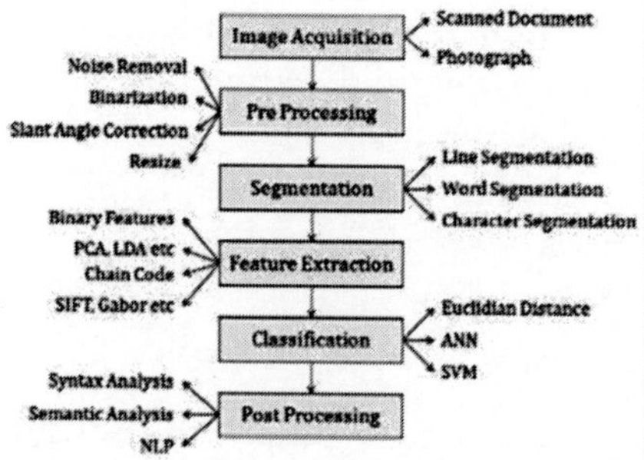

Figure 11.2: Different Steps Involved in Offline HCR System

The scanned document cannot be in a proper size format. It is necessary to resize the large image file to the appropriate dimension without losing the features of the document—similarly requires slant angle correction for perfect horizontal alignment. The document is processed hierarchically; in the first level, the lines are segmented using a row histogram. In each row, the words are extracted using a column histogram. Finally, characters are removed from words. Segmentation accuracy is essential to get a high level of accuracy in the final result.

Feature extraction is the heart of any character recognition. Some feature extraction techniques are Principle Component Analysis (PCA), Linear Discriminant Analysis (LDA), Independent Component Analysis (ICA), ChainCode, Scale Invariant Feature Extraction (SIFT), zoning, gradient-based features and histogram are applied to extract the features of individual characters. These features are used to train the classification system. When a new document image is presented in the HCR system, its features are extracted and given as input to a trained classifier like an artificial neural network (ANN) or support vector machine. The classifiers compare the input feature with the stored input pattern and determine the best matching class for the input. Syntax and semantic analysis or Natural Language Processing (NLP) can be applied in the post-processing step to check the context of the recognized character. Offline HCR is used in postal code recognition, cheque reading, form processing and signature verification.

11.2 TAMIL HANDWRITTEN CHARACTER RECOGNITION

The viability of the character perceives the rate which relies upon the adaptability of the data set utilized for any example/picture planning. The significant obstruction in Indian contents is the non-accessibility of standard information bases for preparing and testing the HCR. Currently, a single online Tamil has a manually written character information base [Hp l-Tamil dataset, 2006] accessible. Acknowledgment of Tamil transcribed characters is intricate because of various styles and shapes.

11.2.1 Image Acquisition

Transcribed report tests are digitalized at 300 dpi goal utilizing a flatbed scanner and put away as 8-bit dim pictures. Detach each line of the text using the upward projection histogram technique. The information base comprises 21600 examples of 72 characters gathered from 300 journalists.

From the dataset, we computed the following properties.

(a) *Aspect Ratio:* Width/height of character images.

(b) Normalized distance of the centroid from the origin (NDCO).

1. Calculate character centroid.
2. Taking top-left origin, find out the distance of the centroid from the origin.
3. Divide distance with diagonal distance [top left to bottom right as shown in Figure 11.3.

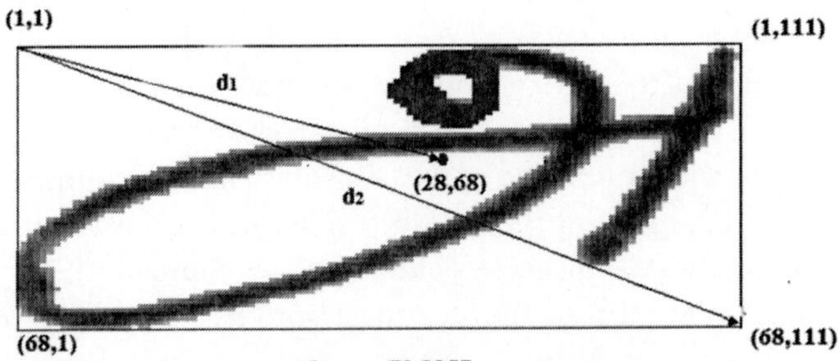

$$NDCO = \frac{d_1}{d_2} = \frac{72.2357}{128.7983} = 0.5608$$

Figure 11.3: Example of NDCO Calculation

11.2.2 Pre-processing

After the document is scanned, various data preprocessing operations need to be applied sequentially to images to make them in a suitable format for feature extraction. The preliminary step for HCR is preprocessing, which involves reducing the noise and simplifying the extraction and statistical features. Scanning the image depends on many factors like age of the document, paper quality, kind of script used and the characters are printed or handwritten and scanned image resolution, amount of skew, the layout of the image and the text. The preprocessing operations include noise removal, slant correction, normalization, thinning, binarization and edge detection to produce less complex images for the feature extraction stage.

Noise Removal

Smoothing is widely used to eliminate the noises from the captured image. The noise of the image degrades image quality in pattern recognition and significantly hinders pattern recognition. Linear and nonlinear filtering and morphological operations are commonly used in noise reduction.

Character Normalization

Character Normalization reduces the within-class variation of characters' shapes and improves classification accuracy. The characters in the images are of different sizes, positions and orientations. In general, linear and nonlinear methods are followed for character normalization.

The segmented character images are cropped, fit into a minimum rectangle and normalized into a standard size 72 × 72, as shown in Figure 11.4 using the nearest-neighbor interpolation method. The standard size is chosen by considering maximum size reduction with minimum loss of information and shape distortion and is fixed by empirical analysis.

Original image size: 68 × 111 pixels *Size normalized image:* 72 × 72 pixel

Figure 11.4: Original Image and Size Normalized Image

Binarization

Binarization is a procedure wherein the examined dim picture is changed into double images, isolating closer view and foundation data. The typical strategy for binarization is to choose a legitimate power limit for the picture. Afterwards, convert all the force esteems over the edge to one force worth and convert all force esteems beneath the edge to one more picked power. Binarization is delegated to two classes: worldwide and neighborhood (versatile) thresholding. The worldwide edge strategy applies one edge worth to the whole picture. Neighborhood or versatile thresholding strategies are acted in one pass utilizing nearby data acquired from the picture. The edge esteem is controlled by the pixel's neighborhood to which the thresholding is applied. Otsu's thresholding determination strategy is more effective for binarization. The algorithm is characterized as below.

1. Read sample image input.
2. Select the intensity value in the range 0.... L–1 as threshold value-k divides the total pixels *S* in the image into two groups.

   C0 = [0, 1... k–1]

   C1 = [k, k+1... L–1] where L is the possible total intensity levels.
3. Compute

   $$W_0 = \sum_{q=0}^{k-1} P_q(r_q)$$

   Where $P_q(r_q)$ = Total pixels with intensity q/Total pixels in the image.
4. Compute W_1, u_0 u_1 and u_t with the following formulas,

   $$W_1 = \sum_{q=k}^{L-1} P_q(r_q)$$

   $$u_0 = \sum_{q=0}^{k-1} qP_q(r_q)/W_0$$

   $$u_1 = \sum_{q=k}^{L-1} qP_q(r_q)/W_1$$

   $$u_1 = \sum_{q=0}^{L-1} qP_q(r_q)$$
5. Find the class variabilityu_0, λ 2 between C_0 and C_1 where

   $$\lambda^2 = W_0(u_0 - u_t)^2 + W_1(u_1 - u_t)^2$$
6. Until with maximum class, variability is found, repeat the above steps.
7. Choose Otsu's threshold value (k) with maximum class variance.

Otsu's thresholding algorithm can effectively apply to the Tamil handwritten image database for threshold selection. Figure 11.5 shows the binary output using Otsu's thresholding algorithm.

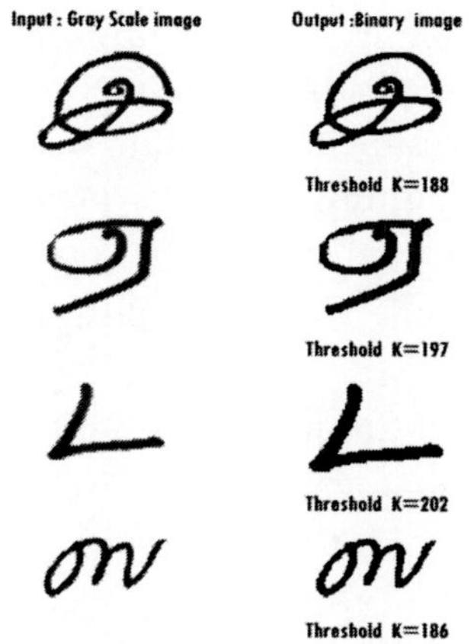

Figure 11.5: Input Grayscale Image and Binary Output Obtained using Otsu's Algorithm

Thinning

Thinning is a cycle to decrease an article in an advanced picture to the base size vital for machine acknowledgment. HCR has brilliant varieties in character thickness. Thinning dispenses with the impact of character thickness on highlight extraction. The Thinning calculations should save the topological and mathematical properties of the first item. It additionally incorporates connectedness of parts, no misleading endpoints and no over-the-top disintegration of the first article. The Thinning algorithm can be named below in Figure 11.6.

Non-iterative diminishing techniques utilize consecutive pixel sweeps of a picture. Iterative thinning calculations erase progressive layers on the edges of an example until a skeleton remains. Although many diminishing

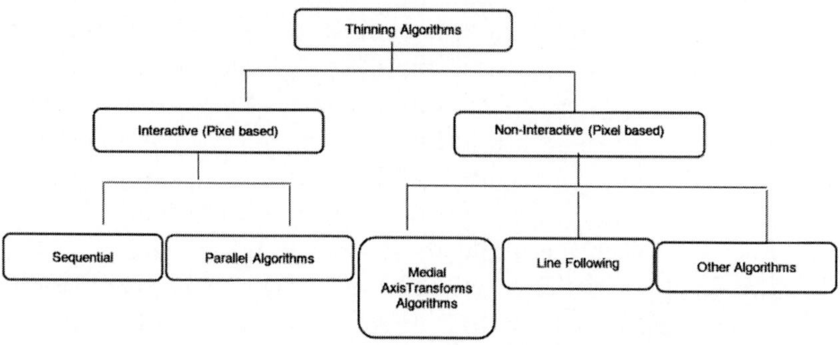

Figure 11.6: Classifications of Thinning Algorithms

measures like Parallel Thinning, Rotation Invariant Thinning, Zhang Suen Thinning, NWG Thinning, Parker Thinning and Stentiford Thinning are accessible, the proposed adjustment to Stentiford Thinning (MST) calculation can be utilized for diminishing. This calculation additionally uses pre-processing, thinning and post-processing.

Pre-processing

Hole expulsion is finished utilizing six examples of pieces or formats, as displayed in Figure 11.7. Smoothing is the expulsion of dark components, has under three dark neighbors and connectivity 1.

X	1	X
1	0	1
X	1	X

H_1

X	1	1	X
1	0	0	1
x	1	1	X

H_2

X	1	X
1	0	1
1	0	1
x	1	X

H_3

X	X	1	1	1	X	X
X	1	1	1	1	1	X
X	1	1	1	1	1	X
1	1	1	0	1	1	1
X	1	1	1	1	1	X
X	1	1	1	1	1	X
X	X	1	1	1	X	X

H_4

X	X	1	1	1	X	X
X	1	1	1	1	1	X
X	1	1	1	1	1	X
1	1	1	0	1	1	1
1	1	1	0	1	1	X
X	1	1	1	1	1	X
X	1	1	1	1	1	X
X	X	1	1	1	X	X

H_5

X	X	1	1	1	1	X	X
X	X	1	1	1	1	X	X
X	1	1	1	1	1	1	X
1	1	1	0	0	1	1	1
X	1	1	1	1	1	1	X
X	X	1	1	1	1	X	X
X	X	1	1	1	1	X	X

H_6

0 = white pixel **1 = black pixel** **X = don't care**

Figure 11.7: Patterns of Hole Removal in Stentiford Thinning Algorithm

The Stentiford thinning algorithm calculation utilizes Yokoi's eight network numbers and doesn't protect all the availability in a Tamil character picture. Thus, the proposed MST thinning algorithm uses Zhang Suen's eight network number. A 3×3 layout window is used to characterize the preprocessing venture, as shown in Figure 11.8, where P1 is a current pixel of interest and P2 to P9 are neighbor pixels. Preprocessing step is applied with value 1. A choice worth is registered as the times the local pixel esteem changes from 0–1 when the neighbors are visited in the request P2, P3, P4, P5, P6, P7, P8, P9 and P2. A choice worth is figured as the occasions the local pixel value changes from 0–1 when the neighbors are visited in the request P2, P3, P4, P5, P6, P7, P8, P9 and P2.

Thinning

This algorithm continuously deletes contour pixels satisfying several conditions until a one-pixel vast 8-connected skeleton is obtained. It is a parallel method, meaning the new pixel value can be computed only using the values known from the previous iteration. 3 × 3 window is used and each element is connected to its eight neighboring elements. The pixel in the label will be labeled as Figure 11.7.

Table 11.1: Identifications 9 Pixels in 3 × 3 Window

P9	P2	P3
P8	P1	P4
P7	P6	P5

Let NT (P1) be the number of zero (white) to nonzero (black) transitions in the ordered sequence <P2, P3…P9, P2> and NZ (P1) be the number of nonzero neighbors of P1. Pixel P1 is deleted (set to zero) if it stratifies the following conditions.

1. $2 \leqslant$ NZ (P1) $\leqslant 6$
2. NT (P1) = 1 and P2.P4.P8 = 0 or
3. NT (P2) $\neq$ 1 and P2.P4.P6 = 0 or
4. NT (P4) $\neq$ 1

The process must repeat until no more changes are present in the image. Though the Zhang Suen Thinning algorithm has advantages like speed and topological preservation has disadvantages also like necking and line fuzz, as shown in Figure 11.8.

Figure 11.8: Zhang Suen Thinning Algorithm Applied on Character Image அ

Post Processing

The additional lines in thinned pictures are eliminated utilizing endpoint evacuation grids. The endpoint expulsion lattices (Mi, Bi, Ci) are looked over the character and at any place a grid fits, the focal dark pixel is set apart for erasure. The proposed MST calculation utilized two new networks Bi and Ci and Mi, where i = 1, 2, 3 and 4. Since Mi examines lattices, eliminate just left, right vertical and descending additional lines. The MST calculation utilizes Bi and Ci output networks to eliminate extra lines, as displayed in Figure 11.9. All grids are looked over the character and at any place a network fits, the focal dark pixel is set apart for erasure. When every one of the four lattices of Mi, Bi and Ci have been checked like this, all stamped pixels are erased and the interaction is rehashed until any longer disintegration can't occur.

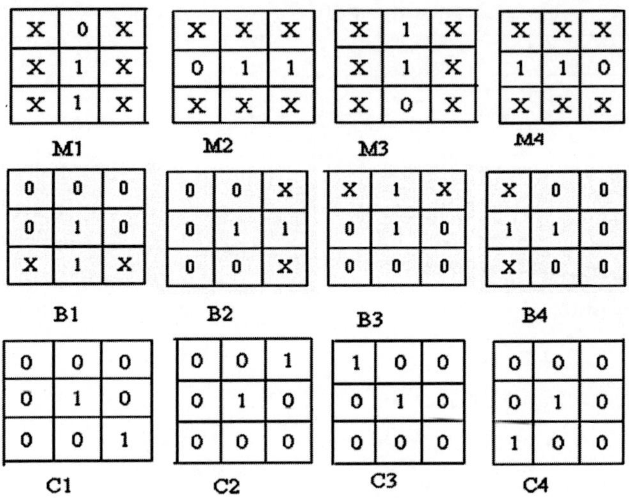

Figure 11.9: Endpoint Removal Matrices

The pixel deletion processes are sensitive to both the order of application of the scan matrices (Mi, Bi, Ci) and the direction of the scan in Table 11.1. The proposed MST algorithm follows the steps below.

Step 1: Scan matrix M1 across characters according to Table 11.2 and identify the next fit position.

Step 2: If the central element at a fit is not an endpoint and has a connectivity value, mark it for deletion.

Step 3: Repeat Steps 1 and 2 for all fit positions.

Step 4: Repeat Steps 1–3 for each scan of matrix M2, M3 and M4.

Step 5: Delete all marked elements.

Step 6: If one or more elements are deleted in Step 4, then return to Step1.

Step 7: Repeat Steps 1–6 for scan matrices Bi and Ci.

Step 8: Exit.

Table 11.2: Matrix Ordering and Scanning Directions of Modified Thinning Algorithm

Order of Application	*The Direction of the Single Scan Line*	*The Direction of the Successive Scan Line*
M1, B1, C1	Left to Right	Downwards
M2, B2, C2	Upwards	Left to Right
M3, B3, C3	Right to Left	Upwards
M4, B4, C4	Downwards	Right to Left

11.2.3 Contour Tracing

Contour extraction is essential to represent the region of the image in terms of its external characteristics (boundary) or internal characteristics (the pixels comprising the region). The external representation is selected when shape characteristics are interesting. An internal model is preferred when regional properties such as color and texture are interested.

A Novel Contour Tracing Algorithm

This section describes a novel contour tracing algorithm using maximal disk and eight sequential Euclidean distance maps and connectivity criteria based on maximal disk. The connectivity criterion is based on a set of point pairs along the image boundary pixels are the nearest point under consideration and its neighbors. The proposed method generates the contour of an image with a smaller number of iterations; execution time, image shape and classification performance are satisfying when compared with two existing contour tracing algorithms—the Moore method and the Canny edge detection method. The connectivity criteria are based on the maximal disk and sequential Euclidean distance mapping.

The proposed Framework applies 8ED mapping and connectivity criteria to achieve the correct contour point of an image. Figure 11.10 shows the flow chart of the new contour tracing algorithm. In this algorithm, background point is 0 and it is in black; the value of the object point is one and represented as white color. A traverse of an image is required to find the contour of the image. Select the background pixel at random and set its value to 1 (set it as the foreground pixel, say P). This pixel can be far from the foreground pixel. Then compute the 8ED mapping and set Q = DM (P). The 8 -point sequential Euclidean distance (8SED) mapping of an image as Figure 11.11. The corresponding point for every eight neighboring points determines

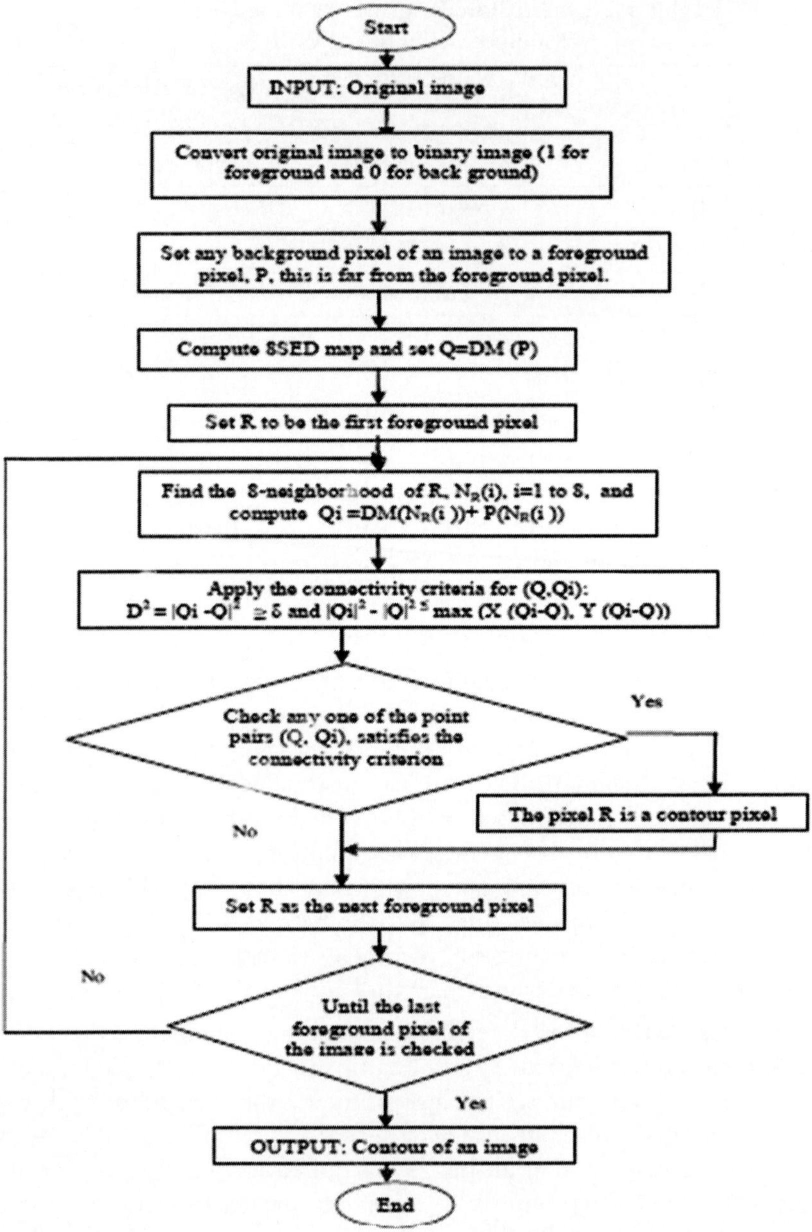

Figure 11.10: Flowchart of the New Contour Tracing Algorithm

whether a pixel point is a contour point. The connectivity criterion is then applied to eight-point pairs. The 8SED map obtains the relative position of the nearest point of each pixel. The eight neighboring points of the pixel under consideration form an eight-point team by adding the relative position of its closest point to the relative position of its neighborhoods. If the point pair satisfies the connectivity criteria, the pixel will be declared a contour point; else, the pixel is not a contour point.

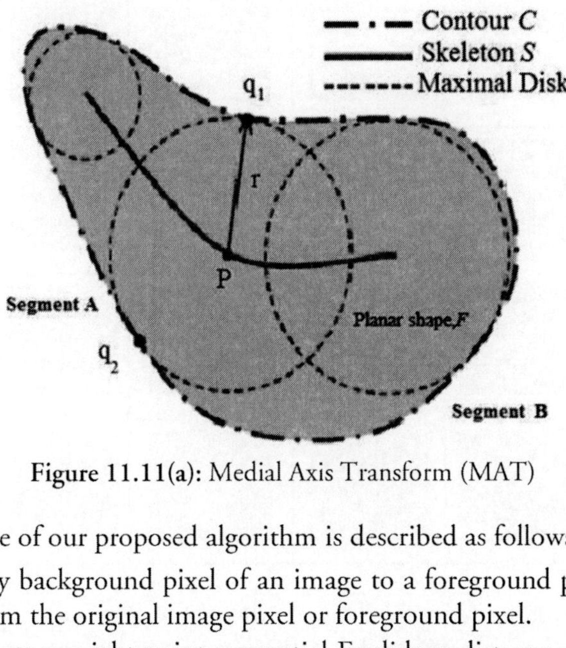

Figure 11.11(a): Medial Axis Transform (MAT)

The procedure of our proposed algorithm is described as follows.

Step 1: Set any background pixel of an image to a foreground pixel P; this is far from the original image pixel or foreground pixel.

Step 2: Compute an eight-point sequential Euclidean distance map and setQ = DM (P), where DM (.) represents the 8SED map.

Step 3: Set R to be the first foreground pixel.

Do

1. Find the 8-neighborhood ofR $N_R(1)$, i =1 to 8 and

   Compute $Q_i = DM\ (N_R\ (i) + P(N_R(i)))$, where $P(N_R(i))$ is the relative position of the ith neighborhood concerning the pixel R.
2. The eight-point pairs are formed by the pixel P and eight neighbors of the pixel R, which are denoted as (Q, Q_1)
3. Apply the connectivity criteria for (Q, Q_i):

   $D^2 - |Q_i - Q|^2 \geq \delta$ and $|Q_i|^2 - |Q|^2 \leq \max\,(X(Q_i - Q), Y(Q_i - Q))$
   where X(.) and Y(.) represent the *x* and *y* coordinates of the pixel.

4. If one of the points(Q, Q_i), satisfies the connectivity criterion, then the pixel R is a contour point.
5. Until the last foreground pixel of an image is checked.

Table 11.3: Results of Different Contour Tracing Algorithms Applied to Tamil Handwritten Characters

Samples	Ch1	Ch2	Ch3	Ch4	Ch5
Original image/ method					
Moore	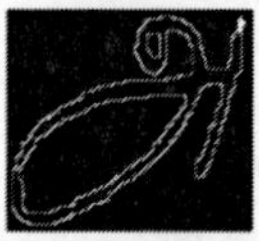	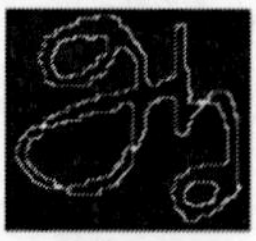			
Canny					
Proposed					

If the foreground pixel is started, the above algorithm discontinues in contour near the starting pixel. So the background pixel is selected as the starting point. The result of the proposed contour algorithm applied to Tamil handwritten characters is displayed in Table 11.3. It is visible that the proposed method did not lose its connectivity.

11.3 SEGMENTATION

Text line segmentation is an essential preprocessing stage for offline handwriting recognition. It is essential because inaccurate text can lead to errors in the recognition stage. Segmentation in handwriting recognition follows the projection-based, smearing, grouping, Hough-based, graph-based and Cut Text Minimization (CTM) approach. Figure 11.11b. Segmentation representation of a character.

Figure 11.11(b): Segmentation

11.4 FEATURE EXTRACTION

Feature extraction estimates those credits of examples more applicable to a given assignment grouping. The specialists must choose the elements that permit viable and productive acknowledgment designs.

11.4.1 Feature Extraction Methods

The primary point of element extraction is to discover a subset of components that recognize the characterization cycle and are consistent with the unimportant information change. A bunch of parts assists with separating between classes while staying compatible with attributes contrasts inside the class. Diverse extraction strategies are displayed in Figure 11.12. Format coordinating and relationship techniques are coordinated pixel by pixel for ID. The factual or mathematical elements approach considers mathematical proportions of picture districts like pixel densities drafting, crossing, course elements and minutes and so forth. The underlying element approach considers strokes, bends, endpoints, convergence focuses and circles. The

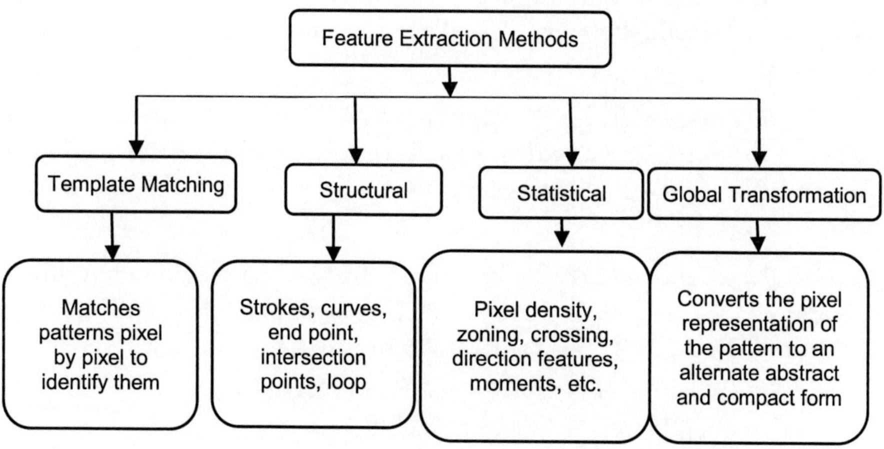

Figure 11.12: General Approaches to Feature Extraction

worldwide changes convert the pixel portrayal of the example into a more dynamic and conservative substitute structure. It likewise lessens the element vector dimensionality.

The blend of two methodologies can be liked to cover inside the class and between-class changeability of the examples to give a productive and complete portrayal of characters. The accompanying provisions can be joined and another model can be made for highlight extraction.

Zero Crossing Features (ZC): The input image is divided into nine equal blocks. Each block is a zero-crossing value for each row and the column is computed. Then calculate RSNZCp and CSNZCp using equation one and equation: 2. These values are used as features and for nine blocks, 2 × 9 = 18 features of the character are acquired (equations 1&2).

$$RSNZC_P = \sum_{i=1}^{m} NZCR_i \qquad \dots (1)$$

$$CSNZC_P = \sum_{i=1}^{n} NZCC_i \qquad \dots (2)$$

Chain Code Includes (CH): The preprocessed character picture is partitioned into four equivalent squares. For each square, the course chain codes for each frontal area pixel are figured. The frequencies of these codes for four squares 4 × 4 = 16 components.

Gradient Descent (GD): A diminished picture of manually written Tamil characters is separated into four squares. For each square, we determined the frequencies of inclination esteems. The frequencies can be 4 × 4 = 16 components.

Mesh View Thinned Image Feature (MVTI): The initially thin picture is divided into four squares, with five perspectives on each square registered. For each view, figure the number of foundation pixels as SBPv and from 4 squares, we get 4 × 5 = 20 elements.

Division Point Highlight (DP): The diminished person pictures are utilized. Consider 72 × 72 pictures and the picture is gone through the recursive region till the third level. The 42 provisions are extricated at the subsequent level.

- Area (A), Euler No (EN) and Aspect Ratio (AR).
- Number of endpoints (EP) and Branch Point (BP).
- Distance from Character Centroid to Top Left Origin (DCTLO).

11.5 CLASSIFICATION

Classification of the method involved tracking down a model dependent on the investigation of a bunch of preparing information to portray the ideas (or classes) and the motivation behind utilizing the model to foresee the class of item whose class name is obscure. Group the accessible dataset to arbitrarily separate the two fundamentally unrelated sets into preparing or test sets by concentrating on the connection between the restrictive and choice properties. The inferred model can be introduced in forecast rules, choice trees, numerical formulae or neural organizations. Then, at that point, the model is utilized to anticipate the class of every information occasion in the test set. The objective is classification assignments to boost the characterization precision rate. The arrangement precision rate is the proportion of a few right expectations to the datasets of several forecasts.

11.6 CLASSIFICATION METHODS

The objective of a classification system is to assign a class to a pattern using a feature vector (list of attributes). The different classification methods are listed in Figure 11.13.

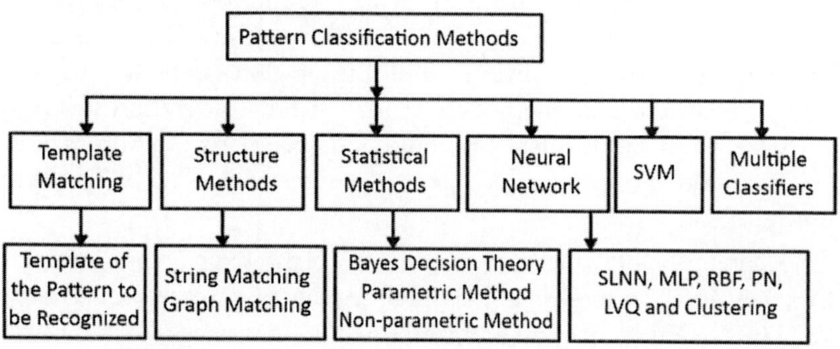

Figure 11.13: Different Classification Methods

Choosing the classifier depends on factors like available training set, number of free parameters, nature of learning, etc. The general approaches for pattern recognition can be template matching, syntactic or structural techniques, statistical classification and neural networks.

Usually, pattern recognition follows two types of strategies.

- ***Supervised Classification:*** The input pattern is identified as a member of a predefined class.

- *Unsupervised Classification:* The input pattern is assigned to an unknown class.

We can select the hybrid model with the Artificial Neural Network (ANN) technique and Hidden Markov Model (HMM).

11.7 POST-PROCESSING

The post-processing text correction is very complex. Maintaining the vocabulary constraint is the biggest problem. It can be solved by identifying the erroneous text of post-processed text and followed by the rectification process. The most widely used OCR post-processing method is based on probability and statistical models, based on dictionaries and mixed-method. The popular hidden Markov Model (HMM) is a statistical model in which the modeled system is assumed to be a Markov process with an unobserved state.

11.8 THE HYBRID MODEL WITH HMM AND ANN TO RECOGNIZE TAMIL OCR

HMM, the technique is based on a mathematically solid foundation and is suitable for recognizing the sequence of observation in speech and handwritten documents. The main advantage of HMM framework is performing the segmentation and recognition simultaneously. Also, it is suitable for designing and training the individual model using global data. It is also proved that ANN is an efficient methodology for pattern recognition in OCR. A hybrid system can be designed for audio and speech recognition. The same hybrid methodology can be incorporated to recognize Tamil handwritten documents.

The core idea of handwriting is left to right sequence of ink signals. HMMs are good at modeling temporal sequences with less discriminative power. The Neural Networks (NN) discriminate shapes from different classes but do not model temporal sequences. The hybrid model is proposed with HMMand NN to yield better results. The sliding window system transforms a two-dimensional array into a one-dimensional array for the fast segmentation process. The word image is sliced from left to right into frames with a width determined relative to the core height of the word image.

11.8.1 Preprocessing

They are preprocessing important step which helps to promote a better recognition rate.

Slant Estimation and Correction

The slant correction process uses a contouring algorithm for each connected component. Each external contour of the connected part is described as a list of contour vectors, each of which is classified as horizontal (n_h), vertical (n_v), diagonal +45° (n+), or diagonal –45° (n.). Count the contour vectors of each class and compute the slant (θ) as the average orientation of the vertical parts of the word.

$$\theta = arctan\left[\frac{n_+ - n_-}{n_+ + n_v + n_-}\right]$$

Slant corrections are applied to the whole word image by shearing the image horizontally.

$x' = x - y \sin\theta$ and $y' = y$

Reference Line Detection

Reference lines help normalize the image size and extract the geometrical features related to the position of letters concerning their context. Input word images can be taken to find individual posts using four parallel straight lines as mentioned in Figure 11.14—the ascender area refers to the position of the top letters. The core area represents the center position of the letters. Descender area refers to the bottom of letters.

Figure 11.14: Reference Line Detection

Run the contour algorithm of the input word image to extract the local minima and maxima of the handwriting signal. The local minima and most of the images given below are in Figure 11.15.

Figure 11.15: Local Minima and Maxima of the Input Image

Use Expectation-Maximization (EM) algorithm to estimate the position and slant of the four straight parallel reference lines.

Segmentation and Letter Hypothesis

The simple vertical slicing method segments the word image into a left to right sequence of vertical slices. The width of the slice (w) depends on the height (h) of the core zone. Each frame has the same width $w = 0.4h$.

Figure 11.16: Window Sliding Left to Right

The exact slicing points are determined by a search of minima of ink pixels in each column. The left frames segmentation graphs to the right ordered sequence of slices and a combination of several consecutive lines. Segmentation graphs show the possible way to segment a word into letters. In Figure 11.17, the word image is cut into eight slices. Figure 11.17 shows the segmentation graphs of an image.

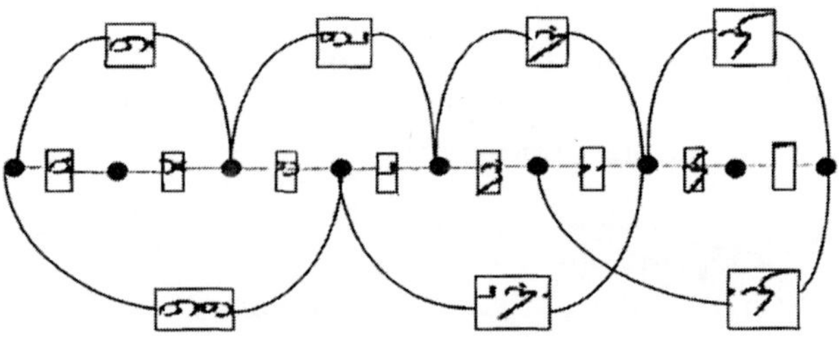

Figure 11.17: Segmentation Graph of an Image

11.8.2 Feature Extraction

The feature extraction will transform the normalized text image into a suitable format for the selected recognition scheme. It captures the most relevant and discriminant characteristic of character to recognize. Nearly 139 geometrical features can be extracted from each frame or letter hypothesis. The features can be the Dimension and aspect ratio of the bounding box of ink pixels in a frame, the canter of gravity, Distance to the core zone, Profiles in 8 directions and Number of transitions from non-ink-pixel to ink-pixel for vertical, horizontal, +45° and –45° diagonal direction. To make the features invariant concerning handwriting size, all the features need to be normalized by the height of the core zone (h).

11.8.3 Hybrid System

After the segmentation graphs and feature vector of each letter hypotheses are generated, a trained neural network system that observes probabilities for each letter. Apply the Viterbi backtracking algorithm to segment the training word database into individual characters, which can be used as training data for NN. Figure 11.16 shows the hybrid Tamil handwritten recognition system.

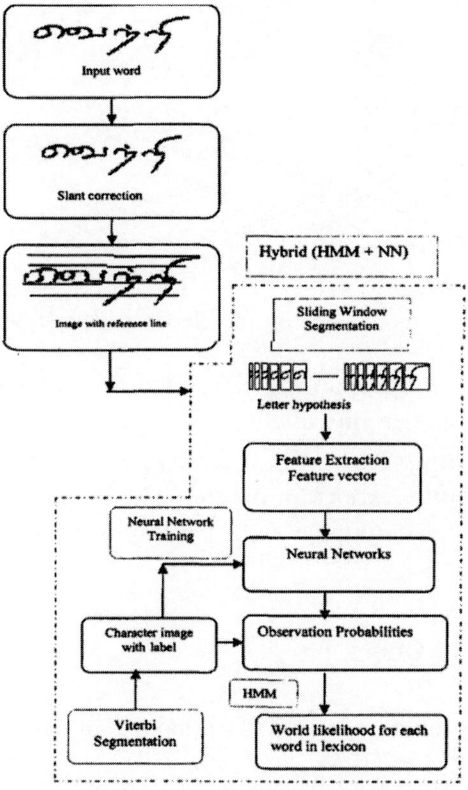

Figure 11.18: Hybrid Tamil Handwritten Recognition System

Neural Networks

The segmentation process generates the character hypotheses that contain characters with parts of characters, multiple characters and single characters with elements of other characters attached. The role of NN is to recognize the character and be capable of rejecting character hypotheses learned through the training process.

The three-layered feed-forward Multilayer Perceptron (MLP) is used for training the model. The network topology MLP is in Figure 11.19.

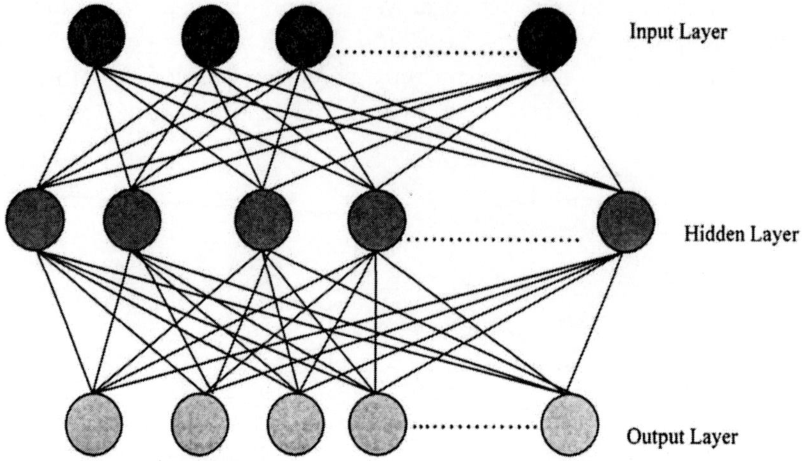

Figure 11.19: Neural Network Topology

The extracted 139 geometrical features can be used as 139 neurons in the input layer, 190 neurons in the hidden layer and 105 neurons in the output layer. The input of the NN is the feature vector $\bar{f}$, where $\bar{f}$. It is the ith feature of the feature extraction process. The output of the jth hidden unit is obtained by first forming a weighed linear combination of the *I* input values to give,

$$u_j = \sum_{i=0}^{I} w_{ji} \bar{f}_i \forall \text{ One} \leq j \leq J$$

The activation of hidden unit *j* is obtained by transforming the linear sum to a function g(.) to give,

$$x_j = g(u_j) \forall 1 \leq j \leq J$$

The activation function at the hidden layer, *g(.)*, is the hyperbolic tangent function which is defined as,

$$g(x) = \tanh(x) = \frac{e^x - e^{-x}}{e^x + e^{-x}} = \frac{1 - e^{-2x}}{1 + e^{-2x}}$$

The network's outputs are obtained similarly to the previous layer by transforming the activation of the hidden units using the second layer of processing elements. For each neuron *k,* we obtain,

$$v_k = \sum_{j}^{J} s_{kj} x_j \ \forall\, 1 \le k \le K$$

The activation function gives,

$$y_k = G(v_k) \forall\, 1 \le k \le K$$

The output of the NN for a particular character class k, given an observation, O is therefore defined as,

$$NN_k(O) \equiv G(v_k)$$

The *NN* is trained to recognize complete letters and reject the candidates who do not look like letters in the training data set. The likeliest path is selected by using forward-backward and Viterbi algorithms.

The Neural Network outputs divided by the corresponding letter class prior are used directly as observation probabilities for the HMM.

P(letter\Segmented candidate)/*P*(letter)

The training of a hybrid recognition system is divided into two stages: Bootstrap and Refine.

Bootstrap

The initial step is to train the neural network to recognize characters. It is done by manually segmenting word images into isolated character images with class labels. It is a time-consuming process. The automatic approach uses the trained baseline recognizer to segment the word images into a training set of isolated character images. The Viterbi backtracking algorithm is used to select the best segmentation path and Baum-Welch training is performed to estimate the transition probabilities.

Refine

The initial bootstrapped recognition result is better than the baseline recognizer because of the discriminant power of NN. The training procedure is iterated using the obtained hybrid to segment the word images into letters for NN.

Results

Ten thousand words are taken for the experiment, 4900 words are used for the training set and 5100 words are used for testing. The lexicon size like

150, 200, 250 and 300 is considered. The recognition performance is displayed in Table 11.4.

Table 11.4: The Recognition Performance Table

Database Age Groups	*Lexicon Size*	*Recognition Rate (%) Hybrid System (HMM + NN)*	
		Bootstrap	*Refine*
6–12	150	82.5	84.3
	200	82.7	85.4
	250	84.3	86.9
	300	84.9	87.2
13–20	150	92.4	93.1
	200	93.9	94.7
	250	95.1	97.2
	300	96.5	98.9
30–45	150	91.9	93.6
	200	93.1	94.3
	250	93.7	95.6
	300	95.4	96.9
Above 50	150	73.4	74.7
	200	75.1	75.9
	250	76.8	77.3
	300	77.9	79.6

The results are better when a hybrid system is used for both bootstrap and refining stages.

11.9 CONCLUSION

Recognizing handwritten characters using a machine is necessary in today's modern world. A computer system should be intelligent enough to receive and interpret handwritten input. The logic of a complete handwritten character recognition (HCR) system must adopt steps like formatting, correct segmentation of characters and determining possible words. The whole chapter described character recognition through different processes such as image acquisition, preprocessing, post-processing, feature Extraction, segmentation, classification and Hybrid model with HMM and ANN to recognize Tamil OCR and suitable methods.

CHAPTER 12

Input/Output and Computing in Tamil

12.1 INTRODUCTION

One essential thing in handling Natural Language Processing is providing a facility for inputting and outputting. It is difficult to take in Asian languages because of the glyph-based approach. To get a character from the keyboard, one should perform many operations like mapping the keyboard to the particular language and installing the appropriate language drivers. Secondly, mapping and installing fronts for the specific language can perform inputting and outputting operations.

First, in Microsoft Windows, one can install the language and proceed with the processing. One should move to the settings, then the language setting and install the Tamil language in the system. Then, the user can do the inputting in Tamil by changing the language selection on the right side of the screen. This section explains the inputting, outputting and computing methods in detail. The python code is used to demonstrate the inputting and outputting functions.

12.2 INPUTTING/OUTPUTTING IN TAMIL

Developers frequently connect with people to obtain data or offer a solution. Most programs today employ a dialogue box to prompt the user for information. In contrast, Python has two built-in routines for reading data from the keyboard. Inputting and rendering the character is an important activity. This section's first program is designed to get two numbers, add them and then print the numbers on the screen. This program is designed to print the Tamil sentence. It is shown in the following schedule.

```
# Program to check input
        num1 = input ("முதல் எண்ணை உள்ளிடவும்:")
        num2 = input ("இரண்டாவது எண்ணை உள்ளிடவும்: ")
        sum = int(num1) + int(num2)
        # Printing type of input value
```

```
print ("முதல் எண்:", num1)
print ("இரண்டாவது எண்:", num2)
print ("மொத்த எண்ணிக்கை:", sum)
```

This second program gets the Tamil character as input from the keyboard and displays the same on the screen. It is essential to remember that the installation of the language is necessary for typing the character in Tamil. It is shown in the following program.

```
# Program to get Tamil input
    from Tamil import utf8
    print ("உங்கள் உள்ளீடுகளை பதிவிடவும்:")
    while True:
        user input = input (":")
        print (user input)
```

12.3 COMPUTING IN TAMIL

Computation is an important activity in the system. It's a goal-oriented action that necessitates, benefits from, or requires generating a computing program to achieve our aim. It entails the investigation and testing of algorithmic procedures and the development of both hardware and software. It encompasses parts of science, engineering, mathematics, technology and society. The following python program demonstrates the simple calculator performing various computing operations. It gets the two different types of inputs that are in character and float.

```
# -*- coding: utf-8 -*-
    while True:
      print("தேர்ந்தெடு:")
      print("கூட்ட'கூட்டு' எனதட்டச்சிடவும்")
      print("கழிக்க'கழி; ' தட்டச்சிடவும்")
      print("பெருக்க'பெருக்கு' எனதட்டச்சிடவும்")
      print("வகுக்க'வகு' எனதட்டச்சிடவும்")
      print("வெளியேற'வெளி' எனதட்டச்சிடவும்")
    user input = input(":")
      if user input == "வெளி":
        break
    elifuser_input == "கூட்டு":
        num1 =float(input("ஒருஎண்ணை உள்ளிடு:"))
```

```
        num2 =float(input( "மற்றொரு எண்ணை உள்ளிடு: "))
        result = str(num1 + num2)
        print("விடை " + result)
    elifuser_input == "கழி":
        num1 =float(input("ஒரு எண்ணை உள்ளிடு: "))
        num2 =float(input("மற்றொருஎண்ணைஉள்ளிடு:"))
        result = str(num1 - num2)
        print("விடை " + result)
    elifuser_input == "பெருக்கு":
        num1 =float(input("ஒரு எண்ணை உள்ளிடு: "))
        num2 =float(input("மற்றொரு எண்ணை உள்ளிடு: "))
        result = str(num1 * num2)
        print("விடை " + result)
    elifuser_input == "வகு":
        num1 =float(input("ஒரு எண்ணை உள்ளிடு: "))
        num2 =float(input("மற்றொரு எண்ணை உள்ளிடு: "))
        result = str(num1 / num2)
        print("விடை " + result)
      else:
        print("தவறான உள்ளீடு")
```

12.4 REGULAR EXPRESSIONS

A regular expression (RE) is a language for specifying text search strings. Regular Expressions (REs) provide a mechanism to select specific strings from a set of character strings.

The Regular Expression helps us to match or find other strings or sets of strings, using a specialized syntax held in a pattern. Regular expressions are used to search texts in different text-driven tools identically.

Regular expressions are context-independent syntax that can represent various character sets and character set orderings, where these character sets are interpreted according to the current locale. While many regular expressions can be interpreted differently depending on the recent string, many features, such as character class expressions, provide contextual invariance across strings.

Properties of Regular Expressions

Followings are some of the essential properties of RE:

- American Mathematician *Stephen Cole Kleene* formalized the Regular Expression language in 1956.
- Regular Expression is a formula in a particular language, which can be used for specifying simple classes of strings, a sequence of symbols. In other words, we can say that Regular Expression is an algebraic notation for characterizing a set of strings.
- Regular expression requires two things: the pattern we wish to search and the corpus of text we need to search.

Mathematically, A Regular Expression can be defined as follows:

- **ε** is a Regular Expression, indicating that the language has an empty string.
- **φ** is a Regular Expression that denotes that it is an empty language.
- If X and Y are Regular Expressions, then
- X, Y
    - X.Y (Concatenation of XY)
    - X+Y (Union of X and Y)
    - X*, Y* (Kleen Closure of X and Y)

are also regular expressions.

A Regular Expression can be recursively defined as follows:

- **ε** is a Regular Expression that indicates the language containing an empty string. (L (**ε**) = {**ε**})
- **φ** is a Regular Expression denoting an empty language. (L (**φ**) = { })
- **x** is a Regular Expression where **L** = {x}
- If X is a Regular Expression denoting the language L(X) and Y is a Regular Expression denoting the language L(Y), then
    - X + Y is a Regular Expression corresponding to the language L(X) **∪** L(Y) where L(X+Y) = L(X) **∪** L(Y).
    - X. Y is a Regular Expression corresponding to the language L(X). L(Y) where L (X.Y) = L(X). L(Y)
    - R* is a Regular Expression corresponding to the language L(R*) where L(R*) = (L(R)) *

Regular Set

Regular Expressions	*Regular Set*
(0 + 10*)	L = { 0, 1, 10, 100, 1000, 10000, … }
(0*10*)	L = {1, 01, 10, 010, 0010, …}
(0 + ε)(1 + ε)	L = {ε, 0, 1, 01}
(அ + இ)*	Set of strings of அ and இ of any length, including the null string. So L = { ε, அ, இ, அஅ, அ இ, இஇ, இஅ, அஅஅ …….}
(அ + இ)* அஇஇ	Set of strings of அ and இ ending with the string அஇஇ. So L = {அஇஇ, அஅஇஇ, இஅஇஇ, அஅஅஇஇ, அஇஅஇஇ, இஇ அஇஇ, இஅஅஇஇ, அஅஅஅஇஇ …….}
(11)*	Set consisting of even number of 1's including empty string, So L= {ε, 11, 1111, 111111, ……….}
(அஅ)*(இஇ)* இ	Set of strings consisting of an even number of அ followed by an odd number of இ, so L = {இ, அஅஇ, அஅஇஇஇ, அஅஇஇஇஇஇ, அஅஅஅஇ, அஅஅஅஇஇஇ, ………….}
(அஅ + அஇ + இஅ + இஇ)*	String of அ and இ of even length can be obtained by concatenating any combination of the strings அஅ, அஇ, இஅ and இஇ including null, so L = {அஅ, அஇ, இஅ, இஇ, அஅஅஇ, அஅஇஅ, ………….}

12.5 AUTOMATA THEORY

Automata Theory is a branch of computer science that designs abstract self-propelled computing devices that automatically follow a predetermined sequence of operations. An Automata with a finite number of states is called a **Finite Automata.**

Automata

The term "Automata" is derived from the Greek word "αὐτόματα" which means "self-acting." An Automata (Automata in plural) is an abstract self-propelled computing device that automatically follows a predetermined sequence of operations (Recognise the strings automatically).

An Automata with finite states is called a **Finite Automata** (FA) or **Finite State Machine** (FSM).

The formal definition of a Finite Automata

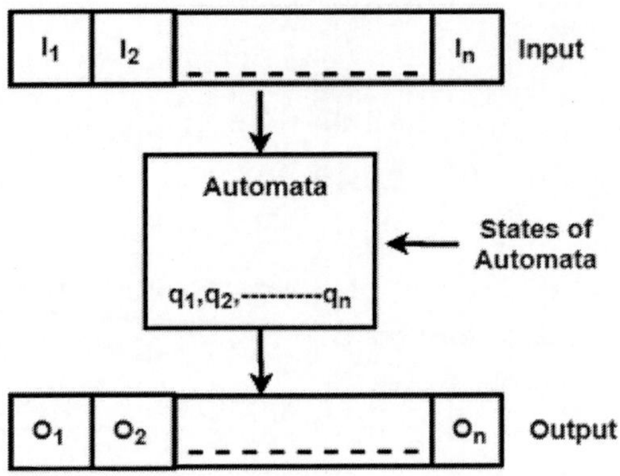

An Automata can be represented by a 5-tuple (**Q, ∑, δ, q_0, F**), where:

- **Q** is a finite set of states.
- **∑** is a finite set of symbols called the **alphabet** of the Automata.
- **δ** is the transition function.
- q_0 is the initial state from where any input is processed ($q_0 \in Q$).
- F is a set of final state/states of Q ($F \subseteq Q$).

Finite Automata can be classified into two types:

- Deterministic Finite Automata (DFA)
- Non-deterministic Finite Automata (NDFA/NFA)

12.5.1 Deterministic Finite Automata (DFA)

In DFA, one can determine the state to which the machine will move for each input symbol. Hence, it is called **Deterministic Automata.** As it has a finite number of states, the machine is called **Deterministic Finite Machine** or **Deterministic Finite Automata.**

Formal Definition of a DFA

A DFA can be represented by a 5-tuple (Q, ∑, δ, q_0, F) where:

- Q is a finite set of states.
- ∑ is a finite set of symbols called the alphabet.
- **δ** is the transition function where $\delta: Q \times \Sigma \rightarrow Q$
- q_0 is the initial state from where any input is processed ($q_0 \in Q$).
- F is a set of final state/states of Q ($F \subseteq Q$).

Graphical Representation of a DFA

A DFA is represented by digraphs called a **state diagram:**

- The vertices represent the states.
- The arcs labeled with an input alphabet show the transitions.
- An empty single incoming arc denotes the initial state.
- Double circles indicate the final state.

Example

Let a deterministic finite Automataaton be →

- Q = {a, b, c},
- $\sum$ = {அ, இ},
- q_0 = {a},
- F = {c}, and

Transition function δ as shown by the following table:

Present State	*Next State for Input 0*	*Next State for Input 1*
a	a	b
b	c	a
c	b	c

Its graphical representation would be as follows:

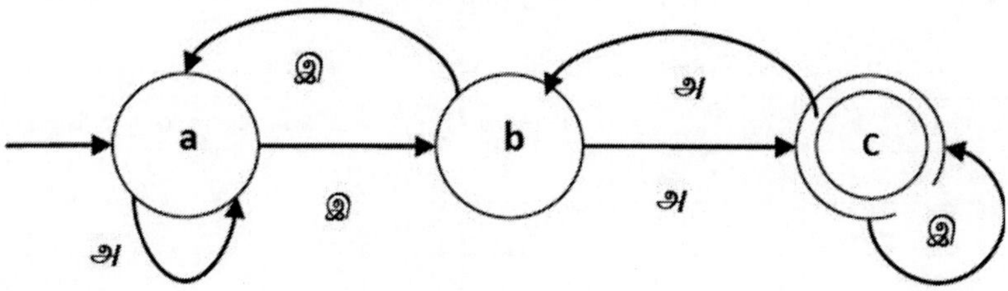

12.5.2 Non-deterministic Finite Automataaton

In NDFA, for a particular input symbol, the machine can move to any combination of the states in the machine. In other words, the exact state to which the machine moves cannot be determined. Hence, it is called **Non-deterministic Automataaton.** As it has a finite number of states, the machine is called **Non-deterministic Finite Machine** or **Non-deterministic Finite Automataaton.**

Formal Definition of an NDFA

An NDFA can be represented by a 5-tuple (Q, ∑, δ, q_0, F) where:

- Q is a finite set of states.
- ∑ is a finite set of symbols called the alphabet.
- **δ** is the transition function where δ: Q × ∑ → 2^Q
- (Here, the power set of Q (2^Q) has been taken because, in the case of NDFA, from a state, the transition can occur to any combination of Q states).
- q_0 is the initial state from where any input is processed ($q_0 \in Q$).
- F is a set of final state/states of Q ($F \subseteq Q$).

Graphical Representation of an NDFA: (same as DFA).

An NDFA is represented by digraphs called a state diagram:

- The vertices represent the states.
- The arcs labeled with an input alphabet show the transitions.
- An empty single incoming arc denotes the initial state.
- Double circles indicate the final state.

Example

Let a non-deterministic finite Automataaton be →

- Q = {a, b, c} • ∑ = { அ, இ} • q_0 = {a} • F = {c}

The transition function δ as shown below:

Present State	*Next State for Input 0*	*Next State for Input 1*
a	a, b	b
b	c	a, c
c	b, c	c

Its graphical representation would be as follows:

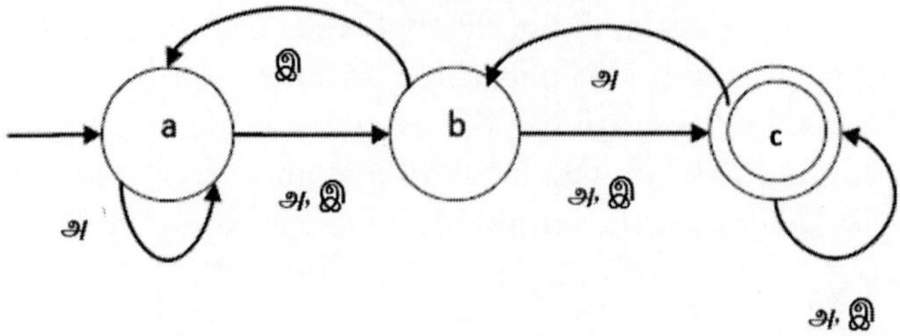

12.5.3 DFA vs. NDFA

The following table lists the differences between DFA and NDFA.

DFA	*NDFA*
The transition from a state to a particular next state for each input symbol. Hence it is called *deterministic.*	Each input symbol can transition from one state to multiple following conditions. Hence it is called *non-deterministic.*
Empty string transitions are not seen in DFA.	NDFA permits empty string transitions.
Backtracking is allowed in DFA.	In NDFA, backtracking is not always possible.
Requires more space.	Requires less space.
A DFA accepts a string if it transits to a final state.	An NDFA accepts a string if at least one of all possible transitions ends in a final state.

12.6 CONCLUSION

This chapter introduces the main issues of "Inputting, Outputting and Computing." Most programs in Tamil employ a dialogue box to prompt the user for information. In contrast, Python has two built-in routines for reading data from the keyboard. Inputting and rendering the character is an important activity. The program gets the Tamil character as input from the keyboard and displays the same on the screen. It is essential to remember that the installation of the language is necessary for typing the character in Tamil. Computing in Tamil entails investigating and testing algorithmic procedures and developing hardware and software. The python program of Tamil demonstrates the simple calculator performing various computing operations. It can deliver two different types of inputs that are in character and float. In addition, a simple calculator is used to perform the essential functions. Most importantly, getting the information and rendering text on the screen is crucial for Tamil Computing, clearly demonstrated in the chapter.

CHAPTER 13

Customize Windows Operating System for Tamil Computing

13.1 INTRODUCTION

In Windows Operating systems, it supports more than 100 different languages. English is beneficial as it is a common language to interact with maintainers, inventors and users worldwide. However, in the case of a country like India, where the majority of the people do not understand English. The availability of such software in the native Language is of crucial significance as it would assist in taking advantage of the "information revolution" to acknowledge proper social use of information technology. Therefore, the operating system is fundamental for system operation. Such local language characteristics might involve the cultural pacts of the state, the date and time format, language-specific scripts (fonts), numbers representation, currency symbols, etc. The recognized portrayal of these characteristics and the linked translations of a native language establishes the *Locale* for that specific language or state. This chapter explains how to customize the Windows Operating System in the Tamil Language.

13.2 CUSTOMIZE OPERATING SYSTEM

The customizable operating system increases and improves the efficiency of the functionality and performance. Language customized operating systems are always in demand for several years of development. However, they have to appear in the commercial market. This chapter explains the operating system customizability and examines the existing approaches' limits. First of all, one must do the language configuration. To do the language configuration, the user should perform the Language enabling and keyboard language selection/enabling. The following steps should be performed.

The first step is to go to the Windows setting, as shown in Figure 13.1.

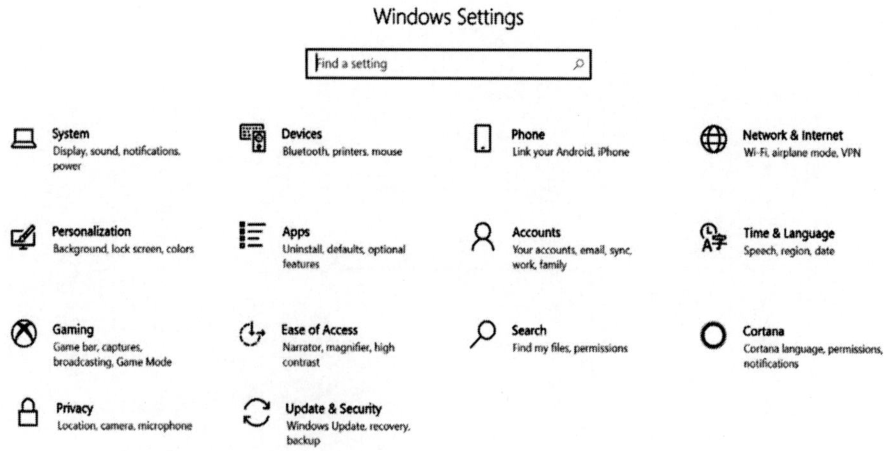

Figure 13.1: Windows Setting

The second step is to select the Time and Language setting. It is shown in Figure 13.2.

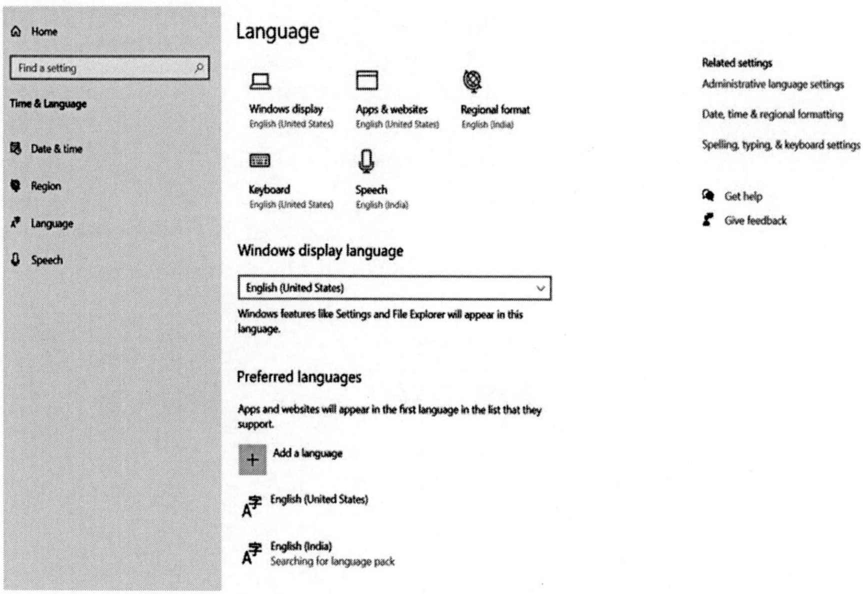

Figure 13.2: Time and Language Setting

Then, the third step is to select Tamil as the preferred Language. It is shown in Figure 13.3.

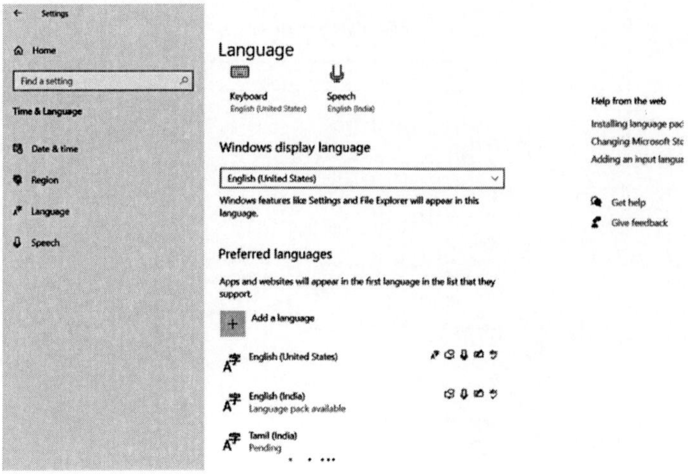

Figure 13.3: Time and Language Setting

If the preferred language already appeared in the time and language setting, one can select the preferred language or otherwise; it has to be installed in the language options by pressing add language option in the Tamil language setting. If the language keyboard is not installed, then one must select the Tamil Language Keyboard and install it, or it has to be installed. It will allow one to install a particular language keyboard mapping in the system. Two types of Tamil language options are available in MS Windows. One is Tamil (India) and the second option is Tamil (Sri Lanka). After the selection, one has to select the options available for typing and spoken languages. Based on the requirements, the user has to choose one of them and install it into the system. It is shown in Figure 13.4.

Figure 13.4: Language Option Selections

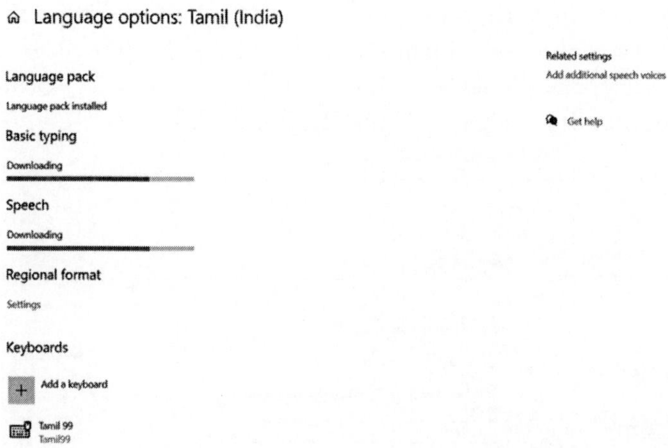

Figure 13.5: Language Options Installation

Once installed, one can select the Tamil language keyboard for the language setting from the desktop itself. Typically, two kinds of keyboards are available with Microsoft. One is the language keyboard and another is the glyph-based keyboard, which permits the user to type contents in Tamil using English voice. If one does the font setting without keyboard mapping, one cannot access the Language for inputting. One should perform the keyboard preference selection on the screen's right side bottom. Once it is selected, then inputs can be given in that Language. It is shown in Figure 13.6

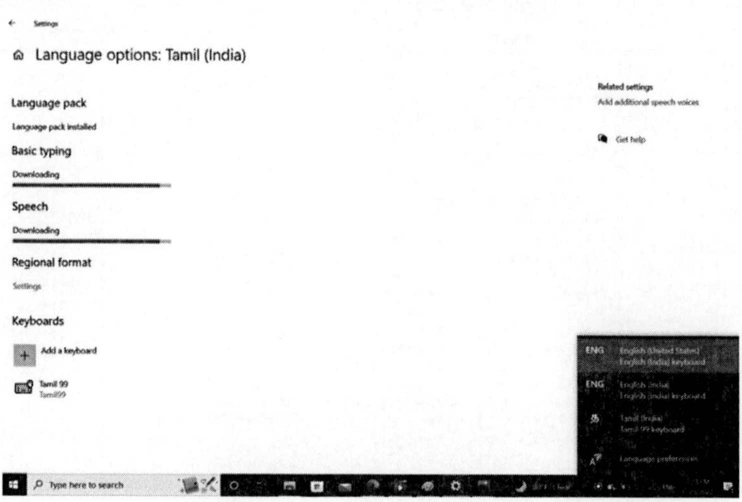

Figure 13.6: Input Language Option Selection

In addition, the user can also map the language enabling. To do that, one should go to the control panel and allow the display language as follows. To do the same, one should select the control panel option and then go to the language option. It is shown in Figure 13.7 and 13.8.

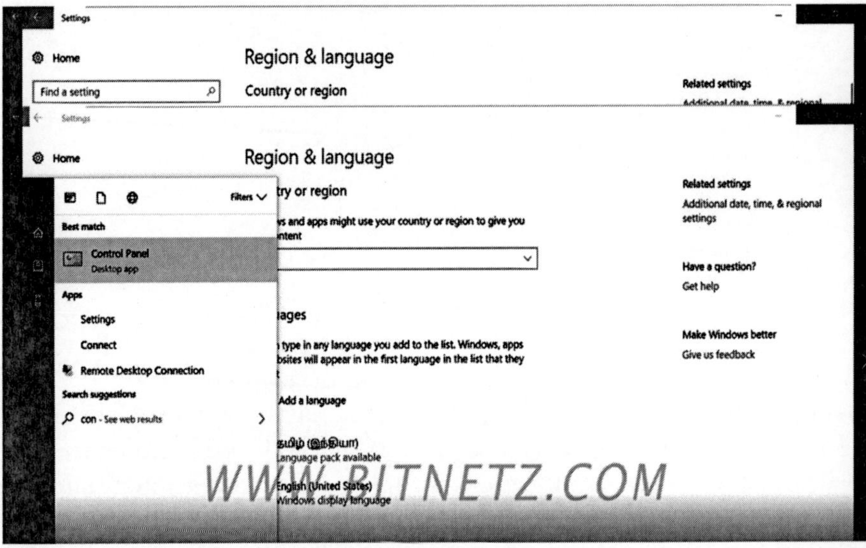

Figure 13.7: Input Language Option Selection

Figure 13.8: Control Panel Language Selection Setting

After selecting the language option, it will show the language preferences to the user. It is shown in Figure 13.9.

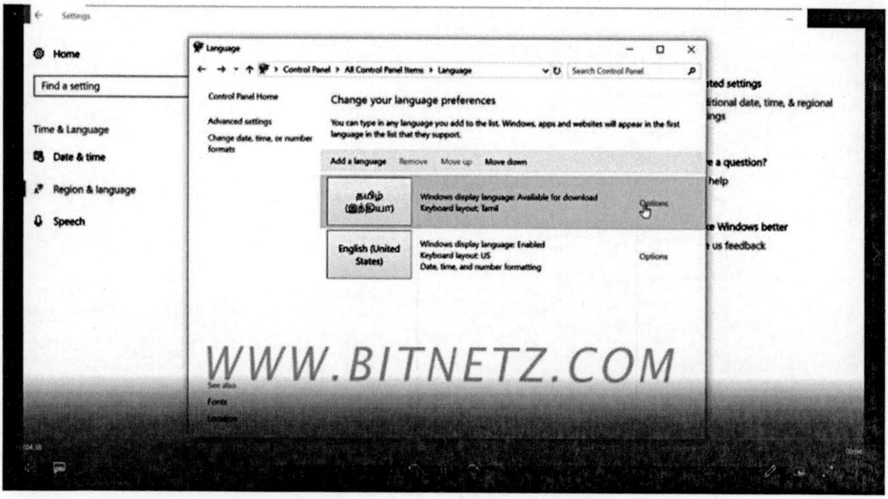

Figure 13.9: Control Panel Language Preferences Setting

After that, one can go to the advanced setting, then the display language setting and the input method language also one can define. After changing these settings, the display and keyboard are entirely adjusted to Tamil, as shown in the following diagrams. It is shown in Figures 13.10 to 13.13.

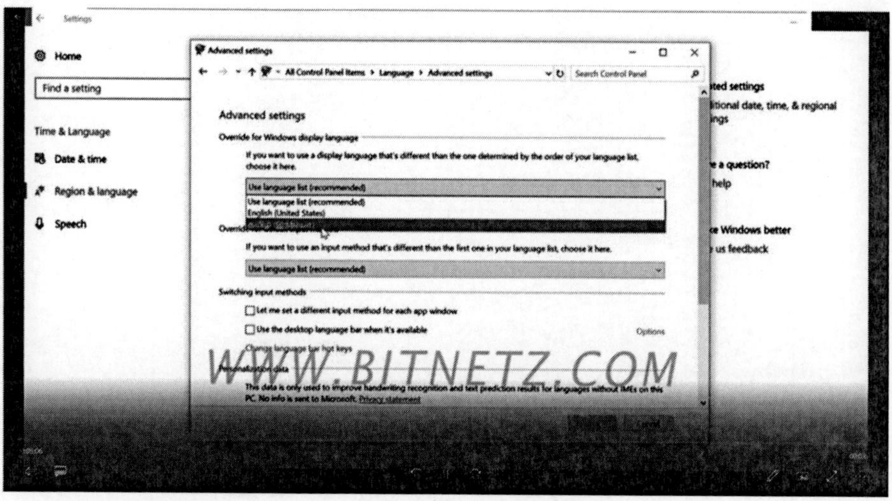

Figure 13.10: Control Panel Language Advanced Setting

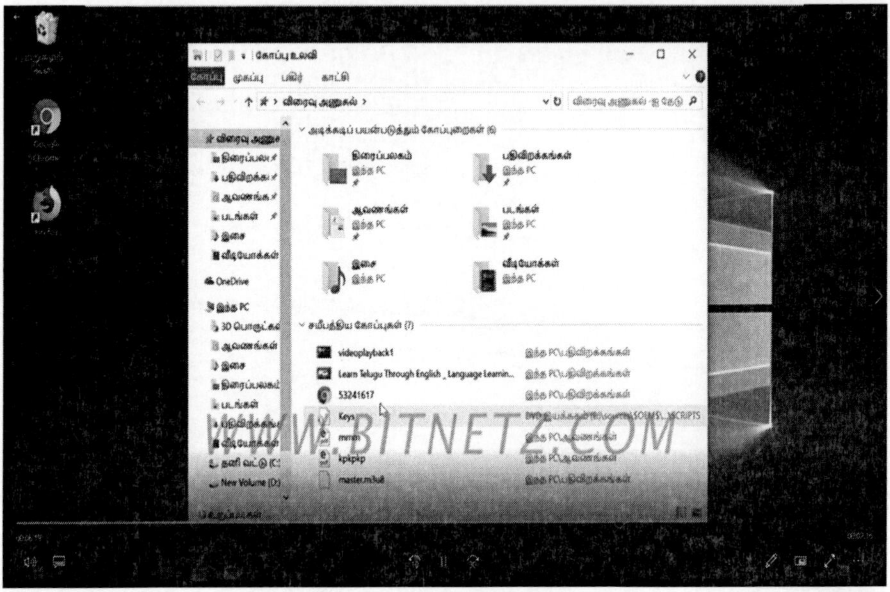

Figure 13.11: File Display in the Tamil Language

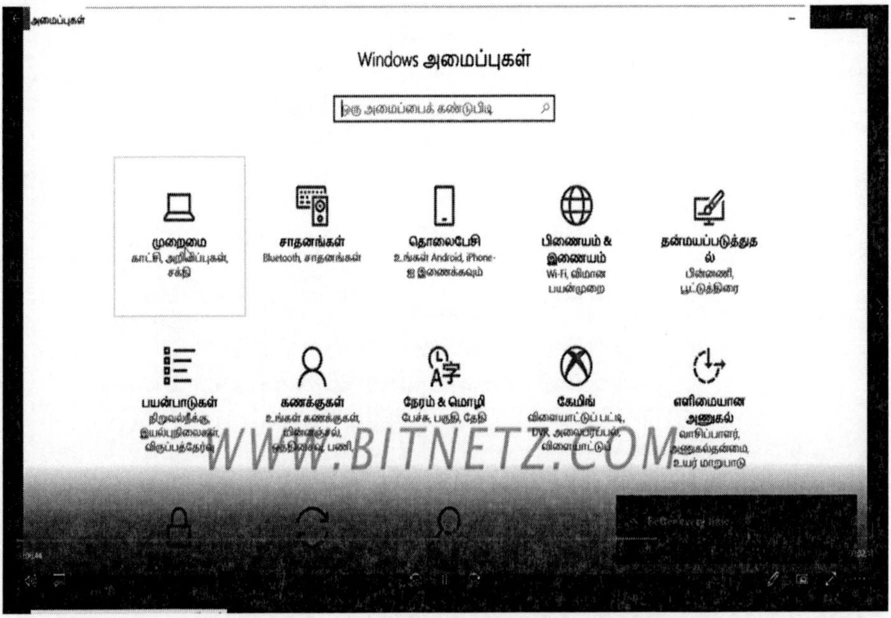

Figure 13.12: Windows Setting Display in the Tamil Language

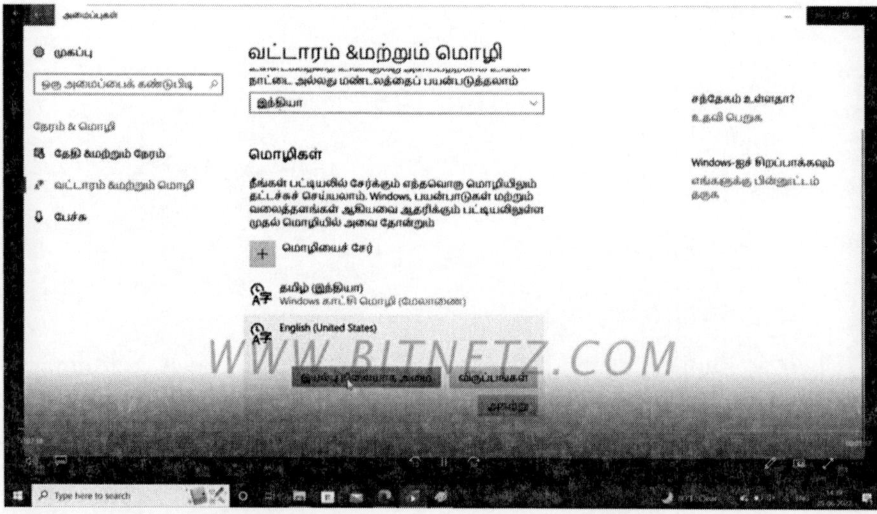

Figure 13.13: Language Setting Display in the Tamil Language

13.3 CONCLUSION

This chapter gives an outline and method of customizing Tamil as the preferred Language and uses it as the Operating System Language in Windows. Even though it is the corporate software, it gives outstanding support to Tamil Computing. It will also enable us to use the Tamil tools effectively. These approaches will not provide a detailed, standard and easy-to-use method of communication for everyone. For the long-term expansion of the Tamil language for electronic processing, it is vital to approach the problem from data processing.

CHAPTER 14

Tamil in Indic Libraries

14.1 INTRODUCTION

There are support methods for the Indic Languages through their libraries. In specific, Python famously supports these language libraries. These libraries include iNLTK, Indicnlp, Stanford NLP, etc. This chapter discusses these two libraries (iNLTK and Indicnlp) in detail.

14.1.1 iNLTK: Natural Language Toolkit for Indic Languages

In Python, the popular NLP library NLTK (Natural Language Tool Kit) is used to perform diverse NLP tasks and operations. NLTK, however, is limited to dealing with English Language only. This chapter will explore and discuss iNLTK, Natural Language Tool Kit for Indic Languages. As the name suggests, iNLTK is a Python library that performs NLP operations in Indian languages. This library is built to provide features that an NLP application developer will need.

iNLTK provides features that modern NLP tasks require, like generating a vector **embedding** for input text, tokenization, sentence similarity, etc., in a very **intuitive** and easy API interface.

14.1.1.1 *Languages Available in iNLTK*

iNLTK covers almost all the most common Indian languages. Following is the list of languages, along with their codes available in iNLTK:

Language	*Code*
Hindi	hi
Punjabi	pa
Sanskrit	sa
Gujarati	gu

Language	*Code*
Kannada	kn
Malayalam	ml
Nepali	ne
Odia	or
Marathi	mr
Bengali	bn
Tamil	ta
Urdu	ur

14.1.1.2 *Installation*

iNLTK can be easily installed using pip as follows.

pip install inltk
conda install pytorch = 1.3.1 -c pytorch

14.1.1.3 *Setup the Language*

From inltk.inltk import setup

setup('<code-of-language>') // if you wanted to use hindi, then
setup('ta')

Note: You need to run Setup ('<code-of-language>') when you use a language for the FIRST TIME ONLY. This will download all the necessary models required for inference for that language.

From inltk.inltk import setup.

setup('ta') // This will set up the Tamil Language.

If it is completed, it will send the message "Done!".

After doing the same, one can run the program and see the outputs as per their requirements.

14.1.1.4 *Tokenization*

Words are like the atoms of natural language. They're the smallest unit of meaning that still makes sense. Tokenizing your text by word allows you to identify words that come up particularly often. The following program will tokenize the given Tamil sentence as follows.

From inltk.inltk import tokenize

text = '''நான் இன்று காலை நேரம் சென்று எழுந்தேன். அவன் நன்கு ஓய்வு எடுக்கட்டும். நீங்கள் வருகைதந்தமைக்கு மிக்கநன்றி.'''
print(tokenize(text, 'ta'))

Output:

['_நான்', '_இன்று', '_காலை', '_நேரம்', '_சென்று', '_எழுந்த', 'ே◌ன்', '_அவன்', '_நன்கு', '_ஓய்வு', '_எடுக்க', 'ட்டு', 'ம்', '_நீ', 'ங்கள்', '_வருகை', 'த', 'ந்த', 'மை', 'க்கு', '_மிக்க', 'ந', 'ன்றி']

14.1.1.5 *Identify Language*

We can give the Tamil text as input or any language mentioned above. The identifying language method will automatically recognise the language of the text.

 # Example - Identify Language of Text
from inltk.inltk import identify_language
print(identify_language('நான் இன்று காலை நேரம் சென்று எழுந்தேன்.'))

Output:

tamil

14.1.1.6 *Get Similar Words and Sentences*

We can use iNLTK to predict the next *'n'* words, get similar sentences, get sentence encoding, identify language, etc. One of the most common tasks of NLP is to generate similar words and sentences to a given input sentence. iNLTK's predict_next_words(text, n, language_code) and get_similar_sentences(text, n, language_code) do exactly the same. It takes the input text, the number of sentences to be generated (n), and the language code as the arguments.

In the example below, we will be using iNLTK to predict next 'n' words and get similar sentences. For an input like *"It's been a long time since we met"* in Tamil, we get a prediction for the following 'n' words as *"And, due to this"*. And the results for similar sentences task is also impressive.

 # Example: Predict Next 'n' Words, Get Similar Sentences

from inltk.inltk import setup
from inltk.inltk import predict_next_words
from inltk.inltk import get_similar_sentences

Note: You need to run Setup ('<code-of-language>') when you use a language for the FIRST TIME ONLY.

This will download all the necessary models required for inference for that language.

```
setup('ta')
example_sent = "உங்களைப் பார்த்து நிறைய நாட்கள் ஆகிவிட்டது."
# Predict the next 'n' tokens
n = 5
pred_sent = predict_next_words(example_sent, n, 'ta')
# Get 'n' similar sentence
n = 2
simi_sent = get_similar_sentences(example_sent, n, 'ta')
print("Predicted Words:", pred_sent)
print("Similar Sentences:", simi_sent)
```

Output:

Predicted Words: உங்களைப் பார்த்து நிறைய நாட்கள் ஆகிவிட்டது. மேலும், இதற்கு காரணமாக

Similar Sentences: ['உங்களைத் பார்த்து நாட்கள் ஆகிவிட்டது', 'உங்களைப் பார்த்து ஏராளமான நாட்கள் ஆகிவிட்டது']

14.1.1.7 *Get Sentence Similarity*

We can also check the similarities between two sentences using iNLTK. It can be done using iNLTK's **get_sentence_similarity**(text1, text2, language_code) function, which takes two text inputs to be compared and the language code as the arguments.

From inltk.inltk import get_sentence_similarity

```
text1 = 'உங்களைத் பார்த்து நாட்கள் ஆகிவிட்டது'.
text2 = 'உங்களைப் பார்த்து ஏராளமான நாட்கள் ஆகிவிட்டது'.
print(get_sentence_similarity(text1, text2, 'ta'))
```

Output:

0.918816089630127

14.1.1.8 *Text Embedding Generation*

In NLP, text embeddings refer to a vectorized representation of text. It is necessary to convert text to embeddings as we cannot directly feed Machine/ Deep Learning models with the raw text. It can be done using iNLTK's **get_embedding_vectors**(text, language code) which takes input text and its language code as the arguments.

```
from inltk.inltk import get_embedding_vectors
from warnings import filterwarnings
from IPython.display import display
filterwarnings("ignore")
text = 'நான் இன்று காலை நேரம் சென்று எழுந்தேன்'.
vectors = get_embedding_vectors(text, 'ta')
print(vectors)
```

Output:

```
[array([–0.627435, –0.399016, 1.00325, –0.017604, ..., –0.865197, –0.207182, 0.255426, 0.129037], dtype=float32),
array([–0.283198, –0.188771, –0.243825, 0.322327, ..., –0.798777, 0.090669, –0.224787, 0.429571], dtype=float32),
array([ 0.061534, –0.161824, –0.226856, –0.161438, ..., –0.214605, –0.468564, 0.20361, 0.203198], dtype=float32),
array([–0.62115, –0.46205, 0.073921, –0.017392, ..., –0.42998, 0.966334, 0.775764, 0.928268], dtype=float32),
array([–0.582462, –0.098368, 0.52979, 0.428812, ..., –0.359963, 0.116916, 0.403835, –0.030496], dtype=float32),
array([–0.207138, –0.218409, 0.80212, –0.349639, ..., –0.654393, 0.300697, 0.154763, 0.668422], dtype=float32),
array([ 0.943783, –0.797455, 0.371784, 0.442829, ..., –0.445079, 0.074518, –0.966617, 0.385461], dtype=float32)].
```

14.2 INDIC NLP LIBRARY

The Indic NLP Library aims to build Python-based libraries for standard text processing and Natural Language Processing in the Indian languages. The Indian languages share many similarities in terms of script, phonology, language syntax, etc., and this library is an attempt to provide a general solution to very commonly required toolsets for the Indian language text.

The library provides the following functionalities.

Text Normalization
Script Information
Tokenization
Word Segmentation/Morphological Analysis

Script Conversion
Romanization
Indicization
Transliteration
Translation

This library supports the following languages.

Language Support

Indo-Aryan			Dravidian	Others
Assamese (asm)	Marathi (mar)	Sindhi (snd)	Kannada (kan)	English (eng)
Bengali (ben)	Nepali (nep)	Sinhala (sin)	Malayalam (mal)	
Gujarati (guj)	Odia (ori)	Sanskrit (san)	Telugu (tel)	
Hindi/Urdu (hin/urd)	Punjabi (pan)	Konkani (kok)	Tamil (tam)	

Tasks

Monolingual	Indo-Aryan													Dravidian			
	san	hin	urd	pan	nep	snd	asm	ben	ori	guj	mar	kok	sin	kan	tel	tam	mal
Script Information	✓	✓	✗	✓	✓	✓	✓	✓	✓	✓	✓	✓	✗	✓	✓	✓	✓
Normalization	✓	✓	✗	✓	✓	✓	✓	✓	✓	✓	✓	✓	✗	✓	✓	✓	✓
Tokenization	✓	✓	✓	✓	✓	✓	✓	✓	✓	✓	✓	✓	✓	✓	✓	✓	✓
Word segmentation	✗	✓	✗	✓	✗	✗	✗	✓	✗	✓	✓	✓	✗	✓	✓	✓	✓
Romanization (ITRANS)	✓	✓	✗	✓	✓	✓	✓	✓	✓	✓	✓	✓	✓	✓	✓	✓	✓
ITRANS to Script	✓	✓	✗	✓	✓	✓	✓	✓	✓	✓	✓	✓	✓	✓	✓	✓	✓

Bilingual

- **Script Conversion:** Amongst the above mentioned languages, except Urdu and English
- **Transliteration:** Amongst the 18 above mentioned languages
- **Translation:** Amongst these 10 languages: (hin, urd, pan, ben, guj, mar, kok, sin, kan, tel, tam, mal) + English

14.2.1 Installation

Indic NLP Library can be easily installed using pip as follows.

Pip install indic-nlp-library

Next, you must download the resources folder containing the models for different languages. You can do that by cloning the **indic_nlp_resources** repository from GitHub.

 # download the resource

git clone https://github.com/anoopkunchukuttan/indic_nlp_resources.git

Apart from its API, this library provides specific scripts for NLP. You can clone the GitHub folder itself to get them.

 # download the repo

git clone https://github.com/anoopkunchukuttan/indic_nlp_library.git

Now that all the files are downloaded, you can set the path so that Python knows where to find these on your computer.

14.2.2 Tokenizing

Tokenization is breaking a stream of textual content into meaningful elements called tokens. These tokens can be words, terms, symbols, etc. Generally, tokenization happens at a word level, but sometimes it's tough to define what's meant by a 'word'. Standard tokenizers use simple heuristics like.

- Punctuations and whitespace may or may not be returned with the tokens.
- Contiguous strings of alphabetic characters or numbers are considered as a single token.
- Tokens are separated using whitespace characters or punctuation characters.

```
from indicnlp import common
from indicnlp import loader
from indicnlp.tokenize import indic_tokenize
# The path to the local git repo for Indic NLP Resources
INDIC_NLP_RESOURCES = r"C:\Users\hp\anaconda3\lib\site-packages\indicnlp"
# Export the path to the Indic NLP Resources directory programmatically
common.set_resources_path(INDIC_NLP_RESOURCES)
# Initialize the Indic NLP library
loader.load()
# Tokenization
indic_string = 'புத்துணர்ச்சியான சுவாசம் மற்றும் பளபளப்பான பற்கள் தங்களின் தோற்றத்தை நிர்ணயிக்கிறது.'
print('Input String: {}'.format(indic_string))
print('Tokens:')
for t in indic_tokenize.trivial_tokenize(indic_string):
print(t)
```

Output:

Input String: புத்துணர்ச்சியான சுவாசம் மற்றும் பளபளப்பான பற்கள் தங்களின் தோற்றத்தை நிர்ணயிக்கிறது.

Tokens:

புத்துணர்ச்சியான
சுவாசம்
மற்றும்
பளபளப்பான
பற்கள்
தங்களின்
தோற்றத்தை
நிர்ணயிக்கிறது.

14.2.3 Morphological Analysis

Morphological analysis (MA) produces information regarding the morphosyntactic properties of a word; it is an essential component of performing Machine Translations.

```
from indicnlp import common
from indicnlp import loader
from indicnlp.morph import unsupervised_morph
# The path to the local git repo for Indic NLP Resources
INDIC_NLP_RESOURCES = r"C:\Users\hp\anaconda3\lib\site-packages\indicnlp"
# Export the path to the Indic NLP Resources directory programmatically
common.set_resources_path(INDIC_NLP_RESOURCES)
# Initialize the Indic NLP library
loader.load()
# Morphological Analyser
analyzer = unsupervised_morph.UnsupervisedMorphAnalyzer('ta')
indic_string = 'புத்துணர்ச்சியான'
analyzes_tokens = analyzer.morph_analyze_document(indic_string.split(' '))
print(analyzes_tokens)
```

Output:

['புத்துணர்ச்சி', 'யான']

14.2.4 Transliteration

Transliteration is the 'transcribing one alphabet to another or replacing letters/ characters to another language with the same phonetic sound'. Unlike translation which gives the meaning of a given word in a different language, transliteration represents the characters of a given script to characters of another. It only gives an idea of how that word is pronounced.

The following program t*ransliterates* the given Tamil input sentence into English.

```
Import requests
    from indicnlp import common
    from indicnlp import loader
    from urllib.parse import quote
    from indicnlp.transliterate.unicode_transliterate import Itrans Transliterator
    # The path to the local git repo for Indic NLP Resources
    INDIC_NLP_RESOURCES = r"C:\Users\hp\anaconda3\lib\site-packages\
    indicnlp"
    # Export the path to the Indic NLP Resources directory programmatically
    common.set_resources_path(INDIC_NLP_RESOURCES)
    # Initialize the Indic NLP library
    loader.load()
    # Transliteration
    input_text = 'புத்துணர்ச்சியான சுவாசம் மற்றும் பளபளப்பான பற்கள்
    தங்களின் தோற்றத்தை நிர்ணயிக்கிறது.'
    lang = 'ta'
    print('iTrans transliteration: ')
    print(ItransTransliterator.to_itrans(input_text, lang))
```

Output:

iTrans transliteration:

*puttuNarchchiyaa*na chuvaacham maRRum paldapaldappaa*na paRkald ta-Nkaldi*n toRRattai nirNayikkiRatu*

Similarly, we can transliterate from one Indic language to another. The following program will transliterate the 'Hindi' sentence into Tamil Sentence.

```
From indicnlp.transliterate.unicode_transliterate import UnicodeIndic Transliterator.
#input text 'Today the weather is good. Sun is bright and there are no signs of rain. Hence we can play today.'
input_text = 'आज मौसम अच्छा है। सूरज उज्ज्वल है और बारिश के कोई संकेत नहीं हैं। इसलिए हम आज खेल सकते हैं!'
# Transliterate from Hindi to Tamil
print(UnicodeIndicTransliterator.transliterate(input_text2, "hi", "ta"))
```

Output:

ஆஜ மௌஸம அச்சா ஹை। ஸூரஜ உஜ்ஜ்வல ஹை ஔர பாரிஷ கே கோஈ ஸஂகேத நஹீஂ ஹைஂ। இஸலிஏ ஹம ஆஜ கேல ஸகதே ஹைஂ!

14.2.5 *Understanding the Phonetics of a Character*

The phonetics of a character describe the speech property of that character (like how it will sound, how much tongue should be rolled to pronounce it, etc.). The Indian Sub-Continent languages have strong phonetics for their alphabet, so in the Indic NLP Library, each character has a phonetic vector associated with it that defines its properties.

How is this useful? Well, you can take the character of a new language and just learn almost everything about it—from whether it is a vowel or consonant to how the tongue is rolled to pronounce that word.

Here is an example of a phonetic property that defines how the character "அ" and 'ந' are spoken.

```
From indicnlp.langinfo import *
# Input character
c1='அ'
c2='ந'
# Language is Tamil or 'ta'
lang='ta'
print('First Letter:', c1)
print('Is vowel?: {}'.format(is_vowel(c1,lang)))
print('Is consonant?: {}'.format(is_consonant(c1,lang)))
print('Is velar?: {}'.format(is_velar(c1,lang)))
```

```
print('Is palatal?: {}'.format(is_palatal(c1,lang)))
print('Is aspirated?: {}'.format(is_aspirated(c1,lang)))
print('Is unvoiced?: {}'.format(is_unvoiced(c1,lang)))
print('Is nasal?: {}'.format(is_nasal(c1,lang)))
print('Second Letter:',c2)
print('Is vowel?: {}'.format(is_vowel(c2,lang)))
print('Is consonant?: {}'.format(is_consonant(c2,lang)))
print('Is velar?: {}'.format(is_velar(c2,lang)))
print('Is palatal?: {}'.format(is_palatal(c2,lang)))
print('Is aspirated?: {}'.format(is_aspirated(c2,lang)))
print('Is unvoiced?: {}'.format(is_unvoiced(c2,lang)))
print('Is nasal?: {}'.format(is_nasal(c2,lang)))
```

Output:

```
First Letter   :  அ
Is vowel?      :  True
Is consonant?  :  False
Is velar?      :  False
Is palatal?    :  False
Is aspirated?  :  False
Is unvoiced?   :  False
Is nasal?      :  False

Second Letter  :  ந
Is vowel?      :  False
Is consonant?  :  True
Is velar?      :  False
Is palatal?    :  False
Is aspirated?  :  False
Is unvoiced?   :  False
Is nasal?      :  True
```

14.3 CONCLUSION

Various individuals have developed libraries in the open world to support fundamental language processing. In this case, only two libraries are discussed; it provides the basic operations also. However, the authors can explore the complete functions available under these libraries.

CHAPTER 15

Exploring Generative AI and Large Language Models for Tamil

15.1 INTRODUCTION TO LANGUAGE MODELING AND GENERATIVE MODELS

Language modeling is a critical task in NLP that involves predicting the probability of sequences of words or letters in a particular situation. The aim is to capture the structure and patterns of the Tamil language. The model needs to understand and predict the probability of different linguistic structures of the Tamil language to facilitate applications like speech recognition, machine translation, and text generation.

15.1.1 Generative Models in Tamil NLP

The NLP models are designed to generate new, coherent, and contextually relevant text. These models are trained using the large data set to learn Tamil language syntax, semantics, and patterns. These models can be used for creative and practical applications like translation, summarization, text completion, and writing. The pre-trained large-scale programs enhance reliability, resulting in linguistic awareness and fluency. Some notable generative models present for English can be trained and fine-tuned for the Tamil language.

Here are some popular generative models in the NLP domain that can be considered for Tamil:

GPT (Generative Pre-trained Transformer)

The GPT series is a powerful generative model, including GPT-2 and GPT-3. GPT-3, in particular, has been used for various creative text generation tasks. Fine-tune these models on Tamil data to make them suitable for specific applications.

BERT (Bidirectional Encoder Representations from Transformers)

BERT is best known for its effectiveness in capturing context and bidirectional relationships between words. It is commonly used in tasks like

Named Entity Recognition and Text Classification. It can be used in generative Tasks with proper modifications.

T5 (Text-to-Text Transfer Transformer)

T5 is pre-trained on large-scale datasets to learn general language patterns. It is a skilled model that forms all NLP tasks such as summarization, translation, question-answering, and converting one kind of text to another into a text-to-text format. This pre-training step helps the model understand syntax, semantics, and context better. This feature allows us to fine-tune Tamil data and make them suitable for specific applications.

mT5 (Multilingual Text-to-Text Transfer Transformer)

An extension of T5 is mT5, designed to handle multiple languages. It is not explicitly trained for Tamil, but it can be fine-tuned on multilingual data to generate text in various languages, including Tamil.

When working with generative models for Tamil, consider the following steps:

- Preprocess Tamil text data, tokenize, and prepare for training.
- Fine-tune a pre-trained model on the Tamil dataset for specific generative tasks.
- Evaluate the fine-tuned model on relevant metrics and adjust as required.

15.1.2 Importance of Language Models to Understand and Generate Human-Like Text

Language models play an essential role in understanding and generating text like humans. It is used in many applications, from everyday communication to advanced NLP processing.

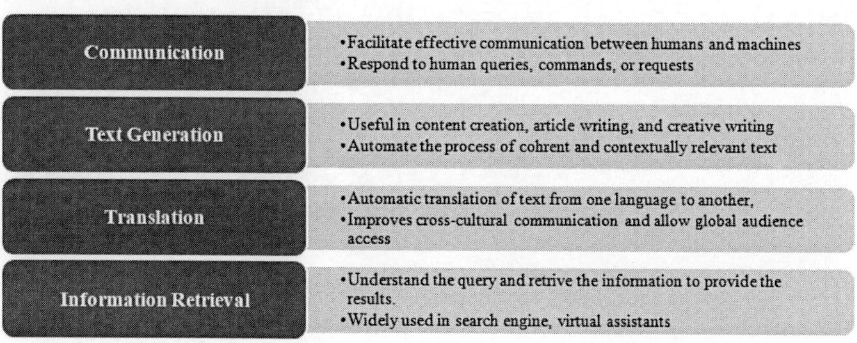

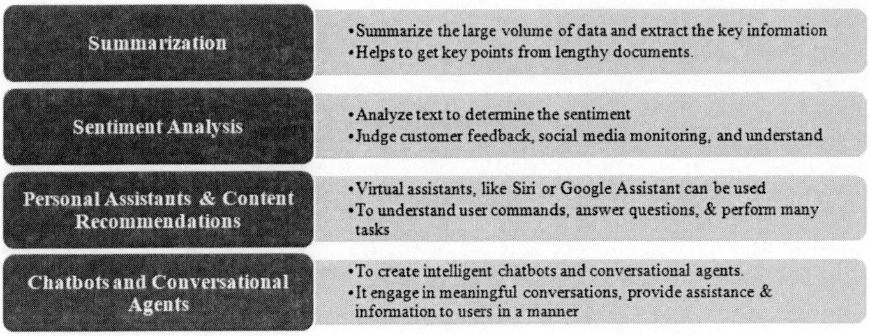

Figure 15.1

15.2 TRANSFORMER ARCHITECTURE OVERVIEW

The Transformer architecture, introduced in the paper "Attention is All You Need" by Vaswani *et al.* in 2017, has become a foundational model in NLP and various other tasks within machine learning. The Transformer architecture is known for its parallelization capabilities, scalability, and ability to capture long-range dependencies in sequences efficiently. The critical components of the Transformer architecture:

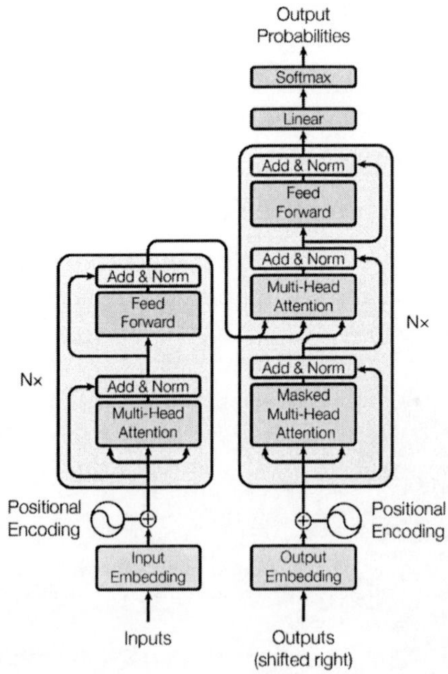

Figure 15.2: Transformer Architecture from "Attention is All You Need"

Input Embedding

The input to the Transformer model is a sequence of tokens, such as words or subworlds. Each token is initially embedded into a high-dimensional vector space. These embeddings serve as the input to the subsequent layers of the model.

Positional Encoding

Since the Transformer does not inherently understand the order of tokens in a sequence, positional encoding is added to the input embeddings to provide information about the positions of tokens. It allows the model to consider the sequential nature of the data.

Encoder Stack

The encoder stack consists of multiple identical layers, typically six in the original Transformer. Each layer in the encoder has two main components:

Self-Attention Mechanism

This mechanism allows each element in the input sequence to focus on different parts, capturing dependencies regardless of their distance.

Feedforward Neural Network

After the self-attention mechanism, the output passes through a position-wise feedforward network consisting of fully connected layers independently applied to each position.

Residual Connections and Layer Normalization (Encoder)

After each sub-layer (self-attention or feedforward), a residual connection is added, allowing the original input to bypass the sub-layer. It helps mitigate the vanishing gradient problem and facilitates the training of deep networks. Layer normalization is applied to the output of each sub-layer to stabilize the training process.

Multi-Head Attention

The self-attention mechanism is enhanced by employing multiple attention heads in parallel. Each attention head operates on a different linear transformation of the input, and their outputs are concatenated and linearly transformed. It enables the model to capture various aspects of the relationships between words.

Position-wise Feedforward Networks

The feedforward neural network in each layer is applied independently to each position in the sequence. It consists of two linear transformations with a ReLU activation in between.

Encoder Output

The output of the final encoder layer is the contextualized representation of the input sequence. This representation retains information about the relationships and dependencies between tokens.

Decoder Stack

The decoder stack also consists of multiple identical layers, typically six in the original Transformer. Each layer in the decoder has three main components:

- **Masked Self-Attention Mechanism:** Similar to the encoder, but during training, it is masked to prevent attending to future tokens. It ensures that the model generates one token at a time autoregressively.
- **Encoder-Decoder Attention Mechanism:** This mechanism allows the decoder to attend to different parts of the encoder's output, incorporating information from the input sequence.
- **Feedforward Neural Network (Decoder):** Similar to the encoder, a position-wise feedforward network follows the attention mechanisms in each decoder layer.

Residual Connections and Layer Normalization (Decoder)

Residual connections and layer normalization are applied similarly in the decoder and encoder.

Output Projection

The output of the final decoder layer is linearly transformed into a vector representing the probabilities of different words in the vocabulary. This output is then used to generate the predicted sequence.

Softmax Activation

A softmax activation is applied to the decoder output to convert the logits into probabilities. It allows the model to generate a probability distribution over the vocabulary for each position in the output sequence.

Training and Inference

The model is trained to minimize the cross-entropy loss between the predicted probabilities and the target sequence during training. The model generates sequences autoregressively in inference, feeding its predictions as inputs for subsequent steps.

The Transformer architecture revolutionized the field of natural language processing and has been widely adopted in various applications due to its parallelization capabilities, scalability, and ability to capture long-range dependencies in sequences. Its modular design allows for easy adaptation to different tasks and domains.

15.3 ATTENTION MECHANISM IN TRANSFORMERS

The attention mechanism is a crucial component in the Transformer architecture, allowing the model to weigh the importance of different parts of the input sequence when processing each element. The attention mechanism was introduced to address the limitations of traditional sequence-to-sequence models that struggle with capturing long-range dependencies in sequences. Here's an overview of how the attention mechanism works in Transformers:

15.3.1 Key Components

Query (Q), Key (K), and Value (V)

Each input token is associated with three vectors: Query (Q), Key (K), and Value (V). These vectors are learned during the training process.

These vectors are used to calculate attention scores, determining how much focus each element in the input sequence should place on the others.

15.3.2 Calculation of Attention Scores

Score Calculation

The attention score between a query and a key is calculated using a dot product or another similarity measure. The scores indicate the relevance or importance of a particular element in the sequence to the current element being processed.

Scaled Dot-Product Attention

The square root of the dimension of the critical vectors often scales the attention scores. It helps prevent the gradients from becoming too small during training.

Softmax Activation

The attention scores are passed through a softmax activation function to convert them into a probability distribution. It ensures that the weights assigned to different elements sum up to 1.

15.3.3 Weighted Sum of Values

Weighted Sum Calculation

The softmax-normalized attention scores are used to calculate a weighted sum of the corresponding value vectors. This weighted sum represents the context or information on which the current element should focus.

Weighted Sum Formula:

$$\text{Attention } (Q, K, V) = \text{softmax}\left(\frac{QK^T}{\sqrt{d_k}}\right)V$$

Here, d_k is the dimensionality of the key vectors.

15.3.4 Empirical Modelling of Self-Attention Modelling

In a human brain, when you read a sentence, a process happens for each word as your eyes progress through the sentence. For example, the sentence "ராஜா ஆப்பிரிக்கா வந்தார்". When your eyes see ராஜா, your brain looks for the most related word in the rest of the sentence to understand what ராஜா is about (query). Your brain focuses or attends to the word வந்தார் (key).

This process is implemented through scaled dot-product attention; the input sequence was transformed using three matrices representing the query, key, and value.

The first MatMul implements an inquiry or question-answer system that imitates this brain function, using Vector Similarity Calculation.

Think of the MatMul as an inquiry system that processes the inquiry: "For the word q that your eyes see in the given sentence, what is the most related word k to understand what q is about?" The inquiry system provides the answer as the probability.

Table 15.1: Query – Key Probability Matrix

q	*k*	*probability*
ராஜா	வந்தார்	0.94
வந்தார்	ஆப்பிரிக்கா	0.86
ஆப்பிரிக்கா	வந்தார்	0.76

The next word to be generated is computed in a self-attention system and calculated using the above model. It is shown in Figure 15.3 below.

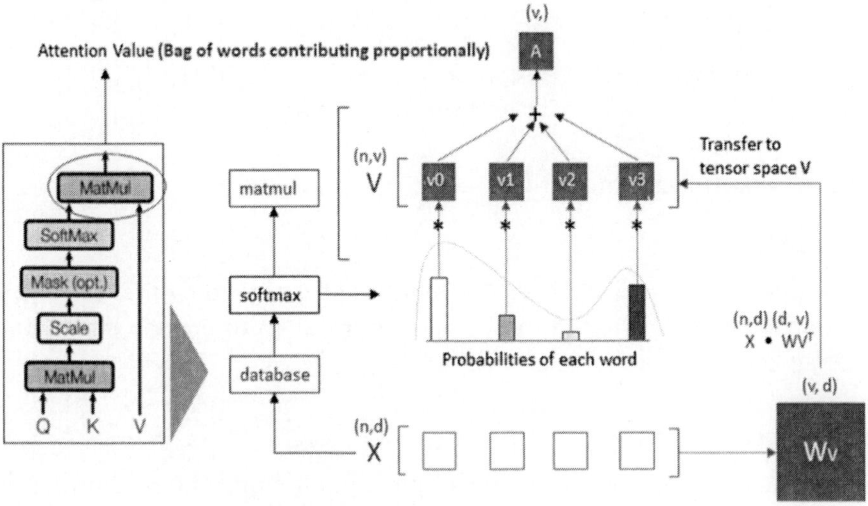

Figure 15.3: Attention Value Computation

15.3.5 Multi-Head Attention

Motivation

The Transformer uses multiple attention heads in parallel to capture different aspects of the relationships between tokens.

Parallel Heads

Each attention head has its set of learned Query (Q), Key (K), and Value (V) weight matrices.

The outputs of all heads are concatenated and linearly transformed to provide a richer representation.

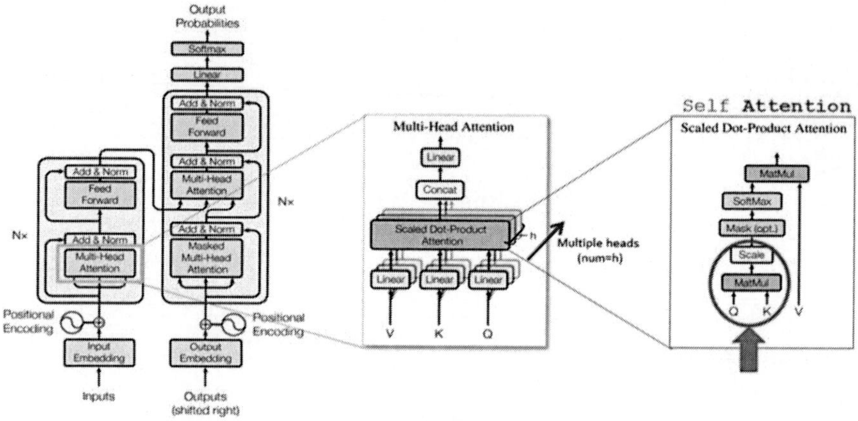

Figure 15.4: Transformers Architecture – Multi-Head Attention and Self-Attention Model

15.3.6 Positional Encoding

Importance

Since the Transformer does not inherently understand the order of tokens, positional encoding is added to the input embeddings to provide information about token positions.

Additive Combination

Positional encoding is added to the original input embeddings, allowing the model to consider the sequential nature of the data.

15.3.7 Masked Self-Attention (Decoder)

Autoregressive Decoding

During training, a masking mechanism is applied to the self-attention mechanism in the decoder. This prevents attending to future tokens, ensuring autoregressive generation during decoding.

15.3.8 Encoder-Decoder Attention (Decoder)

Connection to Encoder Output

An additional attention mechanism in the decoder allows it to attend to different parts of the encoder's output. This connection helps incorporate information from the input sequence during decoding.

The attention mechanism in Transformers has proven to be highly effective in capturing long-range dependencies, enabling the model to process sequences more efficiently than traditional models. It has since become a fundamental component of many state-of-the-art models in natural language processing and other domains.

15.4 GENERATIVE MODELS AND THEIR ROLE IN LANGUAGE GENERATION

Generative models play a fundamental role in language generation, allowing machines to create new, coherent text that resembles human language. These models are designed to capture a given dataset's underlying patterns and structures and generate novel samples similar to the training data. In language generation, generative models are beneficial for tasks such as text completion, dialogue generation, machine translation, and creative writing. Two prominent types of generative models used for language generation are autoregressive models and generative adversarial networks (GANs). Let's explore each of these:

Autoregressive Models

Overview: Autoregressive models generate sequences one element at a time, with each element's probability distribution conditioned on the previously generated elements. These models are often used for sequential data, such as text.

Example Models

- **Recurrent Neural Networks (RNNs):** A type of neural network designed for sequential data, where each step's output influences the next step.
- **Long Short-Term Memory (LSTM) Networks:** A variant of RNNs with a memory mechanism that helps capture long-range dependencies in sequences.

- **Gated Recurrent Unit (GRU):** Another variant of RNNs, similar to LSTMs but with a more straightforward structure.
- **Transformer Models:** While designed initially for attention-based sequence-to-sequence tasks, Transformers can also be used auto-regressively, generating one token at a time during decoding.

Training and Inference

During training, autoregressive models learn to predict the next element in a sequence given the context of the preceding elements.

In inference, the model generates sequences by sampling from its learned probability distribution at each step.

Generative Adversarial Networks (GANs)

Overview: GANs consist of a generator and a discriminator. The generator generates samples (in this case, text), while the discriminator evaluates whether a given sample is actual (from the training data) or generated. The generator and discriminator are trained iteratively in a game-like fashion.

Example Models

GANs don't have a specific architecture like autoregressive models, but they can be applied to various neural network architectures, including recurrent or convolutional networks.

Training Process

The generator aims to produce realistic samples to deceive the discriminator, while the discriminator seeks to distinguish between actual and generated samples.

The adversarial training process improves the generator over time, producing samples that are increasingly difficult for the discriminator to differentiate from accurate data.

Applications in Language Generation

GANs can be used for text-generation tasks by training the generator to produce realistic sentences or paragraphs.

GANs are particularly useful when paired with reinforcement learning, where a reward signal guides the generator to produce high-quality and diverse text.

Whether autoregressive or based on GANs, generative models have been applied successfully in various language generation tasks. They are used to generate creative content, complete sentences, enhance dialogue systems, and even assist in tasks like machine translation. The choice of generative model often depends on the Task's specific requirements and the data's characteristics.

Practical Demo: Training a Language Model with Transformer Architecture

Creating a language model for Tamil using the Transformer architecture involves several steps, including training and fine-tuning. Unfortunately, training a state-of-the-art generative model from scratch requires significant computational resources, and it's not feasible to provide a practical demonstration within the constraints of this platform.

However, the process uses a pre-existing model and a smaller dataset for fine-tuning. Ensure that you have the necessary libraries installed:

```
pip install transformers torch
```

```
from transformers import GPT2LMHeadModel, GPT2Config,
GPT2Tokenizer, GPT2ForSequenceClassification
from transformers import TextDataset, DataCollatorForLanguageModeling
from transformers import Trainer, TrainingArguments

# Load the pre-trained GPT-2 model and tokenizer
model_name = "gpt2" # You can replace this with a different GPT-2 variant
or use GPT-3 if available
model = GPT2LMHeadModel.from_pretrained(model_name)
tokenizer = GPT2Tokenizer.from_pretrained(model_name)

# Load your Tamil dataset
with open("tamil_dataset.txt", "r", encoding="utf-8") as file:
 dataset = file.readlines()

# Tokenize the dataset
tokenized_dataset = tokenizer(dataset, truncation=True, padding=True)

# Create a TextDataset
text_dataset = TextDataset(
```

```
 tokenizer=tokenizer,
 file_path="tamil_dataset.txt",
 block_size=128,
)

# Create a DataCollatorForLanguageModeling
data_collator = DataCollatorForLanguageModeling(
 tokenizer=tokenizer,
 mlm=False
)

# Training arguments
training_args = TrainingArguments(
 output_dir="./tamil_text_model",
 overwrite_output_dir=True,
 num_train_epochs=5,
 per_device_train_batch_size=8,
 save_steps=10_000,
 save_total_limit=2,
)

# Initialize Trainer
trainer = Trainer(
 model=model,
 args=training_args,
 data_collator=data_collator,
 train_dataset=text_dataset,
)

# Train the model
trainer.train()

# Fine-tuning (Optional)

# Load the pre-trained model
pretrained_model_name = "gpt2" # You can replace this with your pre-
trained model path or name
pretrained_model =
GPT2ForSequenceClassification.from_pretrained(pretrained_model_name)
```

```
# Fine-tuning arguments
fine_tuning_args = TrainingArguments(
 output_dir=“./tamil_text_finetuned_model”,
 overwrite_output_dir=True,
 num_train_epochs=3,
 per_device_train_batch_size=4,
 save_steps=5_000,
 save_total_limit=2,
)

# Initialize Trainer for fine-tuning
fine_tuner = Trainer(
 model=pretrained_model,
 args=fine_tuning_args,
 data_collator=data_collator,
 train_dataset=text_dataset,
)

# Fine-tune the model
fine_tuner.train()
```

This example uses a smaller dataset, and for better performance, an extensive and diverse dataset must be used for training. Training and fine-tuning a model, especially with large datasets, may require substantial computational resources, including GPUs or TPUs.

15.5 FINE-TUNING FOR SPECIFIC TASKS

Fine-tuning a pre-trained language model for specific tasks involves adapting a model previously trained on a large dataset to perform a more particular task. This process allows us to use the knowledge and language understanding encoded in the pre-trained model while tailoring it to a specific task. Here's a more detailed elaboration on the steps involved in fine-tuning for particular tasks:

1. Choose a Pre-trained Model

Select a pre-trained language model that aligns with the Task and requirements. Common choices include BERT, GPT, RoBERTa, and others, depending on the nature of the Task (e.g., classification, sequence labeling, translation).

2. Define Task

Clearly define the Task that needs to be performed, such as sentiment analysis, named entity recognition, text classification, machine translation, etc.

3. Prepare Task-specific Data

Collect or prepare a labeled dataset specific to the Task. This dataset should represent the language and domain in which your model will be applied.

4. Tokenization and Input Formatting

Tokenize your task-specific data using the same tokenization scheme used during pre-training the chosen model. Ensure that the input data is properly formatted to match the requirements of the pre-trained model.

5. Fine-tuning Architecture

Modify the pre-trained model to suit your Task. Depending on the Task, you may need to add task-specific layers, modify existing layers, or adjust the model's architecture. For instance:

- For text classification, add a classification head.
- For sequence labeling, adapt the output layer for entity recognition.

6. Loss Function

Choose a loss function that is appropriate for your Task. Common choices include cross-entropy for classification tasks, mean squared error for regression, or specialized losses for tasks like sequence labeling.

7. Hyperparameter Tuning

Fine-tune hyperparameters such as learning rate, batch size, and the number of training epochs. These hyperparameters may differ from those used during the pre-training phase.

8. Fine-tuning Procedure

Follow a fine-tuning procedure that typically involves the following steps:

- Initialize the model with the pre-trained weights.
- Freeze or partially freeze layers from the pre-trained model to retain generalization.
- Train the modified model on task-specific data.

9. Regularization and Monitoring

Incorporate regularization techniques, such as dropout, to prevent overfitting. Monitor the model's performance on a validation set during training to detect signs of overfitting.

10. Evaluate and Adjust

Evaluate the fine-tuned model on a separate test set to assess its performance. Adjust hyperparameters and model architecture as needed based on the evaluation results.

11. Inference

Once fine-tuned, your model is ready for inference on new, unseen data for your specific Task.

Tips

Experiment with different layers for fine-tuning. Sometimes, using earlier layers of the pre-trained model may be more beneficial.

Consider using transfer learning techniques, such as gradual unfreezing, where you progressively unfreeze and fine-tune different model layers.

Fine-tuning is a powerful technique that allows you to leverage the knowledge encoded in pre-trained models for your specific NLP task, saving computational resources and time compared to training a model from scratch.

15.6 CHOOSING HYPERPARAMETERS AND MODEL SELECTION

When choosing hyperparameters and model selection for tasks in Tamil, follow a similar process for other languages for Tamil.

Data Preparation

Tamil Corpus

Ensure a substantial and representative corpus of Tamil text data for specific NLP tasks. The quality and diversity of data play a crucial role in training effective models.

Tokenization and Preprocessing

Use appropriate tokenization and preprocessing techniques for Tamil. Consider libraries like SentencePiece or other language-specific tokenization tools.

Hyperparameter Selection

Learning Rate

Start with a moderate learning rate (e.g., 0.001) and adjust based on performance. Smaller learning rates might benefit stability, especially when dealing with languages with fewer resources.

Batch Size

Experiment with batch sizes suitable for your hardware. Smaller batch sizes can be more advantageous for languages with limited resources.

Number of Epochs

Monitor the training and validation performance over epochs. Adjust the number of epochs based on convergence and potential overfitting.

Dropout Rate

Use dropout for regularization. Start with a moderate rate and fine-tune based on validation performance.

Weight Decay (L2 Regularization)

Apply weight decay for regularization. Tune the weight decay parameter based on the sensitivity of your model to regularization.

Model Architecture Parameters

Choose a model architecture suitable for your Task and the complexity of the Tamil language. Transformer-based models have demonstrated effectiveness for a wide range of NLP tasks.

Model Selection

Transfer Learning

Leverage pre-trained models if available for Tamil. For example, models pre-trained on large English datasets can often be fine-tuned for specific tasks in Tamil.

Task-specific Considerations

Choose a model architecture and hyperparameters based on the specifics of your NLP task in Tamil. Different tasks (classification, sequence labeling, translation) may require different architectures.

Evaluation Metrics

Select evaluation metrics relevant to your Task and consider any language-specific nuances. For example, the F1 score might be crucial for named entity recognition.

Cross-Validation

Use cross-validation to assess model performance robustly. Ensure that the evaluation process reflects the characteristics of Tamil data.

Practical Constraints

Consider any practical constraints such as computational resources and time. Choose models and hyperparameters that align with the available resources for training and inference.

Language-specific Features

Depending on your Task, consider incorporating language-specific features. For instance, if working on sentiment analysis, understanding sentiment expressions in Tamil might require specific considerations.

Fine-tuning Pre-trained Models

If using pre-trained models in English, consider fine-tuning them for Tamil to transfer knowledge from a related language.

Remember that experimentation is crucial, and it may be necessary to iterate through different combinations of hyperparameters and models to find the most effective configuration for your specific Task in Tamil. Additionally, take into account the availability of language-specific resources and the unique characteristics of Tamil language data.

15.7 EVALUATION METRICS AND BEST PRACTICES

In order to evaluate NLP models for tasks in Tamil or any other language, it's important to choose appropriate evaluation metrics which can align with the specific characteristics of the language and the Task.

15.7.1 Classification Tasks (e.g., Sentiment Analysis, Text Categorization)

Assigning predefined labels or categories to input text in NLP is called a classification task, which is a fundamental task. It can be used in applications of various domains like sentiment analysis, text categorization, spam detection, and more. The metrics followed in classification tasks are

Accuracy

Best Practice: Suitable for balanced datasets. Suppose the dataset is imbalanced, as high accuracy cannot be achieved and cannot represent good performance in minority classes.

Precision, Recall, F1 Score

Best Practice: Especially applicable for imbalanced datasets. The F1 score is a good overall measure to balance precision and recall.

Confusion Matrix

Best Practice: Visualization of the confusion matrix provides insights into the model's performance in different classes and helps identify specific areas of improvement.

15.7.2 Sequence Labeling Tasks (e.g., Named Entity Recognition)

Assigning labels to individual elements within a sequence of Tamil text is called sequence labeling tasks. The metrics followed in sequence label tasks are.

Example

Input Sequence (Tamil): "அரசின் அறிவியல் துறையில் அந்நிய நிரலாக்க நிறுவனம் பங்கு பெற்றது."
Label Sequence: (ORG, O, O, O, O, O, O, O, O)

The metrics followed in classification tasks are:

Precision, Recall, F1 Score for Each Entity Type

Best Practice: To evaluate the model's performance for each named entity, type individually to understand if the model performs well across all classes.

Entity-Level Metrics

Best Practice: Consider entity-level metrics, such as entity-level precision, recall, and F1 score, which provide a more refined view of the model's performance.

15.7.3 Machine Translation:

Machine Translation (MT) focuses on developing a system that automatically translates text or speech into Tamil. The main aim is to enable effective communication between people who speak different languages.

BLEU Score

Best Practice: Commonly used for machine translation tasks. However, it has limitations and may not capture all aspects of translation quality. Consider using additional metrics like METEOR, TER, or human evaluation.

Word Error Rate (WER) and Character Error Rate (CER)

Best Practice: Useful for evaluating the accuracy of translated text at the word or character level.

15.7.4 Text Generation (e.g., Language Modeling)

Perplexity

Best Practice: Measures how well the model predicts the data. Lower perplexity indicates better performance.

Diversity and Coherence

Best Practice: Use human evaluation to assess the diversity and coherence of the generated text. Automated metrics might not capture these aspects well.

15.7.5 Best Practices for Evaluation in Tamil

Language-specific Considerations

Consider language-specific nuances and characteristics of Tamil. Certain evaluation metrics might need customization based on the specifics of the language.

Data Quality

Ensure that the evaluation dataset is of high quality and representative of the tasks in Tamil. Biased or low-quality datasets can lead to misleading evaluation results.

Cross-validation

Use cross-validation to evaluate the model's performance robustly. Ensure that the evaluation process reflects the characteristics of Tamil language data.

Human Evaluation

In addition to automated metrics, consider human evaluation, especially for tasks that involve subjective judgments, creativity, or cultural context.

Fine-tuning

If leveraging pre-trained models, fine-tune them on task-specific data in Tamil for better alignment with the language's characteristics.

The cultural nuances, context, and linguistic variations impact the performance of NLP models in Tamil. So, choose evaluation metrics that align with the goals and challenges of specific tasks in Tamil.

15.7.6 English to Tamil Neural Machine Translation Demo

The following example demonstrates the English to Tamil translation. The dataset provided on the website "https://www.manythings.org/anki/" offers a diverse collection of language pairs suitable for various natural language processing tasks. It encompasses translation datasets in multiple languages, including English, Spanish, French, German, Tamil, and more. The dataset consists of aligned sentences, making it ideal for training and evaluating machine translation models, language generation algorithms, and other NLP applications. With its wide range of language pairs and ample data volume, the dataset serves as a valuable resource for researchers, developers, and language enthusiasts alike seeking to explore and advance the field of multilingual communication.

KerasNLP provides building blocks for NLP (model layers, tokenizers, metrics, etc.) and makes it convenient to construct NLP pipelines. In this example, we'll use KerasNLP layers to build an encoder-decoder Transformer model, and train it on the English-to-Tamil machine translation task. This example demonstrates the English-to-Tamil NMT. The original example is more low-level and implements layers from scratch, whereas this example uses KerasNLP to show some more advanced approaches, such as subword tokenization and using metrics to compute the quality of generated translations.

This model is the simple deomonstration for the English to Tamil translation, it needs more training and finetuing to improve the accuracy.

```
!pip show keras
!pip install --upgrade keras

Name: keras
Version: 2.15.0
Summary: Deep learning for humans.
Home-page: https://keras.io/
Author: Keras team
Author-email: keras-users@googlegroups.com
License: Apache 2.0
Location: /usr/local/lib/python3.10/dist-packages
Requires:
Required-by: tensorflow
Requirement already satisfied: keras in
/usr/local/lib/python3.10/dist-packages (2.15.0)
Collecting keras
  Downloading keras-3.0.5-py3-none-any.whl (1.0 MB)
━━━━━━━━━━━━━━━━━━━━━━━━━━━━━━━━━━━━━━━━1.0/1.0 MB 11.6
MB/s eta 0:00:00
ent already satisfied: absl-py in
/usr/local/lib/python3.10/dist-packages (from keras)
(1.4.0)
Requirement already satisfied: numpy in
/usr/local/lib/python3.10/dist-packages (from keras)
(1.25.2)
Requirement already satisfied: rich in
/usr/local/lib/python3.10/dist-packages (from keras)
(13.7.1)
Collecting namex (from keras)
  Downloading namex-0.0.7-py3-none-any.whl (5.8 kB)
Requirement already satisfied: h5py in
/usr/local/lib/python3.10/dist-packages (from keras)
(3.9.0)
Requirement already satisfied: dm-tree in
/usr/local/lib/python3.10/dist-packages (from keras)
(0.1.8)
Requirement already satisfied: ml-dtypes in
```

```
/usr/local/lib/python3.10/dist-packages (from keras)
(0.2.0)
Requirement already satisfied: markdown-it-py>=2.2.0 in
/usr/local/lib/python3.10/dist-packages (from rich-
>keras) (3.0.0)
Requirement already satisfied: pygments<3.0.0,>=2.13.0 in
/usr/local/lib/python3.10/dist-packages (from rich-
>keras) (2.16.1)
Requirement already satisfied: mdurl~=0.1 in
/usr/local/lib/python3.10/dist-packages (from markdown-
it-py>=2.2.0->rich->keras) (0.1.2)
Installing collected packages: namex, keras
  Attempting uninstall: keras
    Found existing installation: keras 2.15.0
    Uninstalling keras-2.15.0:
      Successfully uninstalled keras-2.15.0
ERROR: pip's dependency resolver does not currently take
into account all the packages that are installed. This
behaviour is the source of the following dependency
conflicts.
tensorflow 2.15.0 requires keras<2.16,>=2.15.0, but you
have keras 3.0.5 which is incompatible.
Successfully installed keras-3.0.5 namex-0.0.7

# We set the backend to TensorFlow. The code works with
# both `tensorflow` and `torch`. It does not work with
JAX
# due to the behavior of `jax.numpy.tile` in a jit scope
# (used in
`TransformerDecoder.get_causal_attention_mask()`:
# `tile` in JAX does not support a dynamic `reps`
argument.
# You can make the code work in JAX by wrapping the
# inside of the `get_causal_attention_mask` method in
# a decorator to prevent jit compilation:
# `with jax.ensure_compile_time_eval():`.
import os

os.environ["KERAS_BACKEND"] = "tensorflow"

import pathlib
import random
import string
import re
import numpy as np
```

```
import tensorflow.data as tf_data
import tensorflow.strings as tf_strings

import keras
from keras import layers
from keras import ops
from keras.layers import TextVectorization

from tensorflow.keras.models import Model
from tensorflow.keras.layers import Input, LSTM ,Dense
import numpy as np

batch_size =64 #Batch size for training
epochs= 100 # Number of epochs to train for
latent_dim= 256 # Latent Dimensionality of the encoding
space
num_samples=10000 # Number of samples to train on
#Path to the data txt file on disk
text_file="/content/tam.txt"

with open(text_file) as f:
  lines = f.read().split("\n")[:-1]
  text_pairs = []
  for line in lines:
    # Split the line, assuming single tab delimiter
    parts = line.strip().split("\t")
    eng, tam = parts[0], parts[1]
    tam = "[start] " + tam + " [end]"
    text_pairs.append((eng, tam))

for _ in range(5):
    print(random.choice(text_pairs))
```

```
('Do you know when he will come?', '[start] அவன் எப்ப
வருவான் என்று உனக்குத் தெரியுமா [end]')
('None of your business.', '[start] இது உங்களுக்கு
சம்பந்தமில்லாத விஷயம் [end]')
('He arrived after the bell rang.', '[start] மணி ஒலித்தப்
பிறகு அவன் வந்தான் [end]')
('She has 2,000 books.', '[start] அவளிடம் 2000 புத்தகங்கள்
உள்ளன [end]')
('We ran after the thief.', '[start] நாங்கள் திருடனுக்குப்
பின்னால் ஓடினோம் [end]')
```

```
random.shuffle(text_pairs)
num_val_samples = int(0.15 * len(text_pairs))
num_train_samples = len(text_pairs) - 2 * num_val_samples
train_pairs = text_pairs[:num_train_samples]
val_pairs = text_pairs[num_train_samples :
num_train_samples + num_val_samples]
test_pairs = text_pairs[num_train_samples +
num_val_samples :]

print(f"{len(text_pairs)} total pairs")
print(f"{len(train_pairs)} training pairs")
print(f"{len(val_pairs)} validation pairs")
print(f"{len(test_pairs)} test pairs")

207 total pairs
145 training pairs
31 validation pairs
31 test pairs

strip_chars = string.punctuation + "¿"
strip_chars = strip_chars.replace("[", "")
strip_chars = strip_chars.replace("]", "")

vocab_size = 15000
sequence_length = 20
batch_size = 64

def custom_standardization(input_string):
    lowercase = tf_strings.lower(input_string)
    return tf_strings.regex_replace(lowercase, "[%s]" %
re.escape(strip_chars), "")

eng_vectorization = TextVectorization(
    max_tokens=vocab_size,
    output_mode="int",
    output_sequence_length=sequence_length,
)
tam_vectorization = TextVectorization(
    max_tokens=vocab_size,
    output_mode="int",
    output_sequence_length=sequence_length + 1,
    standardize=custom_standardization,
)
train_eng_texts = [pair[0] for pair in train_pairs]
train_tam_texts = [pair[1] for pair in train_pairs]
```

```
eng_vectorization.adapt(train_eng_texts)
tam_vectorization.adapt(train_tam_texts)

def format_dataset(eng, tam):
    eng = eng_vectorization(eng)
    tam = tam_vectorization(tam)
    return (
        {
            "encoder_inputs": eng,
            "decoder_inputs": tam[:, :-1],
        },
        tam[:, 1:],
    )

def make_dataset(pairs):
    eng_texts, tam_texts = zip(*pairs)
    eng_texts = list(eng_texts)
    tam_texts = list(tam_texts)
    dataset =
tf_data.Dataset.from_tensor_slices((eng_texts,
tam_texts))
    dataset = dataset.batch(batch_size)
    dataset = dataset.map(format_dataset)
    return dataset.cache().shuffle(2048).prefetch(16)

train_ds = make_dataset(train_pairs)
val_ds = make_dataset(val_pairs)

for inputs, targets in train_ds.take(1):
    print(f'inputs["encoder_inputs"].shape:
{inputs["encoder_inputs"].shape}')
    print(f'inputs["decoder_inputs"].shape:
{inputs["decoder_inputs"].shape}')
    print(f"targets.shape: {targets.shape}")

inputs["encoder_inputs"].shape: (64, 20)
inputs["decoder_inputs"].shape: (64, 20)
targets.shape: (64, 20)

import keras.ops as ops

class TransformerEncoder(layers.Layer):
    def __init__(self, embed_dim, dense_dim, num_heads,
**kwargs):
        super().__init__(**kwargs)
        self.embed_dim = embed_dim
```

```
        self.dense_dim = dense_dim
        self.num_heads = num_heads
        self.attention = layers.MultiHeadAttention(
            num_heads=num_heads, key_dim=embed_dim
        )
        self.dense_proj = keras.Sequential(
            [
                layers.Dense(dense_dim,
activation="relu"),
                layers.Dense(embed_dim),
            ]
        )
        self.layernorm_1 = layers.LayerNormalization()
        self.layernorm_2 = layers.LayerNormalization()
        self.supports_masking = True

    def call(self, inputs, mask=None):
        if mask is not None:
            padding_mask = ops.cast(mask[:, None, :],
dtype="int32")
        else:
            padding_mask = None

        attention_output = self.attention(
            query=inputs, value=inputs, key=inputs,
attention_mask=padding_mask
        )
        proj_input = self.layernorm_1(inputs +
attention_output)
        proj_output = self.dense_proj(proj_input)
        return self.layernorm_2(proj_input + proj_output)

    def get_config(self):
        config = super().get_config()
        config.update(
            {
                "embed_dim": self.embed_dim,
                "dense_dim": self.dense_dim,
                "num_heads": self.num_heads,
            }
        )
        return config


class PositionalEmbedding(layers.Layer):
    def __init__(self, sequence_length, vocab_size,
```

```
embed_dim, **kwargs):
        super().__init__(**kwargs)
        self.token_embeddings = layers.Embedding(
            input_dim=vocab_size, output_dim=embed_dim
        )
        self.position_embeddings = layers.Embedding(
            input_dim=sequence_length,
output_dim=embed_dim
        )
        self.sequence_length = sequence_length
        self.vocab_size = vocab_size
        self.embed_dim = embed_dim

    def call(self, inputs):
        length = ops.shape(inputs)[-1]
        positions = ops.arange(0, length, 1)
        embedded_tokens = self.token_embeddings(inputs)
        embedded_positions =
self.position_embeddings(positions)
        return embedded_tokens + embedded_positions

    def compute_mask(self, inputs, mask=None):
        if mask is None:
            return None
        else:
            return ops.not_equal(inputs, 0)

    def get_config(self):
        config = super().get_config()
        config.update(
            {
                "sequence_length": self.sequence_length,
                "vocab_size": self.vocab_size,
                "embed_dim": self.embed_dim,
            }
        )
        return config

class TransformerDecoder(layers.Layer):
    def __init__(self, embed_dim, latent_dim, num_heads,
**kwargs):
        super().__init__(**kwargs)
        self.embed_dim = embed_dim
        self.latent_dim = latent_dim
        self.num_heads = num_heads
        self.attention_1 = layers.MultiHeadAttention(
```

```
            num_heads=num_heads, key_dim=embed_dim
        )
        self.attention_2 = layers.MultiHeadAttention(
            num_heads=num_heads, key_dim=embed_dim
        )
        self.dense_proj = keras.Sequential(
            [
                layers.Dense(latent_dim,
activation="relu"),
                layers.Dense(embed_dim),
            ]
        )
        self.layernorm_1 = layers.LayerNormalization()
        self.layernorm_2 = layers.LayerNormalization()
        self.layernorm_3 = layers.LayerNormalization()
        self.supports_masking = True

    def call(self, inputs, encoder_outputs, mask=None):
        causal_mask =
self.get_causal_attention_mask(inputs)
        if mask is not None:
            padding_mask = ops.cast(mask[:, None, :],
dtype="int32")
            padding_mask = ops.minimum(padding_mask,
causal_mask)
        else:
            padding_mask = None

        attention_output_1 = self.attention_1(
            query=inputs, value=inputs, key=inputs,
attention_mask=causal_mask
        )
        out_1 = self.layernorm_1(inputs +
attention_output_1)

        attention_output_2 = self.attention_2(
            query=out_1,
            value=encoder_outputs,
            key=encoder_outputs,
            attention_mask=padding_mask,
        )
        out_2 = self.layernorm_2(out_1 +
attention_output_2)

        proj_output = self.dense_proj(out_2)
        return self.layernorm_3(out_2 + proj_output)
```

```
    def get_causal_attention_mask(self, inputs):
        input_shape = ops.shape(inputs)
        batch_size, sequence_length = input_shape[0],
input_shape[1]
        i = ops.arange(sequence_length)[:, None]
        j = ops.arange(sequence_length)
        mask = ops.cast(i >= j, dtype="int32")
        mask = ops.reshape(mask, (1, input_shape[1],
input_shape[1]))
        mult = ops.concatenate(
            [ops.expand_dims(batch_size, -1),
ops.convert_to_tensor([1, 1])],
            axis=0,
        )
        return ops.tile(mask, mult)

    def get_config(self):
        config = super().get_config()
        config.update(
            {
                "embed_dim": self.embed_dim,
                "latent_dim": self.latent_dim,
                "num_heads": self.num_heads,
            }
        )
        return config

embed_dim = 256
latent_dim = 2048
num_heads = 8

encoder_inputs = keras.Input(shape=(None,),
dtype="int64", name="encoder_inputs")
x = PositionalEmbedding(sequence_length, vocab_size,
embed_dim)(encoder_inputs)
encoder_outputs = TransformerEncoder(embed_dim,
latent_dim, num_heads)(x)
encoder = keras.Model(encoder_inputs, encoder_outputs)

decoder_inputs = keras.Input(shape=(None,),
dtype="int64", name="decoder_inputs")
encoded_seq_inputs = keras.Input(shape=(None, embed_dim),
name="decoder_state_inputs")
x = PositionalEmbedding(sequence_length, vocab_size,
embed_dim)(decoder_inputs)
```

```
x = TransformerDecoder(embed_dim, latent_dim,
num_heads)(x, encoded_seq_inputs)
x = layers.Dropout(0.5)(x)
decoder_outputs = layers.Dense(vocab_size,
activation="softmax")(x)
decoder = keras.Model([decoder_inputs,
encoded_seq_inputs], decoder_outputs)

decoder_outputs = decoder([decoder_inputs,
encoder_outputs])
transformer = keras.Model(
    [encoder_inputs, decoder_inputs], decoder_outputs,
name="transformer"
)
epochs = 15

transformer.summary()
transformer.compile(
    "rmsprop", loss="sparse_categorical_crossentropy",
metrics=["accuracy"]
)
transformer.fit(train_ds, epochs=epochs,
validation_data=val_ds)
```

Model: "transformer"

Layer (type)	Output Shape	Param #	Connected to
encoder_inputs (InputLayer)	(None, None)	0	-
positional_embedding (PositionalEmbedding)	(None, None, 256)	3,845,120	encoder_inputs[0][0]
decoder_inputs (InputLayer)	(None, None)	0	-
transformer_encoder (TransformerEncoder)	(None, None, 256)	3,155,456	positional_embedding[…
functional_5 (Functional)	(None, None, 15000)	12,959,640	decoder_inputs[0][0], transformer_encoder[0…

```
 Total params: 39,920,434 (152.28 MB)

 Trainable params: 19,960,216 (76.14 MB)

 Non-trainable params: 0 (0.00 B)

 Optimizer params: 19,960,218 (76.14 MB)

Epoch 1/15
3/3 ━━━━━━━━━━━━━━━━━━━━23s 5s/step - accuracy: 0.9673 -
loss: 0.1266 - val_accuracy: 0.8032 - val_loss: 2.0857
Epoch 2/15
3/3 ━━━━━━━━━━━━━━━━━━━━2s 60ms/step - accuracy: 0.9535 -
loss: 0.1559 - val_accuracy: 0.8032 - val_loss: 2.0974
Epoch 3/15
3/3 ━━━━━━━━━━━━━━━━━━━━0s 39ms/step - accuracy: 0.9515 -
loss: 0.1739 - val_accuracy: 0.8000 - val_loss: 2.1462
Epoch 4/15
3/3 ━━━━━━━━━━━━━━━━━━━━0s 39ms/step - accuracy: 0.9511 -
loss: 0.1600 - val_accuracy: 0.7968 - val_loss: 2.1267
Epoch 5/15
3/3 ━━━━━━━━━━━━━━━━━━━━0s 37ms/step - accuracy: 0.9546 -
loss: 0.1704 - val_accuracy: 0.7984 - val_loss: 2.1252
Epoch 6/15
3/3 ━━━━━━━━━━━━━━━━━━━━0s 38ms/step - accuracy: 0.9592 -
loss: 0.1361 - val_accuracy: 0.8000 - val_loss: 2.1585
Epoch 7/15
3/3 ━━━━━━━━━━━━━━━━━━━━0s 40ms/step - accuracy: 0.9657 -
loss: 0.1155 - val_accuracy: 0.7984 - val_loss: 2.1692
Epoch 8/15
3/3 ━━━━━━━━━━━━━━━━━━━━0s 47ms/step - accuracy: 0.9781 -
loss: 0.0723 - val_accuracy: 0.8016 - val_loss: 2.1516
Epoch 9/15
3/3 ━━━━━━━━━━━━━━━━━━━━0s 48ms/step - accuracy: 0.9792 -
loss: 0.0679 - val_accuracy: 0.7984 - val_loss: 2.1035
Epoch 10/15
3/3 ━━━━━━━━━━━━━━━━━━━━0s 54ms/step - accuracy: 0.9772 -
loss: 0.0739 - val_accuracy: 0.7968 - val_loss: 2.1647
Epoch 11/15
3/3 ━━━━━━━━━━━━━━━━━━━━0s 37ms/step - accuracy: 0.9621 -
loss: 0.1287 - val_accuracy: 0.7984 - val_loss: 2.1514
Epoch 12/15
3/3 ━━━━━━━━━━━━━━━━━━━━0s 38ms/step - accuracy: 0.9759 -
loss: 0.0845 - val_accuracy: 0.8000 - val_loss: 2.1817
Epoch 13/15
```

```
3/3 ━━━━━━━━━━━━━━━━━━━━━━━━━0s 37ms/step - accuracy: 0.9801 -
loss: 0.0745 - val_accuracy: 0.7984 - val_loss: 2.1647
Epoch 14/15
3/3 ━━━━━━━━━━━━━━━━━━━━━━━━━0s 38ms/step - accuracy: 0.9784 -
loss: 0.0815 - val_accuracy: 0.8000 - val_loss: 2.1915
Epoch 15/15
3/3 ━━━━━━━━━━━━━━━━━━━━━━━━━0s 43ms/step - accuracy: 0.9767 -
loss: 0.0789 - val_accuracy: 0.8016 - val_loss: 2.2003

<keras.src.callbacks.history.History at 0x78e3b455f820>
```

```
tam_vocab = tam_vectorization.get_vocabulary()
tam_index_lookup = dict(zip(range(len(tam_vocab)),
tam_vocab))
max_decoded_sentence_length = 20

def decode_sequence(input_sentence):
    tokenized_input_sentence =
eng_vectorization([input_sentence])
    decoded_sentence = "[start]"
    for i in range(max_decoded_sentence_length):
        tokenized_target_sentence =
tam_vectorization([decoded_sentence])[:, :-1]
        predictions =
transformer([tokenized_input_sentence,
tokenized_target_sentence])

        # ops.argmax(predictions[0, i, :]) is not a
concrete value for jax here
        sampled_token_index = ops.convert_to_numpy(
            ops.argmax(predictions[0, i, :])
        ).item(0)
        sampled_token =
tam_index_lookup[sampled_token_index]
        decoded_sentence += " " + sampled_token

        if sampled_token == "[end]":
            break
    return decoded_sentence

test_eng_texts = [pair[0] for pair in test_pairs]
for _ in range(30):
    input_sentence = random.choice(test_eng_texts)
    translated = decode_sequence(input_sentence)

test_eng_texts
```

```
['You keep out of this.',
 'She glanced through the magazine.',
 'Who knows?',
 'I know what to do.',
 'Charge it to my account.',
 'If Tom ran away, where could he go?',
 "Don't listen to her.",
 'Where are we?',
 'Tom was in Australia a year ago.',
 'He is sure to come.',
 "He's afraid of the sea.",
 'She stood close to him.',
 "I'm short of money.",
 'We ran after the thief.',
 'I know how to ski.',
 'I have to dress up.',
 "There's no easy way out of here.",
 "I'm proud of my son.",
 "Don't drink and drive.",
 'Be kind to old people.',
 'She gave him a book.',
 "I'm not sharing this with Tom.",
 'Those are my CDs.',
 'May I speak to you?',
 "It's free of charge.",
 "Don't tell Tom you're a cop.",
 "That's our house.",
 'She danced with him.',
 'Beware of the dog!',
 'Do you want to be rich?',
 'I live on the bottom floor.']
```

We are going to test our model now!

```
# Define your own English sentence ----- epoch 100
my_english_sentence = "play with me"

# Translate the sentence
translated = decode_sequence(my_english_sentence)

# Print the translated text
print(translated)

[start] அவள் பியானோ வாசிக்கிறாளோ [end]
```

```
# Define your own English sentence -----epoch 32
my_english_sentence = "run"

# Translate the sentence
translated = decode_sequence(my_english_sentence)

# Print the translated text
print(translated)

[start] என்னால் ஓட முடிகிறது [end]

# Define your own English sentence -----epoch 15
my_english_sentence = "lie down"

# Translate the sentence
translated = decode_sequence(my_english_sentence)

# Print the translated text
print(translated)

[start] என்னிடம் பொய் சொல்லாதே [end]

# Define your own English sentence
my_english_sentence = "i slept"

# Translate the sentence
translated = decode_sequence(my_english_sentence)

# Print the translated text
print(translated)

[start] நான் தூங்கினேன் [end]

# Define your own English sentence
my_english_sentence = "I got down from the taxi"

# Translate the sentence
translated = decode_sequence(my_english_sentence)

# Print the translated text
print(translated)

[start] நான் டாக்ஸியிலிருந்து இறங்கினேன் [end]

# Define your own English sentence
my_english_sentence = "I came before others"
```

```
# Translate the sentence
translated = decode_sequence(my_english_sentence)

# Print the translated text
print(translated)

[start] மற்றவர்களுக்கு முன்னே நான் வந்தேன் [end]

# Define your own English sentence
my_english_sentence = "Beware of scammers"

# Translate the sentence
translated = decode_sequence(my_english_sentence)

# Print the translated text
print(translated)

[start] ஜேப்படிகாரர்களிடம் ஜாக்கிரதையாக இருக்கவும் [end]

# Define your own English sentence
my_english_sentence = "Of course"

# Translate the sentence
translated = decode_sequence(my_english_sentence)

# Print the translated text
print(translated)

[start] நிச்சயமாக [end]

# Define your own English sentence
my_english_sentence = "Tom looks younger than you"

# Translate the sentence
translated = decode_sequence(my_english_sentence)

# Print the translated text
print(translated)

[start] டாம் உங்களை விட இளையவராக தெரிகிறார் [end]

# Define your own English sentence
my_english_sentence = "talk to me"

# Translate the sentence
translated = decode_sequence(my_english_sentence)
```

```
# Print the translated text
print(translated)
```

```
[start] என்னிடம் பேசு [end]
```

15.8 CONCLUSION

This chapter comprehensively explores the operational characteristics of Generative Models and Large Language models, specifically focusing on the bootstrapping process for large language models across different languages, notably Tamil. Comprehending the holistic design of Generative Models necessitates delving into diverse components and learning methodologies. The model leverages supervised, unsupervised, and reinforcement learning techniques while elucidating the Transformer's intricacies. A pivotal aspect of Transformer learning is the acquisition and computation of attention. The self-attention model, grounded in learning, is expounded along with an illustrative example.

References

1. Tholkaappiyam: Phonology and Morphology, Albert, International Institute of Tamil Studies, First Edition, 1985.
2. The Oxford handbook of computational linguistics, Mitkov, R., Oxford University Press, 2022.
3. Translation Theory and Application, M. Valarmathi, N. Murugaiyan, Syed Abdur Raheem, International Institute of Tamil Studies, 1999.
4. A progressive grammar of common Tamil, Arden, Albert Henry, 5th edition, 1942.
5. A reference grammar of spoken Tamil. Cambridge University Press, Schiffman, H.F. and F., H. 1999.
6. A grammar of modern Tamil, Lehmann, T. 1989.
7. Tamil grammar, Wikipedia, the free encyclopaedia. https://en.wikipedia.org/wiki/Tamil_grammar
8. Rajam, V.S. and Rajam, V. (1992). A reference grammar of classical Tamil poetry: 150 B.C. -pre-fifth/sixth century A.D. American Philosophical Society.
9. Tamil Electronic Library—A comprehensive site on Tamil Language, Tamil Culture, Tamil Literature, Carnatic Music, Hindu Temples, Tamil Books, Tamil Radio and Television, ,.. https://tamilelibrary.org
10. தமிழ் இணையக் கல்விக்கழகம் Tamil Virtual Academy, தேமதுரத் தமிழோசை உலகமெலாம் பரவும் வகை செய்தல் வேண்டும். https://www.tamilvu.org
11. UNICODE, http://www.unicode.org/
12. Wibjorn, Microsoft learn: Build skills that open doors in your career. https://learn.microsoft.com/
13. Indian Language Technology Proliferation and Deployment Centre - Home. https://tdil-dc.in/
14. Internet Assigned Numbers Authority. https://www.iana.org/assignments/charset-reg/TSCII
15. An overview of different approaches to word-processing in Tamil and a proposal towards standardisation of tamil computing, K. Kalyanasundaram, Talk delivered at TamilNet'97:

    http://www.oocities.org/Athens/5180/sintalk1.html

16. A Proposal for a Tamil Standard Code For Information Interchange (TSCII), K. Kalyanasundaram and M. Nedumaran, Internet Working Group for the Tamil Standard Code. https://www.oocities.org/athens/5180/tscii.pdf
17. Report on the Final Recommendations of the Task Force on TACE16 http://www.tamilvu.org
18. https://nlp.stanford.edu
19. http://www.languageinindia.com/april2003/verbalcomp.html
20. http://www.kuralsoft.com/kural-tamil-software.html
21. மென்தமிழ் பயனர் வழிகாட்ட, http://www.lingsoftsolutions.com/mentamizh-2017
22. Computational Linguistics and Technological Development in Tamil, Rajendran S., Language in India, www.languageinindia.com Vol. 19 Issue 11, Nov. 2019.
23. Word Classes OR Parts of Speech in Tamil, S. Rajendran, Language in India, www.languageinindia.com, Vol. 5: 6 June 2005.
24. Word Classes OR Parts of Speech in Tamil, S. Rajendran, Language in India, www.languageinindia.com , Vol 5 : 6 June 2005.
25. English to Tamil machine translation system using universal networking language. Sridhar, R., Sethuraman, P. and Krishnakumar, K., Sādhanā, 41(6), 607–620. 2016 https://doi.org/10.1007/s12046-016-0504-9.
26. Morphology based prototype statistical machine translation system for English to Tamil language, M. Anand Kumar, Computer Science, Linguistics, May 2013.
27. http://www.acharya.gen.in
28. Tamil Computing: the present and the future, N. Anandakrishnan, https://www.thehindu.com/news/cities/Coimbatore/Tamil-computing-the-present-and-the-future/article16265648.ece
29. https://www.geeksforgeeks.org/working-csv-files-python
30. https://www.homeandlearn.uk/python-database-rows.html
31. https://www.geeksforgeeks.org/python-create-and-write-on-excel-file-using-xlsxwriter-module
32. https://xlsxwriter.readthedocs.io/tutorial01.html
33. https://xlsxwriter.readthedocs.io/example_chart_line.html
34. https://www.oreilly.com/library/view/access-2007-for/0596528337/ch01.html
35. https://www.onlinetutorialspoint.com/mysql/install-mysql-on-windows-10-step-by-step.html

36. https://www.geeksforgeeks.org/python-mysql-create-database/
37. https://www.datacamp.com/tutorial/mysql-python
38. https://github.com/Marumugam/deeptamil
39. https://github.com/RanchMobile/Tamil-AI
40. Anaphora resolution in Tamil novels, Akilandeswari, A. and Lalitha Devi, S., Mining Intelligence and Knowledge Exploration, 268–277, 2014. https://doi.org/10.1007/978-3-319-13817-6_26.
41. Pattern based bootstrapping technique for Tamil POS tagging, Ganesh, J., Parthasarathi, R., Geetha, T.V. and Balaji, J., Mining Intelligence and Knowledge Exploration, 256-267, 2014,. https://doi.org/10.1007/978-3-319-13817-6_25
42. A novel knowledge—engineering based approach for anaphora resolution of Tamil pronouns, Padmamala, R., International Conference on Smart Technologies and Management for Computing, Communication, Controls, Energy and Materials (ICSTM). 2015, https://doi.org/10.1109/icstm.2015.7225386
43. Anaphora Resolution in Hindi, A M.S. thesis submitted at Praveen Dakwale, at Language Technologies Research Center (LTRC), International Institute of Information Technology, 2014.
44. Chunker for Tamil, Dhanalakshmi V., Padmavathy P., Anand Kumar M., Soman K.P., Rajendran S. 2009 International Conference on Advances in Recent Technologies in Communication and Computing, 2009.
45. Building a part of speech tagger for the Tamil language, Sarveswaran, K., Dias, G., International Conference on Asian Language Processing (IALP), 2021 https://doi.org/10.1109/ialp54817.2021.9675195
46. POS Tagger and Chunker for Tamil Language, V. Dhanalakshmi, M.A. Kumar, S. Rajendran, TIC 2009.
47. Handling Noun-Noun Coreference in Tamil, Vijay Sundar Ram and Sobha Lalitha Dev, Proceedings of the WILDRE5–5th Workshop on Indian Language Data: Resources and Evaluation, pages 20–24 Language Resources and Evaluation Conference (LREC 2020), Marseille, 11–16 May 2020 organized by European Language Resources Association (ELRA), 2020.
48. Co-reference Resolution in Tamil Text, Vijay Sundar Ram R. and Sobha Lalitha Devi, *Proc. of the 14th Intl. Conference on Natural Language Processing,* pages 392–401, Kolkata, India. December 2017.
49. Domain Focused Named Entity Recognizer for Tamil Using Conditional Random Fields, Vijayakrishna R., Sobha L., 2008, *Proceedings of the IJCNLP-08 Workshop on NER for South and South East Asian Languages,* pp. 59–66, Hyderabad, India, January 2008.

50. Named Entity Recognition in Tweets: An Experimental Study, Alan Ritter, Sam Clark, Mausam and Oren Etzioni, Proceedings of the 2011 Conference on Empirical Methods in Natural Language Processing, pages 1524–1534, Edinburgh, Scotland, UK, July 27–31, 2011.
51. Tamil NER—Coping with Real Time Challenges, Malarkodi, C.S., Pattabhi, RK Rao and Sobha, Lalitha Devi, Proceedings of the Workshop on Machine Translation and Parsing in Indian Languages (MTPIL-2012), pages 23–38, COLING 2012, Mumbai, December 2012.
52. Approaches to Named Entity Recognition in Indian Languages: A Study, Prakash Hiremath, Shambhavi B.R., International Journal of Engineering and Advanced Technology (IJEAT) ISSN: 2249-8958, Volume 3 Issue 6, August 2014.
53. Named-entity-Recognition (NER) for Tamil language using margin-infused relaxed algorithm (MIRA), Theivendiram, P., Uthayakumar, M., Nadarasamoorthy, N., Thayaparan, M., Jayasena, S., Dias, G. and Ranathunga, S. Computational Linguistics and Intelligent Text Processing, 465–476, 2018. https://doi.org/10.1007/978-3-319-75477-2_33
54. Part of Speech Tagging for Tamil using SVM Tool—A M.Tech. thesis, Anand Kumar M, Amrita Vishwa Vidyapeetham, Coimbatore, 2008.
55. Hidden Markov model based part of speech tagger for Sinhala language, Jayaweera, A., Dias, N., International Journal on Natural Language Computing, 3(3), 9–23, 2014. https://doi.org/10.5121/ijnlc.2014.3302
56. HMM based POS tagger for Hindi. Joshi, N., Darbari, H. and Mathur, I., Computer Science & Information Technology (CS & IT), 2013. https://doi.org/10.5121/csit.2013.3639
57. Pos Tagging for Classical Tamil Texts. Akilan R., Naganathan, E.R., International Journal of Business Intelligents, 5(1), 15–17, 2012. https://doi.org/10.20894/ijbi.105.001.001.005
58. Structural parsing of natural language text in Tamil language using dependency model.. Selvam, M., Natarajan, A.M., Thangarajan, R., *International Journal of Computer Processing of Languages,* 22 (02n03), 237–256, 2009. https://doi.org/10.1142/s1793840609002093
59. Semantic Parsing of Tamil Sentences, Balaji J., Geetha T.V., Ranjani Parthasarathi, 2012. Proceedings of the Workshop on Machine Translation and Parsing in Indian Languages (MTPIL-2012), pages 15–22, COLING 2012, Mumbai, December 2012.
60. Tamil Spell Checker, T. Dhanabalan, Ranjani Parthasarathi, T.V. Geetha, TIC2003, Chennai, India, 2003.
61. A multilevel UNL concept-based searching and ranking, Ranjani Parthasarathi, Proceedings of the 7th International Conference on Web

Information Systems and Technologies, 2011. https://doi.org/10.5220/0003334402820289

62. English to Tamil machine translation system using universal networking language, Sridhar, R., Sethuraman, P. and Krishnakumar, K., Sādhanā, 41(6), 607–620, 2016. https://doi.org/10.1007/s12046-016-0504-9
63. Word level translation (Tamil – English) with word sense disambiguation in Tamil using OntNet. Padmamala, R., International Conference on Computing and Communications Technologies (ICCCT), 2015. https://doi.org/10.1109/iccct2.2015.7292744
64. Word Sense Disambiguation in Tamil, Rajendran Sankaravelayuthan, A. Dhanavalli, 2019 Amrita Vishwa Vidyapeetham, Coimbatore, Language in India www.languageinindia.com ISSN 1930-2940 Vol. 19:9 September 2019.
65. Multilingual Text-to-Speech Synthesis using Sequence-to-Sequence Neural Networks—A Ph.D. Thesis, Sivanand Achanta, International Institute of Information Technology, Hyderabad, 2017.
66. Semantic Parsing of Tamil Sentences, Balaji J, Geetha T V, Ranjani Parthasarathi, Proceedings of the Workshop on Machine Translation and Parsing in Indian Languages (MTPIL-2012), pages 15–22, COLING 2012, Mumbai, December 2012.
67. Morpheme and Semantic Based Approach for Tamil Question Answering System—A Thesis by Lakshmana Pandian S, Anna University, Chennai, 2011.
68. https://www.ctnlpr.com/textspeech-processing-and-analytics-platform
69. Neural Approaches Towards Text Summarization—M.S. Thesis, Abhishek Kumar Singh, IIIT-Hyderabad, 2018.
70. Tamil characters recognition and retrieval, Abdol Hamid Pilevar, Proceedings of the 7th International Conference on Software Paradigm Trends. 2012,. https://doi.org/10.5220/0004030504870493
71. Development of Cross-Language Information Retrieval for Resource-Scarce African Languages, A Ph.D. Thesis, Kula Kekeba Tune, IIIT-Hyderabad, 2015.
72. Effective Query Translation Techniques for Cross-Language Information Retrieval, A Ph.D. Thesis, Sethuramalingam S,IIIT-Hyderabad, 2009.
73. Ontological Structure-Based Retrieval System for Tamil. Rajendran, S., Soman, K.P., Anandkumar, M., Sankaralingam, C. Applications in Ubiquitous Computing. EAI/Springer Innovations in Communication and Computing. Springer, Cham, 2021. https://doi.org/10.1007/978-3-030-35280-6_10

74. Text Processing in Information Retrieval System using Vector Space Model, Premalatha, R, Srinivasan, S, ICICES2014, Chennai, Tamil Nadu, India.
75. Textual Representations for Corpus-Based Bilingual Retrieval—A Ph.D. Thesis, Paul McNaee, University of Maryland, 2008.
76. Document Ranking using Customizes Vector Method—A Review, Priyanka Mesariya, Nidhi Madia, Abhishek Kumar, 2016, IJCSMC, Vol. 5, Issue. 3, pp. 287–290, March 2016.
77. Tamil Text Extraction Using Dual Tree Complex Wavelet Transform and A Weighted Hybrid Thresholding Approach—A Ph.D. Thesis, Deepa .S.T, Mother Teresa Women's University, 2013.
78. Semantic information extraction from Tamil documents, Pandian, S. L., Devakumar, J. and Geetha, T, International Journal of Metadata, Semantics and Ontologies, 3(3), 226, 2008. https://doi.org/10.1504/ijmso.2008.023570
79. Phonetics and Phonology, S. Rajendran, Amrita Viswa Vidyalaya, Coimbatore.
80. Syntax and semantics of Tamil, A thesis submitted at University of Poona,S. Rejendaran, 1978.
81. https://www.microsoft.com/ta-IN/download/confirmation.aspx?id=51200
82. Foundations for Analytics with Python, Clinton W. Brownley, August 2016, Publisher(s): O'Reilly Media, Inc. ISBN: 9781491922538.
83. Supporting information extraction from printed documents by Lexico-semantic pattern matching, Wenzel, C., Proceedings of the Fourth International Conference on Document Analysis and Recognition, 1997, https://doi.org/10.1109/icdar.1997.620605
84. https://github.com/SAZZZO99/Student-Database-Management-System
85. https://tamilpesu.us/en
86. https://pypi.org/project/Open-Tamil
87. Syllable Modeling in Continuous Speech Recognition for Tamil Language—A Ph.D. Thesis, R. Thangarjan, Anna University, 2009.
88. An improved tamil text to speech synthesis system with annotated dual corpora, Ph.D. thesis by S. Kiruthika, Anna University, Chennai.
89. Novel Approaches to Machine Recognition of Handwritten Tamil Documents, Doctor of Philosophy Thesis, Sobhana Mari. S., Mahatma Gandhi University Kottaiyam, 2014.
90. Natural language processing with Python, Bird, S., Klein, E. and Loper, E. O'Reilly Media, 2009.
91. https://www.microsoft.com

92. https://www.microsoft.com/en-in/bhashaindia
93. https://inltk.readthedocs.io/en/latest/index.html
94. http://anoopkunchukuttan.github.io/indic_nlp_library
95. https://narvidhai.github.io/tamil-nlp-catalog
96. Acoustic phonetics and Text to Speech Processing and Speech to Text Processing, Rajendran Sankaravelayuthan, Language in India. www.languageinindia.com , ISSN: 1930-2940 Vol. 19:10 October 2019.
97. Computational Linguistics and Technological Development of Tamil, Rajendran Sankaravelayuthan, Language in India www.languageinindia.com Vol. 19 Issue 11, Nov 2019.
98. தரவுத்ததொகுதி மொழியியல் (Corpus Linguistics), Rajendran Sankaravelayuthan, Language in India www.languageinindia.com ISSN 1930-2940 Vol. 20:8 August 2020.
99. இயந்திரம மொழிபெயர்ப்பும் அதற்கொன கருவிகள் உருவொக்க-மும் (Machine translation and preparation of tools for machine translation), Rajendran Sankaravelayuthan, Tamil University, Thanjavur.
100. Machine Translation – Yesterday, Today and Tomorrow (இயந்திர மொழி-பெயர்ப்பு – நேற்று, இன்று, நாளை), Rajendran Sankaravelayuthan, Language in India www.languageinindia.com ISSN 1930-2940 Vol. 20:1 January 2020.
101. Text Conversion from TSCII 1.7 to Unicode, Muthu Nedumaran, Muthu@Murasu.com
102. The TSCII 1.7 Code Chart, http://www.tamil.net/tscii/charset17.gif
103. Unicode 4.0, Tamil Code Chart, http://www.unicode.org/charts/PDF/UOB8O.pdf
104. Tunstall, L., Werra, L.V. and Wolf, T. (2022). Natural language processing with transformers. O'Reilly Media.
105. Nazir, A. and Wang, Z. (2023). A comprehensive survey of ChatGPT: Advancements, applications, prospects, and challenges. Meta-Radiology, 100022. https://doi.org/10.1016/j.metrad.2023.100022.
106. Raj, R., Singh, A., Kumar, V. and Verma, P. (2023). Analyzing the potential benefits and use cases of ChatGPT as a tool for improving the efficiency and effectiveness of business operations. BenchCouncil Transactions on Benchmarks, Standards and Evaluations, 3(3), 100140. https://doi.org/10.1016/j.tbench.2023.100140
107. Rahman, M.M. and Watanobe, Y. (2023). ChatGPT for education and research: Opportunities, threats, and strategies. https://doi.org/10.20944/preprints202303.0473.v1.

108. Bhardwaz, S. and Kumar, J. (2023). An extensive comparative analysis of chatbot technologies - ChatGPT, Google BARD and Microsoft Bing. 2023 2nd International Conference on Applied Artificial Intelligence and Computing (ICAAIC). https://doi.org/10.1109/icaaic56838.2023.10140214
109. Sakirin, T. and Ben Said, R. (2023). User preferences for chatgpt-powered conversational interfaces versus traditional methods. Mesopotamian Journal of Computer Science, 24–31. https://doi.org/10.58496/mjcsc/2023/006
110. A. Baki Kocaballi, Conversational AI-Powered Design: ChatGPT as Designer, User, and Product, School of Computer Science, University of Technology Sydney, baki.kocaballi@uts.edu.au
111. GPT-3: Building Innovative NLP Products Using Large Language Models, ISBN:9355422024, Sandra Kublik, Shubham Saboo, 2022.
112. Building Transformer Models with Attention: Implementing a Neural Machine Translator from Scratch in Keras. Jason Brownlee, Stefania Cristina, Mehreen Saeed, Machine Learning Mastery, 2022.
113. Babcock, J. and Bali, R. (2021). Generative AI with Python and Tensor Flow 2: Create images, text, and music with vaes, gans, lstms, transformer models. Packt Publishing.
114. https://www.manythings.org/anki/
115. https://keras.io/examples/nlp/neural_machine_translation_with_keras_nlp/
116. https://mitpress.mit.edu/9780262039512/introduction-to-deep-learning/